P9-AOU-473

DISCARDED
THE
UNIVERSITY OF WINNIPEG
PORTAGE & BALMORAL
WINNIPEG, MAN. R3B 2E9
CANADA

# Atlantic Community in Crisis

# Pergamon Titles of Related Interest

Allworth – *Ethnic Russia Today: The Dilemma of Dominance*

Douglass, Jr. – *Soviet Military Strategy in Europe*

Feld & Boyd – *Comparative Regional Systems: West and East Europe, North America, The Middle East and Developing Countries*

Freedman – *World Politics and the Arab-Israeli Conflict*

Link & Feld – *The New Nationalism: Implications for Transatlantic Relations*

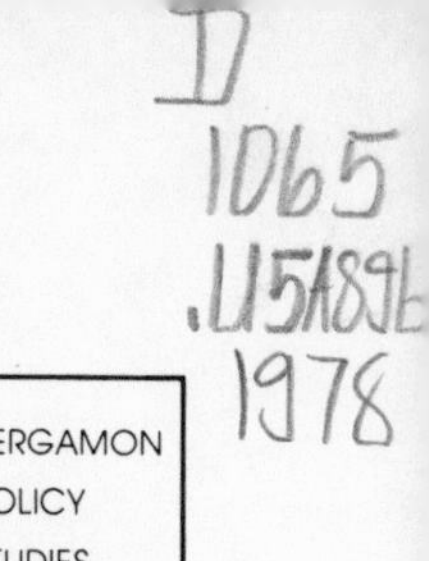


# Atlantic Community in Crisis/A Redefinition of the Transatlantic Relationship

Edited by
Walter F. Hahn
Robert L. Pfaltzgraff, Jr.

An Institute for Foreign Policy Analysis Book

Pergamon Press
NEW YORK • OXFORD • TORONTO • SYDNEY • FRANKFURT • PARIS

*Pergamon Press Offices:*

| | |
|---|---|
| **U.S.A.** | Pergamon Press Inc., Maxwell House, Fairview Park, Elmsford, New York 10523, U.S.A. |
| **U.K.** | Pergamon Press Ltd., Headington Hill Hall, Oxford OX3 0BW, England |
| **CANADA** | Pergamon of Canada Ltd., 150 Consumers Road, Willowdale, Ontario M2J 1P9, Canada |
| **AUSTRALIA** | Pergamon Press (Aust) Pty. Ltd., P O Box 544, Potts Point, NSW 2011, Australia |
| **FRANCE** | Pergamon Press SARL, 24 rue des Ecoles, 75240 Paris, Cedex 05, France |
| **FEDERAL REPUBLIC OF GERMANY** | Pergamon Press GmbH, 6242 Kronberg/Taunus, Pferdstrasse 1, Federal Republic of Germany |



**Library of Congress Cataloging in Publication Data**

Main entry under title:

Atlantic community in crisis.

(Pergamon policy studies)
"An Institute for Foreign Policy Analysis book."
Includes index.
1. Europe--Relations (general) with the United States.
2. United States--Relations (general) with Europe.
3. North Atlantic Treaty Organization. 4. Europe--
Relations (general) with Russia. 5. Russia--Relations
(general) with Europe. I. Hahn, Walter F. II. Pfaltzgraff, Robert L.
D1065.U5A896 1978 301.29'73'04 78-17026
ISBN 0-08-023003-2



*Printed in the United States of America*

# Contents

# Preface

This book represents the findings of a project, completed by the Institute for Foreign Policy Analysis under an original grant from the Fritz-Thyssen-Stiftung, Cologne, the Federal Republic of Germany.

The rationale behind the project can be simply described as follows. In recent years, a variety of strains have loosened the bonds of the Atlantic Community, which emerged in the aftermath of World War II as an association of kindred Western societies and as a military concert in the face of new global dangers. The problems of the Community have been the subject of numerous analyses undertaken in governmental and private sectors on both sides of the Atlantic. These examinations, however, have tended to be selective, directed at immediate and conspicuous problem areas and generally lacking a more comprehensive perspective of the complex interaction of trends affecting the Community. Moreover, this selectivity, although resulting in ample identification of the outstanding problems facing the Community, has left a dearth of broad avenues of proffered solutions.

What seemed to be called for was an analysis in breadth as well as in depth – a searching examination of the evolution of these transatlantic relationships, of the major problems that have asserted themselves, as well as the quest for integrated or, at least, compatible answers to these problems.

In this quest, the authors of this volume benefited immeasurably from the insights and counsel of experts both here and abroad. A listing of those to whom we are indebted would stretch this Preface into an inordinate size; and cannot be acknowledged because of their official positions in the various governments and Atlantic institutions. This applies in particular to the chapters dealing with NATO problems, which reflect the input and review of scores of experts in Washington and other capitals and command centers of the Alliance. Nevertheless, several consultants must receive special mention. The military section of the volume owes much to the conceptual guidance of General Andrew J. Goodpaster, former Supreme Commander, Allied Command Europe. Similarly, the analyses of problems of trade, monetary affairs and resources leaned heavily on the input of experts whose broad knowledge in this complex area has been conditioned not only by academic knowledge but by the leavening of practical policy experience. Particular thanks in this regard is extended to the Honorable J. Robert Schaetzel, former United States Ambassador to the European Economic Community.

All of these contributions, however, would have been to little avail in the absence of the demanding architectural task of placing them into a coherent structure. Robert C. Herber, Associate Director for Publications of the Institute for Foreign Policy Analysis, gave unstintingly of his editorial talents. The equally demanding assignment of translating ideas into typescript was shared by Heidi Anderson, Emily Becker, Marie Burke, Karol Kelliher, Jo Ellen Milkovits and Deborah Roe.

Walter F. Hahn

Robert L. Pfaltzgraff, Jr.

# I

# The Atlantic Community—Conceptual Evolution and Psychological Change

# 1 The Atlantic Community— A Conceptual History

Diane K. Pfaltzgraff

The idea of an Atlantic Community is deeply rooted in the historic relationships among the peoples of the North Atlantic region. It dates from the first European explorations and the establishment of settlements in the New World. It is based upon those shared values of Western civilization founded in humanistic and religious traditions which have placed great emphasis on freedom of speech, opinion, conscience and association. The Atlantic Community idea is indebted to the heritage of Hellenism, the Judeo-Christian religions, Roman law, and the spirit of scientific inquiry – of rational science and toleration of pluralism and diversity.

Western civilization has provided the basis for representative government and for the dual principle of individual liberty and the common good. It has been a civilisation de dialogue – with a continuing exchange of ideas across the Atlantic. The founding fathers of the United States drew heavily upon European political philosophy – principally the tenets of Locke and Montesquieu – in the development of the American Constitution. In turn, the American political experience deeply influenced the shaping of European governmental structures from the French Revolution to the twentieth century.

The Atlantic has hosted the linkage not only of peoples and ideas, but also of commerce. From the founding of the New World settlements in the seventeenth century until the present time, trade across the Atlantic has been vital to the economies of peoples in Europe and North America. The achievement of high levels of industrialization, which distinguishes the North Atlantic area from most of the rest of the world, has heightened the economic interdependence and enhanced the sense of community, or interrelatedness, among Atlantic peoples.

The challenges to Western civilization in the twentieth century have generated efforts to give institutional form to the Atlantic Community. The rise of totalitarianism in the interwar period, a devastating conflict, and the emergence of a new and massive danger in the aftermath of the war spurred the search for strengthened links between the United States and Europe – a search that was rewarded by the postwar evolution of Atlantic political institutions and, within the Atlantic Community, of institutions for West European integration. At both the Atlantic and European levels, several comparable concepts have been developed. They include a federal structure – patterned to some degree on the political model first developed in the United States – as well as more loose-knit organizations providing for collaboration in specific areas of common interest such as economics and trade.

Within the Atlantic Community there have been proponents of a unified Western Europe that could stand as a roughly equal partner of the United States. Advocates of this concept have assigned primacy to the unity of Western Europe as the essential precondition for greater transatlantic unity. Juxtaposed to this has been a concept of Atlanticism, whose underlying assumptions include the likely continued dependence of Western Europe, and the notion of the unity of the Atlantic peoples as the prerequisite for their common and effective involvement in the world-at-large. Europeanism, in contrast, holds that the unification of Western Europe has precedence both in time and importance over the achievement of greater political cohesion within the Atlantic Community as a whole.

Both Atlanticism and Europeanism have given rise to a variety of concepts of institutionalization. Briefly, these may be summarized under three major headings: federal union, confederation, and partnership.(1) This chapter examines the conceptual history of Atlanticism. Its focus is not the institutions of the Atlantic Community, but rather the major concepts that have been proposed for the more effective organization of Atlantic peoples to achieve common purposes.

## FEDERAL UNION

Clarence Streit first proposed the idea of a federal union of Western democracies in his book, Union Now, published in 1939. According to Streit, both the United States – under the Articles of Confederation – and the League of Nations had failed because they lacked a strong central authority to act on behalf of member states. In contrast, Streit held, federalism as evolved in the American political system was worthy of emulation by the Atlantic Community. Admiring the courage of the American Founding Fathers, who created a new union at a perilous time, Streit urged a comparable act of will by the Atlantic nations – specifically Britain, France, and the United States – at the beginning of World War II.

For the postwar period, Streit elaborates his proposal. A union of Atlantic nations was to be established by a constituent assembly of representatives of the members of the Atlantic Alliance.

> Federal Union would start by crossing the political Rubicon and constituting an Atlantic federal government . . . since the political, military, economic, and monetary affairs of Atlantica form an organic whole which should be tacked together by taking first the political decision to set up a 'multination' federal government – one in which all the existing nations of NATO would be directly represented – to handle common affairs in all our fields, and whose first tasks would be to work out the gradual but simultaneous transition to a common Atlantic defense force, market and currency.(2)

Streit urged adoption at the Atlantic level of the Connecticut Compromise formula of 1787, which allowed states of varying sizes to join together via the creation of a bicameral legislature. Representation in one house would be based on population, as in the United States House of Representatives, and in the other on equal representation for the individual state members, as in the United States Senate. Already, in Streit's time, the question of how to achieve a fair representational system among unequal members reflected the magnitude of the problem of inequality between individual West European states and the United States.

A recurrent theme of those who remain skeptical of the wisdom of creating an Atlantic federation has been the concern that in such an undertaking Europe would be in danger of losing its independence and perhaps even its identity. Thus, Hendrik Brugmans, a prominent proponent of European federalism, suggested that West European states would not wish to enter a federation in which one member, i.e., the United States, would be dominant. Such a federation would serve only to grant formal recognition to U.S. hegemony. The problem of physical disparities as well as the historical differences which Brugmans perceived between the United States and Europe led him to support a European federation with sufficient internal autonomy to ensure European pluralism. In this view, a United States of the Atlantic must comprise a United Europe and America.(3)

Although the idea of Atlantic federal union failed to attract widespread popular support either in Europe or in North America, it has elicited sporadic endorsements in the United States Congress. In 1949, Senator Estes Kefauver introduced a resolution calling for the creation of an Atlantic Union.(4) Similar resolutions were introduced subsequently in both houses, but none was adopted. Explaining the consistent refusal of the United States to underwrite the idea of Atlantic Union, one State Department official commented:

> The Department of State shares the goal . . . of attaining an increasingly closer relationship among the Atlantic nations. The reservations which we have about the resolutions (on Atlantic Union) under consideration are not reservations regarding their general philosophy. Rather, our reservations center upon how best to attain the objectives of the resolution and of the specific goal envisaged. . .
>
> The simple, but decisive, fact is that our Atlantic allies do not now wish to move toward any type of federal political relationship with the United States, even as an objective. Until there is an interest on the part of the other states concerned, we cannot do a great deal.
>
> The fundamental reason why there is little European interest in federal union with us at this time is, I think, evident. It is that Europe fears that it would be swallowed by a more powerful United States. . . .
>
> If Europe is hesitant about federation with us because of the inequality between a United States and a divided Europe, we can hope that Europe would be more confident in its relations with us once it

> had attained something approaching equality of power. This hope has been one of the most compelling reasons for our support for European unification. We believe that this is a virtual requirement before political ties with North America of an organic sort can be seriously considered.(5)

Yet, without official American sponsorship, the Atlantic union concept had little chance of being embraced by other Western nations. Even with official U.S. support, it would have faced formidable, perhaps insurmountable, obstacles.

It is unlikely that, without a radical transformation of prevailing attitudes on both sides of the Atlantic, an Atlantic framework could be created along the lines suggested by Streit, that is, by an act of political will. Instead, as many writers have suggested, political institutions result from a complex process of consensus formation. In the case of transatlantic relations, Elliot Goodman notes:

> . . .if there is a dialectical pattern of supranational integration, one must do everything possible to keep the antagonisms between the American thesis and the European antithesis within reasonable bounds. . . . If, as seems likely, it will not be possible to federate the existing individual nations in one step into an Atlantic federal union, neither should one encourage the formation of a European union that will break all Atlantic ties. Whenever, in special circumstances, it may be possible to skip over the intermediate level and create Atlantic institutions directly, this would be highly desirable. In most cases, where this will not be possible, Atlantic ties should serve to reinforce those already created on lower levels even though the Atlantic relations would at first be less well integrated and less supranational than those bonds established among the state units on either side of the Atlantic.(6)

## ATLANTIC CONFEDERATION

The idea of Atlantic confederation provides for cooperation in limited fields. Preferring not to be tied to a single blueprint for the future, the strategy of the advocates of an Atlantic confederation has been to urge governments to accept the principle of gradually pooling sovereignty with respect to matters of mutual interest. The federalist and confederalist approaches also differ regarding the ultimate membership of the communities they seek to create. Atlantic union, for the most part, would restrict membership to NATO participants; the proponents of an Atlantic confederation, however, envisage the possibility of a wider community, including not only NATO members but possibly also the nations belonging to the Organization for Economic Cooperation and Development (OECD) – i.e., a confederation of the industrialized democracies of the North Atlantic area.

NATO represents the oldest existing organization of North Atlantic nations that gives institutional expression to the idea of an Atlantic Community. Although NATO was formed as a defensive alliance against the threat of Soviet attack, there have been sporadic efforts to transform the Alliance into an institutional framework for the achievement of common political purposes transcending defense, as recognized by the framers of NATO in Article II:

> The Parties will contribute toward the further development of peaceful and friendly international relations by strengthening their free institutions, by bringing about a better understanding of the principles upon which these institutions are founded and by prompting conditions of stability and well-being.

In a report to the NATO Council in December 1956, a committee consisting of the foreign ministers of Canada, Belgium, and Norway concluded that the strengthening of NATO depended upon

> the development of an Atlantic Community whose roots are deeper even than the necessity for common defense. This implies nothing less than the permanent association of the free Atlantic peoples for the promotion of their greater unity and the protection and the advancement of the interests which, as free democracies, they have in common.(7)

The Committee did not recommend significant changes in the structure of NATO. Rather, the desired political cooperation was to be pursued through more intensive consultation within the existing framework. In particular, member governments were urged to inform the NATO Council of any matter significantly affecting the Alliance. This was conceived as a preliminary step toward effective consultation. Although these recommendations were adopted unanimously by the NATO Council, member governments in succeeding years have not always honored their commitment to the principle of prior consultation.

Notwithstanding the lack of formal progress toward the goals implicit in Article II, NATO members were able, during the 1950s and 1960s, to create mechanisms for enhancing communication among them. In particular, the NATO Parliamentarians, founded in 1955, brought members of the national legislatures together to discuss Alliance problems. A group of private citizens assembled in London in June 1959 and formulated a document attempting to define the fundamental values of the Atlantic Community.(8) The NATO Parliamentarians Conference helped to organize the Atlantic Convention of NATO Nations held in Paris in January 1962.(9) From this meeting came an appeal for "the creation of a true Atlantic community . . . which must extend to the political, military, moral and cultural fields." The Conference also called for a better definition of the principles for which the Western nations stand and proposed the creation of a Special Commission by the respective governments within two years to study the future organization and means to further the idea of an Atlantic Community.

The 1962 Declaration of Paris was of special significance in the history of the Atlantic Community concept because of its specificity concerning the possible institutionalization of the Atlantic relationship. First, it called for the creation "as an indispensable feature of a true Atlantic Community, of a permanent High Council at the highest political level, to concert and plan, and, in agreed cases, to decide policy on matters of concern to the Community as a whole." In the interim, it recommended the strengthening of the North Atlantic Council. Second, the Declaration called for the NATO Parliamentarians Conference to become a consultative assembly to "review the role of all Atlantic institutions and make recommendations to them." Third, it proposed the establishment of an Atlantic High Court of Justice which would decide legal controversies arising under the treaties. Fourth, to enact its recommendations, the Declaration called upon NATO governments to establish a Special Governmental Commission "to draw up plans within two years for the creation of a true Atlantic Community, suitably organized to meet the political, military and economic challenges of this era."(10)

However, the Declaration of Paris failed to gain the support of the NATO governments to whom it was addressed. To some, the notion of an Atlantic Community was undesirable because any Atlantic organization by definition would appear to subordinate Western Europe permanently to United States hegemony. Others believed it inappropriate, for the term "community" had been preempted by the European Community. Thus, for example, the president of the EC Commission repudiated the concept of an Atlantic Community in the following terms:

> The so-called 'Atlantic Community' cannot be confined to the Atlantic area, for its effects must embrace our other friends and partners in the Pacific and elsewhere. Nor, on the other hand, is it a 'community' in the same sense that this word applies to the European Community – that is, a full economic union with strong political implications. . . . What seems much more likely to emerge, in fact, is a close partnership between two personalities, the European Community and the United States, benefiting not only its 'partners', but the other countries as well.(11)

De Gaulle's attitudes and policies toward NATO were strongly influenced by his concern over American hegemony within the organization. Thus, his memorandum of September 1958 to "create a tripartite organization to take joint decisions on global problems," as well as decisions on the use of nuclear weapons, had it been accepted, would have elevated France to equal status with the United States and Great Britain. To his critics, this initiative meant not so much that De Gaulle wished to cooperate in reaching agreed policies within NATO, but that he desired to find an institutional means to proclaim French grandeur.(12)

Even though French relations with NATO improved somewhat under De Gaulle's successors, the legacy of Gaullist thought, both within France and in other European states, hampers efforts to realize a strong European union or, indeed, to strengthen NATO and Atlantic institutions. While West European nations officially retain their commitment to solidarity with North American in the Atlantic Alliance, as reaffirmed in the Declaration on Atlantic Relations of 1974, there are those who remain attracted to the vision of a "European Europe" capable of being a third force between the two superpowers or who are sympathetic to the anti-American emphasis of De Gaulle's policies. Even in the 1960s, at a time when proposals for the creation of Atlantic Community political frameworks were being put forward, the concept of an Atlantic confederation was in eclipse. Instead, Europeans and Americans focused attention on the concept of partnership, which promoted the idea of a unifying Western Europe acting in concert with the United States.

## ATLANTIC PARTNERSHIP

The concept of an Atlantic partnership between the United States and Western Europe was designed as an alternative to an Atlantic union or an Atlantic confederation, in either of which the discrepancy between U.S. power and that of the European members would remain vast. This discrepancy, it was hoped, would be overcome in a bilateral arrangement between the United States and a more nearly equal and united, or unifying, Europe. Relationships in such a partnership were often described in terms of two pillars supporting a common framework. The United States assumed that a united Europe, stronger economically, would be able to share global burdens.

An essential difference between an Atlantic union or an Atlantic confederation, on the one hand, and an Atlantic partnership, on the other, is that the former would have a multilateral structure and the latter a bilateral one. As Elliot Goodman has observed, efforts to reform NATO as a multilateral organization were pursued until 1962, after which "the bilateral partnership concept had the effect of being viewed as an alternative to NATO, instead of as a complement to it."(13) In Goodman's view, this course was mistaken: "If NATO could have been reformed and strengthened, such plans should have been pursued independently of developments in establishing an Atlantic partnership."(14) Yet officials who supported partnership apparently felt that the reform of NATO would detract from efforts to build a partnership.(15)

A major question posed by the concept of partnership lay in the definition of who was to be "Europe." This problem assumed particular importance because the membership of the European Community did not coincide with that of NATO Europe. Evidently the original supporters of partnership paid little heed to this question because they laid stress upon first developing the bilateral relationship, primarily in the economic field. "The supporters of European unity, both in Europe and in Washington, anticipated a spillover effect from economic union to a political and military one. Consequently, moves toward economic union in the Common Market, functioning in partnership with the United States, were viewed as having political and military implications."(16) Had the European Community been able to act collectively and to function as a unit, it might have gained greater bargaining power in its relationship with the United States. But, as Goodman observed:

> Even after the Community has surmounted the considerable obstacles that stand in the way of achieving a full economic and monetary union, it will be faced with the still greater difficulties of arriving at common agreement in foreign policy and defense affairs, which is essential for a genuine political union. One can only speculate about when, if ever, these more ambitious aims will be achieved.(17)

In addition to the problem of who would constitute Europe in a transatlantic partnership, the concept appeared to neglect the position of Canada. By and large, Canadians rejected this concept because there was no place in it for them; their preference lay instead in a multilateral Atlantic Community. While Lester Pearson was Prime Minister, Canada played an important role in Atlantic relations. Although this role has been reduced since Pierre Trudeau became Prime Minister in 1968, Canada still appears to prefer an Atlantic framework rather than a bilateral partnership.(18)

The concept of an Atlantic economic partnership was voiced as early as 1959 by Jean Monnet, shortly after the formation of the EEC. Monnet called for a new institutional approach to concert policies among the major Western industrial powers on both sides of the Atlantic in several critical areas, including monetary stability, economic growth, aid to underdeveloped areas, world commodity stabilization, and tariff arrangements. Monnet's objective was to encourage joint action among the United States, the United Kingdom, and the European Community. Institutionally, this initiative had led to the reorganization of the OEEC (Organization for European Economic Cooperation) to include the United States and Canada, and renaming it the Organization for Economic Cooperation and Development (OECD). Yet the revised OECD never achieved the objectives set by Monnet. Its failure was attributed to the fact that the Six (France, West Germany, Italy, Belgium, the Netherlands and Luxembourg) refused to sit as a Community, acting as one;

> and a small policy council to bring the United States, Britain, and the Common Market together for joint decisions was never set up. But, above all, what the OECD has lacked has been a mandate for action. The weak OEEC charter, which permitted binding decisions only by unanimity, was watered down further to satisfy the United States; the OECD was not authorized to make binding decisions at all; it can only consult and recommend.(19)

According to Kleiman, another opportunity to foster the concept of partnership was lost during 1961. Again, Monnet, in response to the U.S. dollar crisis during late 1960 and 1961, had taken the initiative by calling for a joint approach by Europe "in partnership with the United States" to promote currency stabilization in the West.(20) While discussions about the U.S. monetary crisis were held within the OECD, action was finally taken within the framework of the International Monetary Fund, an organization then dominated by the United States and Great Britain. In the compromise formula adopted to deal with the crisis

> It was agreed that decisions by the new ten-nation 'Paris Club' could be made by qualified majority votes – the votes of seven countries which had contributed sixty percent of the new reserves. In effect, the agreement was a step toward a limited kind of Atlantic reserve fund. And the same countries, meeting in the OECD monetary committee, thus acquired an added incentive for the day-to-day cooperation by Finance Ministries and central banks that subsequently gave OECD its only significant continuing success.

> Most important, an ad hoc Atlantic institution had been created with decision-making machinery that, for the first time, reflected the new balance of financial power in the West. Sovereignty had been pooled in a way new to the Atlantic area.
>
> This beginning of true Atlantic partnership could have set a precedent for action on other critical economic problems as well as more permanent monetary reform. . . . But the precedent of the 'Paris Club' was not followed up in any field, not even in the field of stopgap monetary measures. . . .(21)

It was largely in recognition of the potential challenge posed by the European Economic Community that the United States made its offer of partnership with the New Europe.(22) On July 4, 1962, in Philadelphia, President Kennedy sought in his "Declaration of Interdependence" to redefine the emerging Atlantic relationship. He asserted: "We do not regard a strong and united Europe as a rival but as a partner. To aid its progress has been the basic objective of our foreign policy for seventeen years."(23) Kennedy envisaged a "Grand Design":

> We believe that a united Europe will be capable of playing a greater role in the common defense, of responding more generously to the needs of poorer nations, of joining with the United States and others, in lowering trade barriers, resolving problems of currency and commodities, and developing coordinated policies in all other economic, diplomatic, and political areas. We see in such a Europe a partner with whom we could deal on a basis of full equality in all the great and burdensome tasks of building and defending a community of free nations.(24)

He also urged the European nations to increase their efforts to achieve political unity among themselves. In fact, it appeared that the building of Europe was a precondition to forming a partnership with the United States. "The first order of business is for our European friends to go forward in forming the more perfect union which will some day make this partnership possible."(25)

Kennedy's speech found a sympathetic hearing among European adherents of a united Europe. Indeed, just a few days earlier, on June 26, 1962, a Declaration of the Action Committee for the United States of Europe had stated:

> While the economic unity of Europe is being consolidated and a start made on its political unification, the cooperation that has already grown up between the United States and European countries should gradually be transformed into a partnership between a United Europe and the United States . . . a relationship of two separate but equally powerful entities, each bearing its share of common responsibilities in the world. This partnership is natural and inevitable because the peoples of Europe and America share the same civilization based on freedom, and conduct their public life in accordance with democratic principles.(26)

It appeared that the United States stood firmly in support of the dual concepts of European integration and Atlantic cooperation as compatible and mutually reinforcing goals. The EEC Commision also issued a statement welcoming President Kennedy's offer of a partnership with Europe.(27) In particular, Walter Hallstein, addressing the European Parliament on June 26, 1963, hailed the U.S. willingness to share its position of world power "with a Europe which is increasingly assuming economic and political proportions comparable to its own. . . ."(28) Pierre Uri, one of the drafters of the Rome Treaty, contended that what made Atlantic partnership attractive to Europeans was, in fact, its recognition that a European entity had begun to exist. With the birth of the Atlantic partnership concept, some former European supporters of an Atlantic Community shifted their loyalties to the former:

> The goal of common institutions spanning the Atlantic, binding Europe and America together, was replaced by the aim of dividing the Atlantic into two distinct parts, each functioning in friendly competition with the other.(29)

Because of this possibility, some believed that partnership could never serve as an adequate substitute to the concept of an Atlantic Community. If the partnership idea was to work, the United States and Europe would have to share a basic consensus on any policy issues they were likely to confront, i.e., they should be partners not rivals.

> The partnership idea . . . embodied the truth that Europe must participate fully in the decisions that would shape its future. The absence of such full discussion could only produce resentment and lead to a continuing crisis in European-American relations. Partnership thus sought to recognize differences and to organize a continuing dialogue so as to produce an institutionalized exchange of each other's views and intentions with the aim of arriving at common decisions. This view of partnership assumed mutual goodwill. . . .(30)

Advocates of the partnership concept never fully examined the question of what would happen should a united Europe wish to play an independent international role, i.e., act as a traditional great power in foreign policy rather than subsume its interests in a transatlantic partnership. François Duchene, in particular, pointed out the potential dangers in a bilateral partnership where the two partners disagreed.(31) Each could, in effect, veto the other. How this problem was to be resolved was never addressed because the supporters of partnership preferred instead to believe that consensus would always exist between the partners.

While the emphasis of the partnership concept appeared to focus on the economic equality of the United States and Western Europe, some tentative steps were taken to extend it to the military and political spheres. In particular, the U.S. proposal for a multilateral nuclear force in the early 1960s represented an effort to satisfy European demands for some form of codetermination in the nuclear strategy of the Alliance – although it also reflected fears of prominent members of the Kennedy Administration of independent nuclear capabilities in Western Europe. The proposal called for a joint Atlantic nuclear force with mixed crews, the deployment of which would be subject to a veto by each member. Given De Gaulle's opposition to all forms of integration and his penchant for French military independence within the Alliance, it was understandable that France objected to the MLF proposal. In De Gaulle's view, the MLF would have given Europe the illusion of codetermination while, in reality, the United States would ultimately preserve control over the Alliance's nuclear forces. He also objected to the idea on the grounds that the United States, because it would retain a large part of its nuclear arsenal outside the MLF, would not relinquish its own independence of action, while the European members would have to forfeit control over their own nuclear forces.

The MLF proposal thus failed to provide the basis for a partnership arrangement in the military realm. The very absence of a distinct European military partner in the scheme constituted a basic reason for its failure. While there were suggestions that the Western European Union, created as an intergovernmental organization consisting of Great Britain and the Six, might fill the role of such a partner, the objections of France to such a proposal prevented its adoption. Thus the partnership concept was limited essentially to the economic field. In 1963, a group of European and American experts proposed a program for transatlantic action through the creation of institutions patterned after the Treaty of Rome: the United States and the European Community were to be represented equally in a Council of Partnership at the ministerial level. In addition to this intergovernmental decision-making body, they proposed to establish a group of three or four "wise men" who, while lacking formal authority, would use their moral influence to focus the attention of governments on the most urgent problems of Atlantic economic relations and submit recommendations to the Council for action.(32)

On June 1, 1964, a similar proposal was advanced by the Action Committee for the United States of Europe, which urged the establishment of a Committee of Detente between the United States and the European Community, composed of high-level representatives from the United States government and from EC member governments. In 1967 and in 1971, the Action Committee repeated its recommendation for the establishment of such a permanent organ for reciprocal consultation, in which the European Community and the United States would be represented on the basis of equality in later years. So far no progress has been made to establish bilateral machinery to carry out these proposals.

## EUROPEAN UNION

A crucial element of the partnership concept is a strong, united Europe, which would be an equal partner to the United States in a broader Atlantic Community. Another perspective, however, sees in this unification the possibility of a Europe independent of the United States and able to assert its own role on the world stage. These two views of a united Europe thus diverge markedly in their attitudes toward Atlantic relationships. Despite the uncertainties over the direction a united Europe might take, the basic concept of European union gained supporters on both sides of the Atlantic in the post-World War II period. This support was based on several assumptions, including the belief that a united Europe would prevent the recurrence of intra-European conflict, promote internal social stability and a democratic order, enable the wartorn European economies to achieve growth and prosperity through economic integration, and build political and military strength through political unification. A key motive behind the unity idea was the desire to harness the West German state tightly to the community of democratic West European societies.

Although the United States lent important support to the concept of a European union, the initiative was undertaken by Europeans. A major step was taken by Robert Schuman, the French Foreign Minister, on May 9, 1950, in his proposal for the integration of the iron, coal and steel industries of Western Europe. By pooling coal and steel production and placing the industries under a joint authority, Schuman sought to "assure the establishment of common bases for economic development, which is the first stage for a European federation. . . ."(33) Schuman's plan thus envisaged the pooling of key industries which would, in turn, create de facto solidarity; ultimately, phased integrative steps in the economic sectors were to culminate in a European federation.

The functionalist strategy was based on the assumption that "the sector approach to the problem would make it possible by gradually widening the area of integration, not only to arrive at an economic union but also, through further extension of this, at political union."(34) The link, as conceived by Schuman and Monnet, lay in the institutional structure proposed as a necessary part of the process of economic integration: once this had proved its worth in purely economic matters, it was believed that it could gradually acquire more explicitly political functions. Once the principle of a certain amount of supranational power had been established and was found to be both effective and essential, it would only be a matter of time before the institutions that wielded this power were given, or could assume, more political power.(35) The creation of the European Coal and Steel Community (ECSC) with its supranational High Authority and the proposal in the Pleven Plan for the creation of a common European army under a supranational commission highlighted the functionalist approach to the unification of Western Europe.

The subsequent success of the ECSC as the first supranational European organization generated other, more ambitious plans for economic integration and political unification. In 1952, the Six established an ad hoc Assembly, composed of the representatives to the ECSC Assembly, to draft a constitution for a European Political Community. In the following year, on March 10, 1953, a draft treaty was submitted to the six governments calling for the creation of a European Political Community. Had this federalist manifesto been adopted by the respective governments, it would have provided for a European authority in charge of foreign policy, defense and trade. Moreover, its declared aim was to establish a supranational, indissoluble union of peoples and states.

But in 1954 the French National Assembly refused to accept the Treaty for a European Defense Community, thereby also defeating the European Political Community. Subsequently, the Western European Union (WEU), an intergovernmental organization composed of the Six, together with Great Britain, was created to replace the EDC. This substitution, WEU for EDC, marked a significant difference not only in structures, but also in basic concepts of European organization and its relationship to the United States. Despite this setback, European leaders, in what became known as the relance européenne organized a meeting of foreign ministers at Messina in June 1955, which eventually resulted in the signing of the treaties of Rome on March 25, 1957, creating the European Economic Community and the European Atomic Energy Community.

The proponents of the supranational European Communities believed that the functional integration in the economic and nuclear sectors would ultimately spill over into unification in the form of a European political federation. According to one writer,

> It was the functionalists who won the race to create the first living unified European reality and, therefore, what there is of the united Europe which was born is neither a Europe of the peoples nor a Europe of states, but rather a Europe of supranational offices.(36)

This fact has had important implications for the course of European unification. In particular, the different routes to European unity – the federal, the confederal, the functionalist – differ in their respective views of the roles that a new European community should play:

> For the federalists, the role of European union consists essentially in the creation of a new political society dedicated to the development of a modern democratic life among peoples. . . .
>
> For the functionalists, political life and institutions are less important superstructures than is normally believed. The proper ordering of men's daily lives is what is fundamental; therefore, the role of European union . . . will not be the ephemeral, superficial, and inconclusive political struggle but the slow, progressive coagulation of customs and interests around an integrated European bureaucracy which is more farsighted and rational than the national bureaucracies.
>
> The confederalists . . . are seeking to recover, at a European level, the glory, power, and grandeur which European national states once had. . . . Because the natural depositories of this glory are the old nation-states, they cannot renounce the fundamental symbol of their status, which is sovereignty.(37)

## A CONFEDERAL EUROPE

An alternative route to a united Europe is that of the confederalists who have emphasized the development of intergovernmental cooperation through the creation of a union of states. This model for European union permits the individual states to retain their sovereignty, but to coordinate decisions on matters of common concern.

The confederal concept of a united Europe was advocated by President De Gaulle. To promote this conception, France introduced the Fouchet Plan for a Union of States. This confederal design for Europe was subsequently rejected by the other five EEC members. De Gaulle conceived of a united Europe des patries in which the individual members would retain their sovereignty. He saw Europe as "a small continental West European bloc of states maneuvering its way between the United States and the United Kingdom on the one hand and the Soviet Union on the other."(38) A European Europe would be capable of acting as an arbiter between the two superpowers. "It appears that Europe, provided it wishes it, is henceforth called upon to play a role which is its own . . . it is a question of Europe's being made in order for it to be Europe. A European Europe means that it exists by itself for itself."(39) Clearly, De Gaulle's vision of Europe left no room for support of either an Atlantic federation or an Atlantic confederation.

Europeans of the Monnet school of thought saw in the EEC's institutions an opportunity to bypass national rivalries by a new concept that accorded all partners legal equality and equal respect. At the same time, its actions were to benefit the broader community of nations. The independent Commission was to transcend narrow national interests and to determine the common interests of the Community. The European Parliament provided a framework in which national parliamentarians could exchange views on common problems. The foundation was being laid for an eventual political union of the separate states into a United States of Europe.

President De Gaulle, while admitting that the EEC's institutional framework had made a positive contribution to Europe, contended that European integration, as it evolved in the postwar period, only contributed to American hegemony. "To him, the Community institutions constituted an arid technocracy without the possibility of developing political roots, and hence they would be susceptible to easy manipulation by the far-reaching schemes drawn up in Washington."(40) De Gaulle's commitment to nationalism prevented him from acknowledging that any political organization other than the nation-state could have political significance.

> Short of conquest, a Gaullist 'European Europe' could not be had. The only possible basis for creating a powerful Europe, truly independent of the United States, fully capable of pursuing independent action, was to renounce the nationalist and imperialist molds of the past and integrate the separate states in a new supranational community. That is, the Monnet school, which he openly scorned, provided the only answer for the kind of institutional strength that would make a truly independent Europe possible. . . .(41)

Given De Gaulle's objections to integration at the European level, it was not surprising that he should also attack NATO as an Atlantic institution which subordinated French interests to those of the United States. Indeed, his long-range conception of a Europe des-patries could be interpreted as envisaging a renversement des alliances under the slogan, "detente-entente-cooperation" between Eastern and Western Europe.

> If the Atlantic Alliance is necessary at present for the security of France and the other free peoples of our old continent, they must

> behind this shield, organize to achieve their joint power and development. . . . France has recognized the necessity of this Western Europe . . . as the indispensable condition of the equilibrium of the independence and the freedom of each nation and taking into account the probable evolution of political regimes, establish a European entente from the Atlantic to the Urals."(42)

In the short term, however, De Gaulle was not averse to pursuing efforts within the Atlantic Alliance to promote French national objectives.

In some circles, it was anticipated that the accession of Valery Giscard d'Estaing to the French presidency in May 1974 would lead to a new French role in the EEC and a less intransigent French attitude toward European union. In August, 1976, the appointment of Raymond Barre, a former Vice President of the EEC Commission, as Premier also encouraged those who hoped for an increasingly pro-European French policy. Domestic events in France, however, including an increasing polarization of French politics between a resurgent Gaullist Right under the leadership of Jacques Chirac and an increasingly powerful Left, have constrained the limited initiatives Giscard made toward a more cooperative French role within the EEC.

Some skeptics in Brussels have doubted that Giscard ever really intended to retreat significantly from the Gaullist stance of his predecessors.

> They concede that the new President withdrew French objections to majority voting in the Council of Ministers and direct elections to the European Parliament. But they argue that these were largely symbolic retreats from positions of Gaullist intransigence made to ensure the adherence of the European-minded Centre Democrats to the new presidential majority. (43)

Another interpretation, less cynical, views Giscard's European policies as having reflected a sincere effort on his part to differentiate his Independent Republican Party from its Gaullist allies, and to take advantage of indications in the 1975 presidential election campaign that the public was more sympathetic to a European policy less obstructionist than that of De Gaulle. (44)

At the very least, France has changed somewhat the style of French diplomacy in regard to European problems. Yet, rather than seeking to strengthen EEC institutions, Giscard has emphasized the importance of bilateral contacts among the four most important members of the organization.

The emphasis upon periodic summits between France and the Federal Republic and between France and Great Britain, (45) as well as apparent interest in a similar arrangement with Italy, suggest that Giscard conceives of some form of board of directors to manage the EEC. (46) The conception of a Paris-Bonn-London-Rome directorate was opposed by the Benelux countries; nevertheless, only these four states participated in the economic summits at Rambouillet in November 1975 and in Puerto Rico in June 1976. Moreover, although all nine member states are represented on the European Council, created at Giscard's initiative, "even here agreement between the 'big four' is the prerequisite to success." (47)

The use of summits and directorates provided Giscard with a means to secure Gaullist support for direct elections to the European Parliament. In presenting the goverment's program to the French National Assembly on October 5, 1976, Raymond Barre had been careful to call for policies toward European union which would be of the confederal type favored by De Gaulle and Pompidou. Moreover, he observed that direct elections to the European Parliament would not augment its powers, a stance long associated with Gaullist attitudes toward that institution.

Meanwhile, the EEC has changed dramatically since 1958. It can boast of some major accomplishments. Paradoxically, however, the success of the EEC appears to have encouraged members to a greater self-assertiveness.(48) As a result, the ultimate goal of a political union still remains in doubt.

At a summit meeting in Paris on October 19 and 20, 1972, heads of government of EEC member-states agreed to establish a European Fund for Monetary Cooperation by April 1973 and a fund for regional development by the end of the same year. The leaders also called for the creation by 1980 of a European union to coordinate economic, social, political and foreign policies among the members, following up on the proposals of the Hague summit meeting in December 1969, which had urged increased political cooperation among the Six (the Davignon Group) and eventual monetary and economic unification.

The Paris communique of 1972 reflected a basic ambivalence about the future direction of the EEC. The summit, while reaffirming the importance of a close European relationship with the United States, took no steps to provide a framework for a transatlantic dialogue. The document reflected support for both a <u>Europe des patries</u> and a federal Europe, the latter envisaged as a unified political structure in which sovereignty would be shared between national and supranational institutions.

Leo Tindemans, the Belgian Foreign Minister, was invited to prepare a report in an effort to resolve the inconsistencies which had permitted these two conceptions of European unity to coexist for the past twenty years. To some, the Tindemans Report begged the question. European union was left largely undefined. Noting the close interconnection between the different facets of European union, Tindemans contended: "The development of the Union's external relations cannot occur without a parallel development of common policies internally."(49) Tindemans avoided specifying the eventual shape of European union or setting a timetable for its completion. In his report, he recommended that the term of the Council presidency be extended to one year to enhance its importance and stature. Moreover, he called for a greater delegation of authority to the Commission under the provision of Article 155 and via the Committee of Permanent Representatives.(50) Finally, Tindemans recommended the direct election of the European Parliament and the expansion of its powers.

These proposals, not unexpectedly, met with hostility from France. Other governments, as well, had reservations concerning the possible loss of sovereignty associated with some of Tindemans' ideas. As a result, the two subsequent summit meetings of the Nine only briefly considered the recommendations, referring them to the foreign ministers for study. When the Tindemans' proposals were presented at the December 1976 Hague meeting of the Nine, most of his suggestions were rejected. The Nine agreed only to request the Commission to make an annual report to the summit on progress toward European union.(51) Thus, as of 1977, further plans toward the creation of a European union, whether of the federal or confederal model, appeared unlikely to win adequate support from European governments. Indeed, one analyst has pointed to

> a risk that the EEC will become increasingly intergovernmental in character and less supranational; and this poses a threat to the smaller members of the EEC. Moreover, any tilt in emphasis toward a non-Treaty body can result only in a relative demotion of Community institutions, especially the Council of Ministers and the Commission.(52)

Thus, it is argued that the Council of Ministers just as easily could have taken the decision, adopted by the European Council in April 1976, to hold direct elections for the European Parliament in 1978. To rationalize European institutions, the proposal was made to absorb European Councils into the Council of Ministers framework.(53) This procedure could easily be followed were the Treaty of Rome to be amended to permit more political cooperation under its jurisdiction, as recommended in the Tindemans Report.

In sum, changes both in the international environment and within the European Community itself have dampened the prospects of further movement toward European political integration.

## THE NIXON DOCTRINE AND ATLANTIC PARTNERSHIP

The Nixon Doctrine was based on the assumption that new power centers – particularly Western Europe, Japan and China – were emerging. It was hoped that such power centers would be able to assume a greater portion of their defense. In successive foreign policy reports to the Congress, the Nixon Administration appeared to welcome the changes in Atlantic relationships which signaled the end of American tutelage and dominance.

> The challenge to our maturity and political skill is to establish a new practice in Atlantic unity – finding common ground in a consensus of independent policies instead of in deference to American prescriptions. This essential harmony of our purposes is the enduring link between a uniting Europe and the United States. . . . European and American interests in defense and East-West diplomacy are fundamentally parallel and give sufficient incentive for coordinating independent policies. Two strong powers in the West would add flexibility to Western diplomacy, and could increasingly share the responsibilities of decision.(54)

While the reference to added flexibility in Western diplomacy appeared to indicate some acceptance of an independent European point of view on issues, Nixon's last foreign policy message to Congress in 1973 contained several reservations regarding the economic policies being pursued by the European Community. Still, Nixon asserted, the

United States supports European unity, as we always have. But now we need to define together the basis of cooperative economic relations between the United States and the European Community in this decade. To do this, we need a new affirmation of our common goals, to give direction to our economic negotiations and promote cooperative solutions . . . .There are new creative tasks for our partnership.(55)

As Secretary of State, Henry Kissinger was often criticized for giving priority to relationships with the Soviet Union, to the relative neglect of NATO. In a major address on the European-American relationship (his ill-fated Year of Europe speech on April 23, 1973) Kissinger alluded to problems confronting the Atlantic nations in their relations with each other:

. . . the problems in Atlantic relationships are real. They have arisen in part because during the fifties and sixties the Atlantic community organized itself in different ways. . . . If we want to foster unity, we can no longer ignore these problems. The Atlantic nations must find a solution for the management of their destiny, to serve the common objectives which underlie their unity . . . the Atlantic nations must join in a fresh act of creation, equal to that undertaken by the postwar generation of leaders of Europe and America.(56)

To that end, the Secretary of State proposed to the Europeans the joint drafting of a new Atlantic charter in recognition that the complex issues facing the European-American relationship required comprehensive treatment. Later, in December 1973, at a time of deep division between the United States and the European Community in the immediate aftermath of the Middle East war and the oil embargo, Secretary Kissinger called upon the European allies to assist America in "finishing the task of renewing the Atlantic community" and stated that "The United States is committed to making the Atlantic community a vital, positive force for the future as it was for the past. . . For we, Europe, Canada and America have only two choices: creativity together or, irrelevance apart."(57)

In calling upon the European states to create the basis for a new Atlantic relationship, Kissinger in his Year of Europe speech of April 23 had been careful to avoid imposing U.S. conditions.Central was the need for reciprocity in U.S.-European relations. In addition, he sought to approach Atlantic problems comprehensively. He noted that

The political, military and economic issues in Atlantic relations are linked by reality, not by our choice nor for the tactical purpose of trading one off against the other. . . . It is the responsibility of national leaders to insure that economic negotiations serve larger political purposes. They must recognize that economic rivalry if carried on without restraint, will in the end damage other relationships.(58)

In Europe, reactions to Kissinger's initiative were mixed and hopes that this step would result in a new conceptual basis for strengthening the Alliance ultimately were not fulfilled.

> There appeared to be emerging two quite different conceptions of a united Europe. One . . . pressed by the French, held that the Atlantic relationship actually impeded the European one. The French conception, illustrated in part by the European Community's September draft declaration on Atlantic relations (primarily of British inspiration), stressed Europe's independence and equality within the Alliance, and emphasized that in those areas where Europe still was weak, notably defense, new efforts would be demanded. The other version, Kissinger's, seemed a new version of the old two-pillar theory . . . some of the phrases in the U.S. document, words like 'partnership' and 'interdependence,' were too strong for the neo-Gaullists (not all of them French), who preferred notions such as 'dialogue' and 'independence.'(59)

The effort to reconcile these two divergent concepts played a dominant role in transatlantic tensions during 1974. In fact, in an address in London in December 1973, Kissinger complained that European unity was defined and measured by the gap between the positions taken by the European Community and the United States, respectively, on problems such as the Middle East. Kissinger objected to the unwillingness of the European Community to consult with the United States in advance of its decisions. "To present the decisions of a unifying Europe to us as _faits accomplis_ not subject to effective discussions is alien to the tradition of U.S.-European relations."(60)

The lack of a consensus among the Atlantic allies during the Middle East crisis in 1973 was not without irony, for in his April 23,1973, speech Kissinger had contrasted a parochial Europe to a United States with global interests and responsibilities. Yet, when the EC succeeded in developing a consensus at odds with U.S. Middle East policy, Washington was unhappy. The irony lay in the fact that this common viewpoint represented the harbinger of a common European position – a European identity of purpose – which the United States had sought repeatedly to encourage. The Nine, at Copenhagen in December 1973, authorized the Danish President to represent them in talks with the United States, following Kissinger's appeal for a new Atlantic charter. This marked the first occasion on which the Nine had spoken through a single spokesman on a foreign policy issue.

> The Middle Eastern Crisis has shown that the international environment conceals dangers that may suddenly threaten disaster. An alliance between America and Europe is an essential element of a safe international system, but that alliance will not be indefinitely maintained in a sort of historical vacuum or without adding to its military core new forms of political and functional cooperation. The emergence of a political Europe must mean a stronger voicing of European interests on the international scene. It also means that changes will be required in the structure of the alliance to accommodate a new political situation. . . . For their part the leaders of America must recognize that the phase of unmodified U.S. leadership of the West . . . is now over and must be replaced by a concept in which the interests of both sides receive equal consideration and there is genuine reciprocity of advantage.(61)

Washington's dissatisfaction contributed to European perceptions that the United States would accept European unity only on its own terms. Europeans objected to the view that they had ganged up on the United States by their preparation of a joint position before meeting with U.S. officials. Moreover, as Karl Kaiser observed:

> A request to consult on all matters with the United States <u>before</u> making decisions would be tantamount to denying the right of further integration if it were meant to be practiced dogmatically. On the other hand, the idea is a sound one if exercised pragmatically through the usual diplomatic channels, i.e., as a process of mutual consultation in which the United States would reciprocate on matters relevant to the Europeans, such as on Soviet-American dealings.(62)

Eventually, the European members of NATO, meeting in Ottawa on June 19, 1974, agreed upon a Declaration on Atlantic Relations. In this document, signed in Brussels on June 26, 1974, NATO members declared that "the Treaty, signed 25 years ago, to protect their freedom and independence has confirmed their common destiny . . . maintained their security, (and permitted them) to preserve the values which are the heritage of their civilization. . . ."(63) They also reaffirmed their conviction that "the North Atlantic Treaty provides the indispensable basis for their security" and that "their common defense is one and indivisible."(64)

On balance, rather than providing the basis for the renewal of the Atlantic Alliance, the Year of Europe seemed to have contributed to a further deterioration in transatlantic relations. It is indicative of the confused state of relations between the United States and the European Community that the latter should have been criticized both for what it had achieved and for what it had failed to achieve.(65)

The Middle East crisis in 1973 affected profoundly the Atlantic Alliance, introducing new strains in the transatlantic relationship. The events of 1973 posed stark questions concerning the continued validity of the post-World War II assumption that there is an identity of interests between the United States and Western Europe. The divergence of views evidenced during the debate over how to respond to the Arab oil boycott created new tensions in the Atlantic relationship. Indeed, many in the United States began to raise serious questions about the premise that American support for European unity continued to be in the best interest of the United States. To be sure, the establishment of the International Energy Agency demonstrated the ability of Western Europe and the United States to overcome some of these differences. On balance,however, the energy crisis, as well as other developments within the Alliance, affected adversely the U.S.-European security relationship.

> . . . the point is that the Europeans together decided on a path during the crisis that was different from the U.S. path, and that is what has worried both sides. Where does identity of interests start and where does it end and how can it be defined? If it is not defined precisely, the value of the alliance is weakened immeasurably, for there can be no allied deterrent where there is no allied credibility. The problem for the alliance today is to find the new definition and its limits, and

where it is different from the old to make the necessary adjustments. But this is a painful process.(66)

Early supporters of a European union and an Atlantic Community had believed that West European economic strength and economic unity would lead to political integration and the creation of a greater European defense capability. Yet, in 1978, Western Europe, lacking its own political unit to raise and command military forces, including a nuclear force, capable of balancing the growing Soviet military threat, remains dependent upon the United States for its security. As one writer has noted:

> The European Community, no matter what its aspirations, will never be the strategic equal of the United States or the Soviet Union. For that reason it is compelled to maintain an Atlantic relationship no matter what it may think of the 'condominium.' Europe should also bear something else in mind: the creation of a European political and defense union is bound to diminish the American presence in Europe. It would be a logical consequence. But by the same token the security of America begins in Europe and will continue to do so even with a more independent Europe and a reduced U.S. presence on the continent.
>
> The Atlantic Alliance has always served both sides. All the interests of the two sides may not coincide, but the basis of the alliance – mutual security – still remains.(67)

## THE PROBLEM OF POLITICAL WILL

As they have since the founding of NATO, the United States and Western Europe today confront many grave problems whose solutions lie beyond the capacity of the individual members of the Atlantic Community. The ideas associated with the creation of an Atlantic Community have represented a response to the common economic, social and military problems shared by the Atlantic nations. The search for new institutional frameworks to encompass the Atlantic nations has signified an attempt to adapt the sovereign nation-state system to contemporary needs.

Yet, some twenty-nine years after the formation of NATO, the Atlantic peoples have still not agreed on a single institutional framework to serve the diverse needs of Atlantic societies. Although lacking consensus in support of any one grand design, the nations of the North Atlantic have established organizations that have begun to link the European and North American peoples. To the extent that the development of a political community results from a dialectical process of consensus formation, the existence of diverse structures may help to provide the basis for the eventual formation of adequate Atlantic institutions and practices.

For the present, the Atlantic Community still lacks an institutional infrastructure capable of translating common needs into joint political action. It exists, in a limited form, in the domain of security as symbolized by the Atlantic Alliance, in the economic and energy field as symbolized by the

OECD and the IEA, and socio-culturally as exemplified by the common beliefs and values of a shared civilization. But in the absence of common political institutions, the Atlantic Community is yet to be fully realized.

Europeanism, too, has yet to find adequate institutional expression. Whether or not the EC will provide the framework for a European political community remains to be seen. Beyond that lies the question of whether this organization, or some other European framework, perhaps yet unborn, will provide the basis for a European entity that could enter into partnership with the United States. The conceptual history of the Atlantic Community, and of its members, is rich in ideas for the building of political institutions. What has been lacking is the political will to translate concepts into programmatic action.

## NOTES

(1) A union is a federation of states, based upon a constitution which divides sovereign powers between a central government and a number of regional authorities, each autonomous in its respective sphere of competence, with the national government in control of foreign policy and defense. A community is a confederation of states, based upon a treaty between sovereign states that delegates certain specified powers to a common authority which exercises them on behalf of, and subject to, the unanimous consensus of the member states. A partnership is an association of sovereign states or regional groupings, linked by a formal agreement or informal understanding, and determined to arrive at a mutually acceptable compromise on all major issues of concern to the partners.

The term "community" lends itself to several definitions. As Frank Munk noted, "An Atlantic Community (with a capital C) may represent only a program, an aspiration, and an idea. A community of history, of basic values, of common interests may or may not be conducive to the creation of a Political Community, but it exists among the people around the Atlantic rim." Frank Munk, Atlantic Dilemma: Partnership or Community (Dobbs Ferry, N.Y.: Oceana Publications, 1964), p. 16.

In modern usage, a community also describes a group held together by common values and beliefs. Then, too, with the birth of such institutions as the European Economic Community (EEC), supranational institutions have acquired the name of Communities. While the term Atlantic Community implies something more than societies which are found on the borders of the Atlantic Ocean, it does not yet imply a political entity entitled to the label of Community. Munk stresses (p. 19) that there is thus a need to distinguish between communities and Communities (capitalized), "the latter representing in current usage a supranational political community. It might be considered a Community of communities, with each state being a political system and the supranational Community a super-system, or alternatively, the Community being the system and national states the sub-systems."

(2) Freedom and Union, April-May 1963, p. 3, and July-August 1963, p. 20.

(3) Hendrik Brugmans, "From Political Defense to World Leadership," Atlantic Community Quarterly, Summer 1964, p. 203. According to Brugmans, "it is unlikely that the medium states of Europe are prepared to enter a federation where one power – America – is predominant. Naturally enough they consider such an enterprise an attempt to institutionalize American hegemony . . . .In fact, the building materials of an Atlantic union are not fifty odd states on one side, and six or sixteen on the other. The material has to be twofold: Europe and America, both united."

(4) For the history of the federal union idea, see Istvan Szent-Miklosy, The Atlantic Union Movement (New York: Fountainhead, 1965).

(5) Statement by John M. Leddy, Assistant Secretary of State for European Affairs before a subcommittee of the Senate Foreign Relations Committee during hearings on S. Con. Res. 128, Department of State Bulletin, April 25, 1966, p. 672.

(6) Elliot R. Goodman, The Fate of the Atlantic Community (New York: Praeger, 1975), pp. 21-22.

(7) Report of the Committee of Three on Non-Military Cooperation in NATO, reprinted in Department of State Bulletin, January 7, 1957.

(8) For the text of the Declaration of this Atlantic Congress, see Ernst Bieri, et al., Basic Values of the Atlantic Community (London: Pall Mall Press, 1962), pp. 132-133.

(9) For the history and achievements of the North Atlantic Assembly, as the NATO Parliamentarians' Conference was later renamed, see Gerhard Mally, The NATO Parliamentarians' Conference (Paris: Secretariat of the NPC, 1966); and The North Atlantic Assembly 1964-1974 (London: The British Atlantic Committee, 1974).

(10) For the text of this Declaration, see Christian A. Herter, Toward an Atlantic Community (New York: Harper & Row, for the Council on Foreign Relations, 1963), pp. 80-82. In regard to other matters, the Declaration urged the harmonization of political, military and economic policies affecting the Atlantic community as a whole. Moreover, it commended the progress being made in the early 1960s toward the strengthening of European economic institutions and "the spirit of President Kennedy's statement that a trade partnership be formed between the Untied States and the European Economic Community, the basis of an Atlantic Economic Community, open to other nations of the free world."

(11) Walter Hallstein, United Europe: Challenge and Opportunity (Cambridge, Mass.: Harvard University Press, 1962), pp. 87-88.

(12) Goodman, pp. 88-91.

(13) Ibid., p. 138.

(14) Ibid.

(15) Ibid., p. 139.

(16) Ibid.

(17) Ibid., p. 141.

(18) Ibid., pp. 141-146.

(19) Robert Kleiman, "Background for Atlantic Partnership," in Karl H. Cerny and Henry W. Briefs, editors, NATO in Quest of Cohesion (New York: Praeger, 1965), p. 439.

(20 Ibid., pp. 438-439. Monnet made his proposal during the course of an interview with Kleiman which appeared in U.S. News and World Report, January 30, 1961.

(21) Kleiman, "Background for Alantic Partnership," p. 441.

(22) Ibid., p. 436. See also his Atlantic Crisis: American Diplomacy Confronts a Resurgent Europe (New York: Norton, 1964).

In Kleiman's view, Kennedy's Grand Design suffered the setback of De Gaulle's veto of British application for Common Market membership in January 1963 because it represented more "a perspective toward the future rather than a concrete program to be implemented."(p. 432.) Specifically, the idea of an Atlantic partnership sprang from Great Britain's Common Market decision in the summer of 1961 and the decision of the United States to try to take advantage of British entry into a united Europe, which would create a partner capable of sharing some of the United States' international burdens.

(23) Department of State Bulletin, July 23, 1962, p. 132. Although John F. Kennedy usually is credited with the "partnership" theme, McGeorge Bundy is also viewed as an initiator of the idea. Bundy, in a speech on December 6, 1961, had spoken of a partnership between the United States and a greater European power. See the Address by McGeorge Bundy at Chicago, December 6, 1961, in Freedom & Union, January 1962.

(24) Deparment of State Bulletin, July 23, 1962, p. 132.

(25) Ibid.

(26) Western European Union: 1962 (Paris: Assembly of Western European Union, March 1963), p. 51.

(27) European Community, No. 55, August 1962, p. 2.

(28) Ibid., No. 64, July-August 1963, p. 2.

(29) Goodman, p. 151.

(30) Ibid., pp. 157-158.

(31) Francois Duchene, Beyond Alliance (Boulogne-sur-Seine: The Atlantic Institute, 1965).

(32) Pierre Uri, et al., Partnership for Progress (New York: Harper & Row, 1963), pp. 100-103.

(33) Department of State Bulletin, June 12, 1950, pp. 936-937.

(34) Roy Price, The Political Future of the European Community (London: John Marshbank, 1962), p. 27.

(35) Ibid.

(36) Altiero Spinelli, The Eurocrats: Conflict and Crisis in the European Community (Baltimore: The John Hopkins Press, 1966), p. 25.

(37) Ibid., pp. 12-13.

(38) Goodman, p. 53.

(39) President De Gaulle's Tenth Press Conference, July 23, 1964. Ambassade de france, New York, Speeches and Press Conferences, No. 208, p. 5.

(40) Goodman, pp. 66-67.

(41) Ibid., p. 67.

(42) Speeches and Press Conferences, op. cit., p. 77. Behind this view of an eventual Europe from the "Atlantic to the Urals" lay De Gaulle's conviction that communist ideology was but a temporary aberration which distorted traditional "Russian" national interests. Thus, Russia, as part of Europe, was in the long run destined to rejoin the other European states in an all-European political construction. See Goodman, p. 73.

(43) Michael Leigh, "Giscard and the European Community," The World Today, February 1977, p. 74.

(44) Ibid., p. 75.

(45) Leigh, p. 75. See also Nevill E. Waites, "Britain and France: Toward a Stable Relationship," The World Today, December 1976, for information on British-French relations.

(46) Leigh, p. 75. This suggestion has been reported in Le Monde, February 10, 1976.

(47) Leigh, p. 76.

(48) E. Moxon Browne, "The EEC after Tindemans: The Institutional Balance, The World Today, December 1976, p. 460. The author notes that "despite the expectations of neofunctionalism, economic integration has stiffened the resistance to political integration. Economic prosperity has been seen in largely national terms: the motivation behind integration thus becomes specifically national aspirations. Since, presumably, the 'founding fathers' established the EEC to transcend national loyalties, the success it has had in reviving national esprit de corps is more than slightly ironic." See R.J. Harrison, Europe in Question (London: Allen & Unwin, 1974), pp. 193ff, for examples demonstrating that discontinuity between economic and political integration had been anticipated by neofunctionalists.

(49) Leo Tindemans, "Report on European Union," Bulletin of the European Communities, Supplement 1/76.

(50) Tindemans, p. 31. See also Roland Bieber and Michael Palmer, "Power at the Top – the EC Council in Theory and Practice," The World Today, August 1975, pp. 312-314.

(51) The Economist, December 4, 1976, p. 64.

(52) Browne, p. 464.

(53) Ibid. A parenthetical suffix could indicate the personnel involved: i.e., European Council (Agriculture) or European Council (Heads of State).

(54) U.S. Foreign Policy for the 1970s (Washington, D.C.: GPO, 1972), p. 40.

(55) U.S. Foreign Policy for the 1970s (Washington, D.C.: GPO, 1973), p. 94.

(56) Address by Henry A. Kissinger, United States Secretary of State and Assistant to the President for National Security Affairs, at New York, April 23, 1973. Department of State Bulletin, No. 1768, pp. 593-598.

(57) Address in London, December 12, 1973, Department of State Bulletin, No. 1801, pp. 778-779.

(58) Kissinger, New York address, p. 596.

(59) James O. Goldsborough, "France, the European Crisis," Foreign Affairs, April 1974, p. 543. Excerpted by permission from Foreign Affairs, April 1974. Copyright 1974 by Council on Foreign Relations, Inc.

(60) Address by Secretary of State Henry A. Kissinger at London, December 12, 1973, Department of State Bulletin, No. 1801, pp. 778-779.

(61) Z, "The Year of Europe?," Foreign Affairs, January 1974, pp. 244-245.

Excerpted by permission from Foreign Affairs, January 1974, Copyright 1973 by Council on Foreign Relations, Inc.

(62) Karl Kaiser, "Europe and America: A Critical Phase," Foreign Affairs, July 1974, p. 728. Excerpted by permission from Foreign Affairs, July 1974. Copyright 1974 by Council on Foreign Relations, Inc.

(63) Atlantic Community Quarterly, Fall 1974, pp. 390-393.

(64) Ibid.

(65) Z, p. 240.

(66) Goldsborough, p. 551. In his Foreign Affairs article (p. 726), Karl Kaiser perceived a tendency in the United States toward growing opposition to a united Europe unless its views accord with those of Washington. He, too, noted the lack of consultation and the unilateralism in action increasingly prevalent between European states and the United States as well as within the Community itself.

(67) Goldsborough, p. 555.

# 2 The Atlantic Community— The Psychological Milieu

James E. Dougherty

A multitude of terms can be used to describe the important psychological factors that crucially affect the Atlantic Community – terms such as political will, credibility, self-confidence and confidence in allies, shared beliefs and values, perceived mutual threats, dependence and interdependence, and above all, sense of community. Psychological factors relate in particular to the perception of past, present, and future realities. These perceptions, in turn, are as important as objective reality itself, for if individuals in the policy process believe their perceptions to be real, they are real in their consequences.

Journalists, in describing the psychological state of the Atlantic Community have used the term as a shorthand assessment of the more important psychological factors affecting the Community at any point in time. This psychological state is often contrasted with previous or anticipated future psychological states. Such a highly abstract concept must be used with some caution. The psychological state of a large social collectivity such as the Atlantic Community is the product of a complex confluence of a host of subjective factors with a large number of objective social, economic, political and military trends – a confluence that influences in a variety of ways the positions taken by governments, political leaders, parties, groups and institutions.(1) No single psychological theory can adequately explain the dynamic processes that define a given psychological state. Yet, theories do exist which can make a contribution toward an understanding of the psychological forces that have helped to shape the Atlantic Community during the last three decades.

*The author wishes to acknowledge the contribution of Dr. Gerald T. West, who first suggested Maslow's hierarchy of needs as a framework for the analysis in this chapter.

## THE MASLOWIAN THEORY

One such theory has been developed by Abraham H. Maslow. Maslow's theory of human motivation is based on an analysis of a hierarchy of needs that most human beings seek to gratify. Although the theory is addressed primarily to individual need gratification, it offers at least an experimental framework for the assessment of primary drives in an aggregate setting, such as that of the Atlantic Community. The experiment in this case seems validated not least by the assumption that by their very definition the salient drives of democratic societies reflect, in good measure, if imperfectly, the aggregate desires of the human constituencies to which they are responsive.

Most psychologists agree that individual human needs can be classified and hierarchically ordered.(2) Maslow has offered a fivefold ordered classification of basic human needs that include:

1. Physical Needs – including, among others, food drink, oxygen and sex.

2. Safety Needs – including not only the need for physical safety, but the need for familiar routines, for order, for protection from noxious stimuli and their threat.

3. Belongingness Needs – including the need for love, affection and the sense of identification with a group or groups, or solidarity with others.

4. Esteem Needs – including the desire for strength, for achievement, for adequacy, for mastery and competence, for confidence in the face of the world, also the desire for reputation and prestige ... status, dominance, recognition, attention, importance or appreciation.

5. Need for self-actualization, including the drive for self-fulfillment.(3)

In his ordering of these five kinds of needs, Maslow argues that some become manifest and demand satisfaction before others emerge. Until the basic physical needs are satisfied, Maslow argues, they will dominate man's attention. Gratifying them permits the next "higher" set of security needs to emerge and to dominate – until they too are gratified and give way to the dominant drive for self-actualization. There is no absolute rigidity in the hierarchical pattern, but the pattern is sequential in the aggregate.

James Davies has noted that while Maslow's hierarchical ordering of man's needs is not ostensibly political, it does enable a description of political motivation in rather broad, but nonetheless discrete, terms.(4) A need hierarchy for nation-states can be developed that corresponds to Maslow's individual need structure. In Table 1 the individual and some selected national need equivalents are presented, along with an identification of specific developments in Western Europe which appear to be relevant. While Table 1

Table 1 Correspondence of Maslow's Individual Need Hierarchy to National Need Hierarchy

| | Individual needs | National Equivalent | W. European Developments | Time Period |
|---|---|---|---|---|
| 1. | Physiological | Basic Economic Needs – provide means to feed, clothe and shelter citizenry | Post War Recovery – Marshall Plan, Reconstruction Politics and Economics | 1946-1955 |
| 2. | Safety Needs | Basic Security and Defense of Citizenry Against Threats Both Internal and External | Creation of NATO – Rearmament of FRG, Berlin Blockage and Soviet Threats, Truman Doctrine | 1948-1965 |
| 3. | Belongingness | Gemeinschaft<br>a) Cooperation integration and homomorphism<br>b) Sense of association through affect, traditions and similarity of values | Formation of Organizations – European Coal and Steel Community, NATO, EEC, OECD, WEU | 1948-1973 |
| 4. | Self-Esteem and Self-Actualization | Independence<br>a) Desire to determine one's own destiny; sovereignty<br>b) Desire for status and prestige | Europeanism – Gaullism/ *force de frappe* – failure to progress more rapidly toward political integration | 1958-1978 |

suggests the usefulness of Maslow's need hierarchy for the analysis of the Atlantic Community, in the next section we shall explore its utility both as a descriptive and diagnostic theory of what has occurred in the Community.

## Europe's Postwar Physiological Needs

The situation that prevailed in Western Europe at the close of World War II aptly fits the initial stage in Maslow's hierarchy. The end of World War II found Western Europe in physical and economic shambles. Much of the industrial base and the transport system had been destroyed. Agricultural production was down by more than a third from prewar levels, and the Europeans lacked the wherewithal to pay the higher prices for food imports from abroad during a period of world shortage. Sources of badly needed energy and replacement parts were similarly beyond reach without external assistance. In every country which had felt the ravages of war, urban populations and camps of homeless refugees were suffering from malnutrition, hunger and severe shortages of food, clothing, shelter and other basic necessities and conveniences. The peoples of Western Europe were preoccupied with the drive for sheer survival. Their governments, such as they were, could focus upon little else besides economic recovery, but were frustrated by their own apparent helplessness to expand production.

Long before the Marshall Plan was conceived, U.S. leaders recognized the dangers posed by physical and economic deprivations to the fragile fabrics of the re-emergent societies of Western Europe. Between June 1945 and December 1946 the United States extended nearly $8 billion in credits to Western Europe. More than half of this amount went to Great Britain. This U.S. response was by no means purely altruistic. There was a recognition in Washington of the threats of continued economic dislocations to the political viability of democratic governments in Western Europe, to the successful operation of the kind of international economic order that had been planned at Bretton Woods (and on which postwar U.S. prosperity would depend), and, perhaps, even to the physical security of West European territory.

Faced with an exacerbation of West European economic woes throughout 1946 and the spring of 1947, and by a severe winter and the prospect of drought and a coal shortage, the Truman Administration drew up the outlines of what was later termed the Marshall Plan for European economic recovery. The essential feature of the plan was that it made U.S. aid contingent upon a joint planning initiative on the part of the Europeans. Theoretically, the offer of American assistance was open to all European states, including the Soviet Union and the East European countries, but the communist-dominated countries rejected the Marshall Plan and attacked it as a form of anticommunist imperialist aggression.(5) Communist abstention made the task of the West European governments easier, and greatly facilitated their eager steps toward coordinating recovery efforts.

## European Security Needs

As Western Europe's basic economic requirements began to be met and economic conditions slowly improved, the needs for physical security and defense against both internal and external threats began to assert themselves more prominently. Indeed, the distinction between Europe's preoccupation with its physiological needs in the early postwar years and its concern over security in the face of Soviet power cannot be sharply drawn. Even though the United States was not yet prepared to give a firm defense commitment, certainly American policymakers, in moving to meet Western Europe's economic requirements, were aware of Europe's vulnerability both to military pressure from the Soviet Union and to political pressure from domestic communist parties, especially in Italy and France. In Europe, a handful of policymakers were well aware of the security threat which was developing in the East, and of the need for the West Europeans to think about integration among themselves. Indeed, even before the war ended, Belgian leaders in London had foreseen the need for a West European alliance under British leadership, supported by the Americans. Shortly after the war, De Gaulle had spoken to the Germans "in the language of Europe," and within a year, Churchill was calling for a partnership between France and Germany as the first step toward the re-creation of the European family. "There can be no revival of Europe without a spiritually great France and a spiritually great Germany," said Churchill in his Zurich speech of September 19, 1946, in which he envisaged a "United States of Europe," that Britain would advocate but not join.(6) By the time the Marshall Plan was being adumbrated at a Harvard commencement ceremony the movement toward the organization of European unity had already been put into motion.

For a relatively modest investment of some twelve billion dollars from April 1948 to January 1952, representing about one percent of its GNP during that period, the United States achieved a remarkable foreign policy success in Europe. Western Europe's production in 1952 was double what it had been in 1938. The Marshall Plan alone, of course, could not possibly have brought about such a remarkable resuscitation; the Europeans themselves provided most of the technological skills and managerial experience needed to ensure economic growth. U.S. assistance speeded up the process by facilitating the flow of imports which the Europeans lacked the necessary dollars to purchase. More importantly, however, the United States induced intra-European cooperation on the planning of recovery, the harmonization of investment policies, and the reduction of trade and payments barriers.

The European governments eagerly accepted the Marshall Plan. Undoubtedly a great many Europeans, remembering the past glories of their nations, were somewhat resentful at the fall from their once high estate and their enforced dependence upon a country which in their eyes embodied the less refined traits of Western civilization.(7) As their physiological needs were met, Europeans could indulge in the luxury of criticizing the United States. The criticism was spearheaded by quasi Marxist (though not necessarily communist) intellectuals who, though not averse to benefiting materially from America's largesse, displayed a fasionable leftist-progressive disdain for anything resembling success in the capitalist, bourgeois system.(8) Even apart from the hypercritical and disgruntled intelligentsia, however, there were undoubtedly others in Europe who contributed a great deal to the postwar economic miracle and who felt that the Americans tended to take too large a share of the credit for postwar European recovery.

By mid-1947 it was becoming clear that the United States intended to commit substantial resources to Europe's economic recovery. West European policymakers were able to turn more attention to security issues, amidst a growing disappointment over the breakdown of great power unanimity on which the United Nations system of collective security had been founded. They had been aware ever since the end of the war that the Soviet Union was consolidating, in permanent form, its control over the countries of Eastern Europe, pursuing an intransigent course in negotiations with the Western Allied Powers (especially over Germany) and applying diplomatic pressure upon Turkey for a revision of the Straits regime on terms satisfactory to Moscow. The Soviets and other communist-dominated governments in Albania, Yugoslavia and Bulgaria had been supporting the communist EAM insurrectionists in the Greek Civil War. Nevertheless, following the war, both the Soviet Union and the United States carried out demobilization. By the end of 1946, Allied strength in Western Europe was down from a mid-1945 peak of five million to about 880,000. By 1948, Soviet military strength had been reduced from more than eleven million to slightly less than three million, but most of those forces were either occupying parts of Europe or facing westward.(9)

The creation of the Cominform in September 1947 by the communist parties of the Soviet Union, the East European satellite countries and France and Italy, followed by a complete deadlock in the Council of Foreign Ministers over the question of Germany, prompted negotiations among Britain, France and the Benelux countries of January 1948 toward the conclusion of a political-military alliance.(10) These negotiations were noteworthy in that the initial impetus for a collective self-defense organization came from the Europeans themselves, not from the United States, which hastened to approve it. Undoubtedly, however, British Foreign Secretary Ernest Bevin was interested, almost from the beginning, in bringing the United States into a European defensive alliance. Two events in the first half of 1948 gave urgency to the psychological issue of security both in Western Europe and the United States. The first was the communist-instigated coup in Prague in February, supported by the Soviet Red Army.(11) The second, several months later, was the Soviet blockade of West Berlin.

American revisionist historians have suggested that the Western nations overreacted to the threat of Soviet military aggression in Europe in the late 1940s, averring that the Soviet Union, too weak at that time to provoke a showdown, had no intention either of mounting a general attack or of trying to push the West out of Berlin. Such verdicts, however, are much more easily rendered in the comfortable light of hindsight than in the context of the times. To anxious leaders in the war-ravaged societies of Western Europe, the events of 1948-1949 pointed to a concerted communist offensive. Their fears were heightened by the rhetoric of communist party leaders in France and Italy, where Maurice Thorez and Palmiro Togliatti were proclaiming in the national parliaments, in identical language, that when the Red Army arrived at the borders of their countries the working classes would greet it as an army of liberation.

Those who contemplated the utter military weakness of Western Europe in 1948 did not doubt that American economic aid alone would be insufficient to bolster Europe. Since an economically reviving Europe would be both a threat to the economically backward communist societies and a more inviting target for Soviet pressure, European policymakers became increasingly convinced that enhanced military security was an essential prerequisite to the stability and self-confidence needed for sustained economic recovery and growth. A comprehensive alliance would provide that security, and U.S. participation was perceived as essential – not least because Western military experts could not conceive of an effective defense without a rearmed Germany, and because only a durable and massive American military presence offered adequate insurance against a resurgence of German strength and militarism.

There was a sufficient consensus among the West European governments to bring NATO into being, but they brought, also, often disparate motives into the Alliance. The British, for example, were interested in maintaining the special Anglo-American relationship that had been developed during the war; their approach to West European defense was calculated to enhance but not to dilute that relationship. A few of the smaller states, especially the Benelux countries, were willing to move toward European unity at a more rapid pace than Britain and France, but even Belgium and the Netherlands disagreed, not over economic cooperation but over how much emphasis should be placed on the anti-Soviet orientation of Western unity.(12) In France, Scandinavia, and the Low Countries, many people were as much (if not more) concerned about the possible future resurgence of an aggressive Germany; while this reflected a genuine fear, its articulation in some quarters was probably designed to make Western defense unity less obnoxious in Soviet eyes.(13)

Europeans in the late 1940s had a vivid image of their own virtual helplessness. Europe, they feared, was a power vacuum waiting to be filled. The strength of the United States was needed to balance that of the Soviet Union. The Europeans hardly had to be lectured on the balance of power, which they had "invented" and which the isolationist elites of the United States had historically disdained until the advent of the Second World War. The invocation of American military power for the maintenance of a stable equilibrium was looked upon as more of a necessity than a desideratum in itself. Nations rarely enjoy dependence on an outside power for protection. No matter how welcome the American GIs had been during the period of liberation, most Europeans undoubtedly would have preferred to be in a position to tend to their own interests instead of relying on a foreign power much stronger than themselves. But in the hierarchy of European needs security obviously was far more important than self-esteem. Faced with the realities of the situation, the West European nations not only accepted but actively sought the status of an American protectorate. At the same time, however, the seeds of subsequent problems were planted.

On the side of the United States, there was by 1948 a widespread recognition by policymakers that U.S. security was inextricably linked to Western European security. America simply could not allow the historic and geographic center of Western civilization to fall under Soviet domination, whether by military or other means. The Sovietization of Western Europe would be a catastrophic blow to democratic government and jeopardize the survival of free political institutions even in the United States; it would render Europe's remaining colonies, bases and spheres of influence throughout the world vulnerable to communist takeover; it would place the growing productive potential of Western Europe at the disposal of totalitarian planners and strategists; and it would greatly reduce the defense-in-depth capabilities of the United States by depriving its air, ground and naval forces of access to the eastern littoral of the North Atlantic Ocean. Whether or not U.S. policymakers anticipated an actively aggressive policy on the part of the Soviet Union, these were nevertheless compelling reasons for the U.S. government to take the position that it could not possibly tolerate a Soviet takeover of the Western region. More pragmatic perhaps, yet less clearly articulated at the time, was the thought in the minds of U.S. policymakers that Western Europe was gripped by an erosive sense of uncertainty and insecurity which had to be removed if the political stability absolutely essential to economic recovery and growth were to be achieved.

## Belongingness

By the mid-1950s Europeans were less concerned about fulfilling basic physiological needs as the European Recovery Plan had begun to bear visible fruit. With the ending of the Korean War, the structuring of NATO (particularly with West Germany's accession to the Alliance in 1955) and the deployment in ever greater measure of American military power to Western Europe, some of the cutting security concerns also began to ease. It became possible for Europeans to give greater expression to what Maslow calls the need for belongingness – to turn, in other words, toward the development of a sense of community. Excessive nationalism had spent itself in the carnage of World War II, and many Europeans became convinced that they had arrived at a deeper understanding of common values as a result of their shared tragedy. The "idea of Europe" began to take root, first among the elites and then in the public consciousness.

Many Europeans perceived the utility of functional cooperation across national boundaries in planning the process of economic recovery in the Organization for European Economic Cooperation. Moreover, they had already undertaken in the seventeen-nation Council of Europe to promote social progress and to safeguard their common cultural heritage. Why could this new attitude of cooperation not be carried forward dramatically with a creative drive toward the European Community? Such a movement, if successful, would transcend the historic enmity of France and Germany and set Europe upon a bold new course. Idealistic impetus was supplied by such Christian Democrats as Schuman, Monnet, Bidault, Adenauer, De Gasperi and others who were convinced that Western Europe must not be allowed again to stray into the blind alley of national particularism that had ended in World War II.

The initial milestone was the Schuman Plan for a Coal and Steel Community. This Community was founded not so much on idealism as on a rational calculus of self-interest. Monnet and other French advocates of economic integration believed in European unity, but they were every bit as much interested in the Schuman Plan as a spur to economic modernization and rationalization. French politicians and military leaders who were still suspicious of Germany looked upon the Schuman Plan as a means of subordinating an important industrial sector of an irrepressibly recuperating Germany to joint planning and control. Chancellor Adenauer regarded the Schuman Plan as an avenue through which West Germany might grope toward international respectability and equality.(14)

Once it became clear that the United States warmly approved of the Schuman Plan, Italy and the Benelux countries were eager to be included. The British, however, although they were major producers of coal and steel, could not be convinced that it would be to their advantage to join. They were unsure of their ability to compete economically with the Germans. The Labourites feared that Common Market policies (reflecting a bias toward free market forces) would interfere with domestic socialist welfare plans; many in both the Labour and Conservative Parties were reluctant to compromise Britain's global role reflected in her Commonwealth ties and the special relationship with the United States by joining Europe. They had misgivings about the loss of sovereign prerogatives, subordination of the nation's independence to supranational law and institutions, and commitment to the long-term political goals of a federal Europe.

Thus, we can see that the desire for belongingness was by no means evenly distributed throughout Europe. There emerged an inner core of what became The Six (France, West Germany, Italy, Belgium, the Netherlands and Luxembourg) who were willing to move further and faster toward integration than the other European states. There was also an outer periphery of The Seven that later made up the European Free Trade Association or EFTA (Britain, Austria, Denmark, Norway, Sweden, Switzerland and Portugal) and showed much more constraint about belonging to and committing themselves to community.(15) Although among leadership and elite groups in Western Europe generally an "idea of Europe" flourished upon a revived sense of shared civilizational values and perceived necessities, nevertheless the idea lacked a coherent political foundation.

Even the Six found that they could not proceed too fast and too far. The European federalists had had their fingers badly burned when they attempted to rush community-building efforts in the defense and political sectors during the early 1950s, and succeeded only in creating, for many groups (including the French Army), an identity crisis which frightened and alienated erstwhile supporters. The federalists, who had been pursuing a strategy based upon economic rationality, encountered the power of irrational, emotional and nationalist elements on the day in August 1954 when the French National Assembly rejected the proposal for a European Defense Community.(16) The Europeanists had seriously miscalculated. They now realized that if they were to make further progress on the practical task of economic integration (which was their forte) they had to devise a new strategy, one which would enable them to advance their community-building objective by maximizing homogeneity and minimizing heterogeneity of national aims, by aiming at closer, more realizable targets and by cushioning unpleasant effects.(17) The federalists became more cautious in their approach. Without renouncing their commitment to foreign policy and defense integration in the long run, they muted it in the short run and intensified their efforts in the economic sector, where support for integration was greatest.

The appearance of a commonly recognized external challenge or threat often provides a spur to the development of a sense of community. To a certain extent, the Suez crisis of late 1956 served just such a catalytic purpose. That crisis roduced both political and economic shocks in Western Europe. The political shock issued from the spectacle of the United States dissociating itself from its allies, Britain and France, and temporarily aligning itself in the United Nations with the principal adversary in order to terminate the war in the Middle East. The economic shock resulted from the impact which the closing of the Suez Canal had upon the oil supplies of Western Europe. Both politically and economically, the West Europeans had been made to feel weak and vulnerable. Monnet, Spaak and other federalists moved quickly in the spring of 1957 to take advantage of the post-Suez mood by pushing through the Rome Treaties for the European Economic Community and the European Atomic Energy Community. But the sense of European Community continued to infuse only the Six, and even though both treaties had definite political implications for the future, the movement for integration remained essentially confined to the economic sector.

Thus, to use the well-known sociological distinction drawn long ago by Ferdinand Toennies, the emerging European Community was more a Gesellschaft based on rational contractual relationships and perception of enlightened self-interest in a world of monetary values than a Gemeinschaft or community of emotion and feeling that results from awareness of likeness, kinship and friendship, as well as of shared life experience.(18) According to Toennies, Gemeinschaft corresponds to the more traditional community of sentiment and affection; Gesellschaft normally comes later, as customary beliefs give way to the dictates of economic utility and efficiency, and the warmth of family and village ties competes with the rising cold of legalistic and commercial associational relationships.(19) The older and more powerful European nationalisms took form in the era of Gemeinschaft. What is perhaps more remarkable about the modern European federalists is their confident expectation that it will eventually be possible to create a community of European sentiment from an association of economic transactions – in other words, that it is possible to move from Gesellschaft to Gemeinschaft. The federalists not only expect that the functional spillover effect will contribute to further integration as the full ramifications of dealing with specific problems in any one area are grasped, but they also hope that the upgrading of common interests will lead to a gradual shifting of elite and popular loyalties toward Community symbols and institutions.(20)

There can be no doubt that Western Europe has become more sociologically and economically integrated since World War II insofar as the mobility of persons, ideas, and goods (capital and consumer) is concerned. It may be true to a considerable extent (as many would contend), that the Common Market has done little more than overcome the excessive nationalist barriers of the archprotectionist period and make available once again the conditions of free movement which prevailed prior to World War I. If so, even this would be no mean achievement, for today's socioeconomic, cultural and technological structures render possible a much more significant intermixing movement than did those of the late nineteenth and early twentieth centuries. What was once freedom for the elites has now become freedom for

Ortega y Gasset's irrepressible masses. Consumer tastes are being homogenized. Businessmen, civil servants, engineers, teachers and professionals of all sorts, students, journalists, athletes, laborers, secretaries and waitresses are traveling through Europe in unprecedented numbers. A substructure for development toward unity is being laid, but the path has been strewn with formidable obstacles.

Europeans, in their striving for unity, have experienced what psychologists call cognitive dissonance, which arises from inconsistencies in knowledge concerning values, environment and behavior.(21) People may believe in the abstraction of European unity as a desirable goal, and pay frequent lip service to it, yet exhibit great caution when it comes to taking practical, concrete steps toward unity because such steps usually bring the goal into either conflict or competition with other values and interests. The ideas of European and Atlantic Community, for example, were complementary in theory, but many people (not only De Gaulle), regarded them as incompatible in actual practical application. The West Germans did not wish to become so fully integrated with the West as to preclude all possibility of eventual national reunification. The neutral countries definitely favored a certain level of European cooperation, but they shunned a unity movement aimed at political goals which might prejudice their neutrality. Socialists and anticlerical republicans in the 1950s and early 1960s were distinctly cool toward a European unity movement which was being guided largely by the leaders of Christian Democracy. Hence no single explanation can be postulated for the differentiation of little Europe from greater Europe.

The dichotomy between British and French policy perspectives was at times overdone, but it was important. For a long time the British manifested an approach-avoidance syndrome toward entering Europe, as if they were unsure of what they wanted to do as their commercial interests were unmistakably shifting from the Commonwealth and EFTA to the European Community. De Gaulle, in an effort perhaps to rationalize his own conservative posture toward European unity and to deflect criticism from France for slowing the integrative process, effected an interesting psychopolitical projection by attributing some of his own political preconceptions to the British. The Germans, who were anxious to offend none of their principal allies, had to balance pro-Atlantic and pro-European policies. While Britain was outside the Community, Frenchmen who dreaded the sublimation of the nation's puissance soveraine into a supranational Europe and Europeanists who disliked De Gaulle's design for a French-led Community took advantage of Britain's absence to argue that there should be no Europe without the United Kingdom.

When Britain finally did arrange to come into the European Economic Community on January 1, 1973, it was almost entirely for reasons of economic necessity, not of political sentiment. Furthermore, the British did not enter on a wave of unshakeable confidence. Hardly was the United Kingdom in when Europe felt the shock of another Middle East crisis, in many respects worse than that of Suez in its repercussions upon the economies and the amour propre of the European countries. The many repercussions of that crisis are described in various sections of this study. Here it is sufficient to say that a series of external threatening events, which should, by all odds, have served to enhance the internal cohesiveness of the recently expanded Community, instead, placed it under a severe strain by complicating all the economic issues which its members were then negotiating. Perhaps even more severe was the political strain imposed upon NATO. The economic-political reaction to the crisis compounded Britain's sense of doubt and confusion concerning the move into Europe, and prompted a lukewarm Labour Government to renegotiate the terms of entry, thereby feeding the suspicions of some Europeans that London was not only opposed to European unity but might try to wreck it.

The shocks of October 1973 and its aftermath can be expected to subside. In one sense, the expansion of the Community from six to nine members can be looked upon as a sign of growth. But thus far there has been no assurance that this expansion will lead to greater cohesiveness in respect to economic, military and political unity. The disparate outlooks and goals of the various governments and national ruling parties toward such issues as energy policy, inflation, international monetary disturbances, the growth of Community institutions and regional development funding make it appear that Europe's governing elites, constrained by many organized interests, are becoming increasingly reluctant to take the bold steps needed to achieve the earlier professed goal of achieving economic-monetary and political union (once hopefully scheduled for 1980). British Foreign Minister James Callaghan has frequently and publicly expressed skepticism of the unity goal. Even after the pro-Common Market vote in the June 1975 referendum, the British remain uncertain about their role in the Community, and they are not at all confident that membership will really help to solve their domestic problems (even though most of them would agree that those problems would be worse if Britain had withdrawn).

The British, it has been suggested, will probably continue to be the most reluctant Europeans, and will be most cautious about creating a European government responsible to an elected parliament. The French now support direct elections to the Strasbourg Parliament, but they do not want an Assembly dominant over the Executive (as embodied in the summit meetings of heads of government), and they can count upon the British to be their allies on that score.(22) The Germans, recognizing that the prospects of federation are not bright at the present time of financial troubles and diverging economic policies, are cautious about committing themselves to costly Community ventures. This is indicative of a serious dilemma which has been described as follows:

> Unless there is a commitment to a form of advanced union, no matter how distant in time, richer states will not tolerate the amount of transfer of resources and the sharing of reserves that are necessary for the poorer members to catch up and for union in economic affairs to be workable.(23)

Such concepts as belongingness, integration, and community, as applied to Western Europe, have to be understood with the complex and diffuse psychopolitical framework just described. The Europeans belong to one set of structures which enable them to pursue their converging and diverging economic interests, and they belong to a different set of structures which enable them to pursue converging and diverging interests of military security. The imperatives of EEC are quite distinct from the imperatives of NATO, despite their complementarity. Within recent years, Europeans have been trying to create or refurbish structures toward a common foreign policy and the Europeanization of defense – whether in the European Community, in the NATO Eurogroup, or the Western European Union (WEU). This leads to the question of whether there is such a thing as a European identity. In an effort to answer the question, we turn to the last two rungs in Maslow's hierarchy – the need for self-esteem and the need for self-actualization.

## Self-Esteem and Self-Actualization

Although Maslow's theory distinguishes between self-esteem and self-actualization, in the context of Atlantic Community politics the two are practically inseparable. Esteem needs are those for strength, adequacy and mastery, while the need for self-actualization pushes the actor toward maximum achievements. In the Atlantic Community, the quest for esteem has been most manifest in the drive by European nations, and especially France, to wrest substantial independence from the United States.

As emphasized earlier, while, in the immediate postwar period, West Europeans looked with some misgivings upon their dependence on American power and largesse, nevertheless such concerns were muted by the stark priorities of recovery and security. Indeed some European leaders saw a positive American role in the political evolution of Europe, agreeing with the formula of Jacques Bainville: "In order to build a federation there must be a federating state." Former French Premier Paul Reynaud, too, expressed the hope in 1950 that the United States would become a more effective _federateur_ than it had shown itself to be up to that time.(24) It is interesting that a Frenchman could suggest that the United States was applying not too much but too little pressure toward European unification. If anti-Americanism became a vogue among European intellectuals after the war, the headquarters of this fashion was clearly in Paris. Nor was this sentiment limited to the Left Bank. In September 1957, nearly a year before De Gaulle came to power, _Sondages_ put the question: "If there were a war between the United States and the Soviet Union, to which camp should France belong?" Those favoring the United States were 15 percent, the Soviet Union, 3 percent; those favoring that France should not take part, 62 percent.(25)

The quest for European self-esteem asserted itself in earnest in France under De Gaulle, and did so because of the peculiar needs of the French people for the restoration of _amour propre_. As has been shown, there was strong support of the European Idea in West Germany, where it reflected in good part the desire to break with a repellant past and to regain a measure of international respectability. Indeed, Konrad Adenauer saw in the European Idea a form of immunization against the virus of nationalism that had produced Nazism and the catastrophe of World War II. The French had not undergone a similar catharsis. Although France had joined the table of the victors in 1945, every Frenchman knew this to be a fiction. Whereas the

Germans had to prove something to Europe and the rest of the democratic world, the French had to prove something not only to the other nations but to themselves as well.

France had many bitter memories to erase – the corruption of democratic institutions in the interwar period, the nation's ignominious collapse in 1940, the Vichy regime and the widespread collaboration with the occupying Nazis during the war. De Gaulle himself never forgot the contempt that he fancied had been meted out to him by Roosevelt, if not Churchill. Many Frenchmen were embarrassed over the Fourth Republic's reputation for political ineffectiveness, instability, internal divisions and foreign weakness. A once imposing colonial empire was crumbling, first in Indochina and later in Algeria. France's voice in NATO seemed weak in competition with that not only of the United States, but of Britain and, increasingly, of West Germany as well. Thus the movement from the Fourth to the Fifth Republic inevitably involved a nationalist effort to elevate the country's self-esteem.

De Gaulle was regarded by many of his countrymen as a follower of Maurras (the integral nationalist) – "a man who exults in the uniqueness of French national values and traditions to the exclusion of all others, a man for whom the destiny of France and French civilization is superior to all other nations. . . ."(26) But if some Frenchmen were inclined to think, cynically, that De Gaulle's pro-European posture was merely a mask for his determination to establish France's hegemony in Europe, nearly half of the French public considered him to be a "dedicated supporter of European unification."(27) A clear majority agreed with him that Western Europe and France were too mature to be totally dependent upon the United States and that some equalization in the roles of France (or Western Europe) and the United States in the development of NATO strategy was logical and necessary.(28)

De Gaulle was not opposed to European economic integration, provided it could be engineered on his own terms to furnish a European confederation led by France. Sometimes his goal was described as making Europe a third force strong enough to reduce the polarization of the world and to arbitrate between Washington and Moscow without, however, necessarily being neutral in the competition between East and West. But Europe could not really be great again unless France restored her former *grandeur*. By inspiring herself to renewed self-confidence, France would similarly inspire Europe.

France would establish her title to the leadership of Europe by resolving the Algerian conflict, which had deeply divided the nation, by building a community of cooperation with the new African states, cementing the Franco-German *rapprochement*, developing a nuclear *force de frappe*, furnishing realistic guidance to the European Economic Community, keeping Britain out until she was ready in French eyes to join Europe, and by undertaking creative new foreign policy initiatives either inside or outside the Atlantic Alliance. De Gaulle never tired of warning that no self-respecting people could rely indefinitely on an outside power for defense or economic prosperity and that Europeans were better qualified than Americans or Russians to decide the fate of Europe.

De Gaulle discerned shrewdly the maneuverability afforded him by the superpower stand off in Europe. He knew that he could go far in asserting

French independence because of the broader ties that bound the United States to Western Europe. Too, he realized that the American deterrent and military presence remained essential to the security of France and Western Europe, and to the maintenance of strategic equilibrium on the continent. A continued U.S.-Soviet military contiguity in Central Europe also represented insurance against a reunified Germany that could challenge France's bid for regional leadership. Thus, De Gaulle was able to take France out of the integrated NATO military command without running any serious risk to his nation's security. He wanted the United States as bodyguard, but not tutor to Europe.

On the European stage, De Gaulle cut a figure that was in turn admirable and ludicrous, grand and poignant. Many Europeans, including some who publicly ridiculed him, agreed that many of the things he was saying needed to be said and that no one else could say them so boldly. But in the final analysis, De Gaulle appeared as a paradox, a symbol of division within both Europe and the Atlantic Community. He wanted France and Europe to recognize their _vocation mondiale_. He wanted Europe to aspire to the status of a superpower. Rather than try to sever the defense bonds between America and Europe, he hoped to bring the two into an equilibrium, which, in his view, would make for a more viable Atlantic partnership. The policies of Washington and London, from his perspective, had been aimed at perpetuating the dominance of _les Angle-Saxons_ within NATO. He was convinced that it would be a great mistake to bring Britain into Europe before she could identify wholeheartedly with Europe as such. When he defined Europe as stretching "from the Channel to the Urals," he seemed less anti-Soviet than anti-British. But he did not exclude the eventual entry of a Europeanized Britain.

With De Gaulle's departure, the most dynamic spokesman for Europe's destiny was gone. Since Britain decided to enter the EEC in the early 1970s, Western Europe has oscillated between optimism and pessimism concerning the prospects for its self-actualization. At times there has been hope that the European Community would be able to produce a considerable political impact on the international system.(29) Pro-Marketeers argued that a Britain inside would be in a much better position than a Britain outside to help shape a new world economic order.(30) In the fall of 1972, at their Paris Summit Meeting, the Nine affirmed their intention to achieve political and monetary union by 1980. Europeans, sensing both their strength in the economic realm and their weakness in the military, reacted rather sharply to Secretary of State Kissinger's call in April 1973 for a new Atlantic partnership, and to his effort to link economic issues (on which they thought they could hold their own) to defense issues (on which they could not). They were particularly sensitive to Kissinger's differentiation between the regional obligations of Europe and the global responsibilities of the United States.(31) The Europeans reached an almost euphoric state in September 1973 when they issued the Copenhagen Declaration – an official, albeit halting, step toward the achievement of a European identity.

But even during this optimistic phase in the early 1970s, many voices expressed doubt over what Europe could accomplish on its own. There was an expectation that the United States, which had long professed support for the European unity movement, would soon lose its enthusiasm as a uniting Europe actually began to exert political and economic weight on the world scene –

not necessarily always in directions pleasing to the United States.(32) This even mingled with the fear that the United States, in an attempt to placate the Soviets for the sake of detente, might tacitly collaborate with the latter in frustrating European unity.(33) Apart from such trepidations, however, among the convinced "Europeans", few believed that Western Europe could ever become a self-sufficient military power.(34) Even those who favored the creation of a European Defense Community did not doubt that it would have to remain linked to the U.S. strategic deterrent.(35)

The October 1973 Middle East crisis and its consequences in the energy and finance sectors drastically jolted all optimistic premises. For the first time, as the International Institute for Strategic Studies put it, "industrial states had to bow to pressure from preindustrial ones."(36) The Europeans, feeling impotent and frustrated, were inclined to blame the United States for assigning a higher priority to the interests of Israel than to those of Europe and the Atlantic Alliance, and for concocting a nuclear confrontation with the Soviets that had more to do with Nixon's Watergate crisis than with any genuine strategic crisis in the Middle East.(37) For a while some observers exaggerated the degree to which European countries were at the mercy of the Arabs, who, allegedly, could use their newly acquired financial resources to preserve or disrupt the political and economic stability of the industrialized West almost at will.(38) Other analysts pointed out more calmly the limits to which Arab oil producers could keep increasing the price of oil, thereby undermining the stability of Western economies, without ultimately hurting themselves.(39) On balance, however, the energy crisis once again led to a shift in the psychological balance within the Atlantic Alliance toward the more energy-self-sufficient United States.(40) The Europeans were compelled to acknowledge that they were not nearly as independent in the economic sphere as they had earlier supposed. Confronted with a United States that was manifestly more robust in both the economic and energy sectors, even the French government formally acknowledged that "a continued and substantial presence of American forces in Europe plays an irreplaceable role in the defense of the U.S. itself as well as in that of the countries of Europe."(41)

Since the fall of 1973, a basic mood of pessimism in Western Europe has eased only marginally. Most Europeans prefer to face the future with a level of self esteem that is strong enough to cope with reality as it unfolds. Those who hold ruling positions in Western Europe seem to be hewing to an unglamorous middle course between the idealists, clinging to the goal of European union, and the dysutopians, concerned that democratic institutions will fall and nationalism will bury the unity movement. They are convinced that their governments can do little more at present than strive for the orchestration of some of their policies in order to ward off disaster in some areas and make marginal gains in others.

The British, now clearly committed to the Community as a result of the June 1975 referendum, still manifest an approach avoidance syndrome when it comes to the strengthening of Community institutions – especially the European Parliament. Discussion about the Europeanization of defense has been intensified, as an unavoidable necessity in light of the perceived decline in U.S. political will. Some efforts have been made to bridge the gap between the Atlantic Community and European institutions through the Eurogroup in

NATO, but France – not a member of the Eurogroup – prefers to work through other channels such as the Western European Union.

The prospects of achieving economic and monetary union now seem dimmer than when the goal was first announced in 1972, largely because the British and Italian economies are even more out of line with those of the hard currency countries than they were five years ago. In the early stages of European integration it was not too difficult for the various governments to reach agreement on what they should abstain from doing; now the situation is much more complex, and it is more difficult to get agreement on specific positive steps to be taken in common.(42)

In the late 1970s, both the Atlantic and European unity movements seem stalled on center. Nearly everyone is saying the right thing, but movement in the direction of progress occurs, when it occurs at all, at a glacial pace. Serious problems persist – the Greek-Turkish dispute over Cyprus; arguments over standardization and the two-way street in arms purchasing; the threat posed by the Eurocommunist parties; disagreements over direct elections to a European Parliament and the strengthening of Community institutions;(43) the political malaise which is worsened by an inability to cope with terrorism; a running controversy, often bordering on the petulant, over the assessment of blame for the West's failure to meet the challenges of energy, inflation, unemployment, trade imbalances and monetary fluctuations; and a gnawing fear that Europe may be drifting toward "Finlandization" because of shifts in the strategic and theater military balances. These and other related issues which make up the present agenda of the Atlantic and European communities will be dealt with in the succeeding chapters of this study.

One wonders whether the countries of Europe and the Atlantic Community, which were not able to achieve unity in the early 1950s when the external catalyst was strong, can now grope for the goal by slow degrees. Perhaps the practical experience of working together and arguing their way through a maze of serious problems will produce results. Perhaps even the constant payment of political lip service to the goal of closer Atlantic unity will have a beneficial conditioning effect similar to that which Henri Saint-Simon, the spiritual father of functional integration, expected to derive from having his valet wake him every morning with the summons: "Arise, Monsieur le Comte, you have great things to accomplish today."

## THE ATLANTIC COMMUNITY AND THE GENERATION GAP

Since the early nineteenth century scientists have been concerned with the concept of generation as a social, historical and political concept. Auguste Comte was the first to argue for conceiving a social generation to be thirty years. Two late nineteenth century historians, Giusepe Ferrari and Wilhelm Dilthey, also found the idea of a generation of thirty years useful for studying the politics and the culture of an epoch. Dilthey concluded that the concept of a generation was both a span of time (an internal metric concept of human life of about thirty years), and a contemporary relation of individuals to each other:

> The relationship between individuals denoted by the term 'generation' is therefore one of simultaneity. We say that certain people belong to 'the same generation' when they have, in a certain sense, grown up together, passed through childhood and youth at about the same time, and enjoyed their period of maturity during more or less the same years. It follows, then, that such people are bound together in another, deeper relationship: they also constitute 'the same generation' because, in their impressionable years, they have been subject to the same leading influences.(43)

To the extent that fundamental human attitudes are shaped by traumatic events, it is often possible to speak of the formation of a distinctive political generation. In this regard, the political generation that was created by World War I was a general European phenomenon. The political generation that experienced World War I (aged approximately 14 to 35 in 1914) by and large filled the leadership positions in Western Europe in the post-World War II years. By the 1960s and 1970s this generation was passing from the scene. This turnover in leadership was unlike any that preceded it. One generation had experienced both World Wars, while the new leaders of the mid-1970s remembered conflict as, at best, a confusing experience of youth. While the shared experiences of World War II may still loom large in the consciousness of some individuals, the passage of thirty years and the traumas of numerous other crises have created national subcohorts in the postwar leadership generation. Among those who do not remember the war, or for whom it was but a dim childhood experience, the slogans of the more immediate postwar period – about the external military menace and the need for tightened community – no longer fit meaningfully into a cognitive framework that was conditioned primarily by economic boom and absence of conflict. The popular indifference to the imperatives of security described in Chapter 3 is as much a generational phenomenon as a product of contemporary trends and circumstances.

Is the generation gap immutable and unbridgeable? Maslow's hierarchy of needs, which has been used analogously in this analysis, applies to the human individual: it thus represents a finite cycle that ends in death. By contrast, unless one takes a Spenglerian view of categorical rise and fall equivalent to birth and death, societies and communities regenerate. The Maslowian cycle thus repeats itself, in whole or in part.

Short of a cataclysmic event, it is difficult to envisage such a regeneration in the immediate and critical period facing the West. If the projection in the following chapter is valid, the shock that might retrigger the cycle, and force a renewed sense of danger and community on the levels of popular opinion and action, may come in the early to middle 1980s.

The narrow bridges that can be erected between the political generations in the meantime can only issue from enlightened leadership. By and large the political generation that occupies the top levels of power in the Atlantic countries is still steeped in values and attitudes shaped by the tragedies of the prewar period, the horrors of fratricidal conflict, and the bold sense of a united purpose in its aftermath. It is the essence of democratic leadership to lead constituent opinion as well as to respond to it. In a pragmatic sense, this means that decision makers, if they recognize the abiding validity of older concepts and ideals, must sustain them even if they no longer find resounding echoes in the corridors of public opinion. The hopes of the Atlantic Community in the critical period ahead thus are hostage to the ability and willingness of present leaders to look beyond narrow political advantage to the accumulating dangers on the horizon, and to the abiding – and even magnified – imperatives of a community approach to meeting them.

## NOTES

(1) Social psychologist Herbert C. Kelman writes: "It is true that the behavior of states ultimately consists of the behavior of individuals, but state behavior is the aggregation of a variety of behaviors on the part of many individuals who represent different roles, interests and degrees of influence on final decisions." "International Relations: Psychological Aspects," International Encyclopedia of the Social Sciences, Vol. 8, p. 76. See also Kelman's essay, "Social-Psychological Approaches to the Study of International Relations," the Introduction to the book which he edited, International Behavior: A Social-Psychological Analysis (New York: Holt, Rinehart and Winston, 1965), especially pp. 5-6.

(2) Robert Lane, Political Thinking and Consciousness (Chicago: Markam, 1969), p. 25.

(3) A.H. Maslow, Motivation and Personality (New York: Harper, 1954), pp. 80-98.

(4) James Davies, Human Nature in Politics (New York: John Wiley and Sons, 1963), p. 9.

(5) Memoirs by Harry S. Truman, Volume II: Years of Trial and Hope (New York: New American Library, 1956), pp. 136-146; Dean Acheson, Present at the Creation (New York: New American Library, 1970), pp. 202-314.

(6) Quoted in Jacques Freymond, Western Europe Since the War: A short Political History (New York: Praeger, 1964), p. 35.

(7) Leo Moulin, "Anti-Americanism in Europe: A Psychoanalysis," Orbis, Winter 1958, p. 451.

(8) Ibid., pp. 451-452.

(9) Wilfrid Knapp, A History of War and Peace 1939-1965, Royal Institute of International Affairs (London: Oxford University Press, 1967), pp. 79-101; Harry N. Howard, Turkey, the Straits and U.S. Policy (Baltimore: The Johns Hopkins University Press, 1974), Chapter VII; Adam Ulam, Expansion and Co-existence (London: Seecker and Warburg, 1968), p. 404; NATO: Facts and Figures (Brussels: NATO information Service, 1971), pp. 12-13.

(10) A.H. Robertson, European Institutions, for the London Institute of World Affairs (New York: Praeger, 1958), pp. 8-9. The Brussels Treaty was signed on March 17, 1948.

(11) Ten years after the Czech coup, Paul-Henri Spaak of Belgium, the second person to hold the post of NATO Secretary-General, wrote: "The determining factor in international politics after the Second World War was the coup d'etat in Prague . . . the bolt of lightning which roused the West. After 1948, everyone . . . understood that the Western nations, for their own safety, had to unite and make clear to Soviet Russia that Prague was the last act of Soviet imperialism on the European continent which we would tolerate." "The Atlantic Community and NATO," Orbis, Winter 1958, p. 511.

(12) See Franz Govaerts, "Belgium, Holland and Luxembourg," in O. De Raeymaeker and others, Small Powers in Alignment (Leuven, Belgium: Leuven University Press, 1974), pp. 300-316. Govaerts makes it plain that the Belgians were more skeptical than the Dutch about the United Nations experiment in universal collective security, and more concerned over the Soviet threat.

(13) Ibid., p. 314.

(14) See Frederick Sethur, "The Schuman Plan and Ruhr Coal," Political Science Quarterly, LXVII (December 1952); and William Diebold, Jr., The Schuman Plan (New York: Harper, 1959), pp. 67-75.

(15) See Achille Albonetti, "The New Europe and the West," Daedalus, Special Issue, "A New Europe?," Winter 1964, p. 9.

(16) See Daniel Lerner and Raymond Aron, France Defeats EDC (New York: Praeger, 1957).

(17) See Amitai Etzioni, "European Unification: A Strategy of Change," World Politics, October 1963.

(18) See Community and Friendship, translated from Ferdinand Toennies, Gemeinschaft und Gesellschaft by Charles P. Loomis (New York: Harper, 1963).

(19) Ibid., pp. 222-233.

(20) For explanations of the Functionalist theory of integration, see Ernst B. Haas, Beyond the Nation-State: Functionalism and International Organization (Stanford, Calif: Stanford University Press, 1964), Chap. 1.

(21) See Leon Festinger, A Theory of Cognitive Dissonance (Stanford, Calif: Stanford University Press, 1957) and Conflict, Decision and Dissonance (Stanford, Calif.: Stanford University Press, 1964).

(22) Donald Chapman, The Road to European Union, Centre for Contemporary European Studies, University of Sussex, Brighton, England, June 1975, p. 6.

(23) Ibid., p. 38.

(24) Paul Reynaud, "The Unifying Force for Europe," Foreign Affairs, January 1950, pp. 262-263.

(25) Cited in Roy C. Macridis, "French Foreign Policy," in Macridis, ed., Foreign Policy in World Politics (Englewood Cliffs, N.J.: Prentice-Hall, 1967, 3rd edition), pp. 75-76.

(26) Karl W. Deutsch and others, France, Germany and the Western Alliance: A Study of Elite Attitudes on European Integration and World Politics (New York: Charles Scribner's Sons, 1967), p. 58.

(27) Ibid., p. 59.

(28) Ibid., p. 61.

(29) Ralf Dahrendorf, "Possibilities and Limits of a European Communities Foreign Policy," The World Today, April 1971.

(30) "The Case for Staying In," The Times, May 28, 1975.

(31) See, e.g., Ian Smart, "The New Atlantic Charter," The World Today, June 1973, and Alastair Buchan, Europe and America: From Alliance to Coalition (Paris: Atlantic Institute for International Affairs, 1973).

(32) Anthony Hartley, "Europe Between the Superpowers," Foreign Affairs, January 1971, p. 274.

(33) "The Hostile Friendship of the Two Giants," Editorial, The Times, June 21, 1974.

(34) Alastair Buchan, e.g., said that Europe could not hope to play the role of Equilibrist. "A World Restored?" Foreign Affairs, July 1972, pp. 649-650. See also Neville Brown, "European Foreign Policy: Myth or Reality," New Middle East, January 1972, pp. 22-27.

(35) Francois Duchene, "A New Europe in Defense Community," Foreign Affairs, October 1971, pp. 80-82.

(36) Strategic Survey 1973 (London: IISS, 1974), pp. 1-2.

(37) See "The Moral Authority of the President," The Sunday Times (London), October 28, 1973.

(38) "Palestinian Coming of Age," Manchester Guardian Weekly, January 4, 1975.

(39) Robert Mabro and Elizabeth Monroe, "Arab Wealth From Oil: Problems of its Investment," International Affairs, January 1974.

(40) Anthony Hartley, American Foreign Policy in the Nixon Era, Adelphi Paper No. 110 (London: IISS, Winter 1974/1975), p. 28.

(41) French Draft for NATO Declaration of Purpose, The New York Times, November 19, 1973.

(42) Andrew Schonfield, Europe: Journey to an Unknown Destination (London: Allen Lane, 1972), p. 11.

(43) Michael Palmer, "The Role of a Directly Elected European Parliament," The World Today, April 1977, pp. 122-130; and Julian Crandall Hollick, "Direct Elections to the European Parliament: The French Debate," ibid., December 1977, pp. 472-480.

(44) Wilheim Dilthey, "Uber das Studium der Geschichte der Wissenschaften vom Menschen, der Gessellschaft und dem Staat," in Wilhelm Dilthey, Gesammelte Schriften, Vol. 6: Die geistige Welt (Berlin: Teubner, 1875 and 1924), p. 87.

# II

# The Atlantic Community— NATO and the Growing Crisis

# 3 Toward a New NATO Consensus

Walter F. Hahn

The North Atlantic Treaty Organization is, first and foremost, a military alliance. As such, it bears unique credentials in mankind's long history of military alignments. It is the first peacetime alliance of truly intercontinental scope to feature a far-reaching integration of the command structures of the participating members. The bonds of NATO have sustained almost three decades of relative peace and stability in Europe. Measured by any yardstick of alliance, these are accomplishments unprecedented in modern history.

## THE NATO BARGAIN

NATO is thus a success story. What accounts for this success? Several years ago, a former United States Ambassador to NATO, Harlan Cleveland, advanced the thesis of NATO as a "transatlantic bargain" – a bargain that exists, in part, as an understanding among the European members of the Alliance, but that is, primarily, a deal between them and the United States. This bargain, Cleveland contended, has been sustained by a fundamental consensus that "Each year the mix of NATO defense forces and the character of allied political collaboration change, adapting to the shifting technology of war and . . . to the tides of politics in each of the fifteen NATO countries. But, while the bargain changes, the constant is a consensus among the allies that there has to be a bargain."(1)

Expressed differently, the Alliance has been bonded in the last analysis by a "consensus of necessity" – by a shared perception that is essentially twofold: (1) while the military threat to Western Europe may wax or wane, the sine qua non of Atlantic security endeavors is their commonality, i.e., an alliance; and (2) while solutions to outstanding economic, social and political problems might conceivably be sought within narrow national compartments or broader European confines, in the security field there is no palpable alternative, at least in the short run, to an Atlantic framework. In other words, the bottom line of the transatlantic bargain is the abiding commitment of the United States to the defense of Europe.

The thesis is plausible up to a point. It helps to explain why, over the years, NATO has weathered crises, both external and internal, that long ago might have shattered an ordinary pact of convenience among nations. The thesis also helps to explain why, while other institutions of Atlantic and European cooperaion have been battered by time and circumstance, the basic structure of NATO has survived relatively intact – at least since France's quasi defection in the mid-1960s.

Yet, it can be argued that NATO is bedeviled in good part by this very success. Because the "bargain" has mastered the trials of nearly three decades, its durability tends to be taken more or less for granted. Occasionally, concerned Western statesmen may sound the alarm about the growing disparity in military power between NATO and the Warsaw Pact and about the sharpening symptoms of erosion within the Alliance itself. Such warnings, however, find few echoes of practical action and tend to be muffled by a pervasive business-as-usual attitude on both sides of the Atlantic.

This attitude has been hardened, not only by the NATO success story, but by circumstances and trends within the broader compass of the Atlantic Community. The purely military issues have retreated from the center stage of Alliance politics. In the 1950s and 1960s, the great questions of military strategy and relationships within the Alliance – of the magnitude of the Soviet threat, nuclear decision-making, "flexible response," and burden sharing – not only dominated the parliamentary chambers of the member countries, but spilled into the public forums. Today, these issues have been shouldered aside by the increasingly complex economic and social problems that, in one measure or another, beset all parts of the industrialized world. In the battle for the allocation of national resources, these new priorities have cut deeply into the muscles of defense.

## THE DWINDLING NATO ELITE

One consequence of the growing disinterest in military matters has been to make the technical questions of military strategy and wherewithal the ever more exclusive domain of what might be labeled the "NATO elite" – a community of experts that includes the military establishments in the member nations, the defense ministries, the national representatives in the councils and integrated commands of the Alliance, an outer circle of knowledgeable people in the various parliaments and their staffs, as well as a scattering of journalists and analysts in academic and research institutions in the NATO countries.

Although no one has kept statistics, there is little question that this body of experts has narrowed substantially over the past decade. This dwindling is particularly evident in Western Europe where, at the official levels (beyond the defense ministries and the military staffs), in most parliaments military affairs engage perhaps only several members and their advisers. The withering of expertise in defense matters reflects, in part, the rising complexity of military strategy and hardware. More significantly, however, it attests to a widespread disinterest in military affairs in most NATO countries

– a disinterest that, unfortunately, abides despite a relatively greater media attention in recent times to the Soviet military threat. Few graduates of European or American universities are disposed to chart careers in strategic analysis. And, among rising young politicians in parties and parliaments, even fewer aspire to the thankless portfolio of the defense ministry, a post that has become marked generally as the graveyard of political careers.

If the NATO elite, broadly defined, has diminished, it can be argued that, in many ways, the elite has become more cohesive on a transnational basis. Perhaps because of the more or less esoteric knowledge they share about force levels, strategies, tactics and intricate modern weapons, defense ministers and their staffs find it easier to talk to counterparts in other NATO countries than to nondefense colleagues in their own national political milieus.

The NATO elite tends also to be united by an increasingly shared fate. To one degree or another, all of the defense establishments in the Atlantic Alliance find themselves at siege within their own societies. They all face continual onslaughts against defense budgets, and staggering difficulties in trying to meet rising defense requirements and costs within the shrinking national allocations doled out to them. Too, they confront political climates that range from disinterest to unremitting hostility from leftwing forces. With some notable exceptions, the West European defense establishments communicate well and cordially with one another. Their increasing sense of common predicament no doubt accounts for the progress made in such institutions as the NATO Eurogroup.

Notwithstanding the tightened cohesion of the NATO elite no strong initiatives have emerged from that quarter toward rationalizing an Alliance posture that, according to all authoritative estimates, is being shaded by the Warsaw Pact in most major categories of military power. The inertia of the NATO elite can be blamed on a number of influences. It partakes of a confused pessimism that has stifled policy initiatives in the West more broadly in recent years. It mirrors, to one degree or another, the standard malaise of entrenched bureaucracies. Undoubtedly, it represents a reaction by defense establishments to the beleaguerment noted earlier – the conviction by embattled ministries that they can best hold the line by maintaining as low a profile as possible in their respective political environments.

But the inertia can be traced to yet another factor: an abiding disparity of perceptions within the NATO elite itself, particularly between the European and American components of that elite. The unhappy truth is that in more than twenty-five years of transatlantic debate inside the Alliance neither side has ever bluntly and honestly spelled out the basic assumptions and expectations invested by it into the Alliance bargain. A number of reasons account for this; notably, the conditioned reflex of diplomats to skate quickly over painful issues in the interest of delicate compromise – especially in recent years, when the fear of American force withdrawals from Europe has tended to blot out other considerations. As a consequence, the Alliance debate has been couched in euphemisms and slogans (conventional pause, flexible response, realistic deterrence, burden sharing, etc.) that have tended to distort the real issues and motivations at stake. These real issues and motivations have to do with the disparate American and European conceptions of the fundamental meaning of military power and its political implications. In any event, the business-as-usual attitude is obscuring a mounting crisis for NATO – a crisis that looms all the more dangerously because it either is not perceived or is ignored.

## THE TIMETABLE OF CRISIS FOR NATO

NATO's crisis is already in train, and it is progressive. It inheres in the shifting military balance in Europe and in the thrust of Soviet intentions behind that shifting balance. The crisis could flare more explicitly at any point in the foreseeable future, depending upon continuing trends in the military and political spheres – in what the Soviets refer to as the "correlation of forces." Yet, the decisive phase in Europe is likely to assert itself in the 1980-1985 time frame. We have that projection from the Soviet leadership itself.

Early in 1973, reports quoted Leonid Brezhnev declaring to restive East European colleagues that detente was a ruse designed to lead to a decisive shift in the balance of power. These reports cited Brezhnev as telling a meeting of East European communist party leaders that the strategy of "peaceful coexistence" would permit the Soviets to build up their military and economic power so that, by 1985, "a decisive shift in the correlation of forces" would enable the Soviets to "exert our will wherever we need to."(2) The report of Brezhnev's remarks had the effect of splitting the NATO intelligence community at the time. Given the apparent reliability of the intelligence sources involved, few seriously doubted the general accuracy of the report. Rather, opinion divided over the issue of motive: did Brezhnev mean what he said, or was he saying it as a bromide to restive East European party leaders?

The likelihood that Brezhnev meant what he said is underscored by other evidence, some of it antedating the Soviet leader's 1973 statements. In February 1968, six months before Soviet tanks rumbled into Prague, Major General Jan Senja escaped from Czechoslovakia to the West. General Senja had been First Secretary of the Communist Party in the Ministry of Defense – in other words, the leading party official in the Czechoslovak armed forces – as well as a member of the Czechoslovak Presidium and a regular participant in the Warsaw Pact planning meetings.

With him, General Senja brought substantial data about the Warsaw Pact. The centerpiece was a planning document, _The Long Term Strategic Plan for the Next Ten to Fifteen Years and the Years After_ – a project that had been initiated apparently by Brezhnev himself at the Warsaw Pact meeting in Moscow in the autumn of 1966.(3) This strategic plan, setting forth the domestic and foreign policy objectives of the Soviet Union and of its East European satellites, was to have been completed in 1968, to coincide with the next series of five-year plans. By the time General Senja defected, in early 1968, the foreign policy section of the plan, consisting of two volumes, was virtually finished. This section analyzed the major target countries in the West, as well as the full panoply of instruments to be wielded by the Warsaw Pact: diplomacy, foreign trade, the armed forces, "disinformation" and cultural exchanges.

The document set forth a strategic plan of four phases. The first phase was retrospective, spanning the period of "preparation for peaceful coexistence" from 1956 to 1959, when Khrushchev's policies of de-Stalinization wedged an opening to the West. The second phase of the plan stretched from 1960 to 1972. The central strategic objectives here were to prod diversity and exacerbate social discord in the West. On the state-to-state level, fears of West German strength were to be played upon to aggravate distrust within NATO, and French nationalism would be manipulated to detach France from the Alliance. On the subnational level, the communist parties were provided with guidelines on the key issues to be exploited for maximum disruption of their respective societies. The trade union and student movements would be used to fan fires of social and industrial unrest and to stampede the forces of radicalism and protest against the "military-industrial complex." In the meantime, the buildup and modernization of Warsaw Pact armed forces would continue apace.

The somewhat familiar picture that this presents of the late 1960s makes it all the more interesting to look at the third phase of the Warsaw Pact plan: the "Period of Dynamic Social Change" covering the decade between 1973 and 1985. The salients here are "to smash the hope of false democracy" and to achieve the total demoralization of the West. Detente with the United States, according to the Warsaw Pact plan, would reap a bounty of economic and technological advantages for the Soviet Union and sap belief in the West in the continued need of military defenses. The fragmentation of NATO was to be quickened with the priority aim of pushing the United States from Europe. In the final phase of the plan – the period of "Global Democratic Peace" _ a beleaguered United States, cut off from Western Europe and increasingly constrained in its access to the raw materials of the Third World, would opt for a "peace-loving" government that would accommodate fully to Soviet power and influence.

There is congenital skepticism in the West about purported Soviet strategic blueprints. In all prudence, however, this one must be taken seriously. It matches fairly closely the picture of the world as it has unfolded in the decade since 1967. It is perfectly consistent with what the Soviets have said about "peaceful coexistence" and the "correlation of forces." It explains the continuing momentum of Soviet and Warsaw Pact military programs amid the chorus of Soviet peaceful intentions. The plan is instructive, not as a detailed blueprint or timetable (the Soviets are not immaculate planners, let alone prophets); rather, the document has to be taken seriously as a statement of fundamental goals and as the phasing of those goals. Lord Chalfont remarked about the plan:

> There is, of course, nothing especially sinister in any of this – nor anything very new to the student of Marxism-Leninism. It is no more than the brutal reality of international power politics. It is, however, an existing plan, initiated by Mr. Brezhnev, and carefully coordinated within the Warsaw Pact. There is no evidence of any kind that the overall strategic aims have changed; indeed every action of the Soviet Union in the international field continues to be consistent with the tactics of the plan.(4)

In the prevailing political climate in the West, where disinterest in matters beyond national borders merges with wistful optimism about the future of detente, statements such as those by Brezhnev in 1973 and corroborating evidence such as the Warsaw Pact plan tend to be either dismissed or attributed to an assumed factional battle inside the Kremlin. Yet, the outward signs suggest that whatever strains may beset the Soviet leadership relate to tactics and timing rather than the basic thrusts of strategy. It is noteworthy, for example, that on October 22, 1974, Mikhail Suslov, the Soviet Union's leading ideologist and an alleged leader of the hard-line faction in the Politburo, indicated why he was giving his support to the Soviet policy of peaceful coexistence. He pointed to the burgeoning crisis in the capitalist countries, asserting that the economic and political problems of the West revealed the lack of future prospects for Western capitalism. He elaborated:

> The number of unemployed is growing, the life of the working people becomes harder, their uncertainty of tomorrow is growing and the entire system of government, monopolistic regimes is bursting its seams . . . the craving of the working class for unity is growing stronger. In a number of countries the position of Communist parties and all leftist forces has been significantly strengthened.(5)

Suslov's remarks echoed similar ones by Party Chairman Leonid Brezhnev in October 1974, in Kishinev. In general, there seems to be a quiet confidence in Moscow that the capitalist world is in the throes of the final, fatal "inherent contradictions" forecast by Marx and Lenin.

Suslov's comments suggest strongly that, whatever factional strife continues at the highest levels of the Soviet leadership, it does not revolve around the basic concept of detente itself, nor does it divide into hawks and doves in a mirror-image of the policy conflicts in Western countries. Instead, it has to do with the question of Soviet exploitation of unfolding opportunities. In effect, Brezhnev has been arguing that a deliberate Soviet policy of forebearance will accelerate the process of unraveling in the West: in dialectical terms, he contends that any manifest Soviet move to exploit the proliferating problems in the West – or even openly to exult about the West's difficulties – would be counterproductive by prompting the West to reconsolidate and raise its guard. The Brezhnevian strategy of detente is thus essentially that of the soft glove over the growing fist. Brezhnev avers that this phase of forebearance not only befits the evolving situation in the West, but is also compatible with the need to cope with remaining problems within the Soviet system and with the China factor.

Brezhnev's rivals (such as there are) can hardly take issue with the basic policy of "peaceful coexistence"; in the Kremlin, as elsewhere, it is difficult to argue with success. But if one reads between the lines of pronouncements by Suslov and other members of what might be characterized cautiously as the more orthodox element in the Soviet leadership, two tendencies are discernible: (1) an assessment of trends in the capitalist world that is even more optimistic than Brezhnev's, and (2) some misgivings about the possible risks of detente for ideological contamination in the communist camp and for Soviet levers of control in Eastern Europe and, more broadly, in the world communist movement. These assumptions, if anything, back urgings for a more active Soviet policy in Europe and elsewhere.

## THE LIKELY SCENARIO OF THE NEXT DECADE

In any event, the factional differences seem marginal at best. There is no reason to assume that Soviet strategy will detour markedly from the basic route that was apparently charted in the late 1960s. On this premise, NATO can look to the following scenario in the next seven to ten years:

1. A continued Soviet and Warsaw Pact buildup in all military categories. The longer-range Soviet goal is the attainment of clear and recognized superiority across the full spectrum of military power. The shorter-term aim is essentially twofold. At the strategic level, the ever mounting arsenal of Soviet intercontinental capabilities serves to sharpen the perception of a "decoupling" of the American strategic deterrent from Western Europe and to inhibit American responses to Soviet thrusts against Western interests in various parts of the world (e.g., in Africa). At the European theater level, the Warsaw Pact buildup is aimed at the achievement of an ever clearer Soviet capability to launch a devastating and lightning "smash grab" attack over substantial areas of NATO territory.

Indeed the Soviet military buildup and deployments trace the pattern of a noose slowly tightening around Western Europe. The continuing amassment of Warsaw Pact capabilities in the central region of Europe is being counterpointed by growing Soviet military pressures along Western Europe's flanks in the Mediterranean and the Baltic Sea. At the same time, Soviet military and political expansion into the Indian Ocean and along the African coasts is gradually pointing the proverbial knife at the economic jugular vein leading from Western Europe's principal raw material sources in the Third World. And the "decoupling" of the American deterrent – mainly through Soviet advances at the strategic level – is arranging the stage for the time when West European nations may discover themselves militarily surrounded, economically beleaguered and psychologically isolated, thereby, having to draw the consequences. This is essentially the specter of Finlandization that concerned European analysts have read into Soviet strategy.

2. Continue Soviet circumspection and restraint – at least until the climactic period projected by Brezhnev. The Warsaw Pact plan cited earlier stressed a continuum of Soviet "peaceful coexistence" policies dating back to Khrushchev, who was credited with prying an opening to the West through de-Stalinization. The major mistake Khrushchev made was that he gambled in Cuba in 1962 and lost. His successors seem determined not to repeat a similar gamble until the odds have become prohibitive in their favor.

The Soviets have pondered not only the lesson of 1962, but also the broader meaning of the dialectic as it has applied to the postwar evolution. That meaning is simple. The Western democracies have banded together – and mustered the sacrifices of defense – in times of stark danger and confrontation; they have tended to lower their guard and to stray into separate ways when the overt danger has, ostensibly, dwindled. What is more, in their desire for relief from the painful burdens of a protracted global competition, Western societies (including substantial segments of their policy elites) have tended to look wistfully toward professed Soviet intentions rather than upon objective Soviet capabilities. In short, the Soviets have learned that so long as they strike a relaxed pose, pay homage to peaceful coexistence and carefully avoid touching exposed Western nerve ends, they can sustain their armament pace and push their global offensive with relative impunity. This is why "peaceful coexistence" and the "changing correlation of forces" have become the interchangeable banners of Soviet strategy.

There is no rational reason why the Soviets should drop their policy of outward restraint, particularly in Europe. Conceivably two contingencies could deflect them: the overpowering pull of opportunities, and the arrival of new Kremlin tenants – or a combination of the two. At least one scenario is popularly invoked for a possible reversion by Moscow to old aggressive habits: a post-Tito succession crisis in Yugoslavia, which would yield to the Soviets the calculation that the political and strategic harvest of direct military intervention would outweigh by far the risks to the longer-range timetable of success. There is no question that the incentives in such a situation would be powerful; the chance to reharness Yugoslavia into the communist camp and to cut the ideological thorn that Titoism has pressed into Soviet control of Eastern Europe, not to speak of the lure of permanent and secure Soviet naval and air bases in the Mediterranean Sea. Yet, from Moscow's vantage point, would military intrusion be necessary – let alone desirable – for the achievement of these ends?

To be sure, much would depend upon the unfolding of the scenario. Perhaps, more importantly, much would depend upon its timing – at what juncture of the power curves in Europe, between now and the mid-1980s, the contingency would arise. If it were to take place in the latter part of the projected period, the Soviets might be tempted not only to exploit the scenario itself, but also to use it for signaling NATO (or what would remain of the Alliance by that time) that the soft glove had been stripped from the first and that the nations of Western Europe must make the final accommodations to the reality of Soviet hegemony over the continent. In the interim, however, there is scant prospect that the Soviets will once again overreach themselves and galvanize the Western Alliance.

Equally frail are the hopes (or fears, depending upon one's viewpoint) of a return by the Soviets to more naked ambitions as a result of leadership changes. Myths die slowly; nevertheless, by now there should be recognition in the West of the bankruptcy of policy investments in supposed factional strife in the Kremlin. In the early 1960s, the argument was prevalent that Khrushchev should be met more than halfway for protection against the hard-liners lurking into the anterooms of the Kremlin. Yet, it fell upon Brezhnev and Kosygin to elaborate Khrushchev's incipient policy of "peaceful coexistence" into a comprehensive strategy. The scoreboard of turnovers and policies in Moscow since the death of Stalin suggests that conflict within the Moscow leadership arena turns more on personalities than on basic issues – particularly basic premises of Soviet foreign policy. The post-Brezhnev leaders in the Kremlin may adjust the latter's strategy in its margins. Conceivably, they may try to accelerate the timetable. But they are not likely to scuttle a strategy that has so clearly spelled ultimate success.

To summarize: Until the "correlation of forces" in favor of the Soviet Union has reached the point of assured dominance, Moscow is not likely to oblige a faltering Atlantic Alliance with a new casus unitas and cement of fear. Rather, the Soviets will continue to exercise relative restraint (more so in Europe than in some peripheral areas) to permit what they deem the historically ordained contradictions of Western capitalism to take their final toll. As the unraveling process continues at the Alliance level as well as in the fabrics of specific Western target countries, the Soviet message will be beamed less subtly and more insistently to Western audiences: "Accept the inevitable and accommodate us in all your policies – foreign, defense and economic – as well as in your domestic processes." Growing Soviet military power will provide the major amplifier for that message.

3. Continued dishevelment of NATO as an embracing alliance and no substantial increases in present levels of Western defense expenditures. This projection depends upon the validity of the previous one, namely, that no new alliance catalyst will emerge. As such, the projection posits the partial correctness of Soviet assumptions. The emphasis is on partial correctness. Soviet expectations continue to be driven by the Marxist-Leninist law of fatal capitalist contradictions. They tend to view both economic and political developments in the West through this ideological prism. Without digging into the roots of recent Western economic malaise – suffice it to suggest that while the entire industrialized world has felt the reverberations of economic shocks, the problems differ from society to society – some of them have shown the symptoms of recovery and there is no cause to sound the deathknell of the free market system.

The preoccupation in the West with economic and social dislocations, however, does reinforce the Soviet premise that the NATO countries will not react to a growing Soviet arsenal by boosting significantly their own armament expenditures or by tightening alliance bonds. Nor, in the foreseeable future, are the prevailing trends and popular attitudes in most of the NATO countries likely to be shaken dramatically by the drum beats of warnings by defense ministers about the rising military threat. To cite the prognosis of British Defense Minister Fred Mulley: "I do not believe that in the foreseeable future the governments of the Alliance will be persuaded that there is an overriding necessity to . . . advance defense expenditure to a higher priority than it has now."(6)

Indeed it is possible to speculate about two cognitive levels in NATO countries with respect to the military threat. At one level, the rising threat is vaguely recognized, but at the same time it tends to be shrugged off with the (by now standard) arguments about Soviet internal constraints and peaceful intentions, as well as with the broader proposition regarding the alleged inutility of military power in the nuclear age. At the other level, the fact of growing Soviet military superiority is already conditioning attitudes and policies of deference to the Soviet Union. In short, the harbingers of Finlandization are already in evidence.

## DIVERGENCES IN NATO: THE AMERICAN PERSPECTIVE

The above projection may seem to spell dire things. If the assumptions about the thrust of Soviet strategy and time frame are valid, NATO faces some five to eight years before a denouement. If present trends in specific NATO countries maintain momentum, the Atlantic Alliance, in any event, will not survive the critical period in its present form. Any NATO planner must heed realistically the hard boundaries within which any short-term salvaging effort may be sought. He faces the constraints of scope: the likelihood that the number of effective participants in the Alliance will dwindle, especially if communist parties ascend to governments in Italy and France. He contemplates the constraints of means: the likelihood that the Alliance will have to find a solution to the challenge somewhere within the present levels of expenditures allocated to defense in the principal NATO countries.

There is still the hope that, notwithstanding these constraints, the Alliance can pull itself together for the dangerous stretch ahead. Yet, a sine qua non is that the NATO elite – in particular, the besieged defense ministries – reach agreement on two things: (1) the recognition that the present drift of NATO strategy and military programs cannot cope with the deepening crisis ahead, and (2) a consensus on the fundamental criteria for an improved NATO posture that can satisfy not only the changing military requirements of the modern battlefield, but also the political and psychological needs of the Alliance.

As was suggested earlier, there has never been such a consensus in NATO. In previous decades, the Alliance could get along on imperfect agreement. It could rely on the luxuries of U.S. strategic superiority and abundance of resources to forgo the airing and clash of basic assumptions and to strike compromises that papered over differences in fundamental attitudes, particularly between the two sides of the Atlantic. Yet, the divergences remain, and they work all the more debilitatingly at a time when the luxuries are gone and the Alliance is in desperate need of a new unifying concept. In order to understand the divergences, it is useful to cast a brief backward glance at the evolution of U.S. and European approaches to security in the postwar period.(7)

In the formative period of NATO, Americans and Europeans agreed that the strategy of the Atlantic Alliance would revolve around two principal pillars: Deterrence and forward defense. Deterrence implied that the potential enemy was to be dissuaded from aggression by a total NATO posture which would make clear to him that the risks entailed by attack would outweigh any foreseeable advantages to be gained. Forward defense meant that, if deterrence broke down, the thrust of the enemy's attacking armies was to be met and contained as far to the east on NATO territory as possible.

Upon these two pillars of strategy the Alliance built up its array of forces in the 1950s; a "shield" of ground armies guarding the forward lines of defense, supported by a growing arsenal of tactical nuclear weapons, and backed, in turn, by the "sword" of atomically armed American bombers. The agreement in the Alliance on basic strategy notwithstanding, ambiguity continued to shroud the relationship between deterrence and defense, particularly in their application to NATO force goals and missions.

Except for the short-lived period of massive retaliation (1953-1957), U.S. policy in NATO has embraced consistently a concept in which effective deterrence has been more or less equated with effective defense – the concept of "that deters best which defends best." In its application to NATO forces, this American concept has been expressed in a relative emphasis on the buildup of effective NATO ground forces. The emphasis preceded the rise of the Soviet strategic nuclear arsenal; it was already reflected in the massive force goals (some ninety-six NATO combat divisions) that the United States pushed for adoption by the Lisbon Conference of NATO in 1952.

The early American stress on shield forces mirrored the traditional notion of matching ground armies with ground armies. The notion gave way to the nuclear emphasis of the Eisenhower-Dulles Administration. Practically from the moment the massive retaliation doctrine was unfurled, however, it was challenged by intellectual opposition in the United States. This opposition was animated to a large extent by an antinuclear bias, but it also found rationalization for its arguments in the developing changes in the global environment, particularly the Soviet achievement of nuclear capabilities of intercontinental range. Thus emerged the concept of limited war, steeped in the belief that potential conflict in Europe should be confined to European battlefields without exploding into general conflagration between the United States and the Soviet Union.

The limited war concept was elevated into U.S. policy with the advent of the Kennedy Administration in 1961. Theoretically, the doctrine of flexible response propounded by United States Secretary of Defense Robert McNamara described a total strategy for NATO. It proposed that for every aggressive option available to the Warsaw Pact NATO should muster a countervailing option – a response to aggression in kind and scope. The focus of flexible response, however, was on conventional forces. This focus was made clearer by American pronouncements, notably Secretary McNamara's warnings to the European allies (e.g., in Athens in 1962) that the Alliance could no longer rely categorically on the American nuclear sword to deter all levels of aggression. It was implicit in the downward revisions of American estimates of the Warsaw Pact's conventional threat, thus suggesting the viability of a NATO conventional strategy. And it was demonstrated in the careful constraints placed on American tactical nuclear weapons in Europe. Furthermore, it was primarily from the platform of conventional strategy that the American campaign for greater European burden-sharing was waged. The basic themes of that campaign have been that the West European nations should either shoulder a greater share of the conventional military burden or help defray the costs of maintaining American forces in Europe, or should do both.

## EVOLVING EUROPEAN PERSPECTIVES

The general view of the West European NATO elite, as it evolved after 1950, has been quite different. In tracing this view, it must be remembered that NATO was founded just four years after the end of conflict in Europe. Numbed by a new and massive danger from the east, the nations of Western

Europe, still clearing away the rubble of World War II, eagerly grasped for the American offer of alliance in 1949. Primarily what they reached for was the U.S. commitment to pit its weight into the European balance – a commitment that was spelled out in Article V of the NATO treaty and radiated from America's relatively undamaged national power, her victorious armies and her armadas of bombers, now armed with atomic weapons. From the beginning, deterrence in NATO was equated by the West European members with the American commitment and the nuclear dimensions of that commitment.

There was no eagerness in Western Europe for new standing armies. Nevertheless, the Europeans went along with the early American plans for massive conventional forces. They did so largely with the recognition that their contributions to these goals represented their part of the NATO bargain, their payment for the American commitment. The bargain was explicit in the case of Konrad Adenauer's nascent Federal Republic of Germany, which saw in rearmament the road to respectability and acceptance by the Western democracies. The willingness to pay the price, however, was tempered by deep apprehensions. These fears reflected a number of motives; predominantly, reluctance to wrest additional sacrifices from painfully recovering economies, as well as the conviction that in any event it would be impossible for the Alliance to match Soviet power on the ground. Perhaps the most telling and elementary fear related to the spectacle of a new conventional conflict rolling back and forth over Western Europe's already devastated landscape.

These motives explain the relative sense of relief in Western Europe that greeted the Eisenhower Administration's doctrine of massive retaliation in 1953. This was the great, harmonious period in NATO strategy in which every NATO government knew exactly what would happen in a major situation. The harmony was short-lived; it began to break down in 1956-1957 when the Soviets installed missiles in Europe, tested their first intercontinental rocket and orbited Sputnik. The European fears mingled with those in America during the assumed "missile gap" of 1958-1961.They eased when the gap proved to be illusory, but reemerged with the Kennedy Administration's modifications of U.S. NATO doctrine.

The impact in Europe and the American doctrinal shift to flexible response was sharp and unsettling. Henry Kissinger described the European reaction in the January 1963 issue of <u>Foreign Affairs</u>:

> To our European allies, the shift in emphasis in American defense thinking after January 1961 was a cause of profound concern. Ideas about conventional warfare which we decided as outdated not three years previously were suddenly resurrected. The tactical nuclear weapons which we had introduced with the argument that they would offset Soviet superiority in weapons were now sharply downgraded.(8)

The 1960s were marked by bitter debate in NATO, climaxed by the retreat of France from the integrated commands of the Alliance in 1966. NATO weathered that crisis, but this effective loss of one of its most important members was a severe setback. The remainder of the Alliance struck ostensible harmony again in 1967, when, after some six years of wrangling, it formally adopted flexible response as the new NATO strategy.

## THE CHIMERA OF FLEXIBLE RESPONSE

The harmony of 1967, however, was only ostensible. The European partners of the United States once again catered to American predilections. They did so partly with a view toward the new realities of the global environment which Washington pressed upon them. But they accepted the doctrine of flexible response with grudging reservations and with an interpretation that continued to place a premium on the strategic-nuclear deterrent as the sentinel of Western Europe's security. Above all, they accepted the new American doctrine out of the fear, already developing in 1967, that failure to accommodate could encourage a progressive American withdrawal from Europe. Indeed, the West Europeans, since 1967, have used flexible response as a subtle means of hanging the United States on its own petard. What they have been saying in effect is: "All right, we accept the need for conventional capabilities that can enhance the flexibility of the Alliance's response to any potential form and scope of attack by the Warsaw Pact. But this means, in the first instance, that there cannot be any reductions in the number of American forces encamped in Europe."

The dichotomy between the European emphasis on the deterrent forces (that is, primarily the nuclear dimensions) of the Alliance and the American stress on war fighting capabilities (that is, primarily conventional ones) can be overdrawn. After all, the West European nations have not made more than twenty-five years of heavy investments in conventional military manpower and hardware simply as a sop to the United States for the American protective guarantee. Moreover, the stark growth in Soviet strategic nuclear capabilities has more recently nudged some European views in favor of more serious consideration of a conventional alternative for NATO. This trend has been particularly noticeable in the pronouncements of the West German Defense Ministry since 1969.

Yet, even if the logic of strategic trends has influenced some European attitudes marginally in the direction of the American position, the logic tends to founder against the perceived realities. In the final analysis, most European strategic analysts cannot accept the primacy of a conventional strategy for NATO because they do not deem such a strategy viable in the face of ever mounting Warsaw Pact capabilities. They are drawn more and more to the conclusion that, as NATO defenses are presently configured, Warsaw Pact forces could smash across substantial parts of the North German Plain within a matter of hours or days. And, to the degree that any resort by the Alliance (i.e., the United States) to a nuclear response is thrown increasingly into doubt, they question glumly the inherent flexibility of flexible response.

It seems fair to generalize, therefore, that even while lip service is paid to flexible response, in large parts of Western Europe's NATO elite the strategy is considered, at best, a useful fiction. It is useful as a rationale which caters to American notions and helps keep American forces tethered to the defense of Western Europe. It is useful as a blanket over divergent views on strategy within the Alliance. It is perhaps useful in trying to persuade the adversary that the Alliance retains unity of purpose and the means to repel aggression. Yet, the fiction is becoming debilitating as the military balance in Europe tilts ever more conspicuously toward the East.

## THE CONCEPT OF MILITARY-POLITICAL BALANCE IN EUROPE

The preceding pages have traced some of the basic divergences in transatlantic attitudes on NATO strategy. The divergences, however, go beyond simple strategic and tactical preferences. Rather, they find their roots in fundamental differences between the two sides of the Atlantic with respect to the meaning of military power and its psychopolitical implications.

It is a truism that national attitudes are shaped significantly in the crucible of historical experience. The American experience reflects the luxury of independent and insular nationbuilding, relatively free of the impingements of international power politics. Indeed, it can be argued that the American ethos still mirrors antipathy toward the dirty politics of the Old World – an attitude that was conveyed by waves of immigrants fleeing the perceived injustices of European societies. The American rejection of old style power politics found clear expression in the Wilsonian idealism following World War I and in the United Nations universalism that inspired American expectations in the immediate post-World War II period. The universalist ideal succumbed to the realities of a new struggle after World War II – a struggle in which the United States found itself in the novel position of manager of power on a global scale. Never before having been compelled to harness military force to national strategy, except in sporadic bursts of continental expansion, self-defense and arbitration of existing conflict, the United States after World War II faced the unfamiliar task of fashioning a rationale for tying peacetime military power to a long-range global policy, a task compounded by the new and awesome dimensions of nuclear weapons.

Not surprisingly, historical experience and the terrifying implications of nuclear power were responsible for a rationale that put an overwhelming premium on war prevention – on deterrence theory. Although there have been variations to deterrence theory as it has been nurtured by American strategic thinkers in the postwar period, it has been marked by three basic denominators. The first, as we have suggested, has been that a new global conflagration must be avoided. The second denominator has centered upon a model of rational interaction among potential adversaries – upon the notion of military capabilities that are objectively perceived by the parties concerned. The third denominator of deterrence theory has been less explicit: it involves the concept that so long as military power (even marginally superior military power) is deterred, it cannot be translated into political gain. American deterrence theory has thus focused upon an essentially mechanistic relationship between war fighting capabilities and war prevention. As such, it has tended to ignore the political arena beneath the dynamics of the strictly military competition. In its application to Europe, the general verdict of deterrence theory tends to be simple: so long as they are likely to be restrained from direct military attack, the Soviets cannot use even superior military power on the continent for political profit.

European views are conditioned by a different historical experience. As the heirs of Talleyrand, Castlereagh and Bismarck, Europeans are sensitive to the subtle political shadows cast by military power. For centuries, these shadows have played upon the chessboard of European politics. There is recognition in Europe of the revolution that modern destructive weapons have wrought in military power and its political utility. Yet, while appreciating (and, indeed, heavily relying on) the blanketing effect of mutual nuclear deterrence on conflict, Europeans have not lost sight of the political implications of shifts in the military balance of power – at the strategic nuclear level and progressively at the level of theater capabilities.

This view explains in large part the preoccupation in Western Europe with the concept of military balance on the continent as a prerequisite of security and what might broadly by characterized as "stability in political relations." Indeed, it can be argued that the imperative of balance rather than mechanistic deterrence motivated the European members from the beginning of NATO. They accepted the need for a conventional forward defense. Yet, recognizing the futility of trying to match Soviet power on the ground in Europe, they accepted eagerly American strategic nuclear power and tactical nuclear power as the essential balancing elements in the European military equation.

There is little question that in key European perceptions (that is, perceptions from the sensitive vantage point of policymaking) this balance is unraveling in major categories. The U.S. "strategic sword" as a mainstay of balance has been blunted and is in danger of being forfeited in its relevance to Europe. The efficacy of the U.S. stockpile of tactical nuclear weapons, emplaced originally as a direct means of redressing the conventional imbalance in favor of the Warsaw Pact, is endangered by the amassing of Soviet theater nuclear capabilities and by self-impositions of American constraint. At the same time, the disparities in conventional forces continue to widen.

Perhaps the best way to contrast military balance with simple deterrence is that the former has political connotations beyond the mere absence of conflict. It has to do with the difficult to define measure of self-confidence which military power donates to a society in its dealings with a competing society. To cite a prominent West German defense expert:

> The rationale of military efforts for the Soviet Union does not have to do predominantly with waging war, but rather with winning political terrain in peacetime. Therefore, the greatest danger that the West faces in its neglect of its own military power is not one of getting involved in war – although this, too, cannot be completely excluded – but rather of gambling away the peace. For this reason, the real danger lies in a military-political imbalance between East and West.(9)

Military imbalance is thus equated with Finlandization. Implicit in this kind of equation is the widespread belief in Europe that some of the current trends in Western Europe, including the gathering strength of leftwing forces as well as the deferential policies toward the Soviet Union by some West European governments, have already been influenced, consciously or not, by the growing military imbalance on the continent. There is nothing mysterious in this process in the eyes of a seasoned observer of European politics:

> The history of mankind offers endless illustrations in every age of

> small countries adjusting themselves toward their powerful neighbors. What applies to big powers in general is true, a fortiori, with regard to a big power which still believes in a political mission. Sometimes this is stated openly, as happened in a recent debate in the British House of Commons when the leader of the leftwing of the Labour Party, in an unguarded moment, said that if the Soviet Union is as strong militarily as maintained, appeasement would be the only sensible policy. But usually the process is far more subtle.(10)

To this should be added that political climates and governmental policies are not fashioned solely by current perceptions; they tend to trade also on futures. Even European analysts who tend to take a more comfortable view of the present military equation in Europe and its implications evince worry about the trends. And to the extent that the trends point to the kind of future scenario that the Soviets have adduced, the tendency becomes ever more compelling to cast for policies of accommodation and reinsurance.

## THE CRITERIA FOR AN IMPROVED NATO POSTURE

The preceding discussion can best be summarized, as well as pushed forward, with the help of the following premises:

1. The nations of the Atlantic Alliance must take seriously the articulated Soviet goals of overall military superiority, the separation of the United States from Europe, and Soviet hegemony in Western Europe by the mid-1980s. The trends thus far bear out the general validity of the Soviet timetable.

2. There is little likelihood that the Alliance can be regalvanized at the subgovernmental levels in the critical period suggested by the Soviet timetable. Some of the at-large trends within the Atlantic Community will probably continue. This means, at the very least, that we can expect no additional resources, relatively speaking, to be allotted to the common defense.

3. The only hope is a reshaping of the NATO posture within the limited means available and on the basis of a new consensus among the NATO elite on both sides of the Atlantic. The previous pages have emphasized that such a consensus has been lacking in the twenty-eight years of NATO's existence and that divergences in perceptions have been obscured by compromises on strategy, notably flexible response. Yet, the viability of flexible response, already strained by differing interpretations in the alliance, has been put into sharpening doubt by the realities of the shifting military equation at the strategic nuclear level as well as within the European theater.

4. A new consensus of the NATO elite must cater to the political military requirements implicit in the European concept of military balance. These requirements go beyond the criteria of deterrence and defense. They connote the maintenance of a counterbalancing military weight vis-a-vis the growing power of the Warsaw Pact – one that will not only deter aggression but will also donate to the governments of Western Europe the necessary self-confidence in their dealings vis-a-vis the East.

5. Although this weight must be sought also in improvements in the conventional capabilities of the Alliance, such improvements cannot be found realistically in numerical increases in NATO capabilities, particularly conventional manpower. Indeed for psychological reasons NATO has to get away from the numbers game of gauging relative capabilities – a game in which the Alliance cannot hope to prevail. Rather, the remedies must be found in the qualitative realms in which NATO still enjoys advantages, particularly in new weapons technologies and their adaptation to strategy.

6. More general, military balance requires that posture improvements not be regarded in separate compartments of the NATO triad – conventional, tactical nuclear and strategic nuclear – but rather within an organic whole of capabilities that span the spectrum of potential conflict. The task is to link integrally those capabilities to the point where the potential adversary cannot demonstrate, let alone invoke, clear superiority in any one. This notion may run counter to current American predilections to separate the legs of the triad – to widen the firebreak between conventional and nuclear warfare, and between tactical nuclear conflict and the strategic exchange. Nevertheless, if the preservation of the Alliance is to have priority in the American agenda for the critical period ahead, the United States must forfeit these predilections in favor of a coherent and credible NATO strategy.

7. Above all, military balance requires the unstinting U.S. strategic commitment to the defense of Europe. There can be no balance in Europe without the strategic weight of the United States on the scales. This means that decoupling – perceived or real (in the form of U.S.-Soviet agreements) – must not only be prevented, but that the strategic linkage must indeed be strengthened. The succeeding chapters address these priorities.

## NOTES

(1) Harlan Cleveland, NATO: The Transatlantic Bargain (New York: Harper & Row, 1970), p. 5.

(2) A recent summary of Brezhnev's 1973 remarks was supplied by William Beecher, "Brezhnev Termed Detente a Ruse, 1973 Report Said," Boston Globe, February 11, 1977.

(3) The following information was provided by Lord Chalfont in "Moscow's Brutal Reality," The Times (London), July 28, 1975. Lord Chalfont drew directly from conversations with General Senja.

(4) Ibid.

(5) "Soviet Sees Gains for Reds in West," The New York Times, October 23, 1974.

(6) C.L. Sulzberger, "Ourselves as Russia Sees Us," The New York Times, March 5, 1977.

(7) The following synopsis of U.S.-European divergence draws in part upon an analysis adduced by the author in another context in "Nuclear Balance in Europe" Foreign Affairs, April 1972, pp. 502-506.

(8) Henry A. Kissinger, "Strains on the Alliance," Foreign Affairs, January 1963, p. 274. Excerpted by permission from Foreign Affairs, January 1963. Copyright 1962 by Council on Foreign Relations, Inc.

(9) Manfred Worner, Chairman of the Defense Committee of the West German Parliament, in Die Welt, Hamburg, August 19, 1975.

(10) Walter Laqueur, "Perils of Detente," The New York Times Magazine, February 27, 1977, p. 34.

# 4 The U.S.-European Strategic Linkage

Walter F. Hahn

One of the most challenging problems for a nation in the modern era is to adjust its strategic posture to changes in the world environment. Difficult as this adaptation may be for an individual state, it is enormously more complex for an alliance which must accommodate the strategic objectives of its members while reconciling frequently divergent interests among them. As pointed out in Chapter 3, this problem is not new for the Atlantic Alliance, through its nearly three decades of existence, NATO has been a constantly adapting "bargain." Yet, in no aspect of the NATO posture is this challenge greater today than in what may be regarded as the foundation of the "bargain": the American strategic nuclear protective guarantee for Western Europe.

Explicitly or implicitly, concern about the declining credibility of this ultimate deterrent – or what has become popularized under the horrendous term coupling – has been center stage in the Atlantic dialogue in recent years. This chapter will begin by reviewing the key developments that have impacted on the credibility of the U.S. strategic nuclear commitment. Subsequently, it will examine Soviet efforts to erode this credibility – to the point where the fear of "decoupling" has become pervasive in the councils of Western Europe. The Western alliance, however, is not without recourse for strengthening its strategic posture or reknitting the strategic linkage. Recognizing that "coupling" is not simply a function of actual military capabilities, but depends meaningfully also on the perceptions of both adversaries and allies, this chapter will focus on ways to enhance the strategic linkage.

## NATO'S STRATEGIC DILEMMA

The principal anchors of NATO have been deterrence and forward defense. Almost from NATO's inception the West European members of the Alliance equated deterrence with the threat of U.S. nuclear retaliation against the

Soviet Union in response to any large scale aggression against Western Europe. From the beginning, moreover, the European allies of the United States recognized – often uncomfortably – that the linkage between the U.S. strategic forces and the defense of Europe was not necessarily automatic, but remained a function of American political resolve. The fear in Western Europe that this resolve might not be forthcoming prompted an almost regular series of visits by U.S. secretaries of state to European capitals in the 1950s with assurances that the United States would stand by its ultimate obligations to the Alliance. So long as the United States enjoyed unquestionable strategic superiority, these anxieties and doubts did not cut deeply into NATO relations. As was alluded to previously, the most harmonious years in NATO came during the short-lived period of the mid-fifties – the period marked by U.S. strategic preeminence and the doctrine of massive strategic retaliation.

The strategy of massive strategic retaliation was based on the notion that NATO would resort early to a strategic nuclear response against major Soviet aggression. The conventional forces of the Alliance were to contain only limited Warsaw Pact incursions; together with the growing stockpile of U.S. tactical nuclear weapons in Western Europe, they were to serve as the tripwire that would activate the American strategic deterrent. By the late 1950s, however, a number of developments prompted questions about this simple strategy. It had become clear that the strategy of massive retaliation offered little flexibility; it basically provided for a choice between an all out response and little or no response. Soviet advances in nuclear weapons technology, moreover, shed a lengthening shadow on the credibility of the American strategic forces to deter limited aggression. Soviet development of an intercontinental nuclear capability, heralded by the launching of the Sputnik in 1957, pointed to the time when a U.S. strategic nuclear strike could risk a similar Soviet riposte on the U.S. homeland. Finally, with the advent of the Kennedy Administration in 1961 a group of policymakers came to Washington who leaned much more than their predecessors on the proposition that even a very limited nuclear strike in Europe inexorably would flare into general nuclear conflict. These considerations were central to the development of the new NATO strategy of flexible response.

As originally conceived in the McNamara era, the flexible response strategy emphasized the conventional defense of Europe. The role of tactical nuclear weapons, which under massive strategic retaliation had been linked essentially with the conventional NATO "shield," became limited largely to deterrence. Under the new perspectives at the Washington policy levels, tactical nuclear weapons would come into play – if, indeed they would come into play at all – only once NATO conventional defenses had failed. At the same time, American policy planners sought to set the nuclear threshold as high as possible.(1) These efforts fueled West European suspicions that the United States was intent upon limiting a war in Europe to a European battlefield, and that the U.S. strategic "sword" had in effect been sheathed.

A logical consequence of the desire to set a high nuclear threshold was the perceived need to tie NATO nuclear forces tightly to central American command and control. Carried to its ultimate conclusion, therefore, flexible response, as developed in the McNamara years, demanded that the United

States retain full control over all the nuclear weapons available to the Alliance and oppose nuclear sharing and the development of independent national nuclear forces by its allies.

The long and bitter debate in NATO over flexible response, with its conventional emphasis for European defense, testified to the deep divisions created by the new strategy in the Alliance. It precipitated France's withdrawal from the integrated NATO commands. To reach agreement on the new strategy required a full six years – from 1961, when the administration in Washington laid down the basic guidelines for the doctrinal revisions, until December 1967, when finally NATO officially adopted the document called MC 14/3, which articulated the flexible response strategy. MC 14/3 recognized ostensibly the need for a balanced posture of conventional and tactical and strategic nuclear weapons. It called for meeting any aggression with direct defense at approximately the same level of conflict chosen by the attacker. If the attack could not be contained, MC 14/3 prescribed deliberate escalation to convince the Soviets of NATO's resolve to resist. Finally, it recommended an appropriate general nuclear response to a major nuclear attack.(2)

MC 14/3 was deliberately phrased in general and somewhat ambiguous terms. The motive behind the ambiguity was not merely to keep the Soviets guessing about the timing and circumstances in which NATO nuclear weapons would be used, but also to allow NATO members a flexible interpretation of flexible response. For the policymakers in Washington, MC 14/3 provided essentially a framework for building a NATO defense that would endeavor to limit a conflict triggered by Soviet aggression – which presumably would start and remain conventional – to Europe. By contrast, the European members of NATO tended to read into MC 14/3 a continued role for tactical nuclear weapons as a link in the chain of escalation to the ultimate use of the strategic nuclear forces. It was not surprising that European leaders, fearful of an American sponsored evolution of a NATO posture and doctrine that emphasized a protracted conventional war on the continent, argued in subsequent negotiations on NATO guidelines for the early use of nuclear weapons to signal NATO resolve and the threat of strategic strikes.(3)

Under the Nixon Administration came a gradual shift in the American interpretation of flexible response. Generally the new policymakers did not share the conviction of their predecessors that any nuclear strike would automatically lead to Armageddon; nor were they, by and large, as emotionally tied to the policy of opposing the nuclear programs of the British and French allies. Stressing the notion that Alliance strategy was based on the triad of conventional, tactical nuclear and strategic nuclear forces, the new officials in the Pentagon (particularly under Secretary of Defense James Schlesinger), were prepared to contemplate a role for tactical nuclear weapons beyond that of deterrence. While they thus agreed with their European counterparts on the importance of the tactical nuclear component, some divergent assumptions were at play. Most European allies continued to focus on the "coupling" aspect of tactical nuclear weapons; for the Americans, tactical nuclear weapons, together with an upgraded conventional defense, offered the best chance for keeping a war in Europe limited and, hopefully, terminable without risk to the U.S. homeland.

While on the surface the disarray over MC 14/3 appeared to be repaired, fundamental disagreement over the nature of deterrence remained and has continued to sap the Alliance. It lay obviously in the European interest to insist on anchoring deterrence to the notion that any Soviet aggression, no matter how limited, would risk escalation to a strategic strike on the Soviet homeland. It remained in the American interest to hedge against that very risk. In practice, the doctrinal differences between these two deterrence concepts could not readily be distinguished in the NATO posture that encompassed a continuum of forces, from conventional through thermonuclear. One West European leader reportedly sought to assuage European concerns by contending that as long as there was a 5 percent chance that the United States would invoke its strategic forces, deterrence would remain effective.

It is probably fair to say that throughout the postwar period the American deterrent was never intrinsically "coupled" to the defense of Europe, just as it is not likely to be categorically "decoupled." In the final analysis, the linkage question boils down to the credibility of the American nuclear commitment – and credibility is as much a function of perception as it is one of objective capabilities. In the 1970s, however, the growing introversion of American politics on the one hand, and the dramatic growth of Soviet strategic capabilities on the other, prompted new cracks in that commitment from the European perspective.

## THE FADING CREDIBILITY OF THE U.S. NUCLEAR PLEDGE

As emphasized in the preceding chapter, the transatlantic dialogue has been lacking in honesty. There has been a panicky reaction in Europe every time the United States has conveyed, through statements or actions, a preference for keeping a conflict in Europe strictly limited to a conventional battlefield. Yet these anxieties were rarely vented at the highest levels of the Alliance, let alone in confrontation with U.S. policymakers. The great inhibitor on the European side has been what might be characterized as the "fear of the self-fulfilling fear" – the notion that challenging or berating the Americans openly on matters of NATO strategy might only hasten the feared contingency of an American retrenchment from Europe.

In the 1970s, however, these fears have both ascended to new heights and pervaded broader domains of European opinion. In Western Europe the shriller denunciations of the American embroilment in Vietnam came principally from the speaker horns of the Old and New Left. Yet, there were deep misgivings in conservative and pro-American circles as well over the protracted American engagement in mainland Asia. It seems fair to generalize that these apprehensions were based less on moral grounds than on the fear that the conflict in Southeast Asia, in addition to sapping the American treasury and inner cohesion, was deflecting American priorities from Europe. Nevertheless, the final collapse of South Vietnam in the Spring of 1975 prompted a shock reaction in Europe. Not so much deploring U.S. disengagement from Vietnam as such, Europeans articulated deep concern over the manner in which the disengagement was carried out. The West European press of various political persuasions expressed a pervasive gloom about the American resolve to sustain global leadership and about the effect of Vietnam on American public opinion and on the U.S. Congress. Throughout Europe, newspapers gave prominent play to a poll in the United States indicating that only 39 percent of the Americans would be prepared to fight even for the defense of Europe.(4)

The reactions to the Vietnam debacle were amplified by West European pangs of impotence and insecurity in the wake of the lingering economic dislocations generated by the 1973 oil embargo, governmental crises in Great Britain and West Germany, and a marked political drift to the left in Italy, France and other West European countries. And, of course, these doubts about America's resolve and staying power mingled with growing apprehension regarding the ever expanding Soviet arsenal of strategic nuclear weapons.

Largely because the United States was fairly scrupulous in keeping its allies informed, the first round of strategic arms negotiations between the superpowers did not generate undue anxiety within the Alliance. At least in Bonn, the SALT I Accords of 1972 were greeted as a framework in which the strategic equation between the superpowers could be stabilized. Influential voices in Paris and other NATO capitals, however, warned that the "extended deterrent" of U.S. strategic power – the backbone of the American nuclear commitment to Europe – was being blunted. More importantly, perhaps, European observers and press began to take greater notice of the details of the unfolding strategic nuclear equation – particularly Soviet adantages in throwweight and the stark differences in the numbers of permitted Soviet and U.S. missile launchers under SALT. Except in limited circles of experts, the superior performance and greater technical sophistication of U.S. weapons, notably their greater accuracy, failed to register very strongly on European views. The conclusion began to take root that Washington was prepared to concede strategic superiority to Moscow.

Moreover, European fears both of the general direction of trends at the strategic nuclear level as well as "decoupling" were sharply exacerbated by reports in late 1977 about the basic outlines of an impending SALT II accord. Particularly disquieting to Europeans was a contemplated three-year protocol that would limit the deployment and testing of American cruise missiles, as well as a proposed no-transfer clause that would bar the United States from making cruise missile technology available to its allies.

More will be said about the cruise missile in other contexts below and in the chapter that follows. The essential point to be made here is that the reported SALT II provisions go to the heart of European decoupling fears, and the outcry in Western Europe that greeted the SALT II reports gave ample evidence of this. The United States was accused not only of casting once again for superpower accord with disregard for Alliance interests, but this time of actually and directly forfeiting such interests on the U.S.-Soviet bargaining table. Moreover, the Alliance interests ostensibly being squandered away involve precisely the theater nuclear capabilities of the United States that constitute in European eyes the last real strands in the weakening U.S.-European strategic linkage.

## SOVIET EFFORTS TO SEVER THE TRANSATLANTIC LINKAGE

The Soviets have, understandably, been alert to opportunities for driving wedges between the United States and its European allies. A variety of diplomatic initiatives and proposals in the arms control arena have been aimed clearly at undermining directly or indirectly the American nuclear guarantee in the eyes of the European members of the Alliance.

A recurring theme in Soviet arms control diplomacy has been the notion of a nuclear-free zone in Central Europe. Originally advanced by Polish Foreign Minister Adam Rapacki in 1957, versions of the denuclearized zone proposal have been tabled by Soviet and East European representatives at Warsaw Pact meetings, arms control gatherings and other forums. These initiatives have been turned aside by NATO with a clear recognition of the obvious pitfalls of a denuclearization scheme. It would leave the critical NATO Central Region at the mercy of numerically superior conventional Warsaw Pact troops. A mutual U.S.-Soviet nuclear withdrawal from the region would penalize primarily U.S. nuclear artillery and forward-based systems, while affecting in no way Soviet IRBMs, MRBMs, Backfire bombers and other weapons systems targeted on Western Europe. Finally, it would be perceived by the European members of NATO as a major move in the folding of the American nuclear umbrella over Western Europe.

A Soviet stratagem with similar intent is the proposal for a reciprocal pledge by the two superpowers not to be the first to use nuclear weapons against aggression. At the November 1976 meeting in Bucharest of the Warsaw Pact Political Consultative Committee, Moscow again dusted off the no-first-use proposal that has been part of the Soviet arms control arsenal throughout the sixties. This time the Soviets recommended that the signatory states of the Conference on Security and Cooperation in Europe (CSCE) conclude a no-first-use agreement. While NATO paid scant attention to the proposal, the prospects point to an intensified Soviet propaganda barrage on this score.

Clearly, Soviet no-first-use gambits are devoid of any sincere substance, and bear the obvious design of prying wider the credibility gap between the United States and Western Europe. It is worth noting that in 1972 the Soviets had unveiled in the United Nations a variant of a no-first-use agreement which combined a general renunciation of force commitment with a nonuse of nuclear weapons pledge. This plan implied the legitimacy of using nuclear weapons against a conventional attack and reflected an effort to placate Western objections to a simple no-first-use arrangement. The reversion in the Bucharest declaration to the simple formula reflects the apparent recognition by the Soviets that they need no longer sugar coat the proposal.

The Soviets are keenly cognizant of the potential harvest of this propaganda line. Allied suspicions that Washington might be disposed to accede to Soviet no-first-use initiatives surfaced in West European reactions to the Nixon-Brezhnev Agreement on the Prevention of Nuclear War of June 1973. Under the agreement the superpowers promised to consult each other in crises that risked escalation to the use of nuclear weapons. The June 1973 accord was widely interpreted in Western Europe, and particularly in West Germany, as a no-first-use of nuclear weapons agreement in disguise and a major step toward decoupling. Allied spokesmen argued that the agreement threatened to neutralize NATO's tactical nuclear component. From a West European vantage point, the agreement appeared to give priority to superpower stability at the expense of the NATO deterrent and loomed as the harbingers of a superpower condominium.

Indeed the effort to promote the image of a superpower condominium, in which the Soviet Union and the United States would in effect preside over the fate of the lesser powers without their direct participation, was clearly evident behind several Soviet initiatives in SALT. Illustrative was Moscow's demand in SALT I to count, under the limits of the provisional agreement, the nuclear forces of Britain and France. Washington rejected any discussion of allied forces in Britain's and France's absence from the forum. Side-stepping this rejection, the Soviets issued a unilateral declaration in SALT I in which they stated that they would not be bound by the force level ceilings if Great Britain and France were to expand their nuclear forces. The gambit was aimed not only at obtaining Soviet advantage in the mathematics of SALT, but also at creating a situation in which Washington would be held accountable for the nuclear programs of its allies. In the SALT II rounds the Soviets reportedly raised again the issue of French and British missiles without in any way suggesting constraints on Soviet missile forces targeted against Western Europe.(5)

A similar Soviet ploy to induce the United States to ride roughshod over allied interests has been the demand to include the U.S. forward based systems (FBS) in the strategic arms negotiations. The FBS, which are mostly the nuclear-armed aircraft, are the only visible forces in the European theater that can reach Soviet territory. For this reason, they carry special political significance as palpable evidence of U.S. fidelity to the nuclear component of the NATO triad. Unmistakably, the FBS are moored to European security. If the United States were to strike an accord with the Soviets which would explicitly or implicitly affect the FBS, the fear of a "decoupling" would become all too real to the Europeans. Although the Soviet Union finally dropped the FBS issue in SALT I – and while renewed Soviet pressures on this score were resisted apparently by the United States in the SALT II negotiations – Moscow has made it clear that the issue will remain an active one on the agendas of East-West negotiations.

Indeed West Europeans charge that the United States already has opened the door wider to Soviet initiatives against FBS by agreeing to bring cruise missiles into the purview of SALT. Although the cruise missile has the potential of use in a number of variants – as a strategic weapons system launched from long-range bombers as well as a tactical system deployed on land and seabased platforms – the appeal of the system to NATO planners attaches primarily to its theater role. In fact, West German analysts have argued that, by accepting restrictions on cruise missiles (which could become permanent after the expiration of the three-year protocol), the United States may be preempting the future of FBS. In this view, cruise missiles loom as the logical replacement for manned aircraft, which are becoming highly vulnerable in deep interdiction missions.

More generally, the Soviet Union has endeavored to create, through the SALT process, a broad climate that will facilitate Moscow's attainment of a maximal strategic posture without, in the process, raising the ante of a strong U.S. counter-effort. Soviet doctrinal writings and strategic programs point clearly to the development of a nuclear war waging and war winning capability that will permit the Soviet Union to survive as a viable national entity should deterrence fail.(6) The Soviet commitment to a war fighting and war winning posture reflects an abiding principle of Soviet military doctrine that any war, including a nuclear war, can be fought and won.

The Soviet Union is intent upon a so-called damage limiting strategy. In terms of its offensive arsenal, this means building forces that not only can carry massive destruction to U.S. population centers and industrial bases, but can also knock out weapons systems in the United States poised against the Soviet Union. Stated in another way, Moscow is fashioning a counterforce capability that can substantially degrade, if not eliminate altogether, U.S. strategic weapons systems, notably landbased Minuteman missiles, and command and control centers. U.S. defense estimates indicate that unless Washington takes appropriate action, the Soviet Union could have, by the early 1980s, a posture which would permit Moscow to destroy with only a fraction of its ICBM forces, the majority of the U.S. landbased ICBMs, the U.S. submarines in port and the non alert bombers.(7)

Barring a breakthrough in Soviet anti-submarine capabilities, the United States could still, in the event of a Soviet preemptive blow, turn to its nuclear-armed submarines on station as well as much of its strategic bomber force. Yet sealaunched missiles cannot match their landbased counterparts in the needed accuracy to strike at hardened, high value targets in the Soviet Union. Strategic bombers cannot respond as quickly as the ICBMs and are vulnerale to interdiction. Moreover, the scenario of potential Soviet superiority depicts a situation in which the Soviet Union launches a preemptive blow with only a fraction of its strategic forces, then holds the surviving U.S. forces at bay with the threat of a massive nuclear barrage against American population centers – whereupon Moscow dictates the terms of surrender.

Even if the Soviet Union were to scale this pinnacle of strategic nuclear superiority, the disastrous scenario may never be played. The very capability to carry it off could be used by Moscow as a political battering ram to coerce Western nations toward broad accommodation with the USSR. As has been pointed out in the preceding chapter and will be elaborated upon in a succeeding one, the Soviets in their Finlandization drive are banking clearly upon European perceptions of a shifting military balance. In the words of one analyst, "It is thus through the uncertain medium of others' perceptions that strategic arsenals generate political power."(8)

In sum, the Soviets have two options for slashing the strategic linkage between Western Europe and the United States. One is the indirect one of whittling away at the physical tokens of the American strategic deterrent in Western Europe and furthering the image of decoupling through superpower accommodations, addressed ostensibly to mutual restraint (e.g., a no-first-use agreement). The second option is the direct road to the kind of clearcut military predominance that will crush any lingering doubt about the outcome of a major conflict, let alone any residual validity of American nuclear commitments, in Europe or elsewhere. These two options are by no means mutually exclusive; rather, they characterize intertwining strands in a single long-range Soviet effort.

## THE REQUIREMENT FOR STRATEGIC FLEXIBILITY

As long as the Soviet Union concentrates upon a war fighting and war winning strategy, it will not accept any real or durable constraints on its strategic programs which will impede the attainment of its strategic objectives. In spite of the SALT I accords, Soviet strategic programs have continued unabated.(9) Since SALT I the Soviets have started to deploy an entire new generation of ICBMs: the SS-17, SS-18 and SS-19. They have developed a new mobile two-stage Intermediate Range Ballistic Missile (IRBM), the SS-20, which, if another stage is added, can be converted relatively quickly into an ICBM. They have deployed versions of a new nuclear-armed submarine, the Deltas, which are equipped with 4,200-mile-range SLBMs. The ICBMs are MIRVed; a new SLBM, the SS-NX-18, is under development and is expected to be fitted with three MIRVs. The Backfire, the new Soviet bomber, has the capability of strategic missions against the United States.

Meanwhile, strategic hardening programs for Soviet strategic forces and command and control centers as well as redundancy of communications are being emphasized. Soviet R&D efforts on the Anti Ballistic Missile have not been relaxed. ABM test firings have continued. The aggressive Soviet effort in the ABM area has raised questions of violations of the ABM treaty. Evidence also suggests that a new strategic air defense system is under development. Soviet civil defense programs, which since 1972 have been placed under military control, are growing. In addition, a new generation of ICBMs is in the R&D stage. More recently, Soviet acivities in space technology have become more pronounced. The Soviets have resumed their antisatellite development. A Soviet capability to interfere with the U.S. early warning and other intelligence satellites would have profound implications for the U.S. ICBM force and intelligence collection capability more generally. Moscow is working on other space applications for support of military forces.

Moreover, the Soviet Union, is clearly searching for breakthroughs in other areas of advanced weapons technology. According to Dr. Malcolm R. Currie, the former Director of Research in the United States Defense Department, the Soviets are pursuing a vigorous program in antisubmarine warfare, directed energy weapons and high energy lasers, and long-range radar surveillance. There are indications of Soviet concentration on particle beam technology which could have advanced weapon implications.(10) In short, the overall thrust and momentum of Soviet force development and deployment programs do not connote in any way Moscow's willingness to settle for the principles of strategic stability – objectives that have provided the main roadmarkers for the United States in the strategic arms negotiations.

In the early 1970s, as the depth, scope and momentum of Soviet strategic programs began to register more sharply in Washington, a reassessment of U.S. deterrent strategy was undertaken. It became painfully evident that the U.S. strategic posture, based on assured destruction or the threat to destroy much of the Soviet urban industrial base, might no longer have compelling deterrent value, or operational logic. Such a posture in effect narrowed the strategic options open to the United States, in the event of a Soviet attack, to a massive response or none at all; and aimed deterrence against essentially the least likely threat, namely, a Soviet nuclear attack against American cities and population. The credibility of the U.S. posture for deterrence of threats below that level, let alone at the European Theater level, was progressively crumbling.

In this light, the United States in early 1974 announced a new doctrine that called for flexible options to meet a variety of threats. The new doctrine, as explained by the then Secretary of Defense, James R. Schlesinger, called for a change in targeting rather than in the basic configuration of the U.S. strategic force structure. According to Schlesinger, U.S. strategic planning would incorporate employment options for selected, controlled strikes that would limit collateral damage and enhance the credibility of deterrence against a broad spectrum of conflict.(11) The new U.S. strategy of flexible options was welcomed in West European defense circles, where it was recognized clearly as a measure designed in part to shore up extended deterrence.(12) For that very reason, the so-called Schlesinger Doctrine was denounced in Moscow.

Greater flexibility in the employment of U.S. strategic forces by striking limited targets represents only a marginal (albeit significant) measure that can be taken to bolster deterrence, including extended deterrence. Even more, the United States needs to ensure the survivability of its forces and the flexibility of its options. Beyond the obvious step of hardening U.S. silos, and command and control centers, survivability and flexibility can best be advanced through a greater versatility in the U.S. force posture and an adequate degree of counterforce capability.

It is against the background of this imperative that more recent trends in U.S. strategic programs take on some ominous implications. The decision by the Carter Administration in 1977 to forego production of the B-1 bomber has been interpreted by disquieted analysts as in effect the abandonment, over the longer run, of the bomber leg of the strategic triad. In this view, present generation U.S. long-range aircraft are not likely to survive in the lethal environment of constantly improving Soviet air defenses. Moreover the proposed alternative of arming bombers with airlaunched cruise missiles, thus giving them a stand-off capability outside the immediate barriers of Soviet air defenses, is cast in doubt by the vulnerability of the bulky present generation air frames to interception. The doubt is enhanced by the range limitations likely to be imposed upon airlaunched cruise missiles in SALT II.

Indeed the decision on the B-1 as well as other moves by the Carter Administration – for example, halting the production line of Minuteman II missiles, and the apparent agreement with the Soviet Union in SALT II to impose a three-year moratorium on the deployment of new mobile ICBMs (in the American case, the MX missile) – have encouraged the suspicion that the United States has made the basic decision to move toward primary reliance on a seabased strategic deterrent.(13) If this suspicion is valid, then the outlook for the future of the strategic-nuclear balance is all the more bleak. Seabased strategic offensive systems have advantages of relative invulnerability over their landbased and airborne counterparts. Yet, as has been emphasized, this invulnerability is at the sufferance of the state-of-the-art in antisubmarine warfare – and, if the United States invests most of its strategic assets in seabased systems, the Soviets can be counted on to redouble their search for a breakthrough in ASW. In the meantime, seabased missiles have neither the accuracy nor the flexibility to deal effectively with counterforce targets in the Soviet Union.

In short, the answer to the perceived weaknesses of two legs of the strategic triad is to strengthen those legs rather than to abandon the triad concept. This strengthening can be accomplished through the introduction of new weapons and the improvement of existing systems. The cruise missile is a case in point. Cruise missile technology will be detailed in the subsequent chapter; suffice it to say in this context that the long-range cruise missile – both in its air- and sealaunched variants – with its high accuracy and low vulnerability as well as cost effectiveness, is one of the most promising candidates for enhancing the U.S. strategic posture. The cruise missile would provide U.S. strategic forces with a survivable, hardtarget kill capability and would thus represent a major stride toward restoring and broadening U.S. deterrence. The development and deployment of a heavier and more accurate ICBM than the Minuteman III, such as the MX, as well as enhanced accuracy in the existing Minuteman force (e.g., through the installation of improved guidance systems and Mark 12A warheads), would generate a greater measure of counterforce than is currently available in the U.S. strategic panoply.(14)

The best safeguards for a viable U.S. deterrent force in the critical decade ahead are diversity and flexibility. A variety of flexible strategic options inherent in a diverse U.S. posture would make it impossible to calculate with confidence the U.S. response and the risk that a given Soviet action would incur. Second, a miltiplicity and diversity of U.S. military targets are much more difficult to destroy than a single set of targets. Soviet force planning would be complicated by a great deal of uncertainty about potential U.S. deployments.

## STRENGTHENING THE NATO POSTURE

A U.S. effort to develop greater flexibility in the American strategic shield would help to reinforce the credibility of the strategic linkage at the upper end of the deterrence spectrum. The preceding chapter has pointed to the untoward emphasis that the United States has placed upon the "local countervailing deterrent" in Europe, notably the conventional component. Nevertheless, clearly the credibility of the strategic linkage is also a function of the credibility of NATO's defense posture in Europe.

In the past ten years the Soviets have been engaged in a steady effort to upgrade the Soviet-Warsaw Pact forces in both quantitative and qualitative terms. These advances are detailed in the succeeding chapter. Suffice it to say here that improvements in Soviet general purpose forces and theater nuclear weapons have greatly boosted Soviet capabilities for fighting a conventional or nuclear war – or, what is more likely, an integrated conventional and nuclear offensive.

For deterrent purposes, it is particularly imperative that measures be taken to strengthen those components of NATO's arsenal that bear more directly on the strategic linkage – notably, the American nuclear systems located in Europe. From a West European vantage point, the American theater and battlefield nuclear forces are an integral part of NATO's forward strategy. The long-range, nuclear armed aircraft fulfill a crucial role in the chain of deterrence. Most important in European eyes are the Quick Reaction Alert (QRA) aircraft. Because of their capability to strike targets in the Soviet Union, the QRA aircraft are high value targets for Soviet preemption and are viewed in some U.S. circles as destabilizing. But it is precisely their capability to strike Soviet territory, if necessary, that endows the QRA aircraft with a psychological value that transcends their military missions of interdiction and striking other targets relevant to the battlefield. They derive additional political value from the participation of several West European allies, including nonnuclear members, in the QRA mission.

The above does not imply that the QRA aircraft are totally irreplaceable. As has already been alluded to in connection with European concerns about SALT, modern technology is expected to render the future battlefield and Warsaw Pact airspace increasingly inhospitable to manned systems. But any substitution for the QRA aircraft should be phased carefully in close consultation with the NATO allies. To assuage European concerns, replacements should be visible in the European theater and should possess a nuclear capability as well as the range to cover some targets in the USSR.

In light of these considerations, airlaunched and landbased cruise missiles offer NATO a significant capacity for interdicting Pact supply lines, striking airfields and storage facilities, as well as blunting the spearhead of an enemy thrust into Western Europe. The cruise missile has the potential of unprecedented versatility. For example, the long-range cruise missile armed with nuclear warheads could complement admirably the QRA mission and provide a penetration capability for striking targets deep in Warsaw Pact territory. The land-attack cruise missile offers uncanny accuracy, less vulnerability, and much greater cost-effectiveness than the QRA aircraft. It could replace effectively part of the QRA force, freeing the latter for close air support operations and interception of Warsaw Pact aircraft. The airlaunched missile, furthermore, could give the shortlegged and older versions of the QRA aircraft a new lease on life. Equally important, the cruise missile would cater to the political and psychological needs of the European allies. The land- or airlaunched version would be a nuclear system in place in Western Europe that could reach the Soviet Union.

This brings us to the larger question of U.S. tactical nuclear warheads in Western Europe and the relationship of TNW to the strategic-nuclear linkage. Already, mention has been made of divergent European and American perspectives of TNW. European strategists have focused essentially on the deterrent effect that the very presence of TNW on European soil conveys to the potential aggressor; they have been understandably reluctant to look closely at the actual war fighting functions of theater nuclear weapons, particularly in immediate support of the battlefield. For their part, American analysts have tended to regard TNW at best as a counter to and deterrent against the Soviet initiation of nuclear warfare in Europe, and/or a last resort in the event of a crumbling of NATO defenses against a Warsaw Pact conventional attack. In face of the shifts in the strategic nuclear equation as well as the growth in Soviet theater nuclear capabilities, even the last resort rationale has dwindled conspicuously in the eyes of some prominent American analysts. There is no question that fears concerning the implications of nuclear war in Europe have sharply motivated various proposals in the United States to substantially reduce the number of nuclear warheads emplaced in Europe.(15)

A common denominator of American and European views has thus been the tendency (although prodded by different motives) to leave the issue of tactical nuclear weapons deliberately vague and undefined. Yet, the dramatic shifts in the military equation relevant to Europe have forced even West European analysts to face more squarely the need to rationalize the role of TNW both as explicit rungs in the ladder of escalation and in support of battlefield operations.(16) Rationalization pertains primarily to the credibility of the use of TNW in actual battlefield situations. The principal blur on this credibility has come from the nature of the TNW stockpile; the predominance of relatively large-yield and "dirty" nuclear warheads that render it inherently difficult to target enemy formations without, in the process, endangering NATO forces and civilian populations. Clearly, the stockpile requires modernization with "cleaner," smaller, and more accurate systems.

One means of modernization might be the so-called enhanced radiation weapons – popularly dubbed neutron bombs. An emotional debate has been generated by the advent of such weapons, whose lethality relates to the effects of radiation rather than blast. The debate has fastened misleadingly on the fact that enhanced radiation weapons kill people without destroying the material surroundings. The key to the promise of such weapons, however, is that they kill fewer people than most of the present weapons in the NATO inventory that rely on blast – that their smaller and more controllable lethal radius enables them to be targeted more discretely on attacking forces with minimum harm to civilians and minimum collateral damage to the surrounding environment.(17)

In general, tactical nuclear weapons bear upon the critical requirement in NATO's posture for a continuum of forces responsive to a strategy which deliberately obscures a firebreak or nuclear threshold. At no level of contemplated attack or conflict should the Soviet Union be able to calculate in advance NATO's response. If anything, NATO's strategy and posture must compound the element of uncertainty in Soviet calculations with respect to the type of response and the timing and circumstances in which the United States would resort to nuclear weapons.

Inevitably, the shifting strategic nuclear equation, with respect to Europe, points a new spotlight upon the role of British and French nuclear forces. It was precisely as an insurance policy against an abandonment of the American nuclear commitment to Western Europe that Britain and France originally constructed their own nuclear forces. Despite concerted American efforts in the 1960s to discourage independent British and French nuclear programs, both countries established their credentials as members of the nuclear club.(18)

Britain's strategic deterrent consists of four nuclear armed submarines, each with 16 Polaris A-3 missiles of some 200 kilotons. The range of the

Polaris is 2,500 nm, sufficient to cover the major cities in the Western USSR. Britain's nuclear bomber fleet has shifted from its erstwhile strategic mission to a primarily tactical role in the NATO theater.

France's strategic arsenal comprises 36 Mirage-IV bombers armed with 100 kt nuclear bombs and supported by a KC-135 tanker fleet for inflight refueling; two IRBM squadrons with nine launchers, each armed with the S-2 nuclear missile with a 150 warhead; and four nuclear armed submarines, equipped with 16 M-1, M-2 and M-20 missiles.(19) The Mirages are scheduled to remain operational until approximately 1985. The S-2 missile of the IRBM squadrons is expected to be replaced by the S-3 missile fitted with a thermonuclear warhead. The fifth nuclear submarine is scheduled for operation in the late 1970s; the building of a sixth submarine has been announced as one of a new generation, thereby implying clearly that more are to follow.(20) The new version will be equipped with the M-4 missile with significantly increased ranges from 2,000 to 2,500 nm, and with multiple warheads. The French tactical nuclear forces include nuclear armed tactical aircraft and the 60-mile range surface-to-surface Pluton regiments, of which a total of five are to be placed in service.

The determination of both countries to maintain their independent nuclear forces has weathered both external crises as well as internal controversies and pressures against defense budgets. The question that has become more marked in recent years is why, in the face of the shifting strategic environment and in the light of their improved relationships within the European Community, the two nations have not taken steps to pool their nuclear resources. The answer relates to a complexity of technological and political issues (with emphasis upon the latter). Suffice it to say that the prospect remains bleak for any meaningful merger of British and French nuclear forces, let alone for the emergence of a European deterrent.

In the absence of such a merger – or more generally of a new infusion of resources – are French and British nuclear forces likely to remain viable in the rapid technological currents of the 1980s? The answer to that question depends again upon a complex matrix of considerations: the assumption against which the effectiveness of the respective forces is gauged (particularly the validity of the concept of "proportional deterrence"), the likely progress in Soviet antiballistic missile defenses, advances in antisubmarine warfare, and a host of other factors. It seems accepted generally, however, that Great Britain particularly has to reckon with the likely obsolescence of its Polaris-based forces by the early 1980s, and thus already faces the agonizing question of whether to proceed to the development of expensive new generation weapons systems.

Here again the cruise missiles come squarely into the picture. Both France and Great Britain have evinced strong interest in long-range cruise missile technology as a relatively inexpensive expedient for both shoring up their present strategic nuclear panoplies and extending the viability of their deterrents well into the next decade. The question then becomes: Will the United States make this technology available to its allies – at least to Great Britain? Or will it deny the technology?

This question invokes the whole tortuous history of U.S. policy toward the nuclear ambitions and programs of its allies within the broader thrust of U.S.

nonproliferation efforts. Beyond the myriad political, emotional, legal, and technical factors involved, the question boils down to an essentially strategic one of risk versus gain from the American perspective, and Alliance versus narrow national interests.

On the one hand, French and British nuclear forces represent, from the U.S. vantagepoint, a diminution of American control over her ultimate destiny. These forces embody the risk that, conceivably, they may be unleashed in a crisis situation responsive to French or British interests which might not coincide in kind and intensity with U.S. interests. In the process, the United States could be pulled inexorably into a nuclear conflagration. Indeed, this triggering function – or what might be termed an insurance against ultimate American irresoluteness – has been at least implicit in the rationality behind the French and British forces.

On the other hand, against the background of strategic parity, is this not precisely what gives French and British forces greater prominence on the terrain of deterrence? The Soviet Union, at least, seems to think so, judging by the Kremlin's inordinate anxieties and its efforts directed against the European forces, some of which have been noted in this chapter. And, if the above is valid, from the American vantage point is the remote risk of an irrational act by France and/or Great Britain greater than the danger of Soviet aggression in Europe? To repeat the question posed in the previous chapter: What risks <u>are</u> the United States willing to accept in behalf of the Alliance?

All this is not to recommend the highly implausible: namely, a 180-degree turn in U.S. policies toward a complete nuclear embrace with France and Britain. However, the shifting strategic environment would seem to dictate an American reassessment of partial and inexpensive ways to help prop up the nuclear establishments of its allies. At the very least, the door must not be shut categorically on this option, as seems to be dangerously implicit in the SALT negotiations.

## A NEEDED CHANGE IN BASIC PREMISES

The various proposals in the previous pages to strengthen the strategic linkage of the Atlantic Alliance may be adjudged on their individual merit. In the aggregate, however, they amount to an admittedly ambitious prescription. They call for an escape from some of the major premises that have imprisoned Western (and particularly American) strategic precepts during the past two decades – premises that emerged, validly or not, in another time and another context – and for a new and realistic framework for coping with a new and critical situation.

One of those premises relates to the concept of minimum deterrence – a concept that bloomed in the comfortable heyday of American strategic superiority in the early 1960s, speeded (or at least rationalized) the relative decline of American strategic power, and continues to infuse (or rationalize) current U.S. strategic planning and programs. Expressed in shorthand, the concept holds that mutual deterrence is really not a function of equality in numbers and means – that merely the reasonable threat by one side, if necessary, to lash out destructively against the other is enough to sustain a semblance of "stability" (meaning the absence of conflict).

This concept has not been put to the test at the strategic nuclear level. Hopefully, it will never be put to the test. In the meantime, however, shifts at the strategic level have propelled some salient trends in the political-military arenas beneath. The danger is that these trends could overwhelm the United States and its vital interests long before the concept of minimum deterrence is ever called into account. As pointed out in the previous chapter, that seems to be the Soviet expectation.

The second major premise which has conditioned American perspectives on NATO – even more conspicuously in recent years – is implicitly a recognition of the penalties of the first premise. Briefly, this premise reads that precisely to the extent that the strategic nuclear equation becomes fraught with greater risks to the United States, it becomes all the more imperative to remove the direct fuses of possible strategic nuclear conflict from Europe. This premise is clearly behind proposals to withdraw elements of the American nuclear presence from Western Europe or (what tends to amount to the same thing) to consign them to the U.S.-Soviet arms control bargaining table. It is less explicitly, but no less meaningfully, behind the U.S. drive to summon the Alliance toward the objective of a viable conventional defense of NATO Europe – an objective whose frailty is recognized by even the more sincere advocates.

But let us face the facts. If we assume that, despite the recommendations made in this chapter, the central strategic nuclear balance continues to tilt in favor of the Soviet Union – and if we assume, furthermore, that maintaining the Alliance remains vital to U.S. interests – then the imperative is for ever more visible fuses of nuclear escalation in Europe and for more pronounced tokens of American willingness to contemplate such escalation.

This proposition can be explained in terms of nebulous elements of deterrence theory – particularly the elements of certainty and uncertainty of response to aggression. It can be explained more simply in terms of superior and inferior military power and the relative risk-taking incumbent upon each. A superior and aggressive military power is tempted to bank confidently upon the weight of its overall military strength to preempt all risks. It is up to the defending power to disrupt that comfortable calculus by selectively and ingeniously enhancing those risks. In essence, that is the task for NATO strategy in the critical decade ahead.

## NOTES

(1) The role of tactical nuclear weapons, as seen by defense officials in the Kennedy-Johnson era, has been spelled out in retrospect by Alain C. Enthoven, a principal proponent of the conventional strategy, and his assistant K. Wayne Smith, in How Much is Enough? (New York: Harper and Row, 1971), pp. 128-129.

(2) The basic principles of MC 14/3 can be found in several official and professional publications, including NATO: Facts and Figures (Brussels: NATO Information Service, 1971), p. 92, and Richard Hart Sinnreich, "NATO's Doctrinal Dilemma," Orbis, Summer 1975, pp. 461 ff.

(3) European efforts to stress the need for rapid escalation have been discussed in more detail in Wynfred Joshua, Nuclear Weapons and the Atlantic Alliance (New York: National Strategy Information Center, 1973), Chapter 4.

(4) See, for examples, The Economist, April 5, 1975; The Times (London), April 7, 1975; Le Monde, April 11, 1975. Many West German papers carried the result of the poll (Christian Science Monitor, March 27, 1975).

(5) See the testimony of Dr. Fred C. Iklé, former Director of the Arms Control and Disarmament Agency, as cited in The Washington Star, January 14, 1977.

(6) Secretary of Defense Donald H. Rumsfeld, in his Report to the Congress on the FY 1978 Budget, January 17, 1977, points throughout his report to Soviet efforts to acquire a war-fighting and war-winning capability. He also cites the findings of the Central Intelligence Agency in this respect (p. 59). Leon Gouré, et al., in The Role of Nuclear Forces in Soviet Strategy (Coral Gables, Florida: Center for Advanced International Studies, University of Miami, 1974), has made the case for a Soviet war-fighting and war-winning strategic effort on the basis of Soviet doctrinal writings.

(7) Ibid., p. 71.

(8) Edward N. Luttwak, Strategic Power: Military Capabilities and Political Utility (Washington, D.C.: The Center for Strategic and International Studies, Georgetown University, Washington Papers, No. 38, 1976), p. 7.

(9) The data on the Soviet strategic buildup have been drawn from General George S. Brown, USAF, Chairman of the Joint Chiefs of Staff, United States Military Posture for FY 1978, January 20, 1977.

(10) Department of Defense Program of Research, Development Test and Evaluation, FY 1978. Statement by Dr. Malcolm R. Currie, Director of Defense Research to the Congress, January 18, 1977, pp. II-23 - II-25.

(11) Secretary of Defense James R. Schlesinger, Annual Defense Department Report, FY 1975 (Washington: march 4, 1974), Chapter II.

(12) Testimony by James R. Schlesinger in Hearings before the Subcommittee on Arms Control, International Law and Organization of the Committee on Foreign Relations, U.S. Senate, March 4, 1974, p. 8.

(13) See the article by Jacquelyn K. Davis, "End of the Strategic Triad?," Strategic Review, Winter 1978.

(14) For a strategic and technical analysis of the role and advantages of the cruise missile, see Robert L. Pfaltzgraff, Jr., and Jacquelyn K. Davis, The Cruise Missile: Bargaining Chip or Defense Bargain? (Cambridge: Institute for Foreign Policy Analysis, Inc., 1977).

(15) Thus, Jeffrey Record proposed a reduction of 5,000 warheads from the current stockpile of some 7,000. See his study, U.S. Nuclear Weapons in Europe: Issues and Alternatives (Washington, D.C.: The Brookings Institution, 1974), p. 69. Paul C. Warnke argued for a reduction of more than 6,000. See his testimony in U.S. Congress, Senate, Committee on Foreign Relations, U.S. Nuclear Weapons in Europe and U.S.-USSR Strategic Doctrines and Policies, Hearings before the Subcommittee on U.S. Security Agreements and Commitments Abroad and the Subcommittee on Arms Control, International Law and Organization, 93rd Cong., 2nd sess., March 7, 14 and April 4, 1975 (Washington, D.C.: Government Printing Office, 1975), P. 57.

(16) See, for example, Manfred Worner, "NATO Defenses and Tactical Nuclear Weapons," Strategic Review, Fall 1977.

(17) For a thorough discussion of this issue, see S.T. Cohen, "Enhanced Radiation Weapons: Setting the Record Straight," Strategic Review, Winter 1978.

(18) For a detailed discussion of British and French strategic concepts that provided the rationale for the British and French nuclear programs, see Wynfred Joshua and Walter F. Hahn, Nuclear Politics: America, France, and Britain (Washington, D.C.: Sage Publications, for the Center for Strategic and International Studies, Georgetown University, 1973), Chapter 2.

(19) International Institute for Strategic Studies, The Military Balance, 1976-1977 (London: 1976), p. 21.

(20) Gerard Villant, "La programmation 1977-1982: sous le signe de l'equilibre," Revue de Defense Nationale, June 1976, p. 151.

# 5 The Shifting Euro-Atlantic Military Balance— Some Avenues of Redress

Jacquelyn K. Davis
Robert L. Pfaltzgraff, Jr.

The Soviet Union has been engaged in a military build up which has no parallel for a major power in peacetime since that of Nazi Germany in the 1930s. With an economy less than half the size of that of the United States, the Soviet Union has consistently devoted a larger percentage of its GNP to defense spending than has the United States. With at least 14 percent of its GNP allocated to defense spending – compared with the U.S. figure of 5.2 percent in 1977 – the Soviet Union has emerged as a global military power, capable of competing with the United States in every region of the world.

Concentrating simultaneously on quantitative and qualitative improvements in its military capabilities, the Soviet Union has moved, in little more than a decade, from a position of strategic inferiority in relation to U.S. forces to at least parity with the United States,(1) and in some strategic indicators, such as missile throwweight and numbers of strategic systems deployed, to a position of superiority. Despite the SALT I agreements of 1972, and the attempt to negotiate NATO-Warsaw Pact force reductions in Central Europe, the momentum of Soviet military research, development and deployment of forces has continued unabated, giving rise to concern in the West that by the 1980s the Soviet Union will attain "a potentially destabilizing asymmetry in missile hard target capability."(2) With such a capability, the Soviet Union would possess the potential means to hold hostage the population of the United States and to deter the employment of U.S. nuclear weapons against the Soviet homeland in retaliation for a Soviet-Warsaw Pact attack upon Western Europe. Under such circumstances, the phenomenon faced by many in Western Europe and the United States – the decoupling of the American strategic nuclear force from European security – would have taken place, if indeed it has not already occurred. (This issue is considered in greater detail in Chapter 4.) Under conditions in which the U.S. strategic force was decoupled from the defense of Europe, the European regional-theater balance would become even more important than it has been to the security of Western Europe and its survival outside the Soviet sphere of influence.

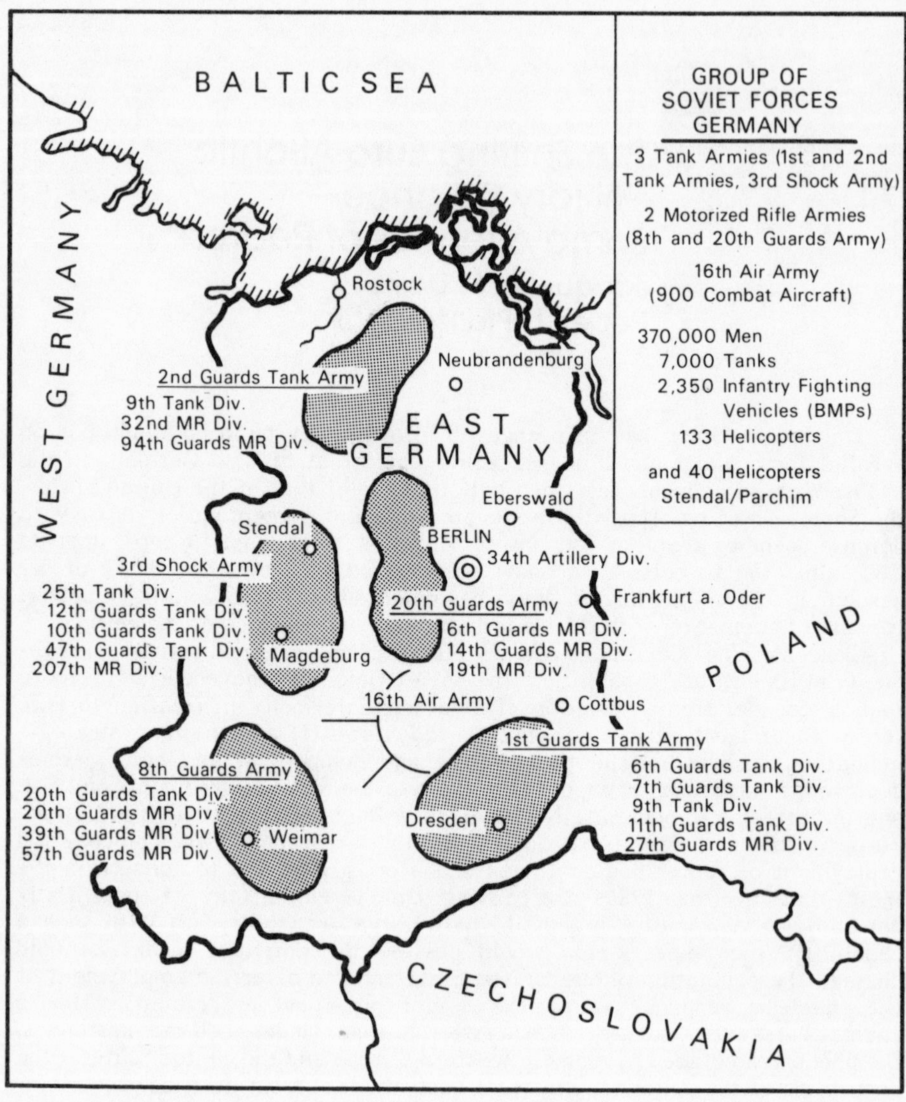
BALTIC SEA
GROUP OF SOVIET FORCES GERMANY
3 Tank Armies (1st and 2nd Tank Armies, 3rd Shock Army)
2 Motorized Rifle Armies (8th and 20th Guards Army)
16th Air Army (900 Combat Aircraft)
370,000 Men
7,000 Tanks
2,350 Infantry Fighting Vehicles (BMPs)
133 Helicopters
and 40 Helicopters Stendal/Parchim
WEST GERMANY
Rostock
Neubrandenburg
2nd Guards Tank Army
9th Tank Div.
32nd MR Div.
94th Guards MR Div.
EAST GERMANY
Eberswald
Stendal
BERLIN
34th Artillery Div.
3rd Shock Army
25th Tank Div.
12th Guards Tank Div.
10th Guards Tank Div.
47th Guards Tank Div.
207th MR Div.
Magdeburg
20th Guards Army
6th Guards MR Div.
14th Guards MR Div.
19th MR Div.
Frankfurt a. Oder
POLAND
16th Air Army
Cottbus
1st Guards Tank Army
6th Guards Tank Div.
7th Guards Tank Div.
9th Tank Div.
11th Guards Tank Div.
27th Guards MR Div.
8th Guards Army
20th Guards Tank Div.
20th Guards MR Div.
39th Guards MR Div.
57th Guards MR Div.
Weimar
Dresden
CZECHOSLOVAKIA

For this reason, the continued growth of Soviet-Warsaw Pact forces represents an ominous trend which, if projected without compensating NATO action, will lead to an imbalance that will be destabilizing for Western Europe. Whereas NATO forces have always been numerically inferior to those deployed by the Warsaw Pact, the overall superiority of Western, and especially American, technologies has been invoked as the means by which the Alliance putatively could offset the quantitative advantages possessed by Soviet forces in Europe. However, the situation has changed dramatically; the Soviet Union has now deployed in Europe a new generation of battlefield weapons which not only outnumber those of NATO, but, in many areas, incorporate technologies that are superior to their Western counterparts. The quantitative and qualitative improvements in Warsaw Pact forces have altered substantially the nature of the "deployed Soviet threat" in Europe, and have contributed to modifications in Soviet-Warsaw Pact theater strategy and tactics. Moreover, for the first time, the Soviet Union has attained in the Group of Soviet Forces deployed in Germany (GSFG) a genuine dual capability allowing for a greater flexibility of employment options.

## WARSAW PACT STRATEGIC-MILITARY DOCTRINE AND FORCE POSTURE

The emphasis of Soviet-Warsaw Pact military doctrine and force posture is on the primacy of offensive action.(3) Based on a strategy of high-speed maneuver, but one which also provides increasingly for a sustained combat capability, and utilizing the combined arms concept,(4) massed Soviet-Warsaw Pact mechanized and armor formations – in particular Soviet tanks, armored personnel carriers (APCs), and their extremely sophisticated armored fighting vehicles (BMPs)(5) – are designed to overrun Western Europe in days and weeks, not months, as has heretofore been postulated in NATO planning.(6) (The following chart depicts a typical combined-arms army of the Soviet Union.) In continuous daytime and nighttime operations, the Warsaw Pact would seek to overrun forward NATO positions, especially stocks of tactical nuclear weapons; cut vital supply lines linking U.S. forces in the south of Germany with other NATO units to the north; and prevent resupply from the continental United States, Canada or Britain. The present configuration of NATO forces, based upon the expectation of adequate warning and the effective utilization of warning for mobilization and reinforcement, makes such a Warsaw Pact strategy highly suitable from the Soviet perspective, since it strikes Western forces when they are at their weakest and thus maximizes the opportunities for swift and decisive victory.(7)

### The Attack

The single most important and decisive element of the USSR's theater strategy is the attack in which the objective is to surround and destroy the enemy force.(8) In the opening stages of conflict, to which the Soviet leadership assigns critical significance, the element of surprise is paramount.

SOVIET COMBINED ARMS ARMY

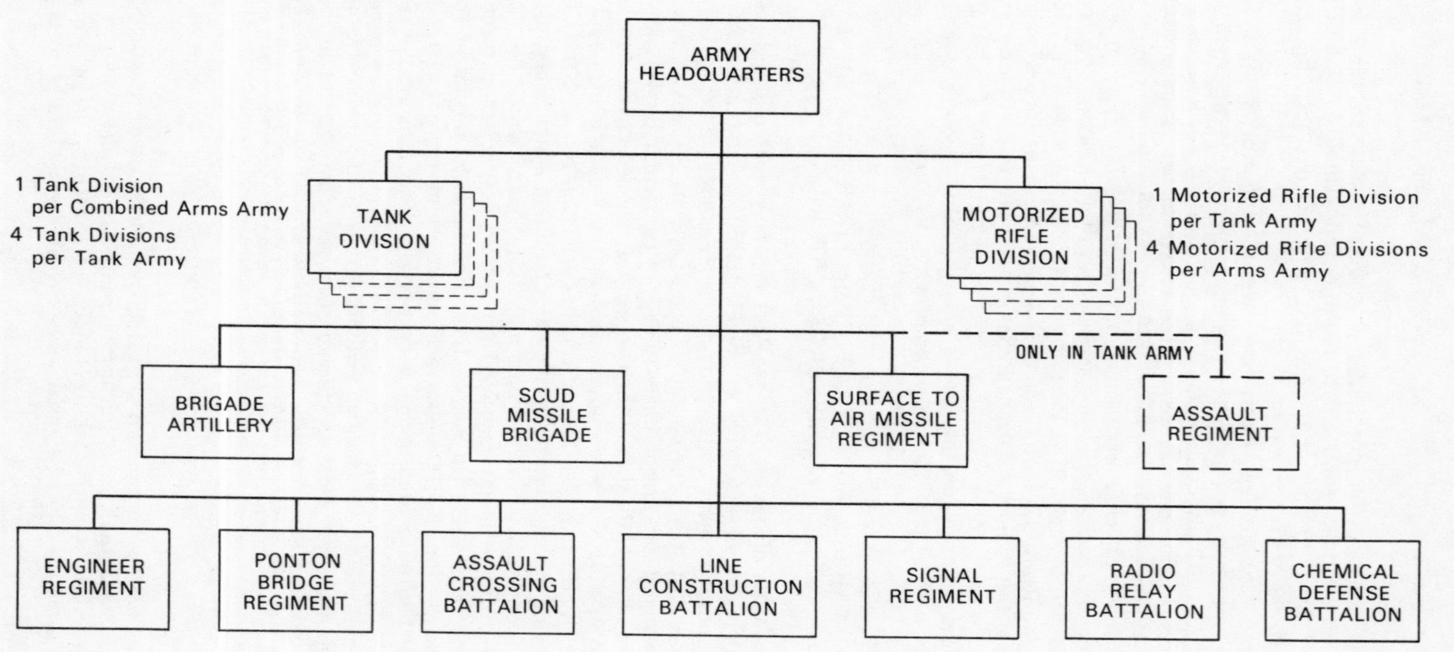


Source: FM 30-40 Handbook on Soviet Ground Forces – 1975, prepared by the Department of the Army (Washington, D.C.: Government Printing Office, 1975).

To achieve surprise, Soviet-Warsaw Pact planning emphasizes troop combat readiness. In peacetime, the first strategic echelon of Warsaw Pact forces(9) is maintained in such a state of combat readiness (about 90 percent) as to be able, according to one estimate, "to march with only two hours notice, when imminence-of-hostilities indicators are received only a short time before."(10) Without question, the Soviet Union faces inherent difficulties in attaining such a high degree of readiness in its first echelon forces. One problem is that there has been a relatively frequent rate of turnover for troops in the GSFG. Since 1967, the conscription term for the Soviet Army has been reduced from three to two years, although the educational level of conscripted troops in the 1970s is significantly higher than in the 1960s, providing a better basis for training in the use of military equipment.(11)

The rapid turnover rate of Soviet forces ("somewhere between 1,200,000 and 1,500,000 are discharged into the reserves each year"), largely the result of extremely poor living conditions and, for those assigned to Eastern Europe, severe restrictions on travel and communications,(12) detracts from the ability of the Soviet Union to sustain combat readiness at the desired high level. Because of problems of conscription, the second strategic echelon is not considered, in peacetime, to be combat-ready, with full mobilization taking as many as thirty days. Nevertheless, in the event of an initiation of hostilities against NATO, the second strategic echelon will probably be at full combat strength, since Soviet-Warsaw Pact planning calls for its mobilization during the precombat phase .

To maximize strategic surprise, Soviet-Warsaw Pact planners might elect to attack under the guise of a field maneuver in order to obtain a "jump-off" point that might not immediately be detected as such by NATO intelligence.(13) Under such circumstances, the Soviet Union might be forced to mount its offensive with both the group of Soviet forces in Eastern Europe and national units of Warsaw Pact countries, inasmuch as Soviet exercises are frequently conducted in conjunction with Pact member nations, or at least with the "host" country. In this situation, problems of language and questions of troop reliability could hamper the rapid movement of offensive forces, although this need not be the case if a third language (English, for example) were used to convey commands, as it was during the 1968 invasion of Czechoslovakia.

In the event that the initial attack were undertaken by Soviet forces alone, to ensure troop reliability, Western intelligence would not necessarily be able to assess Soviet intentions fully, inasmuch as they have been observed frequently conducting exercises unaided by East European units, sometimes at the divisional chain of command within regiments.

Alternatively, the Soviet strategy for Europe may call for attack from Warsaw Pact assembly areas, resembling the Egyptian offensive against Israeli forces in the October 1973 war. This type of attack is rarely discussed in open Soviet military writings, although both Egypt's campaign across the Suez and Syria's operation in the Golan Heights were based on this Soviet command principle. Given their penchant for secrecy and emphasis on surprise, the attack from assembly may well constitute the means by which Soviet planners intend to initiate hostilities against the NATO central front, should circumstances dictate. Like an attack under the guise of troop maneuvers, the attack from assembly has as its objective to break through the enemy's positions rapidly and destroy his tactical reserves. In either instance, the attack may be launched from the march, in which case Pact forces would engage the enemy upon approach, perhaps without the benefit of preparatory fire support from artillery, mortars and rockets. More likely, however, is the situation in which the engagement of NATO forces would be undertaken after forward or reconnaissance units (probably platoons) make contact with the enemy – so-called meeting engagement.(14) Whatever the circumstances of attack, Soviet theater operations place a premium of firepower, mobility and maneuverability.(15)

## Warsaw Pact Attack Capability

Operationally, the tank and associated armored vehicles from the core of the attacking units. Even after detailed analyses of the tactical implications of new weapons technologies for nonuclear combat – in particular those of the October 1973 Middle East war – Soviet military planners have concluded that the tank still offers the most effective means by which to exploit breakthroughs in the enemy's defenses. Although the potential of antitank and precision-guided weapons has been the subject of debate among Soviet theoreticians, the belief persists that:

> an abundance of anti-tank means (weapons) undoubtedly does not exclude successful actions of tanks on the battlefield. A well-trained and coordinated crew can successfully engage in combat and anti-tank means. In close cooperation with infantry, artillery, helicopters, and aviation, tanks are able to successfully solve tasks placed before them, in combined arms battle.(16)

If anything, the problem of the survivability of the tank in a modern battlefield environment has contributed to pronounced changes in Soviet theater tactics to enhance the role of the armored platforms. The tank's capability to exploit a diversity of battlefield situations, including a rapid offensive across vast expanses of territory and defensive ambushes along the enemy's routes of penetration,(17) remains critical to the Soviet employment of the "tactical means of warfare in battle."(18) Faced with the growing emphasis by NATO on the deployment of antitank guided munitions, the strategy of the Soviet Union has been "to field a significantly greater number of armored vehicles than are available to the defense, so that sheer numbers, in conjunction with other suitable weapons, will provide sufficient capability for achieving a breakthrough." (19) In support of its strategy, the Soviet Union, over the last several years, has increased the number of combat-ready battle tanks in each of its armored divisions from 188 to 266 – an increase of about 40 percent – thus improving the prospects for the survival of tank units.

Numerical compensation for the increasing lethality of Western antitank systems represents but one means of countering NATO defenses. Since 1973, all Soviet tanks have been equipped with a full complement of smoke munitions and aerosol generators designed to increase problems of targeting by precision-guided munitions and antitank weapons. Since current antitank guided munitions travel at relatively slow speeds, their flight times are long enough to give warning (by means of radar or laser warning systems) to threatened vehicles. The intorduction to its Warsaw Pact arsenal over the last year of a new and greatly improved tank, designated the T-72, may enable the Soviet Union to reduce further potential effectiveness of NATO's antitank guided weapons. With its improved armor protection, a new hull and turret and suspension systems (while retaining the low profile of previous Soviet tanks), and deploying what is probably a 125mm smooth bore gun, the T-72 augments the maneuverability and firepower of Soviet tank forces.(21) A laser range finder and a variety of infrared devices permit nighttime operations or, with infrared devices, use in inclement weather.

By themselves, deception devices and improved performance do not ensure the survival of the main battle tank as a preeminent theater platform weapon system. However, when combined with changes in operations and tactics, the potential effectiveness of the tank for the offensive, in particular, is perceived to be greatly enhanced.(22) To neutralize the enemy's defenses, especially his long-range antitank weapons, the Soviet Union has evolved tactical concepts which rely primarily on motorized rifle units and massed artillery and airpower.(23) By emphasizing surprise, and relying on daring thrusts along numerous and diverse axes of penetration, the Soviet Union hopes to create a situation in which Western forces are unable to wage an effective defense in the critical, early hours of battle. Soviet troops, particularly those of crew-served weapons, regularly engage in exercises designed to quicken their movement and increase their proficiency in hypothetical situations of tactical employment. Even if NATO forces had received warning of the impending attack, Soviet writers suggest that the use of nuclear weapons by Western forces would be impractical, if not disastrous, from the Atlantic Alliance perspective because of the interpenetration of enemy with friendly forces.

Mechanized infantry divisions, "in which infantry troops are transported in Armored Personnel Carriers (APCs)," and unmechanized infantry divisions, in which infantry troops are transported by truck, move on foot, or are airborne,(24) accompany the Soviet tank offensive, providing the firepower necessary to help defeat NATO's exposed antitank defenses.(25) Together with Soviet Frontal Aviation (FA)(26) and assault helicopter units, Soviet-Warsaw Pact artillery and motorized rifle units are assigned the combined task of breaching the enemy's defenses to allow their exploitation by armored forces and of destroying NATO airpower, artillery, troop concentrations, airfields, ports and transportation systems.(27)

Under all situations of attack, the primary attacking units – tanks and mechanized formations – are held in the extensive rear areas, away from the battle front, for as long as possible as protection against the possible use of its theater nuclear weapons. Once the breakthrough is imminent, however, these same attack units are moved quickly to the battle area, whether or not the enemy has deployed nuclear weapons. Although all Soviet attack units are said to be psychologically and physically prepared to fight in a nuclear environment, the advancing Warsaw Pact forces will depend on tactical airpower to preempt the Western nuclear option by destroying nuclear stockpiles in Western Europe shortly after the outbreak of conflict.

## The Evolution of Soviet Tactical Airpower

As recently as three years ago, Soviet-Warsaw Pact tactical airpower was perceived in the West as having essentially a defensive mission subordinate to the Ground Forces. The primary role of Soviet Frontal Aviation, in conjunction with ground based defenses, was to provide cover and support for advancing forces, with deep strike missions under the command of Soviet Long Range Aviation (dal 'nyaya aviatsiya). Over the last year, however, a new assault transport gunship helicopter (MI-24 Hind) has been introduced to the Group of Soviet Forces in Germany.(28) Comparable to the U.S. Army's advanced assault helicopter, one variant of the Hind, the Hind-D, was observed during the Soviet exercise Karpathy in a close air support role, allowing the release of FA aircraft for other missions, including deep interdiction against enemy territory and support facilities.

The evolution of Soviet Frontal Aviation toward an offensive capability is fully consistent with the emphasis of Warsaw Pact military doctrine on the primacy of the offense.(29) Whereas Soviet air doctrine continues to stress the need for air superiority, "the evolving air order of battle of FA" undoubtedly "accords ground attack (and relatively deep penetration for such attack) at least equal priority with local air superiority." Indicative of this is the introduction into the Soviet tactical air forces of the SU-19 (Fencer A), the MiG-23B (Flogger D), and the SU-17 (Fitter C). (30) Each of these aircraft demonstrates greater payload and range capability than its predecessor model, as well as a low-level penetration capability, making detection by existing generation NATO radars difficult.

Beyond the modifications to these existing generation aircraft, there is mounting evidence of the development by the Soviet Union of three follow-on types of combat aircraft – a new fighter, designated the MiG-29; a new technology, close air support aircraft, the T-58; and a long-range bomber, a supersonic version of the TU-144.(31) Observed in flight tests over the Soviet Union, the MiG-29 appears to be Moscow's answer to the U.S. deployment in Western Europe of the F-15, F-16 and potentially the F-18 aircraft. It is also thought to have an intercept role against low flying aircraft, including the USAF F-111 and the MRCA Tornado. Originally thought by NATO to have been designed to counter the now canceled B-1 strategic bomber, since its radar characteristics and armament appear to be appropriate for the detection and target acquisition of low flying, supersonic aircraft having an extremely small radar cross section, it is now suggested that the MiG-29 is being oriented toward the interception of cruise missiles. Together with the T-58 flying a close air support mission and the enhanced Soviet capability for long-range interdiction in the TU-144 supersonic bomber the MiG-29 will greatly increase the offensive power of Soviet tactical air armies.

## Employment Concepts for Soviet Tactical Air Forces and the Role of Theater Nuclear Weapons

With their reliance on the combined arms concept and the use of the Soviet Ground Control Intercept (GCI) System,(32) the operational control and target designation of Warsaw Pact airpower lies within the purview of the ground commanders. It may well be that the highly centralized system of command and control under which Soviet-Warsaw Pact forces operate is an inherent weakness in posture which could be exploited effectively by NATO in a wartime situation. In any event, the mission priorities of Soviet-Warsaw Pact armies are chosen according to the perceptions of the ground commanders of each group of Soviet forces deployed in Eastern Europe of the tactical needs and opportunities of the unfolding battlefield scenario.

In particular, it is reasonable to assume that the role of Soviet airpower in a European conflict environment will be defined in tandem with that of nuclear weapons. Clearly, the objectives sought by the use of nuclear weapons in a tactical theater situation correspond closely to those accruing from the employment of offensive airpower. Both forces have as their primary objectives: (1) the destruction of NATO's nuclear attack capabilities; (2) the elimination of principal groupings of combat forces and their command and control; (3) the isolation of front line forces in the forward edge of the battle area; and (4) the breaching of supply lines and communications networks. An additional objective, more psychological than strategic in nature, that has been identified with the employment concepts for both types of forces, "is to break the enemy's will to fight."(33)

Despite the symmetry of the objectives sought by their use, it cannot be assumed that the growth and potential offensive power of the Soviet tactical air armies are seen as providing an alternative to the employment of nuclear systems in a European conflict. In contrast to Western strategic thought, the Soviet Union, in its conceptualization of military doctrine and theater force posture, makes no distinction between nuclear and conventional warfare. Concepts such as that of the NATO "firebreak" are totally alien to Soviet military thought.(34) In this context, recent strategic analyses of Soviet military literature, which suggest the "possibility and even the desirability of conducting a prolonged phase of conventional operations in the European theater, as opposed to the 'switch on/switch off,' nuclear-conventional relationship that has so far predominated,"(35) do not (or should not) have as their purpose the denigration of the nuclear option. Nuclear weapons are still regarded by Soviet strategists as the ultimate means by which to influence the outcome of warfare, theater or global.(36) If anything, Soviet reliance on nuclear forces as the decisive means by which to effect the outcome of a conflict in Europe has increased in the last decade.

There are indications that the Soviet Union is undertaking to develop greater precision in its battlefield nuclear systems, with the presumed objective of destroying NATO-related military and industrial sites, while minimizing collateral damage to the West European industrial base.(37) The introduction, for example, of dual capable aircraft in Soviet tactical air armies; the increased production and deployment in Eastern Europe of the Backfire strategic bomber; the deployment of the intermediate-range SS-20,(38) a new generation Soviet ballistic missile whose accuracy (although still the subject of conjecture among military analysts) doubtless is improved greatly over that of older systems; and the modernization and stockpiling of older nuclear surface-to-surface missiles, including Scud, Frog and Scaleboard – all are indicative of a continued emphasis on the role of nuclear weapons in local conflicts. Even more revealing, however, of the importance of nuclear weapons to the theater strategy of the Soviet Union is the recent appearance in Eastern Europe of what is probably nuclear capable, self-propelled artillery.(39) Increasingly, Soviet literature is giving attention to the advantages of nuclear artillery in suppressing NATO defenses. The deployment, at the regimental level, of increasingly accurate artillery having low-yield warheads (thought to be nuclear) could suggest the greater likelihood of their use, even in close proximity to Pact troops.

Nevertheless, it may be that the Soviet Union believes increasingly that it is possible to overcome Western Europe's defenses, including NATO's nuclear weapons and associated stockpiles, without all of the consequences that would result from protracted nuclear exchanges. This has resulted, in part, from the development of weapons – nuclear and conventional – of unprecedented accuracy, and from the growth of Soviet in-theater forces and their vast stockpiles of reinforcement capabilities located close to the forward edge of the battle area. In May 1977, for example, "the Soviet Union flew more than 120,000 troops into Eastern Europe in just one week as part of a regular troop reaction."40 With such a capability Warsaw Pact forces would have the potential to launch an attack against Western Europe, while its troop mobilization would afford NATO as little as three to five days of warning time.(41) From a "standing start," Warsaw Pact forces might be able to destroy high value "counterforce" NATO targets swiftly, without necessarily resorting to nuclear weapons.(42)

In this context, it is suggested that the primary role of Soviet Frontal Aviation will be the nonnuclear destruction of targets located behind enemy lines, with a secondary emphasis on the isolation of the NATO front line forces. At the onset of battle, Soviet fighter aircraft (essentially the MiG-21 PFMA Fishbed-J, the MiG-21 SMT Fishbed-K, and the MiG-23 Flogger B)(43) would be assigned to missions to penetrate NATO airspace, along with fighter bombers (in particular the SU-19 Fencer), in order to ensure aerial superiority over the entire battle area, thereby providing the conditions necessary for interdiction missions against military and industrial targets in Western Europe, especially airfields and logistical structures, supply lines and command posts.(44)

Particularly ominous for NATO is the threat posed by Soviet airpower to prepositioned ammunition and fuel supplies. In Europe today, fuel storage facilities are limited in number, with few protected against the possibility of preemption by Soviet air and missile forces. The vulnerability of existing stores of fuel, together with the great quantities of oil and gas that will be required on a future European battlefield, creates for the Alliance one of its most pressing tactical dilemmas.

The defense problem for NATO forces would become even more acute if Soviet-Warsaw Pact airpower and seapower could effectively forestall North American reinforcements, at least until a sizeable foothold in Western Europe had been attained. Toward that end, Soviet fighter/bomber operations may be supplemented in various ways, including the use of paratroopers, armed reconnaissance flights,(45) and electronic warfare measures. Soviet paratroopers, probably transported behind enemy lines under the cover of night, could be expected to have as their mission the destruction of nuclear missile sites, the occupation of NATO and civilian airfields, surprise attacks against bridges and command centers, and operations to prepare the way for Warsaw Pact forces to cross waterways and harsh terrain.(46) Special troops such as these could also aid in the destruction of NATO's air defense system by means of commando raids against Alliance surface-to-air missile sites (and associated storage facilities) prior to, or in conjunction with, operations by Soviet aircraft designed for electronic warfare.

Essentially, however, defense suppression would be accomplished primarily through the use of low-flying aircraft deploying sophisticated jamming equipment. "The most common Soviet/Pact ECM operations are the direct jamming of NATO radars by superimposition of signals over the full spectrum of military frequency bands and the dropping of ionized foil strips from aircraft to mislead radar detection equipment."(47) The Soviet electronic warfare capability has improved greatly over the last decade, and this factor, together with the deployment of low-flying aircraft, threatens to compound the problems for NATO of detection and diminished warning time of interdiction by air.

At a minimum, Soviet tactical air forces must be able to seize and maintain air superiority over the zone of combat. Soviet doctrine for the employment of tactical airpower emphasizes a sustained capability to ensure the elimination of enemy air forces. Clearly, a decision by Soviet ground commanders to employ nuclear weapons would be related directly to the ability of Soviet-Warsaw Pact air forces to destroy NATO airpower. It can be inferred that if NATO's tactical air forces can reduce drastically the effectiveness of Soviet-Warsaw Pact airpower in the opening stages of battle, the decision to employ Soviet nuclear missiles would be made quickly. It is expected that the SS-12 Scaleboard, with an operational range of approximately 800 km (496 mi.), and the SS-11 Scud-B, having an approximate range of 280 km (175 mi.), will be used against deep targets, including NATO ports, airfields and nuclear sites. The Frog-7, a free-flight rocket having a range of about 70 km (43.4 mi.) and able to carry nuclear or chemical warheads, is to be employed at the division level for use in the immediate area of battle.(48) A new generation surface-to-surface missile now being tested in the Soviet Union is thought to be a follow-on to the Frog, although it is likely that both models will remain operational in Warsaw Pact inventories. In a nuclear environment, Soviet Frontal Aviation can be expected to fly reconnaissance missions as well as undertake interdiction of targets not covered by the rocket forces. Such missions, presumably, would include the delivery of both nuclear and conventional ordnance, and would concentrate on mobile targets, notably enemy air forces which had escaped and/or survived Soviet missile attacks.

## The Tactical Use of Soviet Chemical/Biological Agents

Soviet Frontal Aviation aircraft can also be used for the delivery of chemical/biological (CB) weapons. The chemical warfare capability of the Soviet Union is formidable. Inasmuch as chemical weapons are considered to be integral to Soviet battlefield tactics and the most powerful means of destroying enemy forces under modern combat conditions, over the last decade the Soviet Union has supported extensive programs of research and development of chemical agents and munitions.(49) It is believed in the West that the Soviet Union has developed, standardized and stockpiled highly toxic chemical agents – including nerve and skin agents designed to penetrate protective clothing – as well as psychoactive agents, and binary systems whose toxic substances are produced by a reaction on, or over, the battlefield. Each of these agents maybe disseminated by tactical missiles, aircraft and ground systems, including rockets and tube artillery. Biological agents, if emplaced in the water reserves of major European cities, could within hours incapacitate major pockets of resistance along the planned routes of invasion. Unlike chemical toxins which could threaten – depending on a variety of factors, not the least of which are environmental and wind conditions – friendly as well as enemy forces, the use of biological contaminants would imperil indigenous populations, without necessarily affecting friendly troops.

Together with nuclear missiles as weapons of mass destruction, chemical/biological agents could be deployed in an antipersonnel role and against enemy defensive operations. Their use may complement the employment of nuclear weapons, or they may be used alone, reinforced by conventional firepower. Against an opponent who is virtually unprepared, the use of chemical agents could be decisive. Likely targets of a chemical strike include artillery units, reserve troops, airfields and supply depots, although their use against the cities of Western Europe cannot be dismissed since many of these urban centers contain vitally important NATO-related facilities, includuing command posts and intelligence centers.

The potential effectiveness of chemical agents against high-value enemy targets led Soviet-Warsaw Pact military planners to give highest priority to preparation for military exercises under toxic conditions. Ground troops undergo extensive training in reconnaissance and movement through contaminated areas, including areas simulating radioactive fallout, fires and flooding caused by nuclear strikes. If Soviet-Warsaw Pact troops are forced to pass through contaminated areas, such as cities, protective measures have been devised. All of the newer Soviet mechanzed vehicles, armored personnel carriers, and tanks can be at least partially sealed against chemical/radioactive environments. As a last resort, troops wearing protective garments could be moved quickly through contaminated areas in unprotected vehicles, to be decontaminated later. Decontamination equipment appears to be plentiful and large-scale decontamination exercises are held regularly. Generally, however, Soviet combat techniques stress the necessity of bypassing chemically or radiologically contaminated areas whenever possible, if only to maintain the momentum of the attack.

## Other Factors Affecting the Strategy of Attack: Urbanization and Water Obstacles

Similarly, Soviet tactics for local wars emphasize the importance of bypassing cities if the momentum of the offensive is to be sustained. There can be no doubt that the World War II experience has profoundly influenced Soviet thinking on combat in urban areas. (50) In the event such combat cannot be avoided (i.e., if the enemy has occupied the area and has set up a defense), Soviet literature suggests attacking from the line of march. In this way, forward elements of an approaching regiment are used to draw enemy fire, with the desired objective of revealing their defensive positions. Once under fire, the advance forces (composed basically of motorcycle units) will attempt to outflank the defenders, while a forward security patrol (GPZ) of the battalions moves in to draw fire from the frontal position.

The results of these two essentially intelligence maneuvers will provide the basis for decision by the regimental commander regarding the type of assault to initiate – either an envelopment or frontal maneuver. Whichever option is chosen, the key to its success is rapidity of movement and tactical surprise. Airborne assault troops and paratroopers are expected to participate in city combat, as part of an encircling operation. Such troops dropped behind enemy lines conceivably could employ Soviet chemical grenades and/or engage troops in combat from rear and flanking areas. As is generally the case with Soviet concepts of attack, ground operations would be supported by aerial bombardment and massive fire barrages in order to effect a quick breakthrough. When a breakthrough does occur, second echelon forces would be expected to storm the enemy's defenses in an operation similar to that described in the previous discussion of Soviet attack techniques.

Areas through which rivers or other waterways flow can be traversed quite readily by Soviet combat forces, with the notable exception of artillery and supply troops.(51) Soviet tactical planning emphasizes training and development of equipment for river crossing operations. Its amphibious vehicles at battalion level give the Warsaw Pact the capability of transporting about 600 men across water barriers. At the army level, a pontoon bridge regiment carriers with it over 900 meters of tactical floating bridging equipment. There are about 40 K-61 medium tracked amphibians in the assault crossing engineering battalion at army level, each of which can transport 31 men in a lift. There are additional heavy tracked amphibians (20 PIS-M), each capable of lifting 70 men, and 24 GSP heavy ferries, each with a 52-ton capacity.(52)

As with the attack, Soviet military literature reveals several means for executing river crossings, although these operations are almost always undertaken on a broad front. Under the cover of night or camouflage maneuvers, water obstacles may be executed from the march, before or upon contact with the enemy. In the latter case the operation would be accompanied by heavy air, artillery and missile barrages.(53) In general, however, it is assumed that river crossing operations will be executed after advance units have gained control of the area. Engineering troops, who form the backbone of Soviet bridging operations, have the responsibility to determine the best location and means of forcing the obstacle.(54) Speed is essential in these operations, yet swift river crossings are dependent not only on Soviet force capabilities, but also on the rapidity of the current and the configuration of the river banks. Generally, in western Europe, river currents are swifter than those in Eastern Europe. This, together with the simple defensive action of barricading flat river banks, could slow down the enemy

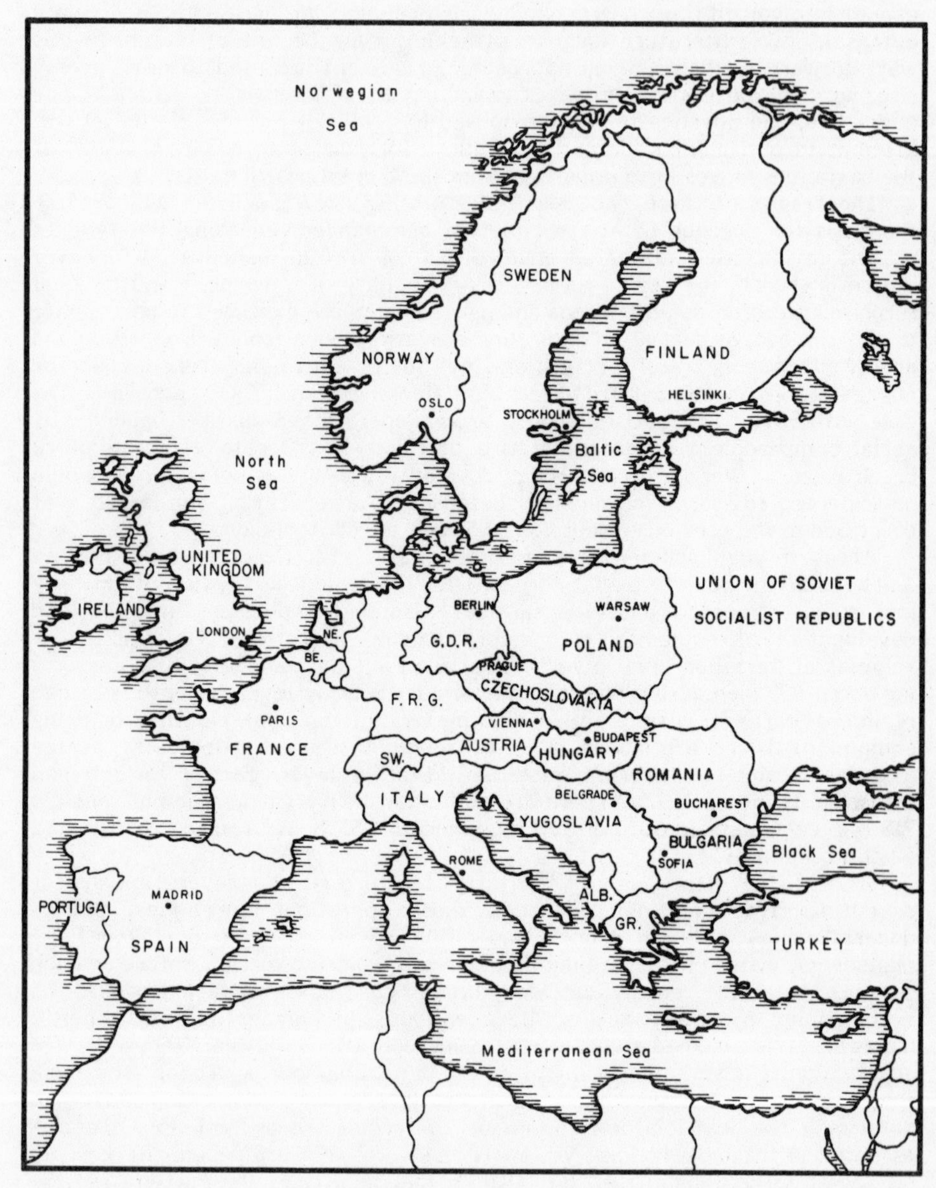


THE EUROPEAN THEATER

offensive, providing time in which friendly forces could marshal their airpower to strike the bulk of Warsaw Pact strength (probably at the division level) in their assembly area. In anticipation of such a defensive reaction, however, the ground assembly and troop movements of Pact forces are protected by an impressive array of mobile defense units composed of tactical air forces, antiaircraft guns and surface-to-air missiles.(55) The recent introduction of the ZSU-23/4 short range air defense gun system, the SA-8 surface-to-air missile, and the follow-on SA-9 SAM system provides significant firepower in protection of ground forces.

## SOVIET THEATER DOCTRINE AND EUROPEAN ATTACK STRATEGY

According to Soviet strategic literature, the attack constitutes the preeminent form of combat for Soviet-Warsaw Pact forces. The tactical application of this military doctrine in the European theater seemingly has been defined as a frontal assault in which the NATO northern and southern flanks have been neutralized – a result of the comparative weakness of Denmark and Norway and the political problems that reduce the effectiveness of the military capabilities of Greece and Turkey. For this reason the flanks can be expected to provide no real obstacle during a frontal assault by Warsaw Pact forces. Hence, the conventional wisdom in the West suggests that the most likely avenues of penetration by Warsaw Pact forces lie through the plains of northern Germany, from Magdeburg to the Cologne-Duisburg region passing through Hanover, Bielefeld and Dortmund.(56) To the South, where the concentration of Warsaw Pact forces is greatest, the route from Erfurt via Eisenach extends directly to Frankfurt and then Mainz. According to one estimate, the Soviet Union could field, for an in-place, unreinforced attack against NATO's central front,

> twenty divisions from GSFG, with 370,000 men, plus 7,000 main battle tanks (at least 600 to 800 of them new T-72s), 2,350 modern infantry combat vehicles and 170 helicopters for assault landings and fire support. Babayev's 16th Air Army would come to full strength at 1,200 aircraft ("topped up" with light bombers and reconnaissance elements, although without the need for extensive pre-attack marshalling).
>
> If we look at this picture in greater detail and include the 3rd Shock Army, this formation can field 55,000 men, 1,198 tanks, 1,100 infantry combat vehicles backed by at least eighteen SCUD missiles and immediate artillery holdings of 408 guns (and about 5,000 vehicles). Linked with Central Group, GSFG could field about 200 battalion-size combat groups, which would provide the resources for some eight to ten breakthrough sectors.(57)

At present levels, Soviet-Warsaw Pact planners speculate that NATO forces, in the event of a surprise enemy attack, probably would be incapable of holding their forward positions without rapid reinforcement. The maldeployment of NATO forces, north/south and east/west, compounds an already dangerous situation. NATO deployments in the Federal Republic of Germany (FRG) are the legacy of the post-war occupation zones, rather than the product of a rational analysis by the Alliance of its current logistical and tactical needs. With a diversity of troop nationalities, the problems of communication and coordination in an alliance of many members would be magnified under conditions of diminished warning of enemy attack. Language barriers have been largely overcome, but problems resulting from lack of standardization and disparate national procurement policies – compounded by inadequate communications facilities – would make the tasks of command, control and intelligence gathering after the outbreak of conflict formidable indeed, especially if Warsaw Pact forces were to precede a frontal assault with a diversionary tactic or major operation elsewhere against NATO. This is a contingency which is increasingly plausible but seldom discussed in the literature of the Alliance.

The combined arms concept, emphasized by the Soviet Union, provides the Warsaw Pact with the option of envelopment in addition to that of the frontal attack. Envelopment, or a maneuver aimed at an open flank, may be directed against one or both of NATO's northern and southern theaters of operation. According to Soviet tactics for a theater operation, the flank envelopment operation may be supported by frontal firepower from the same units that are aiding attacking troops (close envelopment); or involve strikes at NATO flanks or rear echelons by highly mobile forces requiring coordination with the frontal attack force, with the deep maneuver being executed out of range of supporting firepower (deep envelopment) from units attacking NATO's central front. One could argue that because of the centralized nature of Soviet command, control, communications and intelligence systems, the likelihood of a deep envelopment maneuver against NATO Europe by the Warsaw Pact is relatively low. However, the deep envelopment option could be perceived by Pact military planners as increasingly attractive under the circumstances of nuclear and/or chemical/biological warfare, or in conjunction with the offensive employment of Soviet airpower. In a deep envelopment offensive, the Warsaw Pact would have several objectives: (1) frustration of Alliance efforts to mobilize and mount a defense against the associated frontal assault; (2) control of the air space and sea lanes adjacent to the main theater of operations so as to interdict or impede NATO reinforcement; (3) destruction of NATO logistics and industrial supply facilities and civilian assets that could be converted for military use.

## The Envelopment Option

In the last two years the Soviet Union has demonstrated increased interest in the NATO northern and southern flanks. There has been a substantial growth and modernization of Soviet naval and maritime capabilities in the Mediterranean, the Western part of the Baltic, and the North Sea, particularly in the areas of British and Norwegian oil and gas fields.(58) Naval units and air forces assigned to the Soviet Northern Red Banner Fleet, as well as those under the command of the Leningrad Military District,(59) have been reported as conducting maneuvers designed for amphibious operations.(60) With the use of a new-technology hovercraft recently developed by the Soviet Union, Soviet forces are highly mobile and their readiness state is equal to that of other first-line divisions, maintaining full equipment and more than 85 percent of their war establishment.(61) Hence, with only minimal reinforcement, these forces could be brought to full alert, supported, if necessary, by Soviet border guards and the one marine corps brigade that is assigned to the Northern Fleet. Considered in the context of the deep envelopment option, an initial surprise offensive against NATO's northern flank could facilitate a Warsaw Pact frontal assault across Central Europe, initiated either simultaneously or after northern flank operations had begun.(62)

The significance of this region from which the Soviet Navy could control the coastal waters of Northern and Western Europe cannot be overemphasized. NATO clearly lacks adequate resources to fight a European conflict on two fronts. Immediately available to meet an attack against NATO's northern flank would be one Norwegian brigade, one group of three infantry battalions, four squadrons of fighters, and a frigate, some submarines and fast missile boats. The effectiveness of the Norwegian resistance would depend largely on the speed with which Norwegian and NATO forces could be reinforced.(63) Second, if NATO diverted some of its limited resources to the northern or southern theater of operations, a frontal assault across its central front would be facilitated, especially if the initial thrust were to come without adequate warning. In this contingency, NATO's principal hope of defense would depend on its ability to mobilize national reserves and to reinforce front-line troops massively in a matter of days, an option that may very well be denied the Alliance if the Soviet Union controls northern waters.(64)

The strategic value of the Northern Theater is increased by its rich deposits of minerals and other resources. The development of natural resources on the Norwegian continental shelf could yield as much as one to two billion tons of oil and one to two billion cubic meters of gas. North of the sixty-two degree latitude mark there exist enormous deposits of resources which are still unmeasured. In this region, whose sovereignty is disputed by Norway and the Soviet Union, the latter has developed a basing complex, allegedly for the purpose of exploiting oil reserves.(65) Together with basing facilities on the Kola Peninsula, the complex on Svalbard would enable the Soviet Union to undertake military operations far beyond its borders.

The tactical forces that have been deployed to "protect" these northern Soviet bases embody a capability for "seizing and holding any appreciable territorial buffer zone in order to guarantee that self-same 'protection'."(66) The enlarging of the canal that links the Baltic and White Seas enables ships of the Northern Fleet, the Soviet Union's largest naval grouping, to use this inland waterway to reinforce the Baltic Fleet without surveillance from North Atlantic installations on Norway's North Cape or from ships and aircraft operating in the Spitzbergen-North Cape region of the Barents Sea.(67) In any crisis situation the Soviet Union could deploy quickly at least five naval task forces from the Baltic, augmented by airpower from the Kola Peninsula, units from the Baltic and Leningrad Military Districts, and Warsaw Pact airborne units from Poland. Amphibious units could either land on the

Norwegain coast or remain in reserve for use against coastal strongholds.

In this context, maneuvers during the Karpathy exercises held in the summary of 1977 concentrated specifically on amphibious operations, especially designed to overcome coastal defenses. In these exercises the role of airpower was directed primarily against indigenous air defenses, particularly SAM units. On the basis of this set of exercises, but also as indicated in recent Soviet military literature, NATO planners could anticipate, with a high degree of certainty, the use in the Northern Theater scenario of Soviet airpower against Alliance airfields – those housing the FRG's 42 G-91s and 30 RF-4s – and NATO defenses, including the interdiction of Danish SAM units which are composed of 36 Nike-Hercules and 24 Hawk interceptors.(68) If launched in conjunction with a frontal assault, Soviet ground operations in the north "would have to move faster and with greater decisiveness"(69) than those of the central front simply because of the need to ensure Soviet control of the North Atlantic, including its air space, in order to impede Allied reinforcement efforts. Should this occur, the only feasible option remaining to the West would be the employment of nuclear weapons, provided such stockpiles had not been overrun by Soviet forces in the early stages of the war.

No less impressive is the buildup of Soviet capabilities, naval forces in particular, in NATO's southern flank region. AlthoughSoviet naval forces have been deployed in the Mediterranean Sea basin since 1964, only in the aftermath of the 1967 Arab-Israeli war has the Soviet Union undertaken to expand substantially its on-station capabilities in the region. Here, since 1973, the Soviet Union has deployed on the average, some 40 ships of the 3rd Eskadra of its Black Sea Banner Fleet, including approximately 10 submarines, as many as 15 major combatants (a mix of cruisers and destroyers), and a variety of auxiliary craft and amphibious vessels. For the most part, one or both of the two Soviet helicopter carriers (Moskva and Leningrad) have been assigned to the Mediterranean, as has been the Kiev, the new Soviet V/STOL aircraft carrier.

In addition to the V/STOL aircraft aboard the Kiev, Soviet naval capabilities are supplemented by aircraft designed to conduct both reconnaissance and combat missions. Included in the former category are the IL-38 and the Badger TU-16; in the latter class of aircraft is the Backfirestrategic bomber, which participated in the 1975 Okean worldwide exercise of Soviet military forces. The largest exercise ever staged by the Soviet Union, Okean '75 included anticarrier operations in the Tyrrhenian Sea area of the Mediterranean; antisubmarine warfare operations in the North Atlantic and Western Pacific Oceans; and antishipping operations in the Atlantic, Indian and Western Pacific Oceans, as well as in the Caribbean and Mediterranean Seas. In the later area, ships from the Black Sea Red Banner Fleet entered the Mediterranean to reinforce the 3rd Eskadra as it moved to the area off the east and south coasts of Sardinia in a simulated effort to control this Mediterranean chokepoint.(70)

For NATO the significance of Okean '75 and other military exercises, including recent air and sea operations to transfer weapons and technicians to Ethiopia, cannot be overestimated. Clearly, any consideration of Alliance maritime operations in the Eastern Atlantic and Mediterranean areas, including that of wartime reinforcement form North America and even

Britain, must be made under the shadow of the threat posed by the Soviet Navy. Since 1975 the Soviet Navy has become a familiar presence in all of the world's oceans. This factor, together with the now common and frequent Soviet practice of conducting large-scale naval maneuvers, provides the basis from which Soviet military planners could position their maritime forces for a European conflict without arousing undue suspicion among NATO members of an impending attack.

Nevertheless, maintenance and sustained support for maritime operations will be difficult for Soviet naval forces without access to foreign bases. The development of the Soviet basing complex on the Kola Peninsula, together with the beginning of a development of facilities along the West African coast, provides the basis for a logistical infrastructure to service Soviet operations in the Atlantic.(71) Similarly, the USSR's use, albeit limited, of Egyptian facilities together with a reliance on the Syrian port of Latakia, two anchorages in the Mediterranean – one located near Alboran Island (lying off Spain) and one located near Kitheria (lying of Greece) – offer facilities for sustaining Soviet naval operations in the region. Likewise, based on the Soviet use of Ethiopian airbases – an increasingly probable development – landbased, long-range aircraft, such as Backfire, deployed with the Black Sea Fleet, could participate easily in operations against NATO.

To these suppositions about Soviet capabilities must be added the possibility that political developments within the countries along NATO's southern flank may make it difficult for Alliance forces to utilize facilities and bases located in the region. Should a government with communist participation at the cabinet level come to power in Italy, for example, NATO would probably be denied use of facilities located in that country. The loss of Italian bases could take place at the same time as, or be preceded by, a declaration of Greek and/or Turkish neutrality in a European conflict. As a result of the political problems of recent years, many of which are the legacy of the Greek-Turkish conflict over Cyprus, Greece has already withdrawn her military forces from NATO's military command and has closed down several U.S. bases on its territory. U.S.-Turkish relations have cooled considerably since the U.S. Congress voted to embargo arms for Turkey in reaction to her 1974 invasion of Cyprus during which U.S.-supplied forces were used. The damage that has been done to Turkey's relationships with its NATO allies, in particular the United States, should not be underestimated. Should further irritants develop between Turkey and her Alliance partners, it is not inconceivable that Turkey's leaders would seek alternative means of providing for her security, including the signing of a nonaggression pact with the Soviet Union. Such an agreement would mean not just the loss of a valuable NATO ally but what, in effect, woudl amount to the strengthening of Soviet influence, if not Soviet control, of the strategically important Dardanelles Strait.

For the present, however, Soviet military strategists generally agree that preemptive maneuvers against NATO's southern flank represent an unattractive, if not unnecessary, military option. Naval forces alone could not be expected to secure the region. The logistics for operations by ground forces would pose major problems, since Soviet-Warsaw Pact infantry would have to pass through mountainous terrain in order to secure the region. Even if, in a

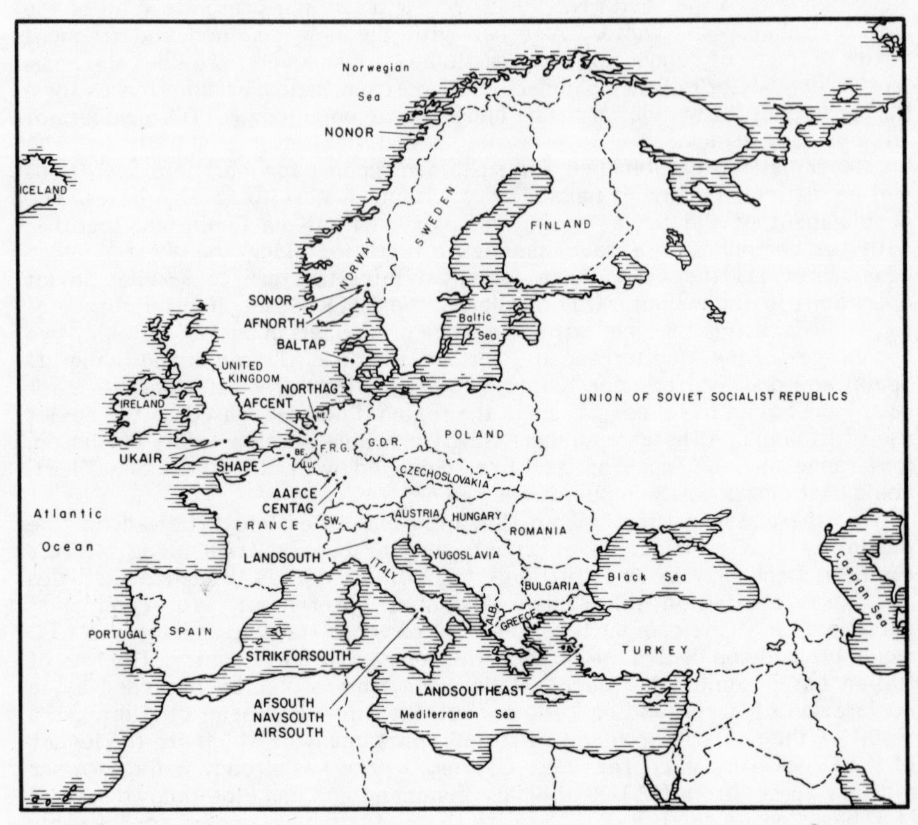


ALLIED COMMAND EUROPE

SUPREME HEADQUARTERS ALLIED POWERS EUROPE – SHAPE

| | | | |
|---|---|---|---|
| ALLIED FORCES NORTHERN EUROPE | AFNORTH | ALLIED FORCES SOUTHERN EUROPE | AFSOUTH |
| Allied Forces Baltic Approaches | Baltap | Allied Land Forces Southern Europe | Landsouth |
| Allied Forces North Norway | Nonor | Allied Land Forces Southeast Europe | Landsoutheast |
| Allied Forces South Norway | Sonor | Allied Naval Forces Southern Europe | Navsouth |
| ALLIED FORCES CENTRAL EUROPE | Afcent | Allied Air Forces Southern Europe | Airsouth |
| Northern Army Group | Northag | Naval Striking and Support Forces Southern Europe | Strikforsouth |
| Central Army Group | Centag | | Ukair |
| Allied Air Forces Central Europe | AAFC | UNITED KINGDOM AIR FORCES | |
| | Centag | | |
| | Aafce | | |

post-Tito Yugoslavia, Soviet forces were deployed in that country, their movement into Italy, for example, would be less efficient in organization and speed than would be an incursion into the West by Soviet forces stationed in East Germany. In all likelihood, therefore, the Soviet Baltic Red Banner Fleet and its 3rd Eskadra would be charged, in a European conflict, with the task of supporting operations in Central and Northern Europe, by depositing troops behind enemy lines and interdicting, as necessary, Allied reinforcement convoys. However, both of these missions would be subsidiary to their primary task of neutralizing NATO's naval capabilities, including the U.S. Sixth Fleet(72) stationed in the Mediterranean, and British,(73) French,(74) and to a lesser extent Italian, Greek, and Turkish naval forces.

## WARSAW PACT FORCE POSTURE: IMPLICATIONS FOR NATO

With the adoption of a strategy of flexible response in 1967, NATO embraced concepts for the defense of Western Europe predicated upon the deployment of strengthened conventional forces to respond to a Soviet-Warsaw Pact attack, without initial resort to tactical nuclear weapons or a strategic nuclear strike by the United States against the Soviet Union. Integral to Alliance conceptions of the flexible response strategy was, and is, the concept of forward defense – halting a Warsaw Pact invasion as close to the East German frontier as possible. Incorporating what can be conceived of as three principal phases, the NATO forward defense relies upon: (1) the use of forces deployed near or at the frontier between the German Federal Republic and the German Democratic Republic (these comprise about one-fourth of NATO forces presently deployed on the Central Front); (2) the rapid mobilization and reinforcement of NATO forces by troops airlifted from the United States, Britain and Canada; and (3) the launching of a NATO counter attack designed to recover territory lost in the initial stage of a Warsaw Pact invasion of Western Europe. Whether nuclear weapons would be used in the second stage would depend, of course, on the breadth and depth of the Warsaw Pact invasion, as well as factors external to the immediate military situation, including national predilections to resort to this option.

The global context in which NATO today must operate is significantly different from that of the 1960s. As a result, the reliance by the Atlantic Alliance on a strategy of flexible response based on present force posture and attendant assumptions raises problems of fundamental importance for the United States and its European allies in their efforts to preserve the security of Western Europe. From the foregoing discussion of Soviet strategy and force capabilities, these can be summarized as follows:

1. Warsaw Pact doctrine provides for the maximum utilization of military power – conventional, nuclear or both – to reach Channel ports before NATO forces can be mobilized to their maximum strength. In short, the Warsaw Pact would stage an offensive designed to deprive NATO of the time required to bring NATO forces to their full strength.

2. The capacity of NATO to achieve full strength quickly would depend upon adequate warning time, as well as the swift mobilization of reserves in Europe and the rapid introduction of reinforcements from the United States,

Canada, and Britain, assuming that ports and airfields will still be usable. Defense analysts are not in agreement as to whether the Soviet Unoin is now able to launch an offensive against Western Europe without prior political-military warning. The Soviet-Warsaw Pact military buildup of recent years seems designed to deprive NATO of warning time and to increase the flexibility of options available to the Soviet Union in Europe. A projection of present trends adverse to NATO in rising Soviet force levels will reduce considerably, if not eliminate, the military warning time available to NATO in advance of a Pact invasion in the next decade. Whether political warning time available to NATO would be adequate, or would be utilized to NATO's advantage, is problematical.

3. The growth of Soviet-Warsaw Pact forces in Europe provides the capability to overrun much, if not all, of West German territory shortly after the outbreak of war. West German forces, the bulk of the ground power available to NATO at the outbreak of war, would either be destroyed or forced to mount a defense at the Rhine or farther west. The Federal Republic would thus be deprived of the opportunity to mobilize reserves whose availability would be vitally important to augment NATO forces at an early stage in a European conflict. The psychological effects, both for the Germans and other West European countries, of the loss of all or substantial parts of West German territory would be profoundly debilitating to the resolve of the Alliance to fight on. This would be especially so in the context of an Alliance decision to resort to its nuclear option.

4. As a result of the growth of Soviet-Warsaw Pact forces and the development of enhanced conventional capabilities, NATO may be faced with the stark option of first use of tactical nuclear weapons, with the prospect of Soviet retaliation against targets in densely populated Western Europe, together with the increasing probability that the United States would not be in a position to invoke its strategic forces in defense of Western Europe.(75) The theater nuclear balance within Europe heavily favors the Soviet Union. British and French nuclear forces are greatly outmatched by existing generation Soviet nuclear forces targeted against Western Europe, in terms both of numerical deployments and the potential effectiveness of their use based upon the extensive Soviet programs for active and passive defense. With the development of the mobile Ss-20 and the Backfire strategic bomber – and possibly a supersonic bomber comparable to the B-1(76) – and the disparity between strategic forces in Western Europe and the Soviet Union will widen greatly in the next decade. If it is deprived of the protection of the American strategic force, NATO Europe will be vulnerable to a greater extent than ever before to Soviet nuclear attack or at least to a form of nuclear blackmail. Under such circumstances the Soviet Union will hold the upper hand in an escalatory process to successively greater levels of nuclear exchange within Europe.

Thus NATO's strategy of flexible response relies on the threat of an escalatory chain that has been weakened greatly, if not neutralized, by the growth and modernization of Warsaw Pact forces and Soviet strategic capabilities. If this is the case, the North Atlantic Treaty Organization's flexible response strategy is in danger of becoming "flexible" in name only. It is the Warsaw Pact that is acquiring a greater flexibility of options –

conventional and nuclear – as a result of its force configuration and deployment.

Almost three decades after its birth in 1949, the North Atlantic Treaty Organization stands at a crossroad. Whatever had been its success in providing for European security, NATO's reliance on outdated defensive concepts, assumptions and force postures provides an inadequate basis from which to safeguard Western interests. Despite the widening of the gap between East-West military force levels in Europe, Western societies, in general, remain consistently reluctant to devote what are regarded as scarce resources to the strengthening of military forces. Military power is regarded by many as obsolete in an era in which global economic issues and problems of resource scarcities dominate naitonal (and multinational) policy agendas. Other problems, too, hinder the functioning of the Alliance, not the least of which has to do with the institutional inability of NATO to command the loyalty and dedication of its member nations. It is within this context that the debate over NATO strategy and force posture is today unfolding. Solutions must be found if the West is to blunt the impact in Europe, and the world at large, of the perceptible changes in East-West force levels and, as a consequence, in the global correlation of forces – a Soviet phrase used to connote the political utility of deploying worldwide superior military forces (i.e., forces able to wage war and prevail in war), whether or not nuclear weapons are used.

The priority task for NATO in the late 1970s, as it has been since its founding, is to provide for Western Europe a credible defensive capability, one that is responsive to the dynamics of the European security environment and the evolving Soviet-Warsaw Pact threat. Strategically, this does not necessarily mean the adoption of a new NATO strategy; flexible response can continue to serve the Alliance well if, and only if, its tactical concepts can be made to accord with the problems delineated above, including a significant reduction in warning time of an impending enemy attack, the loss of air and sea superiority, and the need to operate along several fronts simultaneously.

## Forward Defense: Still an Essential Concept for NATO

In order to mount a defense against a Soviet-Warsaw Pact invasion, it remains essential for NATO to meet the forward attack units as early as possible and thus rob advancing forces of their momentum. Allied forces would probably be less able than in the past to trade substantial space for time with Soviet forces configured as they are for continuous daytime and nighttime operations. In accordance with NATO's tactical concepts, all Alliance resources that could be mobilized quickly would be assigned a role in the forward defense of West Germany, at least until such time as reinforcements arrived at the scene of battle. Immediately available to meet the principal threat on the North German plain would be the British Army of the Rhine (BAOR), Dutch and Belgian contingents, and French Army forces, each of which may have become less effective as fighting units in recent years because of defense budget cuts and decreases in manpower with inadequate compensatory increases in firepower or changes in strategy.(77)

These forces are supplemented by three corps of the Bundeswehr, the bulk of which can reach operational status within three days.(78) Other FRG forces, under national command, operate to the rear of the NATO ground forces and have as their mission the defense of positions close to the West German frontier.(79) As the result of a recent decision, the United States intends to increase its own manpower and equipment deployments to the North German plain in order to improve NATO's capability to defend against the possibility of reduced warning of a Soviet attack.(80) Although there has been no precise indication of the size or composition of the American forces to be assigned to the northernmost sectors of the Federal Republic, some reports suggest that enough equipment, weapons and ammunition for two divisions will be newly assigned to prepositioned depots primarily in West Germany.

Nevertheless, whether the decision calls for transferring one whole U.S. division, or two, to West Germany, NATO forces will still be outnumbered by Soviet ground forces, in terms of manpower alone. Deployed by the Soviet Union currently in East Germany, Poland, and Czechoslovakia are 15 tank and 14 motorized rifle divisions, immediately facing NATO's central region. Moreover, it is important to note that the additional manpower and equipment to be reassigned to Europe will be drawn from Continental United States (CONUS) based reserves, thereby eroding the American capability for European reinforcement and resupply. Also, it behooves NATO to consider that if the preceding analysis of the Soviet penchant for the envelopment option is correct, the repositioning of additional manpower in the northern most areas of the German plains will have virtually no effect upon Pact efforts to direct operations simultaneously against NATO's northern flank in the expectation of reaching the Atlantic coast before effective reinforcements could be deployed. In the circumstances of this scenario, time is of the essence for Pact forces, and their potential for success would depend largely on Soviet capabilities already deployed in the region. Based upon its facilities located on Kola, together with the forces, naval and marine in particular, of Poland and the German Democratic Republic, the Soviet Union would rely on elements of its Northern Red Banner Fleet, including naval air units like the Backfire bomber and marine and army contingents, to sever the Atlantic link and to divert NATO resources from the central front.

Without question, a high priority mission for NATO now becomes the preservation of maritime superiority in order to ensure, in the event of war, the effective and rapid deployment of reinforcements to Western Europe. Clearly, the United States and its NATO allies need to reconceptualize their views of the Alliance's delineation of its theaters of operation, integrating more closely battlefield strategy and tactics. Heretofore, Alliance control of the North Atlantic, and more generally of all the world's sea lanes, was assumed in NATO planning – an assumption which no longer can be taken for granted.

In order to redesign the NATO force posture to accord with the changed milieu in which the Alliance must operate, NATO's three major commands in the North Sea region should be unified if only to provide planning which is consistent with the needs of the entire Northern Theater and its relationship to strategy on the central front. The northern flank, when regarded as the left wing of the defensive front in Europe, should be the object of greater attention by the Alliance than in the past. In addition to unifying the three northern commands and integrating them more closely with planning for the central front and SACLANT, NATO forces assigned to the region must be strengthened and, to a certain extent, diversified if Soviet-Warsaw Pact forces are to be countered. In view of the growth of naval forces deployed to the Soviet Northern and Baltic Fleets, and with the expectation that the Soviet Union will continue to improve and expand its basing structure within the region, at the very least the U.S. Second Fleet must be strengthened – not, however, by the transfer of units from the Pacific Seventh Fleet, but rather by the building of additional naval units.

Improvements in Soviet naval air capabilities – aircraft as well as missile systems – together with the modernization of Polish and GDR naval assets, especially their amphibious forces, will require of NATO both a quantitative and a qualitative growth in its naval capabilities, including ASW technologies. U.S. and FRG amphibious units, working in closer concert than ever before, should evolve new concepts and technologies for maritime operations. New technology weapons and precision guided munitions can greatly augment the NATO posture, especially in a theater of operations such as this which, geostrategically, affords advantage to defensive forces. To exploit fully the factors of geography – for example, as was done during the Second World War – NATO would have to establish a stronger force presence in its northern flank region. This will not be an easy task for the Alliance if Norway and Denmark continue to prohibit foreign military deployments in their countries. Lacking a basing infrastructure in the region, ships of the U.S. Second Fleet would lose precious time in deploying to the region – time in which force must be brought immediately to bear in order to blunt a Soviet-Warsaw Pact offensive across Europe.

In the current situation, unless U.S. Second Fleet units were operating in the waters east of the Icelandic coast at the time of the attack, the Soviet Navy could, with relative ease, gain control of the Norwegian, Barents, and Greenland Seas, facilitating the prospects for control of the Baltic approaches to the Atlantic. These two areas of naval operations, which are included in NATO's Northern Theater, are linked by the North Sea, and NATO might consider deploying some units of the U.S. Second Fleet in this region. Another base in Scotland or an augmented complex at Holy Loch would be useful for the deployment of naval forces to both areas of the northern flank. However, the psychological impact upon the nations bordering the Alliance's Northern Theater of the growth and continued development of Soviet forces and facilities in the region may be such as to neutralize the whole of NATO's northern flank, with the result that, in the event of an East-West confrontation in Europe, the Soviet Union might be more willing to act less cautiously. Only with a concerted Alliance effort to maintain the perception of an "essential equivalence" of East-West forces in the area can this situation be averted. For NATO this means a reassessment of its northern force posture.

## Needed: Greater Alliance Mobility

Against the numerically superior forces of the Warsaw Pact and in the event that an offensive were launched in place, it is probable that Alliance airpower would be forced into a close support role because of the intensity with which the first echelon could be expected to attack. Heavy, close air support would be indispensable to a successful defense by NATO under such circumstances. Several problems, however, are inherent in the early use of NATO airpower in close support. Because of the apparent evolution of Soviet-Warsaw Pact Frontal Aviation, there can be little doubt that the ground offensive will be complemented by comparable air operations. For NATO members, two requirements emerge as crucially important to European security: the deployment of improved low-level tactical surveillance radars, and the procurement of a system like the Boeing E-3A AWACS to provide command, control, communications and realtime intelligence ($C^3I$) including an early warning capability for the Alliance.(81) Without adequate systems of detection, NATO's surface-to-air defenses would be of dubious value. NADGE, NATO's primary warning system, is unable to detect low flying aircraft of the type with which the Soviet forces are now being equipped. Thus, under present circumstances, it is likely that many of NATO's tactical aircraft would be destroyed on the ground during the opening stages of the conflict. Of those which escaped preemption, a large number would not be able to take off because of enemy interdiction of airfields.(82) Although in many instances runways can be made operational after interdiction in a matter of perhaps twelve hours, this elapsed time might be crucial.

Whatever NATO airpower could be launched before a preemptive strike would encounter difficulties in attempting to carry out missions of close ground support and battlefield interdiction because of the growth of Soviet counter-air capabilities. The density of Warsaw Pact ground defenses, especially mobile surface-to-air missile systems and the ZSU-23/24 antiaircraft gun, can seal off the battlefield at high and low altitudes. The overall lethality of the expected battle environment would enhance the prospect of NATO aircraft being shot down by friendly forces (with which communication may be difficult under battle conditions because of the lack of systems interoperability) as well as by enemy forces.

Nevertheless, the flexibility afforded by airpower, together with its ability to apply highly concentrated damage at widely different points at short intervals, must be regarded as a critical asset by NATO, especially if warning time is substantially reduced. However, close air support operations will be costly, and each aircraft lost in the early stages of battle could affect the capacity of Alliance forces to sustain a forward defense before the arrival of reinforcements.

At present, the U.S. Fairchild A-10 close air support aircraft has the task of defending front line NATO forces. In a European conflict, the A-10 would strike against enemy forces (tanks, in particular) "by staying on the friendly side of the battle line and maneuvering hard at low altitudes to bring its own weapons (a full load of GAU-8 cannons and six Maverick air-to-surface missiles) to bear on targets of opportunity for only seconds at a time."(83) The suppression of Soviet mobile SAMs is the primary mission of the U.S.

Army Cobra helicopter.(84) The A-10, however, has a relatively lower performance envelope than other aircraft, and could be expected to have problems in escaping enemy infrared-seeking missiles like the SA-7 Strela and the follow-on SA-9. Even if flares were used to confuse these missiles, as was done in Vietnam, the battlefield environment may be too intense to expect the survival of the A-10 – assuming, of course, it escapes preemption in a surprise attack. Potentially, just as lethal to the A-10 is the growth in Western Europe of high intensity power and communications lines, the newer of which are unlikely to be noted on older NATO maps. Other problems, too, would adversely impact on the performance of the A-10, including the lack of a survivable forward air controller (FAC).

As is the case with the Soviet Union, NATO will need increasingly to develop new means for providing indigenous support for ground forces at the forward edge of the battle area (FEBA). Improved attack helicopters, armed with new generation antitank precision weapons, together with improved artillery and eventually the cannon-launched guided projectile, some with fuse settings to neutralize enemy self-propelled artillery, have been suggested for the ground support role.(85) The effectiveness of the helicopter in amassing firepower against an enemy offensive is inherently limited by the platform's vulnerability to groundfire and airfire,(86) although, if capable of vertical maneuver,(87) its vulnerability to interdiction by Soviet SAM systems would be reduced somewhat. At any rate, NATO armies will need to be restructured so as to be able to fight more independently of close air support than in the past.(88)

As already noted, the essence of the Soviet-Warsaw Pact attack concept rests on the ability of offensive forces to sustain the momentum of their thrusts until breakthroughs occur.(89) In a European scenario this probably means before Allied reinforcements can be mobilized and transported to the areas of battle. For NATO the implications of this are twofold, affecting both ground and air deployments. In addition to those being redeployed from the United States, more alliance ground forces should be transferred, to their forward wartime positions. Other American army forces, in particular mechanized brigade units, as well as troops of the Federal Republic of Germany,would be put to more effective use if redeployed from the southern areas of the FRG to the north along the most likely avenues of Warsaw Pact attack.(90) Bundeswehr forces deployed along the Rhine should be moved eastward, while those brigades designated as covering forces should be strengthened and moved forward. Reserves and national militia could be integrated readily into the NATO defense plan, to supplement and strengthen the firepower available immediately for use against invading forces. So as not to endanger NATO's rear areas, French, Belgian, Dutch, and British forces could be stationed along the eastern bank of the Rhine. These "covering forces" could be strengthened by national units and reserves equipped with weapons capable of greater firepower deployed on the western bank of the Rhine.

The redeployment of NATO units, placing U.S. and FRG forces in forward positions to the north and central areas of Germany, while repositioning those of Belgium and Holland at the Rhine, need not raise apprehensions of American-German bilateralism if undertaken in conjunction with a broader reappraisal of Alliance tactical concepts. Moreover, by stationing the Belgian and Dutch brigades closer to the Rhine in peacetime, their effectiveness would be increased significantly, ensuring their participation at the opening stages of hostilities.

Infantry divisions should be converted into mobile units, since enemy forces emphasize great mobility of maneuver. Clearly, the principal costs will be for the acquisition of tanks and armored personnel carriers. NATO needs a new tank to meet the challenge of the T-72 and the T-80. If, as is likely to be the case, Alliance-wide procurement of a new generation main battle tank is impossible, the variant chosen by each nation should be redesigned wherever possible to include characteristics common to the other systems. In the case of the West German Leopard II, the British Chieftain and the U.S. XM-1 Abrams, areas of commonality have been suggested, such as the type of armament to be used on the tank platform. Thus, with parts interchangeable, spares could be provided as necessary from a common depot or from logistics supplies of national forces other than one's own. If this is not possible – and this may indeed be the case, inasmuch as the standardization and interoperability issues are a function of national policy constraints – the United States, West Germany and Britain should push ahead quickly with their respective national plans for tank production and deployment.

The commitment to create additional heavy divisions is reinforced by the experience of the October 1973 Middle East war in which the importance of the tank for defensive, as well as offensive, forces was demonstrated. But the conversion to heavy divisions will do NATO no good in a situation of surprise attack if these units are stationed in the United States. To the problems posed by the growth of Soviet air and naval power must be added the insufficient American transport capability. If we assume a short war scenario, the 77 C-5 heavy transport aircraft, which compose the entire U.S. inventory of transport capabilities that can carry a main battle tank to the European theater from the United States in a matter of hours (assuming an efficient alert response), have a lift capacity of only one tank per plane. This means, in effect, that each C-5 would be required to undertake three roundtrips to Europe before the 250 tanks of one division could be in place in Europe. For obvious reasons this would be an impractical situation with front line forces awaiting reinforcement. Moreover, the other urgent uses to which such aircraft would have to be put would preclude their total allocation to the airlifting of tanks from the United States to Western Europe. At the very least, the prepositioning of additional tank division sets is called for,(91) to be manned, if necessary, by troops of other NATO nations.(92)

Equipment for additional tank divisions could be stockpiled through the POMCUS (Prepositioned Material Configured in Unit Sets) program, assuming that storage dumps can be protected against enemy covert or overt attack. In this way, the combat readiness of U.S. troops stationed in Europe can be upgraded by stockpiling greater amounts of ammunition and prepositioning equipment to counter the threat of a Soviet launch without warning. This is a critical task facing the Alliance. Stockpiles of tanks, artillery and munitions have been dangerously low since 1973 when the United States resupplied Israel.(93) In Europe today there is prepositioned only enough material to equip one division. Although the United States has announced its intention to add enough equipment for two or three divisions, much more needs to be done.

One serious problem that requires urgent attention concerns the closing down of U.S. army depots in Europe to compensate for the increase in manpower represented by the two newly formed 3,800-man mechanized infantry brigades deployed to North Germany. In recent years, several supply installations have been eliminated with the result that Kaiserlautern, a city located in the Palatinate Hills of West Germany (35 miles west of the Rhine River), has become the major storage and supply depot for U.S. NATO forces. With the concentration of a major portion of U.S. prepositioned material in an area having a radius of thirty miles, the Soviet-Warsaw Pact forces could attack by air to destroy one of the most important facilities in the NATO infrastructure. To the extent possible, NATO supply depots should be dispersed and storage facilities hardened in order to diminish their vulnerability to preemption.

## New Technologies and the Firepower/Manpower Trade-Off

Critical to the Alliance's ability to halt the momentum of the enemy offensive will be the firepower that can be brought to bear in the early stages of the conflict. Faced with societal, budgetary and manpower constraints, NATO's options for upgrading Alliance defenses and thereby bolstering deterence in Europe are not numerous. In the United States and Western Europe, it is generally agreed that NATO's conventional forces can be greatly upgraded if the Alliance places a premium on incorporating new technology weapons into its force posture.

Precision guided munitions (PGMs) describe a growing class of bombs, missiles and artillery projectiles that, because of improvements in guidance techniques, possess greatly increased single-shot kill probabilities. Incorporating advanced radar, electro-optical, infra-red homing, correlation, and/or laser designation technologies to accomplish homing guidance; or systems which find their target using a signature emitted from the target itself, or which rely on inertial guidance, updated by means of radio transmittal, or correlation guidance, especially mapmatching – PGMs have demonstrated accuracies on the order of ten meters or less. Together with developments in weapons design and support, new guidance technologies enable defensive forces, operating in more decentralized formations, to take advantage of the natural benefits that accrue to the defense, including camouflage and hiding.(94) The greater vulnerability to PGMs of large formations, those in operation as well as those in staging areas behind the forward edge of the battle area, makes necessary their dispersal, a tactic that would reduce the inherent shock power of assaulting forces. Under these circumstances, the concentration of forces for the classic breakthrough scenario that forms the basis for NATO planning becomes more risky for Warsaw Pact forces, increasing the plausibility of the thesis that an enemy assault against NATO's Northern and/or Southern Theater(s) of operation might precede an attack on the central front or that a Pact offensive against the central front would be launched with surprise, along several axes of penetration simultaneously.

Against an armored column on the move, highly accurate weapons could interdict highways, thereby forcing the dispersal of enemy armor along less well defined routes of entry into Western Europe.(95) Even seemingly insignificant delays would provide NATO with important time for mobilization and for reinforcement of Alliance front line forces.

If we assume that Warsaw Pact forces were to break through NATO territory across the North German plain, Allied forces equipped with precision-guided weapons, notably the U.S. TOW (tubular, optical, wire-guided) antitank system and new technology, cannon-guided laser projectiles, promise to bring firepower to bear more effectively against an enemy assault. The appropriate force structure by which to exploit to the fullest the promise of precision-guided and other new technology weapons has been demonstrated to be one in which the traditional delineation of the missions and roles of each of the armed services is skewed. Although the source of not a little controversy, a reassessment of the institutional dogma that has provided the parameters for delineating missions and roles among the armed services would be a small price to pay for the revitalization of NATO's defenses. A reconceptualization of the respective missions and roles of Allied air, ground and naval forces is probably the only means by which the Alliance will be able to take full advantage of new technology weapons and to respond to the threat of an enemy surprise offensive across northern Germany and/or one directed against NATO's northern and southern flanks.

Based on an Alliance-wide combined arms concept, NATO's forward deployed forces would identify the main thrust of the attack, confirm the major avenues of approach, and initiate defensive operations designed primarily to destroy or stop enemy armored divisions. Interdiction to the enemy's rear would be provided by standoff aircraft employing cruise missiles or other PGMs, freeing NATO's aircraft for air superiority and close air support missions.(96) The latter would include numerous air-to-ground operations, including tank interdiction and defense suppression.

Even so, by the late 1980s the ability of aircraft to fulfill their assigned deep interdiction missions will be in doubt.(97) In recent years, the Soviet Union has undertaken major programs designed to strengthen Warsaw Pact defenses against Western counterattacks. In particular, it has devoted sizeable resources to the hardening of airfields and the construction of shelters to house aircraft, logistics and munitions, as well as to the defense of command centers, military elites and cadres. In the Soviet Union itself, efforts have been made, and are continuing, to relocate military production plants in its Eastern or Asian regions or to reduce their vulnerability to attack by placing them underground. As a result, many of the most lucrative industrial and military targets within the Warsaw Pact countries have been made largely invulnerable to the munitions deployed currently by NATO's tactical airpower – nuclear and conventional.

Moreover, the growth and modernization of Soviet-Warsaw Pact forces over the last decade, have given Soviet tactical airpower a capability to provide air support for advancing Warsaw Pact forces, thus denying air supremacy to NATO forces in Western Europe. In the future, although the battlefield, especially in European contingencies, will be increasingly inhospitable to manned systems as a result of the greater lethality and accuracy of weapons, landbased and airborne, the situation in the early 1980s will be less critical for Soviet-Warsaw Pact airpower because of the relative dearth of NATO air defenses – and even less so if the Alliance is unable to deploy a sophisticated system of warning and command/control. It will be necessary, therefore, to deploy weapons that can be remotely controlled, or at least launched from points outside the battle area to targets to the rear of enemy front line troops as well as those at the FEBA. New technology weapons, precision-guided munitions, remotely piloted vehicles and cruise missiles, if they can be developed and deployed in quantity fast enough, promise to revolutionize theater warfare, allowing for a flexible and discriminating use of force, conventional and nuclear – requirements that would seem to be critical in any European scenario.

Given their capability for terminal guidance, cruise missiles, among new weapons technologies, have attracted considerable attention in Western military circles. Deployed on land, sea or aircraft platforms, cruise missiles, because of their potential for highly accurate warhead delivery, could assume many of the deep interdiction missions which at present are assigned to NATO's Quick Reaction Alert (QRA) aircraft.(98) The latter could then be released for use against mobile targets, for example, or in other areas of the theater of operations. In a battlefield environment characterized by numerous and noncontiguous fronts, the mobility afforded by airpower emerges as a precious resource, and the use of NATO's QRA assets against, for example, advancing enemy units (in contrast to fixed sites which can be interdicted by other, more efficient, means) promises to yield important advantages to Alliance positions. Thus, while their current requirement for pretargeting restricts the employment options of the cruise missile to use against fixed targets, their flexibility with regard to modes of deployment and versatility of warhead employment promises to provide NATO with a survivable weapon for use against important military and industrial facilities and installations in Eastern Europe.

One of the major shortcomings that potentially could be disastrous to the success of a Soviet offensive against Western Europe relates to the nature and dispersion of the logistical infrastructure of Soviet-Warsaw Pact forces. For example, because the group of Soviet forces deployed in Eastern Europe function (on a daily basis) independently of other Warsaw Pact units – as do each of the national groupings of forces of Pact nations – and use equipment manufactured and produced primarily in the Soviet Union, resupply, spare parts, and, in rare instances, maintenance must be obtained in the USSR. Were Soviet forces engaged in offensive operations, their logistical requirements would extend from within the Soviet Union to the forward edge of battle, providing NATO planners with an extremely lucrative target set whose destruction would limit the effectiveness of Soviet forces with the passage of time. Against high priority targets such as enemy railheads, the major supply point of a front, or logistical facilities – e.g., the major Soviet-Warsaw Pact supply depot located at Grossborn, Poland, with its subsidiary depots in East Germany, Czechoslovakia and Hungary – the employment of cruise missiles would be extremely cost effective. Cruise missiles could be used to strike Soviet-Warsaw Pact airfields, interdicting runways and hardened installations.(99)

Conceivably, one of the most important requirements for NATO in a European conflict will be the destruction of Warsaw Pact energy networks, including the supply of fuel to the FEBA and front line forces. There can be no question that the Soviet Union is concerned about the availability of fuel supplies, as demonstrated by its far-ranging efforts to improve pipeline systems and lines of supply to Eastern Europe. The fuel requirements for Soviet-Warsaw Pact forces configured for rapid advance and highly mobile maneuvers will be stupendous (although less so then if Pact planners emphasized a protracted campaign across Western Europe).(100) Pipelines connecting the oil producing areas in the Soviet Union to the large refineries at Bratislava and Schwedt offer lucrative targets for the cruise missile, as will the pipeline connection between Tyumen and Szczecin currently under construction. Other oil and natural gas pipelines include the recently completed network that stretches from Slovakia across Hungary and Yugoslavia to Fiume (Rijeka) and its correlary system from Hungary to Fiume which, when completed, will transport crude oil from the Middle East. The railroad container service that went into operation in 1975 between Riga-Rostock-Prague, Moscow-Warsaw-East Berlin and Rostock-East Berlin-Prague-Budapest-Belgrade-Sofia provides another potential target for U.S. cruise missiles. To these potential fixed, landbased target sets could be added many others against which the cruise missile could be effectively employed. It remains only for NATO planners to exploit the opportunities provided by such technologies.(101)

Sea attack cruise missiles, as well as other new generation antishipping weapons, such as the Anglo-French Martel and U.S. Harpoon missile systems, could augment greatly the offensive firepower of NATO naval forces and extend, by a factor of five to forty, the submarine attack radius. With regard to the primary wartime naval mission of sea denial and control, cruise missiles deploying warheads incorporating fuel air explosives (FAEs) promise to provide an effective alternative to the use of both nuclear and TNT firepower, based on their peculiar blast effects.(102) On the basis of recent experiments undertaken in the United States, the blast effects of FAEs were demonstrated to linger longer and affect larger areas than did those resulting from the detonation of conventional TNT charges. Inasmuch as masts, spars, radar antennas and displays, directional equipment, radomes, electronic warfare housing, ECM casings, aircraft and hangars are extremely vulnerable to airborne blast waves and overpressures, it has been suggested that cruise missiles employing an FAE warhead could be used effectively against surface ships, in place of nuclear warhead employment. Indeed the Soviet Union has been involved for years in the development of fuel air explosives, providing basis for speculation that the new SS-NX-13 Mach-4 cruise missile may, in one configuration, deploy an FAE warhead for use against U.S. aircraft carriers.(103)

Armed with Captor mines,(104) for example, cruise missiles could block vital choke points or enemy-controlled ports or rivers in areas that might not be readily accessible to U.S. surface naval vessels. As part of a NATO defense/deterrence posture, cruise missiles and other new technology weapons systems provide a potential for blunting Soviet-Warsaw Pact initiatives both on land and on the sea lanes over which vital raw materials and supplies, as well as NATO reinforcements, must be carried.

Notwithstanding their potential, new technology weapons do not provide answers in themselves for NATO's problems of defense against a potential enemy who has advantages in numbers, standardization of weapons, logistics supply, command and control, intelligence, a common doctrine, agreed upon tactical concepts, and, increasingly, superiority in some areas of technological development. For example, new-generation, antitank guided missiles (ATGMs), for the most part, rely on direct link guidance to steer a missile to a tank – by signals transmitted through wires that are played out while the missile is in flight – and thus are distance-constrained. Current generation antitank and precision-guided weapons have a limited ability to operate in adverse environments; thus, their potential effectiveness for European defense is diminished because of regional environmental constraints.

Even if these problems could be overcome by means of new technological developments – as they may well be – it would be unrealistic to assume that the defense implications of new technology weapons have escaped the attention of Soviet military planners. Over the last several years articles have appeared with increasing frequency in Soviet military literature cautioning that "a successful offensive is possible only with the reliable suppression of the enemy's antiarmor defense with ATGM as first priority."(105) It is perhaps with this objective in mind that the Soviets have begun to deploy in Eastern Europe advanced, self-propelled artillery which may be nuclear-capable. Whatever their motives, the introduction of self-propelled artillery enhances the firepower that Warsaw Pact forces could bring to bear against NATO defenses.

Nor can it be assumed that the new Soviet tanks (T-72 and T-80) do not incorporate improved armor, suspension and motor systems, the combined effect of which could be an armed platform somewhat less vulnerable to ATGMs. It is important to recall that the large numbers of tanks destroyed during the October 1973 Middle East war represented, on both sides, older systems. Neither the U.S.-supplied Israeli tanks nor those supplied by the Soviet Union to the Arabs incorporated the latest in tank technologies. For this reason, NATO cannot extrapolate sortie ratios based upon formulas even from the recent past. The potential effectiveness of PGMs against enemy armor, for example, cannot be presumed. Hence PGMs in themselves do not provide an adequate solution to the problem of assuring a military balance in Europe. Technological advantages rarely endure long against the development of countermeasures. Unless NATO members resolve among themselves to preserve what remains of the West's diminishing technological lead over the Soviet Union, the advantage will accrue to the East. On the basis of projected increases in the cost of R&D, these efforts will require greater collaboration among Alliance members at every point in the developmental cycle.

Other problems face NATO in bolstering its capabilities. These include the prospect that the United States will acquiesce, in bilateral arms control negotiations with the Soviet Union for a SALT II treaty, in limitations on the cruise missile, a weapons system which is perceived in Europe to be potentially of great importance in strengthening West European defenses. The U.S. cruise missile has, for some years, been one of the most contentious issues at SALT, with the Soviet Union pressing for its limitation. Of particular concern to the Europeans have been proposals to restrict the cruise missile in such a way as to render impossible its effective deployment in the European theater – whether by means of range limitations, a moratorium on its systems development and/or deployment, prohibiting its technology transfer to U.S. allies, or banning its sealaunched and groundlaunched variants. Any of these suggested restrictions would have the effect of reducing dramatically the potential effectiveness of the deployment in Europe of cruise missiles, either as part of a new generation British, French, or even a European, nuclear force, or under NATO command, providing one cost-effective means to redress the East-West military imbalance.

In this context, recent reports suggesting agreement between the superpowers on a SALT II treaty (with its accompanying three-year protocol and commitment to follow-on negotiations), in which the U.S. cruise missile is to be restricted both in terms of its mode of deployment and its range capability, threaten to have an adverse effect on U.S.-European relations and to reduce the potential for NATO to counter the growing power of the Warsaw Pact.(106) The inability of SALT to modify significantly the buildup of Soviet military forces – nuclear and nonnuclear – provides little basis for hope that future arms control negotiations can be relied on to safeguard Western security interests. In the absence of a viable SALT accord, or for that matter other East-West arms control agreements, the United States and its NATO allies have no alternative but to assign a greater priority to, and concentrate their energies on, the development of a military force posture that provides for the active defense of Western Europe, based upon appropriate, well-reasoned concepts employing all available resources – both in terms of new weapons technologies and manpower, including greater reliance on reserves and other national forces.

## Theater Nuclear Weapons

One means by which the United States can reassure its NATO allies while providing for a credible and responsive defense of Western Europe – the only basis on which deterrence can be maintained – is to revitalize the role, in NATO planning, of U.S. theater nuclear weapons.(107) From the European perspective, theater nuclear weapons furnish the necessary link militarily between the American strategic arsenal and the U.S. commitment to NATO. Whether or not such is the case, theater nuclear weapons provide one option that might enable NATO to slow or to halt an advance by Warsaw Pact forces, in order to permit Alliance mobilization and reinforcement.(108) Theater nuclear weapons, especially the new generation "mini-nukes," offer a particularly effective means of disrupting Warsaw Pact attack formations and forcing a greater dispersion of enemy troops. In general, a Soviet front is about 200 kilometers wide, somewhat narrower than planned for in the West. By their emphasis on deep echeloning, however, Soviet forces are configured so as to allow their main attacking units to be held in rear areas (which for any army ranges from 80-150 km behind the FEBA) for as long as possible as a means of offsetting the threat of NATO's employment of nuclear weapons. In doing so, however, Warsaw Pact troops would be forced to sacrifice mass in the critical early stages of their attack, and this would have the effect of improving the prospects that NATO's conventional capabilities could defeat advancing armored formations.

In the event an attack can be launched without (or with relatively little) warning, the Soviet-Warsaw Pact tactical doctrinal emphasis on the meeting engagement calls for numerous and diverse maneuvers and daring thrusts, based upon a force posture emphasizing smaller units, most likely to be conducted at the regimental level – as opposed to the classic emphasis of blitzkrieg at the division/army level. In this situation the use of theater nuclear weapons by NATO forces may not redound to Western advantage. Relying on multiple, simultaneous penetrations and a high-speed, widely dispersed advance, Pact forces will make target acquisition, and command, control, and communications as well as a nuclear response exceedingly difficult to achieve. Area saturation would likely be ineffective, for any nuclear employment would threaten friendly forces as well as enemy troops. With regard to target acquisition, Allied communication links would be susceptible to enemy jamming, while target designation by air would be hampered by the interpenetration of forces. However, should a nuclear response be chosen by NATO forces in the circumstances of this scenario, the blast, heat, and fallout effects of nuclear detonations – barring a direct hit against enemy armor – would probably have little effect upon Soviet tank and BMP crews whose vehicles are configured for war in a radioactive environment.

Clearly, the potential effectiveness of a nuclear employment by NATO forces depends as much on the circumstances of the attack scenario as on the type of systems used and the level of Allied response. In both of the attack situations described, NATO will be forced by its present force configuration to use nuclear firepower to interdict the Warsaw Pact offensive. However, in a surprise attack characterized by daring thrusts and multiple engagements, the ability of Alliance forces to organize and concentrate nuclear firepower against fast moving enemy targets will be limited. In the situation in which enemy targets are acquired prior to the penetration of a Western line of defense, nuclear firepower would be employed in a variety of ways: for instance, by using Atomic Demolition Mines (ADMs) to block the line of advance of the first-echelon forces, and by using missile and cannon-launched nuclear warheads whose task would be the destruction of the advance guard, main body, flank and second-echelon support. Nuclear artillery would be engaged within ranges of under 100 miles.

In circumstances of surprise, preemptive multiple maneuvers, it is unlikely that ADMs can be emplaced with sufficient speed to be effective against invading Soviet armor. Even assuming that NATO's long-range, landbased missile launchers, nuclear storage sites, airfields, and $C^3$ facilities located to the rear of front line forces have not been engaged by Soviet aircraft and/or long-range, landbased missiles, their use in a situation of diverse fronts and the interpenetration of enemy with friendly troops would be virtually impossible. Without a clear delineation of target sets, resort to nuclear weapons by NATO would likely be contemplated only if Pact forces threatened to overrun or bypass those of the Alliance across a corps front.

If, however, the initial thrusts by the advance guard of the Soviet regiment (probably a reinforced battalion) are unsuccessful and second-battalion forces remain committed to flanking operations, a second-echelon regiment would be directed to undertake another flanking maneuver, this time across a slightly broader front, 10-12 kilometers behind enemy lines. Conceivably, in this situation, existing generation theater nuclear missiles could be used with some degree of success against enemy forces. The success or failure of an operation of this type could depend on the number of meeting engagements within the corps area, the reliability of NATO systems of command, control and communications, and the vulnerability of deployed nuclear systems in the face of the Soviet-Warsaw Pact attack.

The NATO use of nuclear weapons in the meeting engagement scenario would require, however, the modernization of existing generation nuclear systems to emphasize the employment of small packages of low-yield nuclear warheads. To compensate for their reduced yields, theater nuclear systems – if they are to be considered effective war fighting weapons – must benefit from the revolution in guidance technologies to demonstrate increased accuracies against a concentrated target set. In the "mini-nukes," there already exist nuclear systems capable of delivering low-yield warheads with pinpoint accuracies so as to effect a hard target kill, with a minimum of collateral damage. Against key point targets such as bridges and roadways, located in the FEBA, the employment of mini-nukes by NATO forces makes eminent sense, as does the use of longer-range systems against high-value targets just to the rear of the FEBA and deep into Eastern Europe, including perhaps the Soviet Union itself.

## The Neutron Bomb

The immediate issue, however, remains the most effective means by which Alliance forces could counter the threat of multiple, surprise Soviet-Warsaw Pact armored thrusts. Toward this end the deployment of an enhanced radiation weapon might well be the single most important potential contribution in providing for the defense/deterrence of Western Europe, although this is by no means a widely held view. In the second half of 1977, the neutron bomb emerged as a controversial issue among Alliance members, even though the concept of an enhanced radiation weapon is anything but new. Based on a fission-fusion reaction,(109) an enhanced radiation weapon produces reduced levels of heat, blast and fallout, while maximizing the prompt emission of nuclear radiation. Nuclear radiants have the capability to penetrate materials such as steel, providing the basis for a weapons system that could defend against the threat of a Soviet-Warsaw Pact armored attack upon Western Europe. In an all-fission nuclear weapon – the concept underlying almost all existing generation U.S. tactical nuclear weapons – the radiations are virtually identical to those produced by the fission-fusion process of the neutron bomb, the primary difference being the number of high-energy neutrons produced in relation to the weapon yield. What enhanced radiation weapons mean for the NATO defense posture is the development of systems capable of destroying an enemy armored advance with much less physical collateral damage and radioactive wastes. In terms of expected collateral damage and the potential for use in areas close to friendly troops, or in civilian areas, employment of the neutron bomb would be preferable to the high blast effects and waste products produced by nuclear fission weapons.

The neutron warhead has been designed for employment from a landbased missile (Lance) or from artillery shells (8 inches in diameter). The use of existing systems for the deployment of the enhanced radiation weapon provides for an effective and credible means of countering the growth of Soviet armor in Central Europe. Notwithstanding this, the deployment of the neutron bomb has been criticized at two levels: one relates to the morality of using a weapon that is more lethal to living cells and less destructive of inanimate objects; the other concerns the obscuring of Western conceptions of delineation between conventional war and nuclear war. Yet, such arguments hold little substance when juxtaposed to the larger objective of defending and, if possible, deterring the outbreak of conflict in Western Europe. For this reason alone, the neutron bomb should be considered as a desirable and usable war-fighting weapon whose deployment in the European theater would enhance the credibility of NATO's force posture. It would, in fact, be a step toward a return to a war-waging mode based upon minimization of collateral damage.

Western conceptions of strategic doctrine, with their overwhelming reliance on the deterrence of nuclear war, have greatly restricted serious thought about the value of, or the employment options for, theater nuclear systems. Only recently have there been indications of a change in conception with regard to theater deployments of nuclear weapons. In part, this comes as a result of the military buildup by the Soviet Union. In part, it is a function of technological developments which have produced a new generation of theater nuclear systems possessing capabilities for highly accurate and low-yield delivery. Improvements in accuracy, together with reductions in warhead payload, have made available to NATO weapons of great precision in target acquisition while, at the same time, reducing collateral damage from the blast.

Nevertheless, the engagement of enemy targets with nuclear weapons remains a highly controversial issue both among Alliance planners and within member nations. Political anxieties about the nature and extent of a Soviet response to a NATO employment of nuclear weapons, and, for some, moral considerations, argue against their deployment in Western Europe, and even more their use in waging an active Alliance defense. On their own, these considerations might merit cautious debate on the issue. But when considered in the broader context – as indeed they must be – of Soviet strategic doctrine and force posture, the emerging military imbalance in Central Europe, and the available means by which NATO could effectively defend against a Warsaw Pact attack, arguments against the use by NATO of its nuclear systems in the defense of Western Europe are unconvincing. The preservation of West European security and deterrence of war on the Continent are dependent upon constructing and maintaining a credible NATO defense posture.

## Survivability and Vulnerability

However, as has been the case since 1967 when the Alliance officially adopted the doctrine of flexible response (MC 14/3), NATO forces are directed to wage a conventional defense, resorting to the use of theater nuclear weapons only after nonnuclear capabilities have been exhausted. As already noted, resort by NATO to theater nuclear weapons to avoid defeat is premised on the assumption that the advantage in such escalation lies with the Atlantic Alliance. In view of Soviet doctrine and recent Warsaw Pact force deployments, this assumption is of dubious validity. First, it cannot be assumed that Warsaw Pact forces would rely only on nonnuclear weapons in an initial attack against Western Europe. Second, in the event that Soviet-Warsaw Pact planners elect to undertake their initial operations at the conventional level, the employment of nuclear weapons by NATO threatens to evoke an even larger-scale nuclear response from enemy forces. And third, for nuclear weapons not to be used by NATO except as an alternative to defeat raises the likelihood that some, if not most, of NATO's theater nuclear weapons would have been interdicted by invading Warsaw Pact forces.(110) This would be especially true if Pact forces were to launch an attack in place, since U.S. nuclear weapons in Europe and those of France are stored in sites whose locations are presumably known to Soviet intelligence and therefore vulnerable to preemption.(111)

Quite obviously, theoretical conceptualizations of the employment of NATO's nuclear weapons are governed largely by the very real, and practical, issue of their survivability – and the survivability of their logistical and support systems – in a European battlefield environment. Although NATO's theater nuclear arsenal, as presently configured, is composed of several types of systems – nuclear capable artillery, atomic demolition munitions, air-to-surface and surface-to-surface missiles, short-range ballistic missiles, and nuclear gravity bombs – each, for varying reasons, is either vulnerable to, or undefended against, preemption by Soviet-Warsaw Pact forces. Much of NATO's nuclear artillery, while extremely effective at distances under 30 nautical miles, does not possess the range capabilities necessary to afford protection to their launchers. Because these weapons cannot be fired until enemy forces are in relatively close proximity, their vulnerability to enemy suppressive fire would be considerable. In point of fact, about 70 percent of the Alliance's tactical nuclear weapons are tied to delivery systems possessing ranges of under 100 miles. Similarly, with their limited ranges, the Sergeant, Honest John, and Lance surface-to-surface missiles would be confined in their use to targets within NATO territory, inasmuch as the nuclear option presumably would be invoked only after Pact forces had driven deeply into Western Europe.(112)

Those systems capable of long-range targeting, notably NATO aircraft, are even more vulnerable to preemption than shorter-range systems like nuclear artillery or mobile surface-to-surface missiles. Theoretically, NATO's Quick Reaction Alert forces, F-4s and F-111s, could be dispersed to hard hangarettes. However, aircraft dispersal is dependent on adequate warning of an impending attack, and limited in its effectiveness by the number of air bases available in Western Europe. Recently, the Alliance has undertaken to harden NATO air forces in Central Europe. However, without corresponding improvements to NATO's intelligence gathering and assessment capabilities and to its systems of air defenses that would enhance warning of an impending attack, programs of hardening and dispersal, in all probability, will be inadequate for protection against Soviet offensive capabilities, in particular the SS-20, whose combined payload and accuracy potentials would enable Moscow to strike hard targets located in NATO territory. At a minimum, NATO must take steps to enhance the survivability of its nuclear forces.

With regard to protection of airbases, the anticipated deployment of the Patriot and Roland surface-to-air missile systems should be considered a high Alliance priority, if only because the existing NATO air defense capability is ill-equipped to counter lowflying aircraft, such as the Soviet Union is deploying as part of its tactical air forces. Even so, the Patriot/Roland network will be limited in its ability to detect and defend against aircraft flying nap-of-the-earth profiles. Augmented R&D initiatives, for example, in the advanced technologies of laser and sensor detection promise revolutionary developments in the areas of passive detection, tracking and targeting of lowflying hostile aircraft.(113)

The improved defense of NATO airfields and other potential high value targets against Soviet offensive airpower would enhance the survivability and, hence, the credibility, as a deterrent force, of Alliance theater nuclear systems. However, against the threat of Soviet employment of its nuclear rocket forces, in particular medium-range ballistic missiles, the combined capabilities of the Patriot and Hawk systems are clearly inadequate, especially if it is assumed that Moscow will, by the mid-1980s, possess enough reentry vehicles to direct multiple numbers of warheads against each designated NATO target. In this situation, improvements in the mobility of NATO's theater nuclear systems could be crucial to their survivability, especially if the development of new technology systems of ballistic missile defense is foreclosed by political, economic, and/or arms control considerations.

As it is incumbent upon NATO to construct a force posture which incorporates discriminate tactical nuclear weapons, so, too, must the Alliance give greater emphasis to the protection of its ground forces in a nuclear, or CB, warfare environment. With regard to aircraft, for example, the Alliance assuredly needs to improve means of protecting (i.e., hardening) airfields and related facilities. Just as important to providing for the survivability of NATO airpower is the development of additional bases and airfields to which Alliance aircraft can disperse under conditions of attack. Soviet-Warsaw Pact forces are equipped with gear and support vehicles that are designed to protect in a nuclear or chemical/biological battlefield environment; NATO forces are not. The resulting asymmetry detracts from the credibility of NATO's declared posture, while bolstering the perceived war-fighting configuration of Soviet-Warsaw Pact forces. If NATO defense is to be credible – essential for deterrence in Europe – CBR protection must receive greater attention by NATO planners.

## THE HARD CHOICES

If we learned anything from the October 1973 Middle East war and the American involvement in Vietnam, it was that no single type of weapon can survive on the modern battlefield without the support of other systems. In planning for a defense against Soviet-Warsaw Pact forces, Alliance strategists must design a theater strategy, combining the tactics and capabilities associated with the more traditional offensive and defensive battleplans. With its own emphasis on the concept of combined arms, NATO forces could be configured to provide a more vigorous defense, envisaging offensive tactics which would have an important psychological effect on the will and determination of Alliance members to resist an enemy assault, as well as providing more effective military means of bringing force to bear against enemy territory.

Experiences of the recent past suggest that a future conflict on the European continent would be characterized by a flexibility of maneuver in which an active defense may have to be waged from hastily prepared positions, unless adequate warning is received. Within NATO, the United States has been advocating the modification of groundbased radars to interface with the Joint Tactical Information Distribution System (JTIDS) data link on the Boeing Airborne Warning and Control Aircraft (AWACS), the British Hawker-Siddeley Nimrod, and the U.S. Navy Grumman E-2C early warning aircraft. Despite a possible lack of agreement by the West Germans over the specifics of the electronics system,(114) there has emerged an Alliance-wide consensus on the need for upgrading NATO's overall systems of air defense. The Royal Air Force, for example, has embarked on a 15-year program, amounting to well over $3 billion, to rebuild British air defenses.(115) Included in this ambitious program is Nimrod, the procurement of 165 Tornado (MRCA) interceptors,(116) the deployment of the Bloodhound medium-high altitude missile, and a computerized control system. In addition, Britain is participating in a NATO-wide program to harden Alliance airfields against enemy attack and to train engineers in the rapid repair of aircraft runways and the construction of airfield shelters.

Notwithstanding the ambitious scope of NATO's efforts to improve shortcomings in its defensive posture, many of the really crucial programs that are needed to protect against the changing nature of the Soviet-Warsaw Pact threat await political decisions at the highest level. NATO's ability to surmount warning problems depends in part on progress toward standardization even in the area of warning systems – notably the AWACS-Nimrod problem. Yet the debate over Alliance-wide procurement of the U.S. AWACS has been linked to the main battle tank issue,(117) and this, in turn, has been made contingent upon the armament chosen, and so on. Admittedly the competition over dollars and jobs cannot be considered an insignificant problem for the political leadership of Alliance partners; but neither can the problem of revitalizing NATO.

For this reason, the United States should be prepared to work toward greater technological collaboration among member nations, and to achieve increased weapons standardization and interoperability. In this context, we applaud the recent American decision to deploy a German-made tank gun on the XM-1. But more needs to be done. The costs associated with research and development are rising with each passing year. As a result, R&D has become increasingly expensive, and most NATO members cannot support a comprehensive program of military research and development. It makes sense, therefore, for Alliance leaders to attempt to delineate a collaborative program for R&D, based upon who can do what most effectively. This is certainly not a new proposal and studies already exist which suggest means of designating such tasks on an Alliance-wide basis. Neither is the suggestion new that such an effort be undertaken under the auspices of the European Programme Group (of which France is a member) and, for the United States, in an agency such as the Department of Defense's Directorate of Development, Research and Engineering (DDR&E). What is needed is an Atlantic consultative body composed of representatives of all Western industrialized nations to deal with the specific issues of competitive arms development, with authority for their resolution.

Thirty years after the end of World War II, Western Europe remains dependent on the United States for its security. The assumption popular in the United States in the 1960s – that West European economic power and economic unity would lead to political integration and the eventual development of a greater European defense capability – has not come to pass in the 1970s. Although the combined resources of Western Europe surpass by far those of the Soviet Union and, in some respects, rival those of the United States, Western Europe remains far from united in defense. The economic miracle of the past generation has been threatened by spiraling inflation and the heavy West European dependence on energy imports. In the absence of a European political unit capable of dealing effectively with security issues, the United States will remain indispensable to the deterrence of conflict in Western Europe, although the problems confronting NATO are growing as a result of the great expansion of Soviet-Warsaw Pact military power relative to the West. As President Carter noted in his speech at the North Atlantic Summit Meeting in London on May 10, 1977:

> The threat facing the Alliance has grown steadily in recent years. The Soviet Union has achieved essential strategic nuclear equivalence. Its theater nuclear forces have been strengthened. The Warsaw Pact's conventional forces in Europe emphasize an offensive posture. These forces are much stronger than needed for any defense purposes. Since 1965, new ground and air weapons have been introduced in most categories: self-propelled artillery, mobile tactical missiles, mobile air defense guns, armored personnel carriers, tactical aircraft, and tanks. The Pact's build-up continues undiminished.

In short, the growth in Soviet-Warsaw Pact forces the advent of new technologies for nuclear and nonnuclear conflict, and constraints on manpower in Western Europe and the United States lend increased urgency to the need to maintain a NATO force posture and defense doctrine that does not hold Western Europe hostage to Soviet intentions. At the least, the continued shift in the NATO-Warsaw Pact balance toward the Soviet Union will confer upon Moscow unprecedented political leverage. The task confronting NATO is the mobilization of the considerable human and material resources available to the Atlantic Community, together with the political will needed to surmount the formidable and complex challenges to the security of the West in the late twentieth century.

## NOTES

(1) The qualitative improvement of Soviet weapons systems – nuclear and nonnuclear – is perceived in Moscow as a critical factor in determining the correlation of world forces. See, for example, Professor D.M. Proekter, " 'Qualitative' Aspect of Correlation of Forces Stressed," Novoye Vremya, March 18, 1977, p. 21; reprinted in Foreign Broadcast Information Service (FBIS), Soviet Union, March 22, 1977, pp. AA1-2.

(2) As quoted in Report to the Congress by Secretary of Defense Donald H. Rumsfeld, Annual Defense Department Report FY 1978 (Washington, D.C.: GPO, January 17, 1977), pp. 124-125.

(3) "Offensive operations in a future war will be the basic means for solving the problems of armed conflict in land theaters of military operations. They will be conducted by fronts and by combined arms, tank and air armies. The main role in solving the combat problems of an offensive operation will be played by operational tactical rocket troops and frontal aviation using nuclear ammunition and also by tank, motorized infantry and airborne troops." Marshal V.D. Sokolovskiy, Soviet Military Strategy, edited with analysis and commentary by Harriet Fast Scott (New York: Crane, Russak, for the Stanford Research Institute, 1975, 3rd edition), p. 292.

(4) Designated in Soviet literature as the Concept of Combined Arms, Soviet tactical doctrine stresses the coordination and interaction among different military services as well as among different weapons systems and platforms – nuclear and nonnuclear. In other words, motorized rifle squads, operating with tanks and Frontal Aviation (FA), are used to support the ground forces. (In fact, Soviet FA is under the command of the leader of Soviet Ground Forces.) Combat operations are coordinated and sustained by detailed planning which specifies the direction of attack, its objectives and timing. Soviet defenses – surface-to-air missiles and tactical air support – are also directed from the ground.

(5) The Soviet armored fighting vehicle (BMP) was first observed by the West in 1967 and utilized in the Soviet invasion force in Czechoslovakia in August 1968. See Eugene D. Betit, "Soviet Tactical Doctrine and Capabilities and NATO's Strategic Defense," Strategic Review, Fall 1976, p. 99.

In the wake of the October 1973 Middle East war the vulnerability of the BMP to anti-tank weapons emerged as a major concern of Soviet military leaders. (See, for example, Marshal A.A. Grechko, The Armed Forces of the Soviet State: A Soviet View (Moscow, 1975), translated and published under the auspices of the United States Air Force, Soviet Military Thought Series, No. 12 (Washington, D.C.: GPO, 1977)). To solve the problem, the Soviet Union has developed a new armored personnel carrier, designated the GTT M1970. Although its basic design first appeared in the year 1970, the GTT M1970 represents an improved APC, especially in armor protection. See "USSR: Substantial Progress Reported on Artillery Modernization," En Clair section, Defense and Foreign Affairs Digest, No. 7, 1977, p. 32.

(6) For example, Friedrich Wiener writes: "Soviet planning for a campaign in Western Europe allows 10 to 14 days for Soviet forces to reach the Atlantic Coast." See his The Armies of the Warsaw Pact Nations: Organization, Concept of War, Weapons and Equipment, translated by William J. Lewis (Vienna, Austria: Carl Ueberreuter Publishers, 1976), p. 120. The original German title was Die Armeen der Warschauer-Pakt-Staaten, published in 1974.

(7) Increasingly, the threat of decreased warning time for NATO has become the major concern of NATO's Supreme Allied Commander, General Alexander Haig. In testimony before the U.S. Senate Committee on Armed Services, General Haig described the problem of the expansion and modernization of Soviet military power in Europe: "All of these improvements – increased mobility, increased sustaining power, greater strength in the Warsaw Pact divisions – are giving them a greater ability to launch an attack without reinforcement and without these tell-tale indicators that we are seeking to focus on." U.S. Congress, Senate, Committee on Armed Services, Hearings on the Status of United States and Allied Military Forces and the NATO Situation Generally, stenographic transcript, March 1, 1977 (Washington, D.C.: Alderson Printing Company, 1977), p. 32.

Even as NATO officials have conceded a reduction in warning time, there exists no consensus among Alliance planners over the extent to which time has been reduced. General Haig declared in public testimony that warning time for the Alliance has been reduced, although the West still is said to have sufficient "time in which to identify preparations for an attack by the Warsaw Pact and initiate countermeasures." (Kurt Hofmann, "The Battlefield of the 1980s," International Defense Review, June 1977, p. 433.) Conflicting with the Haig assessment is the controversial analysis presented by Belgian General Robert Close in L'Europe Sans Defense (Brussels: Editions Arts and Voyages, 1976), who estimates that Warsaw Pact forces are capable of launching an attack without prior warning and reaching the Rhine in 48 hours.

(8) "Counterforce," in Soviet military doctrine, "is a basic concept in planning strategic and theater operations. Destruction of enemy combat units has priority over acquisition of terrain." (Wiener, op. cit., p. 117). According to Marshal Grechko, "the Soviet Strategic Missile Forces are intended for the destruction of th enemy's means of nuclear attack, large troop formations and

military bases, destroying his defense industry, disorganizing his governmental and military command and control, and paralyzing the operations of his economy and transportation." Quoted in Leon Goure, "Soviet Military Doctrine," Air Force Magazine (Soviet Aerospace Almanac 1977), March 1977, p. 50.

(9) The first strategic echelon is composed of approximately 100 divisions (Soviet and East European nationally composed forces) located in forward areas as well as a number of divisions stationed in the three western-most military districts of the Soviet Union.

(10) Wiener, p. 121. "It can be assumed that the initial forces of the first strategic echelon can cross the Western borders of the Warsaw Pact area prepared for war within four to eight hours after an alert."

(11) See, for example, Colonel Frederick C. Turner, USA, "The Soviet G.I.," Air Force Magazine (Soviet Aerospace Almanac 1977), March 1977, pp. 8283.

(12) David A. Smith, "Soviet Military Manpower," ibid., March 1977, pp. 7881. The Soviet Navy is not, however, included in these figures, inasmuch as the Soviet Navy has a conscription period of three years, as do Border Troops.

(13) Such an option is entirely feasible for Warsaw Pact forces in view of the increased frequency, in the last several years, of Soviet and Soviet-Pact field maneuvers conducted along Western border areas.

(14) According to Wiener (p. 133), "Soviet military planners plan for the use of at least 100 tubes of artillery and mortars with enough ammunition for preparatory fires of 10,000 rounds per kilometer of front to execute the type of attack discussed above."

(15) See Sokolovskiy, p. 255.

(16) Colonel N. Nikitin, "New Developments in the Struggle With Tanks," Zanamenosets, May 1974, p. 38; reprinted in William F. Scott, "Change in Tactical Concepts Within the Soviet Forces," in Lawrence L. Whetten, editor, The Future of Soviet Military Power (New York: Crane, Russak, 1976), p. 89.

(17) The Soviet conception of the role of the tank in a tactical battlefield situation is discussed, for example, in Colonel A. Akimov, "Fighting Tanks,," Soviet Military Review, October 1976, pp. 10-13.

(18) Lieutenant-General V. Reznichenko, "The Role of Tactics in Modern Warfare," ibid., September 1976, p. 9.

(19) As quoted in Hofmann, p. 432, and confirmed by a defector from Czechoslovakia, Major-General Senja, quoted in Lord Chalfont, "Moscow's Brutal Reality," The Times (London), July 28, 1975.

(20) These particular innovations may also serve another purpose, i.e., the Soviet chemical warfare capability against NATO.

(21) The chassis of the T-72 has been redesigned to be shorter and wider than older Soviet medium tanks with a suspension system similar to that of American tanks. The T-72 has six road wheels and carries a combat-loaded weight of some 40 tons. Its improved armor promises increased protection for its three-man crew, and its maximum speed, estimated to be somewhere around 70 kilometers an hour (powered by 700-750hp V-12 diesel engine), allows for greater maneuverability on the battlefield. Beyond this, the Soviet Union reportedly has under development a new generation main battle tank. Designated by NATO officials as the T80, this tank has demonstrated greater maneuverability than the T-72.

(22) The late Soviet Minister of Defense, Marshal Grechko, wrote: "The continuing process of improving antitank weapons has imposed grave tasks for science and technology. These tasks have to do with improving the survivability of tanks and developing more effective means and methods that would be reliable in neutralizing antitank defense measures." Op. cit., p. 155.

John Erickson estimates that "the present 20 divisions in GSFG have the capabilityof some 25 divisions a decade ago." "The Ground Forces in Soviet Military Policy," Strategic Review, Winter 1978, p. 68.

(23) "Until recently the Soviet strategic bomber force, Long Range Aviation, was assigned the burden of attack on Western Europe. Now, Frontal Aviation units can augment, especially in escort and defensive suppression roles." "Eastern Bloc Augments Attack Force," Aviation Week & Space Technology, Special Report on Tactical Air Command, February 6, 1978, p. 58.

(24) Betit, p. 96.

(25) See Colonel A. Rodin, "Struggle between Artillery and Antitank Weapons," Soviet Military Herald, May 1974; quoted in Philip A. Karber, "The Soviet Anti-Tank Debate," Survival, May-June 1976, p. 110.

(26) Frontovaya Aviatsiya (Frontal Aviation) may be provided assistance in its air defense mission by the PVO Strany (Voiska protivovozdushnoi oborony strany) whose major task is the defense of the Soviet Union and the direction of Warsaw Pact air capabilities. See Colin Grey, "Soviet Tactical Airpower," Air Force Magazine (Soviet Aerospace Almanac 1977), March 1977, pp. 6271.

(27) Goure, p. 50.

(28) The practice of numerous troop exercises and the experience of military operations in Indochina and the Middle East testify that, as a result of the mass introduction of helicopters, the combat capability of the land forces, especially their mobility and fire-power, sharply increases and considerable changes in the employment and tactics of their forces take place," Colonel M. Belov, "Helicopters and Land Force Tactics," Soviet Military Herald, December 1976, p. 22.

(29) According to one recent assessment of Soviet Frontal Aviation, "because of this modernization program and the advent of offensive airpower, . . . even without direct Soviet support, Warsaw Pact forces are now capable of dealing a severe blow to the Central Region with some 3,000 fighter/attack aircraft positioned in Europe." "Eastern Bloc Augments Attack Force," Aviation Week & Space Technology, February 6, 1978, pp. 59-60.

(30) The SU-19 can carry a payload of 6,000 pounds, can achieve ranges of up to 600 miles, and incorporates a laser rangefinder and terrain-avoidance radar. According to the Commander of Allied Forces Central Europe, General John W. Vogt, the SU-19 is a "third-generation fighter," and has "a range that covers all NATO bases in central Europe, the most vulnerable territory on the continent since it is without buffer zones." See Laurence Doty, "NATO Reshaping Tactical Air Posture," ibid., March 3, 1975, p. 12.

(31) The MiG-29 reportedly resembles a cross between the USAF F-15 Eagle and the Soviet MiG-25 Foxbat, with a thrust-to-weight ratio, when armed (having four air-to-air missiles and 50 percent internal fuel), exceeding 1:1 – comparable to the USAF F-16 and the USN F-18. "Its size, avionics and flight performance leave no doubts that it will succeed the aging MiG-21 Fishbed with its limited avionics, as the USSR's low and medium altitude air superiority fighter. . . .The MiG-29 could also be usefully deployed in the PVO Strany to provide a defense around the Soviet frontiers against cruise missiles."

Further observation of the MiG-29 has convinced NATO analysts that the primary mission of the MiG-29 will be to intercept cruise missiles. See "NATO Says MiG-29 Being Tested as Cruise Missile Killer," Defense/Space Daily, January 6, 1978, p. 18.

The T-58 is undergoing an extensive program of flight testing. This is a slow, low-flying, armored jet aircraft which is reported to have a large store capability (internal and external) for conventional gravity bombs and air-to-surface missiles, in addition to antitank guided missiles (ATGMs). See "International Defense Digest," International Defense Review, August 1977, p. 607.

(32) The Soviet Ground Control Intercept System is responsible for directing all ground and air operations.

(33) Wiener, p. 119.

(34) See, for example, Richard Pipes, "Why the Soviet Union Thinks It Could Fight and Win a Nuclear War," Commentary, July 1977, pp. 21-34.

(35) John Erickson, "Soviet Military Posture and Policy," in Richard Pipes, editor, Soviet Strategy in Europe (New York: Crane, Russak, for Stanford Research Institute, 1976), p. 174.

(36) See, for example, Grechko (p. 278): ". . . the threat of war involving the use of nuclear weapons has not been removed." See also, Colonel Vasilii

Yefimovich Savkin, The Basic Principles of Operational Art and Tactics (Moscow, 1972); translated by the United States Air Force, Soviet Military Thought Series, No. 1 (Washington, D.C.: GPO, 1974).

(37) From this, one cannot infer, however, that the Soviet Union is seeking to evolve a counterforce targeting strategy based on a "mirror-image" of the U.S. conception of such a strategy (which seeks to avoid employment against population centers) since many of the targets that have been designated in the military literature of the Soviet Union as high-value enemy targets are located in some of the largest cities of the NATO nations. Command posts, for example, are lucrative targets from the Soviet perspective. Most of the vital command functions of NATO are undertaken in facilities located in the urban centers of the German Federal Republic, or in Brussels and its environs.

(38) The SS-20 is a mobile, MIRVed intermediate-range ballistic missile, designed to augment (or perhaps replace) the older SS-4s and SS-5s. Capable of carrying three MIRVed warheads, each of which would have a payload of one mega on, the SS-20 could be given a range of 5,500 miles, or that equivalent to an ICBM, either by the addition of a third stage (i.e., the SS-16) or by "offloading" its MIRVs.

(39) According to one recent source, "One-sixth of Soviet land forces stationed in East Germany have been equipped with self-propelled artillery. . . ." Reportedly, the introduction of improved artillery began last year with the aim of reinforcing the six towed guns in each regiment with 18 self-propelled weapons. "Initially, one regiment in each division will receive the 18 SP guns, and once this has been achieved, the military authorities are thought to be planning to equip two regiments in each division with the new artillery." See "USSR: Substantial Progress Reported on Artillery Modernization," En Clair section, in Defense and Foreign Affairs Digest, No. 7, 1977, p. 32.

(40) "Soviet Sent 89 Subs Into Atlantic," New York Times, July 29, 1977.

(41) According to NATO Supreme Allied Commander Alexander Haig, "the great increases of recent years in Soviet strength, mobility, and firepower are creating a situation in which a Soviet attack without prior reinforcement is becoming for the Soviet Unon a more and more attractive option." Quoted by Lord Chalfont, in "The General Alert We Cannot Ignore," The Times (London), November 9, 1976.

(42) Grechko, pp. 147-148.

(43) The MiG-21 PFMA Fishbed-J is an air superiority/close air support aircraft, with a combat radius of 125 miles (if deployed with a minimum payload).

The MiG-21 SMT Fishbed-K is an air superiority/close air support aircraft which is similar in all respects to the MiG-21J, with the addition of an ECM capability.

The MiG-23 Flogger-B carries a 23mm two-barrel GSH-23 cannon and four infrared and radar homing AA-7 Apex and AA-8 Sphid air-to-air missiles.

(44) Wiener, p. 158.

(45) Possessing a high-speed and a high-altitude capability the MiG-25B is a theater reconnaissance aircraft which gives Soviet Frontal Aviation greater command flexibility in reconnaissance missions. The Soviet Union has deployed about twenty MiG-25Bs at Brieg in Silesia as well as a small contingent of its interceptor version. The MiG-25B has demonstrated more powerful engines and improved radar over its A variant. See, for example, "Insider's View of the MiG-25," Letter to the Editor by Major General George J. Keegan, Jr., USAF (Ret.), Christian Science Monitor, February 1, 1977.

(46) Recent exercises of Soviet-Warsaw Pact forces, including the Karpathy military maneuvers of July 1977, revealed a greater reliance on helicopters and naval craft to insert troops in the enemy's rear areas. See, for example, "Southern Forces Take Offensive in Carpathian Exercises," FBIS, Soviet Union, July 15, 1977, pp. V1-V2; and "Carpathian Military Maneuvers Continue," ibid., July 14, 1977, p. V1.

(47) Wiener, p. 162. The dropping of ionized foil strips in order to jam enemy radars was recently practiced by Soviet Bear reconnaissance aircraft against American naval ships, including those of the Spruance class, operating off the Eastern coast of the United States. See "Pentagon Aides Say Soviet Planes Tried to Jam U.S. Radars," New York Times, October 15, 1977.

(48) FM 30-40 Handbook on Soviet Ground Forces – 1975, prepared by the Department of the Army (Washington D.C.: GPO, 1975), section 5, p. 23.

(49) See Bernard Weinraub, "NATO Fears Soviet Gas Warfare," New York Times, May 17, 1977.

(50) This point is discussed in depth in C.N. Donelly "Soviet Techniques for Combat in Built-up Areas," International Defense Review, April 1977, pp. 238-242.

(51) "Soviet military doctrine allows for the crossing of a narrow water obstacle during the attack every 5-10km, a medium-sized water obstacle every 25 to 30km, and a major water obstacle every 80 to 100km in a war fought in the European theater of operations." Wiener, p. 144.

(52) Ibid.

(53) The Egyptian crossing of the Suez Canal in 1973 was accompanied by barrages of Soviet antiaircraft rockets.

(54) "The chief function of engineer units in the Soviet ground forces is to help combat units keep up the speed of advance by facilitating movement across or around obstacles." (Handbook on Soviet Ground Forces, section 6, p.

73.) "Engineer troops are assigned down through regimental level in all Soviet divisions, and platoons are sometimes detailed to battalions for specific operations." Ibid., section 6, p. 75.

(55) Each of the five Soviet ground armies in East Germany is armed with some 1,000 surface-to-air missiles and 1,000 antiaircraft gun systems. In recent years, "a massive increase in surface-to-air and anti-aircraft systems for ground divisions in the Warsaw Pact area, particularly a low-level air-defense capability, leads officials here to believe that initially the USSR will resort to air defense of the battle area using ground forces alone. The Soviet Union would, under this concept, assume that rear areas would be defended by the non-Soviet Pact fighters and other air defense systems, freeing Soviet airpower for an offensive role." See Clarence A. Robinson, Jr., "Increasing Soviet Offensive Threat Spurs Stronger Europe Air Arm," Aviation Week & Space Technology, August 1, 1977, p. 46.

(56) According to Belgian General Robert Close, this route would be the most direct way of reaching the Ruhr region. Moreover, it is suitable for armored formations and extends for 300 kilometers. The Weser river provides the only water obstacle that must be overcome. See Robert Close, "The Feasibility of a Surprise Attack Against Western Europe" (A Report to NATO Officials), unpublished report, Chapter II, p. 27.

(57) Erickson, "The Ground Forces in Soviet Military Policy," p. 74.

(58) Soviet naval forces are divided into four fleets: (1) The Northern Red Banner Fleet, with headquarters at Severomorsk (also called the Arctic or Polar Fleet), composed of three combat groups and a marine brigade. (2) The Baltic Red Banner Fleet (also called the East Sea Fleet). Comprising about 140,000 men, this is the largest unit in the Soviet Navy. Fleet headquarters is located in Baltisk, with naval air units deployed in Kaliningrad. (3) The Black Sea Red Banner Fleet, with headquarters located in Sevastopol and one combat group (the "Third Eskadra") permanently on station in the Mediterranean Sea. (4) The Pacific Red Banner Fleet (also called the Far East Fleet), is headquartered at Vladivostok. This fleet is divided further into the Northern Battle Group and the Southern Battle Group.

In addition, Soviet naval fleets are reinforced by four squadrons – the Danube Squadron, with its flagship at Latakia, Syria; the Asov Squadron, headquartered at Kertsch; the Caspian Squadron, colocated at Astrakan and Baku; and the Amur Squadron with headquarters at Khabarovsk.

(59) These include "a standing force of two motorized rifle divisions deployed within the Kola Peninsula and emplaced between the Murmansk railway and the Norwegian border. Though of standard Soviet establishments (a motorized rifle division in its modern format with an establishment of 13,000 men and a heavier complement of armor), these northern divisions hold a higher number of amphibious vehicles and transport for movement across snow, plus engineer, artillery and missile support." John Erickson, "The Northern Theater: Soviet Capabilities and Concepts," Strategic Review, Summer 1976, p. 70.

(60) Don Cook, "Massive Soviet Base Built During the Years of Detente," Los Angeles Times, January 24, 1977.

(61) In early December 1977, Soviet forces were observed by NATO in tests of a "large, high-speed hovercraft capable of carrying both infantry and tanks. . . The Soviet hovercraft, if deployed in substantial numbers, could affect the NATO position in the Baltic. Intelligence, working from photographs, estimates that the vessel can carry either 400 naval infantry, the Warsaw Pact's designation for marines, or a mixed force of infantry and tanks." Drew Middleton, "Haig Says New Soviet Hovercraft and Tank Raise Risk of Nuclear War," New York Times, December 8, 1977.

(62) The presence of uncovered flanks "creates conditions for carrying out daring envelopments, deep turning movements, lightning appearances on the enemy's flanks or in the rear, and for delivering suprise and decisive blows from different directions." Lieutenant-General V. Reznechenko, "The Role of Tactics in Modern War," Soviet Military Review, September 9, 1976, p. 10.

(63) See Drew Middleton, "Military Strategy of New Importance in North Norway Near Soviet," New York Times, June 20, 1977.

(64) Erickson suggests ("The Northern Theater. . . .," pp. 74-76) that the Soviet Vesna/Okean worldwide maneuvers of 1975 embodied "some rehearsal of attack procedures on Western shipping, particularly reinforcement for NATO and essential supply."

In July 1977, 89 Soviet submarines – more than a quarter of the Soviet Navy's 325-boat Northern Fleet – swept into the Norwegian Sea and the Atlantic Ocean. Accompanying the submarines was a "large force of surface ships, including the aircraft carrier Kiev. Long-range airplanes, including some of the 400 supersonic bombers designated Backfire that the Russians now operate, flew over the maneuvering fleet from their bases in the Murmansk. . . .American and British submarines that usually trail Soviet submarines were unable to cope with the rush and had to resort to other, less effective means to keep track of many of the boats." See "Soviet Sent 89 Subs Into Atlantic," New York Times, July 29, 1977.

(65) In Svalbard, the Soviet Union is engaged in intensive drilling operations, despite the fact that possession of the Svalbard archipelago has been a source of controversy between the USSR and Norway. "Spitzbergen Issue Defused," The Guardian (Manchester), January 4, 1976.

In recent years, Norwegian Foreign Minister Karl Drydenbund "has sharply denied press rumors that the Soviet Union is putting pressure on Norway to demilitarize the northern border region. Such an action would weaken NATO's position in a strategically important area." Colonel John H. Roush, Jr., "Norway's Significance from a Military Point of View," Military Review, July 1975, p. 21.

(66) John Erickson emphasizes this point in "The Northern Theater. . . ." op. cit.

(67) Drew Middleton, "NATO Hears Soviet Canal is Enlarged for Naval Use," New York Times, October 24, 1974.

(68) The vulnerability of NATO airfields, especially runways, is becoming one of the major problems confronting the Alliance today. According to U.S. General Richard H. Ellis, former Commander, Allied Forces Central Europe, and currently Commander, U.S. Strategic Air Command, "The solution is to develop a new generation V/STOL aircraft. It will take five years to develop the engine technology needed for such a fighter. We should do that work now and not decide on the types of aircraft until later. There may be more than one type available after the propulsion is perfected; that is the secret." Quoted in Robinson, "Increasing Soviet Threat Spurs Stronger Europe Air Arm," p. 46.

(69) Erickson, "The Northern Theater. . .," p. 80. op. cit.

(70) See, for example, "4 Soviet Task Forces in Pacific Part of Global Naval Exercises," New York Times, April 19, 1975, and "Vast Soviet Naval Exercise Raises Urgent Questions for West," ibid., April 28, 1975.

(71) According to a recent report, "The Soviet Union has reportedly asked the Spanish Government for a nonmilitary port for its merchant fleet at Algeciras, Spain, which is just across the bay from the NATO base on British Gibraltar." "Soviets Want Port Near Gibraltar," Defense/Space Daily, December 6, 1977.

(72) The U.S. Sixth Fleet in general has a complement of between 40 and 45 ships, including the flagship, a cruiser, two aircraft carrier task forces, each having its own tactical air wing of about 90 aircraft and six escort ships. In addition, an amphibious assault task group of six vessels with a Marine battalion, several submarines, miscellaneous escort ships not attached to the carrier or amphibious task group, and several auxiliary vessels complement the Fleet.

(73) In its 1975 Defence White Paper, the British government "decided that it cannot in future commit British Maritime forces to the Mediterranean in support of NATO. After 1976, no destroyers, frigates or coastal minesweepers will be earmarked for assignment (in the Mediterranean) and between 1977 and 1979 the Royal Air Force Nimrods and Canberras at present committed to NATO there will be withdrawn. In peacetime HM Ships will, however, visit the Mediterranean from time to time and will continue to participate in exercises there with our NATO allies." Quoted in David Fairhall, "Defense Economies Anger NATO," The Guardian (Manchester), March 29, 1975.

(74) This assumes, of course, that France elects to oppose actively the Soviet military campaign against Western Europe. If, for example, the Socialist-Communist coalition were to come to power, France might adopt a neutral stance in the event of a conflict between NATO and the Warsaw Pact. In general, the PSF supports the view of its leader, Francois Mitterand, who

espouses "general disarmament, worldwide suppression of nuclear weapons and dissolution of blocs." See Flora Lewis, "Atom Defense a Big Issue for French Leftist Alliance," New York Times, August 5, 1977.

(75) In an interview in December 1977, General Haig was reported to have warned, "that an imbalance between the West and the Soviet bloc in conventional weapons 'inevitably' increased the prospect of an earlier employment of nuclear weapons to halt any Soviet attack." Drew Middleton, New York Times, December 8, 1977.

(76) Speculation among Western military analysts has increased in recent months over the possibility that the Soviets are developing a new generation, supersonic-capable, low-altitude heavy bomber, which is not a variant of the Backfire as we know it today. Although the information is scant, reference has been made to the possibility of a joint Sukhoi-Tupolev bomber design. See for example, Jane's All the World Aircraft, (London: Jane's Yearbooks, 1976), pp. 515-516.

(77) The British Army of the Rhine (BAOR) consists of 55,000 men assigned to the first (British) Corps – I(BR) Corps – which forms a part of the Northern Army Group (NORTHAG). The reorganization of the I(BR) Corps, begun in 1976, is scheduled for completion by 1979. When completed, the BAOR will consist of four "new-style armoured divisions, each rather smaller than the three which exist at present, an artillery division, and a new formation (the 5th Field Force) which will take over the reinforcing role of the 39th Infantry Brigade. The reorganized infantry and armoured battle groups will contain four company-size subunits of armour and infantry, and specialist and support functions will be concentrated." Statement on The Defense Estimates 1977, presented to Parliament by the Secretary of State for Defence by Command of Her Majesty (London: Her Majesty's Stationery Office, February 1977), Command #6735, pp. 22-30. France, according to Rapport sur la programmations des depenses militaire et des equipments des forces armées pour la periode 1977-1982 (Paris: Government of France, 1976), plans to cut its Army forces stationed in West Germany by about 25 percent.

(78) See White Paper 1975/1976, The Security of the Federal Republic of Germany and the Development of the Federal Armed Forces (Bonn: Federal Ministry of Defense 1976), p. 80.

(79) Ibid., p. 90.

(80) U.S. Army Chief of Staff Bernard Rogers disclosed that "equipment and manpower from Army units in the United States will be sent overseas to strengthen Western Europe's defenses against any huge, short-warning Soviet ground attack." "Army 'Sacrifices' Some Ground Units to Help Europe," Washington Post, October 19, 1977.

(81) The NATO-wide procurement of an airborne early warning system such as the Boeing E-3A AWACS would provide the Alliance with realtime intel-

ligence over an area of 250,000 square miles. Because of a remarkable development in U.S. miniaturization and computer technologies, the Boeing AWACS is capable of tracking simultaneously up to 2,000 targets. Beyond this, the AWACS is being fitted with a capability for use over the seas in order to facilitate detection and tracking of enemy surface vessels. Although a platform like the AWACS would undoubtedly be designated a high priority target by enemy forces because of its capability for resolution, its ability to stand off at great distances renders it less vulnerable to enemy interdiction than had originally been assumed.

Based upon the incorporation of advanced optics – perhaps an outgrowth of satellite or electron microscope technologies – AWACS could provide the basis for resolution of NATO's forward observer problem.

(82) For use against point and hardened targets, the Soviet Union reportedly has developed a new generation air-to-surface missile, ASX, which has a range of up to 30 miles and has a minimum launch altitude of 500 feet and which uses electrooptical homing guidance with a data link for electrooptical command.

(83) "A-10 Tactics: Hard, Low Altitude Maneuvering on Friendly Side of FEBA," Aerospace Daily, May 24, 1977, p. 132. According to Lt. General Alton D.Slay, Deputy Chief of Staff for Air Force R&D, "other weapons such as iron bombs and Rockeye guided munitions, would not be as effective because they would force the plane to be much closer to its targets. In a typical GAU-8 or Maverick attack . . . the A-10 approaches the Forward Edge of the Battle Area (FEBA) at an extremely low altitude, pops up to 300 or 400 feet to acquire its target – for instance, a simple tank in a charging line – fires, and turns sharply away at low altitude to fly behind terrain where the pilot decides whether to reattack."

(84) See U.S. Congress, Senate Committee on Armed Services, Hearings, Fiscal Year 1978 Authorization for Military Procurement, Research and Development, and Active Duty, Selected Reserve and Civilian Personnel Strengths: Part 9, Research and Development, 95th Cong., 1st sess., especially the testimony of March 29, 1977 (Washington, D.C.: GPO, 1977), p. 6180.

(85) Included in NATO's force improvement programs is the deployment of the new generation U.S. tubular-launched, optically-tracked, wire-guided, heavy antitank system (TOW) which can be fired from aircraft or on the ground. With a speed/range capability of 1,000 kilometers per hour, TOW is most effective when operating against a target 3,000 meters away. However, as enemy tanks close in on defensive positions, TOW, because of its line of sight requirement (for target designation), is less effective against the tank which can fire faster. In this situation, the tank itself, supported by artillery batteries, offers a more cost/effective means of antitank defense. This will have even greater validity with the deployment by the United States and West Germany of their respective new-technology main battle tanks, the XM-1 and Leopard II. See, for example, prepared answers to questions submitted by

Senator McIntyre, in U.S. Congress, Senate, Committee on Armed Services, Hearings, Fiscal Year 1978 Authorization, op. cit. March 8, 1977, pp. 5941-5942.

(86) According to the testimony of Edward A. Miller, Assistant Secretary of the Army for Research and Development, the Army's advanced assault helicopter, carrying 16 Hellfire (Copperhead CLGP) missiles, could be deployed in a defense suppression role, greatly surpassing the capability of the existing Army Cobra attack helicopter which can deploy only three such missiles. Ibid., p. 5336.

There is under development in the United States a new helicopter, which by virtue of advanced engine and rotor technologies may be capable of greater speeds and maneuverability than heretofore had been conceived for such aircraft. This development would have important applications for the European theater, especially in the pursuit of antitank and close air support missions.

(87) The development of V/STOL aircraft for deployment in Western Europe is one of the most critical needs confronting the United States and its NATO allies. V/STOL platforms would be cost effective, for example, in the service of the U.S. Marines, a complement of which could be deployed to Europe for use against enemy operations in the Northern Theater. The Air Force could deploy V/STOL aircraft in close air support along the Central Front, while naval forces could utilize such aircraft in an ASW or antiship role, as does the Soviet Union. V/STOL aircraft can operate from aircraft carriers or from makeshift runways in the event that Allied airbases have been interdicted. For these reasons, we conclude that Secretary of Defense Harold Brown's tentative program decision memorandum for fiscal 1979 to reduce "the pace and scope of the Navy's effort to develop a V/STOL aircraft force," is a mistake. "Washington Roundup – Defense Decisions," Aviation Week & Space Technology, August 22, 1977, p. 11.

(88) It has been suggested by Pentagon officials, and we think it worthwhile, that the U.S. infantry divisions be restructured to include eight gun batteries, with a four-battery battalion.

(89) Charles Messenger, The Blitzkrieg Story (New York: Charles Scribner's Sons, 1976), p. 239.

(90) Already the United States has decided to station a brigade at Garlstedt, just south of Bremerhaven in North Germany. "This brigade will be used to plan and test movement and support arrangements to permit flexible use of U.S. reinforcements in the area. This brigade will also plan and train with British and German forces in that area. Moreover, a U.S. mechanized brigade will move into Garlstedt in late 1978." "Short-Term Initiatives Readied by NATO," Aviation Week & Space Technology, August 15, 1977, p. 54.

"The Federal Republic of Germany is working on facilities to transfer another brigade already deployed in Europe to Northern Germany to reinforce that area in a realignment of forces." Clarence A. Robinson, Jr., "Conventional Force Build-Up Emphasized," ibid., p. 45.

(91) This assumes that the United States is unwilling to raise the total number of U.S. troops deployed on the European continent. It also assumes that reinforcement by air and/or sea from the United States is impossible within the time constraints dictated by enemy offensive operations.

(92) U.S. and West German corps are already participating in joint training exercises which include air defense, mining and countermining operations. A logical extension of these programs would be field maneuvers in which West German reinforcement troops manned U.S. equipment that had been prepositioned in Europe.

(93) U.S. stockpiles of TOW, for example, were depleted by 90 percent during the resupply of Israel. "The Israelis, who also received up to 50 percent of U.S. stockpiles of other types of ammunition, now say stocks in Israel were not as low as first thought. A computer error in the pipeline inventory from domestic suppliers is blamed for the miscalculation." "Industry Observer," Aviation Week & Space Technology, September 16, 1974, p. 9.

(94) A detailed examination of new technologies for nonnuclear warfare and their military impacts is found in Geoffrey Kemp, Robert L. Pfaltzgraff, Jr., and Uri Ra'anan, editors, The Other Arms Race: New Technologies and Non-Nuclear Conflict (Lexington, Mass: D.C. Heath and Company, Lexington Books, 1975).

(95) It has been estimated that if, for example, support maintenance of a mobile force can be delayed by one hour by interdiction, total enemy movement can be checked by as much as three hours. "Modernization of Luftwaffe to Counter Soviet Shift," Aviation Week & Space Technology, March 3, 1975, pp. 13-14.

(96) Rear-area security is a high priority of Soviet strategy since it means, in essence, the uninterrupted and complete resupply of front-line troops.

(97) The Warsaw Pact will face similar constraints with regard to its tactical airpower as time goes on, assuming that NATO members are willing to invest in weapons systems designed to respond to the evolving Soviet offensive threat by air.

(98) Ground-launched cruise missiles are being considered, along with Pershing II ballistic missiles, as cost-effective substitutes for QRA aircraft employed against fixed targets, deep to the enemy's rear. According to published reports of a closed session of the Senate Armed Services Committee, which is looking into this option, Dr. John Walsh, formerly the Defense Department's Director of Strategic Studies, in Defense, Development, Research and Engineering (DDR&E), "did a comparison of F-16 vs GLCM, concluding that the cost of one unit equipped cruise missile would be $2.3 million and that of one F-16, $16.9 million, including operation and support. On a ten-year cost comparison basis, 300 F-16s would cost $5.1 billion vs. $700 million for 300 GLCMs." Aerospace Daily, June 21, 1977, p. 285.

(99) "Along the Western border of the Soviet Union, in East Germany, Poland and Czechoslovakia, are now some 220 operational military airfields. In addition, there are about 140 airfields that are used for flight schools and training units; these fields are large enough to accommodate fighter bombers. The infrastructure in Bulgaria, Romania and Hungary is less solid. Not all of their airfields are constantly manned." Weiner, p. 163.

(100) In this context, it is instructive to recall the efforts of the Soviet Union in the early 1970s to involve U.S. and Japanese firms in the development of the Tyumen oil and natural gas fields. Located in the eastern, Asian portions of the Soviet Union, the sizeable energy reserves of Tyumen could provide the basis for a Warsaw Pact fuel supply network in support of offensive operations against Western Europe.

(101) A detailed analysis of the potential employment modes for the cruise missile are found in Robert L. Pfaltzgraff, Jr., and Jacquelyn K. Davis, The Cruise Missile: Bargaining Chip or Defense Bargain? (Cambridge, Mass: Institute for Foreign Policy Analysis, 1977).

(102) Fuel air explosives are composed of volatile hydrocarbons which do not require oxygen either for spontaneous combustion or for burning. They contain, by themselves, a high proportion of oxygen which, upon contact with a combustible material, causes a violent reaction, even in an atmosphere of moisture at "ambient" temperatures. See Georg Johannsohn, "Fuel Air Explosives Revolutionize Conventional Warfare," International Defense Review, December 1976, pp. 992-996.

(103) Ibid., p. 995.

(104) Captor is an encapsulated torpedo which can be dropped by submarines, surface ships or long-range bombers and is designed to strike enemy submarines from the bottom of the sea. "Once deployed, it could seriously impede the movement of Russian submarines at the points through which they must move to reach the Atlantic and Pacific Oceans and the Mediterranean Sea." They operate by lying dormant until their detection devices are activated by hostile submarines whose engine sounds they are progammed to pick up and to differentiate from friendly engine sounds. In a conventional mode, Captor is based on the technology of the Mark 48 torpedo, which has a range of 25 miles and a speed of more than 50 miles per hour. "Armed with a nuclear warhead (Captor) could destroy a hostile submarine within two miles of the point of detonation." See Drew Middleton, "U.S. and Soviet Expanding Antisubmarine Warfare," New York Times, May 26, 1976.

(105) "The battery destroys ATGMs," Voyennyye Vestnik, August 1974; reprinted in Edward B. Atkeson, "Precision Guided Munitions: Implications for Detente," in National Security and Detente (New York: Thomas Y. Crowell, 1976), p. 137.

(106) In a press conference held in November 1977, Paul H. Nitze, former U.S.

Assistant Secretary of Defense for International Security Affairs, and one of the members of the U.S. delegation to SALT I, disclosed the details of the SALT II agreement under consideration by the United States and the Soviet Union. Nitze's remarks have been reprinted in full in Soviet Aerospace (November 7, 1977, pp. 65-71, and November 14, 1977, pp. 79-80).

(107) In accordance with this view is Manfred Wörner, Chairman of the Defense Committee in the Bundestag of the Federal Republic of Germany and Speaker on defense matters in the parliamentary delegation of the Christian Democratic Union and its Bavarian sister party, the Christian Social Union. In his article, "NATO Defenses and Tactical Nuclear Weapons" (Strategic Review, Fall 1977, p. 17), Wörner concludes that "A nuclear-armed opponent cannot be countervailed with purely conventional capabilities – neither militarily nor politically nor psychologically."

(108) Unlike many military analysts in the West, those of the Soviet Union readily concede the importance of nuclear weapons for use in the theater. See, for example, Reznichenko (pp. 9-10): "Nuclear weapons have radically changed the context of modern all-arms combat for a new element has appeared – a nuclear attack. It makes it possible to inflict almost instantaneously on the enemy such heavy losses that they can sharply change the correlation of the sides' forces and force him to give up one type of combat action, for example, an offensive or a meeting engagement, and pass over to another type – the defensive. A nuclear attack can create conditions for rapidly overcoming enemy resistance and passing from the defensive to the offensive."

(109) Nuclear fission, discovered in the late 1930s by Otto Hahn and Fritz Strassman, is the splitting of a nucleus. Nuclear fusion, the discovery of Hans Bethe (1939), is the union of two nuclei to form a heavier nucleus. See, for example, S.T. Cohen, "Enhanced Radiation Warheads: Setting the Record Straight," Strategic Review, Winter 1978, pp. 9-17.

(110) As presently configured, the Alliance's tactical nuclear weapons "are concentrated in locations and units that are presumably well known to the Soviet Union. . . .The current disposition of these weapons opens them to Soviet attack and destruction." See Drew Middleton, "NATO's Need to Redeploy Nuclear Force," New York Times, February 21, 1977.

(111) A repeated theme found in Soviet military literature emphasizes the importance of preempting NATO's nuclear weapons. The following passage by Reznichenko (p. 11) is illustrative: "In a meeting engagement the significance of delivering preventive nuclear and fire blows with subsequent routing of the enemy both by maneuvering on the flanks and in the rear and by a frontal blow has also increased." Soviet military analyst Colonel A.A. Sidorenko emphasizes this point by stating: "One could not even consider going on the offensive without full knowledge of the location of an enemy's nuclear system." A.A. Sidorenko, The Offensive (A Soviet View) (Moscow, 1970), translated under the auspices of the United States Air Force, Soviet Military

Thought Series, No. 1 (Washington, D.C.: GPO, 1974), pp. 132-133.

(112) In addition, because Lance was designed to have a dual-capability, it is, in effect, a compromise system for optimal performance in neither the nuclear nor the conventional role.

(113) See, for example, Prepared Statement of George H. Heilmeier, Director, Defense Advance Research Projects Agency (DARPA), in U.S. Congress, Fiscal Year 1978 Authorization. . ., Part 9. . ., Hearings, pp. 6177-6322, esp. pp. 6313-6314.

(114) The Federal Republic of Germany may opt to use its own electronics, called MACs, which is not interoperable with either the British Electronic Counter Measures Resistant Communications System or the U.S. JTIDS. See David Fairhall, "Britain Rebuilding Air Defenses," The Guardian (Manchester), July 10, 1977.

(115) Ibid. "The RAF's assessment is based on three main facts: that Soviet reconnaissance bombers (nowadays mainly propeller driven Bears but before long probably Backfires) regularly penetrate the UK Air Defense Region to probe the radar cover and test the response of RAF interceptors from bases like Leuchars; that unless a major European war started without warning, about 40 percent of NATO's combat aircraft strength would probably be assembled in the UK, on RAF and USAF bases mainly in Eastern England; that Soviet as well as NATO military doctrine now seems to assume that an East-West conflict would initially be confined to conventional weapons. . . .Many of the (potential) targets (in the UK for Soviet attack), particularly the airfields, are in Eastern England. But Soviet strikes against them would not necessarily come from the East. If the Backfires now in service with the Soviet Air Force and Navy were refueled in the air, they have the range to loop out into the Atlantic and attack from the West – hence, the recent additions to our radar coverage on that side of the country."

(116) The Multi-Role Combat Aircraft (MRCA) Tornado has been built by a three-nation European consortium of Britain, Italy and the Federal Republic of Germany. A swing-wing aircraft, the MRCA has a thrust of 14,900 pounds at takeoff and has registered speeds of Mach 1.5.

(117) The issue relates to the choice of the FRG Leopard II or the U.S. Chrysler XM-1, and to a lesser extent the British Chieftain, as the Alliance's choice for replacement of older systems.

# III

# U.S.-European Technological Collaboration— The Need for an Atlantic Framework

# 6 Defense Technology and the Atlantic Alliance— The Promises and Realities of European Collaboration

Frank T. J. Bray
Michael Moodie

While most Europeans no longer take seriously the notion of a meaningful Europeanization of nuclear and/or conventional forces, the concept of a Europeanized defense procurement system still fires the imagination. To a large degree it is viewed as a panacea to many of the economic and technological problems facing Europe's more sophisticated defense industries. Support for Europeanizing defense procurement has been spurred, at the same time, by resentment of American domination of the conventional arms market in Europe and in the world generally.

To date, Europeanization of defense procurement has, for the most part, taken the form of collaboration, i.e., the bilateral or multilateral development and production of specific weapons systems. Future European cooperation is likely to be of a similar nature. This chapter examines the prospects for greater Europeanization of Europe's defense from the perspective of collaboration in defense procurement. Special emphasis is placed on the relationship of the United States with any Europeanized defense procurement system. In fact, the central thesis is that whatever progress is made toward greater cooperation in West European defense procurement, a role for the United States will be essential.

A study of this nature is warranted for several reasons. First, technology has been the dynamic generator of NATO's defense posture – the force that has enabled the Alliance to meet its twin requirements of defense and deterrence over three postwar decades. Yet, progressively since the early 1960s when the nations of Western Europe recovered from war and began to build sophisticated scientific and technological establishments of their own, technology also has become a divisive force in the Alliance. While disputes over technology could be as damaging to NATO in the long term as differences over the status of Portugal, troop levels or the Cyprus issue, they have been often overlooked not only by the media but by many NATO analysts as well.

Second, when the United States has considered NATO procurement, it has been largely in the context of West European purchases of U.S. weapon systems to offset American balance of payments deficits. It is important that the United States take a closer look at Europeanization of defense procurement not only for its narrow economic impact on available markets in Europe for American products, but also for its more general implications for political and economic relations within the Alliance.

Third, the need to assess prospects for greater cooperation in defense procurement in Europe has heightened considerably in the wake of the Callaghan Report(1) which has impacted widely on attitudes toward procurement on both sides of the Atlantic. This chapter, which is based in large part on interviews with key governmental and industrial decision makers as well as members of the intellectual defense community in the United States and Western Europe, explores these changes in attitudes as well as their impact on the prospects for and problems of increased collaboration.

Finally, the subject matter has been made more prominent by key developments in the sphere of NATO defense procurement: the British, West Germans and Italians have taken an important step by giving the go-ahead to the production of their jointly developed Tornado combat aircraft;(2) the decision regarding procurement of combat aircraft for the smaller NATO countries has been made in favor of the American F-16; the United States has announced its two-way street policy in procurement decisions. These and other developments could have serious ramifications in the matter of increased European collaboration in the development and production of weapons systems and other defense-related equipment.

The issue of joint development and production of weapon systems will be confronted by NATO frequently in the years ahead. Western Europe and the United States are facing, in the immediate time frame, important procurement decisions that could have repercussions in the Atlantic Alliance for decades. This chapter will seek to provide an assessment of the salient issues that must be addressed in making these decisions and to provide options for promoting collaboration on a transatlantic basis. Its goal is to contribute more generally to a transatlantic dialogue which, in the final analysis, is essential for laying the foundations for a rational long-term NATO strategy.

## MOTIVATIONS FOR EUROPEAN COLLABORATION

Over the last fifteen years the major countries of Western Europe have been gravitating increasingly toward collaboration in the development and production of high-technology goods. Major collaborative efforts have been undertaken by European countries, for example, in civilian aircraft such as the Concorde (Britain and France) and the A-300B (France, West Germany, the Netherlands and Britain). In addition, several permanent international organizations have been established to manage collaborative efforts in missiles (European Space Agency – ESA), satellite communications (Intelstat), space exploration (Euronaut), molecular biology (European Molecular Biology Organization – EMBO), and atomic energy (European Atomic Energy Community – EURATOM; European Council for Nuclear Research – CERN).

Collaboration in Europe, however, has been most evident in the development and production of military aircraft such as the Jaguar (Britain and

France) and the Tornado (Britain, West Germany and Italy). Britain has not developed a combat aircraft independently since the Harrier program. In fact, the era of the nationally produced European combat aircraft may have been cut short in the face of the inability of France's Mirage to compete successfully with the American F-16 in the "arms deal of the century." Forces are also at work pushing for greater collaboration among European countries in missiles, tanks and other sophisticated conventional armaments.

In Europe, the importance attached to collaboration was evidenced in 1972 when members of NATO's Eurogroup agreed to a set of principles aimed at fostering greater collaboration in defense procurement. Among other things, these nations consented to "cooperate in identifying areas where collaboration seems especially important or promising" and to "approach each other when preparing planning requirements to determine whether other members of NATO's Eurogroup have the same or similar intention." Most importantly, each Eurogroup member agreed in principle not to formalize its equipment requirements before that "country has satisfied itself that any substantial possibilities of harmonizing have been exploited."(3) Clearly the goal is to make collaborative development and program management an integral part of the procurement decision-making processes of the Eurogroup members.

## THE PROMISES OF COLLABORATION

A wide variety of incentives can be cited to explain European enthusiasm for collaboration in weapons development and production. Advocates of collaboration have argued that it would permit European nations, by pooling resources, to accomplish technological feats that would be beyond the capacity of any single state. Still others in Europe have pointed to the savings that could be wrested by eliminating wasteful R&D duplication among the various states. In the defense sector alone, waste from duplication of research and production amounts to an estimated $2.95 billion per year.(4) Still others foresee technological collaboration fostering, in the long run, a national division of labor within certain European industries. There is also the political incentive: the notion that technological collaboration represents perhaps the most promising road toward the goal of political unification of Western Europe.

A reading of British, French, and West German press and parliamentary debates, however, supports the conclusion that technological cooperation in Europe generally has been supported in the past, and continues to be supported today, for more narrow economic and political reasons. To a large degree European interest in collaboration is stimulated by the exigencies of modern weapons development, especially the phenomenal increase in the sophistication of weapons systems. Increasing sophistication has been accompanied by a commensurate rise in cost. The F-111, for example, cost approximately 320 times more to produce than the F-51; the cost of an F-5 is seven times that of the F-47.(5)

By and large, the escalation in weapons costs can be tied to the larger research and development (R&D) input needed to develop each succeeding generation of weapons. A relatively simple World War II bomber such as the

Halifax, for example, took only 8,320 design weeks to develop. Today it is not uncommon for a military aircraft to require 200,000 design weeks. Not only are modern weapons more costly, but they take longer to develop, thus compounding the task of projecting the given system's likely effective life span in the face of possible parallel or counter developments by the potential enemy. Defense industries are, accordingly, faced with a dilemma: To remain competitive they must cut costs, while at the same time they must expand R&D capacity to cut lead-times. As a result, they find themselves ever more dependent on a continuous flow of government contracts in order to sustain their expanded R&D capabilities.

Such pressures are particularly intense among European defense industries which cannot aspire to the economies of scale enjoyed by their American counterparts or to the export advantages that economies of scale bring to U.S. armaments industries. European countries sometimes have been forced to rely on additional procurement to fill capacity in an industry during slack periods. For example, on occasion the British government in effect has subsidized the aircraft industry through projects whose need was questionable – such as the Anglo-French variable geometry fighter project and the TSR-2 – only to cancel them when more essential projects were conceived. In the shipbuilding and ordnance industries, contract support sometimes is extended to marginal or inefficient facilities because of the economic repercussions their closing or rationalization would have on specific geographic regions of Britain.

Regardless of the form, however, subsidization has proven at best a stopgap solution to the problems posed by surplus capacity and scale. In many cases, it means simply a postponement of painful decisions and their economic consequences. The cancellation of the TSR-2, P1154, and HS681 projects in 1965, for example, resulted in the redundancy of 8,000 British aerospace employees.(6) Collaboration, and the sharing of total costs offers the potential for reducing R&D and production expense as well as for easing the problems of surplus capacity by providing contracts for weapons that individual governments would be hard pressed to finance unilaterally. This is attractive to political and military leaders faced with tightening defense budgets and public criticism of excessive national defense spending. At the same time, collaboration gives national high technology defense industries an opportunity to stay in business by providing contracts, widening markets and utilizing excess capacity.

Collaboration holds out more subtle political and economic advantages as well. It provides Britain, for example, with a way of demonstrating its desire to become more involved in Europe. This was especially important during the 1960s when Britain was trying to allay European misgivings about its efforts to join the EEC. In addition, to the extent that partners in collaborative efforts become locked in, or committed, to fulfill their parts of an agreement, collaboration offers both the military and industry a hedge or guarantee against the sudden withdrawal of government support from an ongoing project.(7) This is not to say that there is necessarily a direct relationship between collaboration and project stability. Collaboration, however, does subject government officials to international pressures to continue a project that are absent when R&D is being carried out on a purely national level – or at least it enables officials to cite such pressures to keep the project going. It is generally recognized, for example, that French political pressures and heavy penalties for cancellation worked into the original contract kept the British government from withdrawing its support from the Concorde project.

Collaboration offers a variety of incentives, not only to Great Britain, but to the major continental countries as well. Theoretically, France could apply the cost savings in conventional weapons systems wrought from collaboration to the development of the French nuclear force de dissuasion. For West Germany, collaboration offers the opportunity to step up military R&D programs with less chance of criticism from its Western neighbors, who are always apprehensive of unilateral West German military efforts. It also presents the FRG with a convenient vehicle for sidestepping official government regulations restricting arms exports to non-NATO members:

> From the point of view of the FRG's arms producing industry – and possibly also of the federal government – a most attractive side effect (of collaboration) is that the responsibility for export is blurred and, further, that all of the FRG's partners in joint ventures pursue far more permissive policies toward transferring weapons to nations outside NATO. Thus, it becomes possible to cash in on the revenues from the export of weapons, which in part have been designed and built in the FRG but have been sold and exported by some other nation without the West German government ever becoming involved.(8)

Finally, there is a purely military rationale for collaboration. Intensified intra-European cooperation could lead to greater standardization of weapons systems and other equipment, which would help to alleviate the wasteful costs of duplicate R&D efforts, and increase the military effectiveness of NATO's forces. General Andrew Goodpaster, Supreme Allied Commander Europe until December 1974, estimated that NATO loses between 30 and 50 percent of its potential capability through lack of standardization.(9)

The penalties imposed on the military effectiveness of NATO forces by a lack of standardization are illustrated by the ACE (Allied Command Europe) Mobile Force – AMF. This force, to which seven member nations contribute, is meant to symbolize the cohesiveness of the Alliance. However, its weapons inventory includes seven different types of combat aircraft, six different recoilless rifles, four wire-guided antitank weapons, and three types each of mortars, rifles and machine guns.(10) The diversity of these weapons systems means that each of the seven AMF national units must also maintain its own logistical support. The AMF's commander has estimated that standardization within his force could reduce the time required to deploy and be combat ready by more than one-half and could also cut logistic personnel by the same percentage.

The AMF reflects the problems facing NATO military forces as a whole. Lack of standardization, blighting the whole gamut of weaponry from planes and tanks to tire pumps, leads to expensive and chaotic logistics and inefficient joint operations, and even to potential fratricide.(11) In one NATO exercise the absence of common codes for data transmission and standardized systems for identification of friend or foe resulted in the "destruction" of many NATO aircraft by the Alliance's own air defense forces.(12)

Standardization of weapons systems and other equipment in NATO has become, for compelling reasons, a major goal of the Alliance. One way toward standardization would be through large-scale purchase of single types of systems from a single country – meaning in most cases the United States. This option, however, tends to be unacceptable on political as well as economic grounds. Many government officials, professional soldiers and defense analysts in Western Europe therefore look to multinational participation in the development and production of armaments as the principal road to standardization. The more NATO members are involved in development and production, they argue, the greater the number of actions that will introduce the finished products into their arms inventories.

In theory, then, collaboration holds out to the Alliance the promise of greater military effectiveness at substantial economic savings. This promise to Europe's high-technology industries becomes more alluring as governments find it increasingly difficult to keep the flow of contracts in pace with surplus capacity – especially if available funds for R&D investment continue to decline, as they have since the late 1960s. In many instances, collaboration will offer the only cost-effective and, therefore, publicly acceptable means of acquiring needed modern weapons systems. In fact, for the most part, the options open to West European political and military figures are already quite narrow. The alternatives to intra-European collaboration in developing modern weapons systems are to look for them abroad or to do without them. Balance of payments problems, domestic pressures and often national pride increasingly tend to rule out the first alternative to collaboration, while national security and/or domestic requirements make the second one unpalatable.

## THE REALITIES

The logic supporting West European collaboration in weapons development and production is difficult to challenge. In practice, however, many of the benefits associated with collaboration have yet to emerge in tangible form. Nationalism seems to be the major culprit.

Irrespective of the lip service paid to collaboration, neither the politician nor the professional soldier nor the industrialist in Western Europe has shown any real disposition to surrender sovereignty in his respective sector. Technological potential has been and continues to be viewed primarily through national prisms – as an asset to be guarded and developed as much as possible on the national level in order to ensure industrial and military strength as well as maintain the state's competitiveness in the technological marketplace. Collaborative projects are joined only when they embrace clearly national interests. When cost constraints make collaboration essential, design leadership can be obtained, or access to the technological know-how of a more sophisticated partner can be secured. The operative motivations have been those of short-term advantage; for the most part, long-term goals have been overlooked.

The preoccupation with short-term national interests has impeded above all the search for effective management models for collaborative ventures. Indeed, the record of collaborative projects clearly must be a disappointment to those EC planners who, according to John Hoagland, foresaw the 1970s as the decisive stage for technological collaboration on a West European scale:

> According to the formulation of EEC planners, the 1960s were years of rationalizing the different national aerospace industries, involving the consolidation and merger of numerous smaller companies into large, unified national aerospace companies. The 1970s were perceived as a decade in which these large national entities would engage in a series of major collaborative programs, leading to increasing operational unity. As these projects advanced, they would make it possible, in the 1980s, to achieve actual consolidation throughout Europe, through the creation of perhaps two airframe companies and two engine companies for the whole of EEC. Although these views were advanced by EEC planners rather than by national ministries or industries, they were treated with considerable interest.(13)

After a decade of experience, however, Western Europe's collaborative programs have yet to be brought into a regional framework. As a result, such efforts have fallen short of needed efficiency levels, particularly in the areas of project definition, coordination and cost control.

Government hesitance to relinquish sovereignty in defense procurement has led European nations to approach defense collaboration primarily on a project-by-project basis. With the possible exception of Panavia – the British, West German and Italian consortium established to develop the Tornado – the international consortia and related intragovernmental political and economic associations formed to manage the joint development and production of weapons systems have tended to dissolve after the completion of the given project. Research on a particular family of weapons, therefore, is not continued and technological momentum tends to be lost.

Collaborative defense efforts have also suffered from lack of centralized decision-making authority. The technique of having each phase of a single project approved by a new memorandum (as in the case of the Tornado and the Alpha-Jet) is time consuming and industrially inefficient. The development and production delays lower the market value of the item by increasing its costs and artificially aging it before it reaches the market.

These inefficiencies have been compounded by a lack of agreement on the part of collaborative partners on defense perceptions and equipment requirements. Incompatible national requirements, for example, foiled several NATO attempts to develop a common main battle tank. Differing equipment requirements also plagued the development of the Jaguar: both an interceptor and a fighter version of the plane had to be produced to satisfy French and British requirements.

Disagreements on tactical concepts and requirements also have obstructed the standardization or interoperability that should flow logically from collaboration. In fact, it is by no means certain that collaboration between two or more NATO members in the development and production of a weapons system will lead to the introduction of a standardized system by those countries. In some cases, modifications dictated by national requirements and specifications so alter the national versions of a jointly designed and produced system that those versions might as well be considered single-country products. They are not interoperable, cannot be serviced by the logistics crews of the other partners in the venture, and do not have interchangeable subsystems. Despite British and French collaboration in the production of the Jaguar, for example, there was some question whether a malfunctioning plane of one country could be serviced at an airfield of the other.

The need for collaborative parties to rationalize defense perceptions and equipment requirements is best illustrated by the Tornado project. During the conceptual stage of this project (then known as the MRCA), no fewer than five different missions had to be assigned to the Tornado in order to secure British, West German and Italian participation in the project: (1) interdiction of logistics support, (2) support of combat forces on the gound, (3) obtaining and maintaining air superiority, (4) reconnaissance, and (5) nuclear attack. Today, however, one finds growing concern in Bonn and London, at least, that the Tornado will not be as effective militarily as envisaged originally. It may prove capable of serving only the lowest common denominator of combined British, West German and Italian military requirements.

West German and British doubts over the Toronado seem to be reflected in the military aircraft procurement programs of these countries. Bonn's decision in 1968 to purchase eighty-eight American reconnaissance RF-4E Phantoms does not speak well for the FRG's faith in the reconnaissance function of the Tornado. Hesitation in Bonn about the Tornado's ground support and air superiority function also may have led to the FRG's decision in 1971 to purchase 175 intercept/combat F-4F Phantoms from the United States. Similarly, Bonn's decision to procure the Alpha-Jet raises some suspicion concerning its trust in the Tornado's ability to fulfill its close support role.(14)

To be sure, Bonn's purchase of the Phantoms can be explained in part as stemming from the FRG's need to fulfill offset obligations to the United States. Nevertheless, West German sources document the notion that questions about the Tornado's military effectiveness were instrumental in the procurement of the Phantoms:

> Because of its (multiple roles), it has become improbable that the MRCA, fully loaded in slow flight, would be able to support ground forces without high casualty quotas. The achievement of air superiority, on the other hand, had also become obsolete at a time when modern versions of the Soviet MiG-21 had to be considered superior to the MRCAs in all dimensions of aircraft.(15)

British hesitations about the Tornado are more difficult to document. On the one hand, British procurement of the plane has been slowed down; on the other hand, no other aircraft have been procured to fill the roles to which the Tornado was originally assigned. British critics of the Tornado, however, have argued that the United Kingdom could have a more balanced air force by abandoning it in favor of procuring more Harriers, Jaguars and F-16s.(16)

The Tornado project also demonstrates that collaboration does not necessarily enhance cost-effectiveness. Recent estimates place the total R&D cost of the aircraft at $1.15 billion (1972 prices). In 1973 alone, Germany devoted DM 370 million, or 25 percent of its total R&D defense expenditure, to the MRCA project. Production costs for the Tornado have been estimated to run as high as $6 million (1972 prices), not including weapons and spares. This figure has been based on an original projected total British, West German and Italian requirement of 800 aircraft, and could very well be considerably higher in light of British, French and Italian hesitation to give firm production commitments for the Tornado. Defense analysts in Europe have argued quietly that even though the project costs will be divided three ways, it might have been less expensive for one country to have developed the Tornado alone.(17) It should be added, however, that at the outset of the Tornado project Britain was the only one of the three collaborative partners to possess the technological base to develop the Tornado alone, but refrained from doing so for what appeared at the time to be sound economic reasons. West Germany lacked the necessary aeroengine technology, although this may no longer be the case. Italy lacked both technolgoical know-how and resources.(18)

The cost of collaboratively developed weapons systems, of course, could be reduced by expanding production runs through export sales. Experience has shown, however, that industrialized nations with advanced defense industries are often hesitant to purchase costly defense systems unless they, too, have had a stake in its development, or at least in its production. Moreover, no matter how much they may collaborate, the nations of Western Europe simply are not competitive with the United States in expanding exports to the Third World through aid or other inducements. As a result, they face wide fluctuations in demand for their exports. In 1972, for example, French military exports were 27 percent lower than they had been the previous year.

Adding to the problem is the fact that where export opportunities have existed for collaboratively developed weapons, tensions have arisen among collaborating partners over export policies. British efforts to export the Jaguar to the Third World, for example, have run into competition from the Mirage F-1 fighter/interceptor, notwithstanding the fact that France had joined Britain in the development and production of the Jaguar. The profit margin has been at the root of France's preference to export the Mirage rather than the jointly-produced Jaguar. One analyst noted that

> agreement has been reached by London and Paris over the division of revenues resulting from a Jaguar sale, but for France the profits of the division (55 to 45 percent, to the vendor and the partner respectively) are substantially lower than those that can be expected if the Mirage aircraft is chosen by Third World buyers. Thus the interest expressed by the governments of Egypt, Iran, Oman, and Saudi Arabia in the Jaguar has met some resistance in France.(19)

More recently, French efforts to sell the Franco-German Roland II to Israel have been impeded by Bonn's hesitation to sanction the sale.(20)

In the absence of a common export policy, the issue of exports of jointly produced high-technology products is bound to create dissension among collaborative partners – especially in the face of the ever more alluring market for modern military hardware among the oil-rich countries of the Middle East. While the overall impact of increased sales opportunities for West European states in this respect is not yet clear, one could argue that nations that have limited defense industries, such as West Germany and Italy, may be prompted to cooperate more closely in order to secure a portion of the OPEC technology market. On the other hand, there is some evidence that the new market opportunities may prompt countries like Britain or France, which have large and sophisticated aerospace industries, to make a last ditch effort to build military aircraft on their own in the hope of defraying costs through exports. Britain, for example, already is developing the Hawk trainer particularly for this purpose. Also, the French are developing the Delta Mirage 2000 with an eye toward the OPEC market.(21) If such a trend were to proceed unchecked, the arms sales competition would escalate rapidly, thereby seriously compromising future collaborative efforts in Western Europe.

The shortcomings of West European collaborative projects, however, cannot be tied entirely to the Europeans' nationalism. The United States, too, has had a significant influence on the collaborative process. American industrial success and the growing U.S. domination of the European market in the important fields of high technology were, in fact, two of the primary stimulants behind European collaboration. At the same time, however, U.S. policies by and large have impacted negatively on the collaborative process. Most annoying to our European allies is the American practice of protecting its high technology industries almost completely from foreign competition for government contracts. "Buy American" was, in fact, a firm American policy long before the Buy American Act was passed by the U.S. Congress. This Act and a host of other regulations at the federal and state levels have successfully closed the American defense market to European producers and have thus limited their growth potential.(22)

American use of offset agreements to ease balance of payments problems arising from the maintenance of American troops in Europe was another and more subtle means of inhibiting West European collaboration. American pressures on its NATO allies to purchase American military equipment as a means of offsetting the foreign exchange costs of U.S. forces in Europe had the effect of preempting a potential market for European-produced weapons systems. American offset regulations posed particularly difficult problems for West Germany. In the 1974 agreement alone the West Germans agreed to offset American balance of payments costs at a level of about $2.2 billion, with military equipment purchases accounting for almost half of the amount – a great portion of which, many Europeans feel, Germany might otherwise have spent on European-made weapons. The offset agreements thus not only placed a "made in U.S.A." label over a good part of the West German weapons market, but also reduced the incentive for the FRG to enter into collaborative schemes with its continental neighbors. Moreover, the forced weapons sales (as the offset agreements have sometimes been called) tended to sharpen the advantages enjoyed by American arms producers over their

European competitors through the greater efficiencies and lower unit costs that redounded from lengthened production runs. Especially with the growing constraints on European defense budgets, cost considerations have a way of triumphing over political desiderata. The victory of the American F-16 over its European rivals in the NATO procurement market represented a milestone in this trend.

The decision in Bonn in 1976 not to renew offset agreements – particularly in light of the substantial shifts of payments and trade balances in the U.S. favor in the preceding years – may eliminate this American wedge into the European procurement arena, at least in a formal sense. Yet, Europeans complain that there is a less formal, but no less potent, side to this wedge – a side represented by American endeavors to link the U.S. security guarantee in NATO to a resolution of outstanding trade and monetary problems between the United States and Western Europe. Europeans profess to see in this linkage a thinly veiled threat: "Accommodate our economic penchants or you will risk an American retrenchment from Europe." And they complain that, in deference to this threat, they have been forced to render concessions, particularly in the trade of high-technology goods.(23)

In summary, then, the promise held out by collaboration has not been realized fully, largely as a result of nationalism that has exhibited itself on a variety of levels. Individual West European governments and industries have been extremely reluctant to relinquish sovereignty to the degree required by economic, military and industrial logic. While these countries compete among themselves, at the same time they engage individually in head-to-head competition with the United States. In addition, in some cases a quasi-regional competition emerges, with Western Europe having to yield frequently to a better organized and more efficient American defense production system.

## NOTES

(1) Thomas A. Callaghan, U.S./European Economic Cooperation in Civil and Military Technology: An Issues Oriented Report (Arlington, Va.: Ex-Im Tech, Inc., 1974). Prepared for the Department of State, this study examined problems and prospects for collaboration between the United States and Europe in technology. It contributed in part to American acceptance of the concept of the "two-way street" and helped to set the stage for a transatlantic dialogue on defense procurement.

(2) The Tornado was formerly known as the Multi-Role Combat Aircraft (MRCA).

(3) Hugh Green, "Prospects for European Arms Co-operation," in John C. Garnett, editor, The Defense of Western Europe (London: St. Martin's Press, 1974), p. 103.

(4) Robert L. Pfaltzgraff, Jr., "Resource Constraints and the Effects of Arms Transfers: Implications for European Security," Paper prepared for the Conference on the Implications of the Military Build-Up in Non-Industrialized States, International Security Studies Program, The Fletcher School of Law and Diplomacy, Tufts University, May 6-8, 1976, p. 14.

(5) Mary Kaldor, Defense Industries – National and International Implications (Sussex: Institute for the Study of International Organization, ISIO Monograph First Series, Number 8, 1972), p. 2.

(6) Ibid., p. 21.

(7) This latter advantage was quite attractive in Britain during the 1960s when government policy with respect to weapons procurement and the aerospace industry in general had been anything but stable. Between 1955 and 1965 the British government invested $829 million, or approximately 14 percent of its total R&D budget, on projects that were eventually canceled. Many of these cancellations were products of erratic shifts in government policies. With its acceptance of "massive retaliation" in 1951, for example, the British government suddenly cut back its manned military aircraft program only to reinstate it when the strategy of flexible response was accepted in the 1960s. In the interim, the British aircraft industry lost much of its R&D momentum. Similarly, in a questionable attempt at economy the British government canceled the TSR2 program in 1962 after the project had reached the prototype and testing stage. Since Britain's embrace of collaboration in the mid-1960s, however, only one military aircraft project – the Anglo-French Variable Geometry Fighter – has been canceled. Commission of the European Communities, Studies on the Aeronautical and Space Industries of the Community Compared with Those of the United Kingdom and the United States, Vol. 4 (Turin, Italy: SORIS, 1971),pp. 172-173.

(8) Hans Rattinger, "West Germany's Arms Transfers to the Non-Industrial World," Paper prepared for the Conference on the Implications of the Military Build-Up in Non-Industrialized States, International Security Studies Program, The Fletcher School of Law and Diplomacy, Tufts University, May 6-8, 1976, p. 27.

(9) Cited by General Ulrich de Maizere in his study, Rational Deployment of Forces on the Central Front (Paris: Assembly of Western European Union, Document 663, April 2, 1975), p. 51.

(10) Dr. Gardiner L. Tucker, "Standardization and the Joint Defence," NATO Review, January 1975, p. 11.

(11) Ibid., p. 12.

(12) New York Times, May 19, 1975.

(13) John H. Hoagland, "American and European Industry Relations in Military

Exports to the Less Developed Countries," Paper prepared for the Conference on the Implications of the Military Build-Up in Non-Industrialized States, International Security Studies Program, The Fletcher School of Law and Diplomacy, Tufts University, May 6-8, 1976, p. 16.

(14) See Ulrich Albrecht, Luber Burhard, Peter Schlotter, "Das Ende des MRCA?," in Studiengruppe Militaerpolitik, Ein Anti-Weissbuch (Hamburg: Rowohet, 1974), pp. 81-98.

(15) Frankfurter Rundschau, November 7, 1974.

(16) Interviews conducted by the authors with British government officials and defense analysts in the United Kingdom between September 18 and October 11, 1975. Hereafter cited as British interviews.

(17) W.B. Walker, for example, has argued that on the basis of a 50 percent "collaboration premium" for development costs and 15 percent for production and as the market stands at present, the Tornado would have been cheaper to produce domestically. Cited in Roger Facer, The Alliance and Europe, Part III: Weapons Procurement in Europe -- Capabilities and Choices (London: International Institute for Strategic Studies, Adelphi Paper No. 108, 1975), fn. 93.

(18) British interviews.

(19) Pfaltzgraff, p. 18.

(20) "Israel: Interest in Roland II Claimed," Defense and Foreign Affairs Digest, 8-9. 1971, p. 90.

(21) It is interesting that the Delta Mirage 2000 is being developed for the same missions as the Tornado, making these planes likely competitors for the export market. See Aviation Week & Space Technology, December 20, 1976, p. 23.

(22) See Robert E. Baldwin, "Nontariff Distortions of International Trade," in Robert E. Baldwin and J. David Richardson, editor, International Trade and Finance (Boston: Little, Brown, 1974), pp. 143-163.

(23) Interviews conducted by the authors with British, Belgian, West German and European Community (EC) officials in Europe between September 18 and October 24, 1975.

# 7 Defense Technology and the Atlantic Alliance— Modes of Collaboration

Frank T. J. Bray
Michael Moodie

The importance of the U.S. factor notwithstanding, the major impediments to European collaboration in weapons development and production issue clearly from the divergence and clash of national political, military and industrial interests in Western Europe. A meaningful Europeanization of defense procurement can become reality only if European nations can reconcile competing national interests with sound business practices and military logic, as well as with a compelling vision of the longer-range future.

Schemes for improving Europe's defense collaboration have been under consideration by a wide variety of political and military bodies, most notably NATO's Eurogroup, the WEU and, more recently, the European Community's newly formed Independent Program Group (IPG). The IPG promises to be an important forum because, unlike the Eurogroup, it enjoys French support. On the industrial level, Aerospatiale (France), BAC and Hawker-Siddeley (UK), VFW-Fokker (West Germany and Holland), Messerschmitt-Bolkow-Bolhm (MBB) and Dornier (West Germany) have already formed a Group of Six to meet the American challenge head on. The goal of the Group of Six is to make European aircraft industries competitive with the United States not only in technology, but also in spare parts, service, financial resources, restructuring, and management.(1)

Attitudes in Western Europe are crystallizing in favor of strong governmental intervention in the collaborative process, and this is true even among European industrialists, save those in Britain who are now facing the prospect of nationalization of the aerospace industry. There is broad recognition of the need for rationalizing military requirements and procurement agreements as well as for encouraging joint agencies for European standardization and cooperation, preferably through existing bodies such as the Tornado management framework, the proposed European Defence Procurement Agency or, for civil technology, Airbus Industries and the European Civil Aviation Conference (ECAC).(2)

This mounting interest in Western Europe in collaboration – and in the search for a framework that can leaven divergent national defense procurement policies and practices – must be adjudged a positive development. Yet, even if it is assumed that the psychological impetus behind intra-European collaboration is growing – and if it is further assumed that the project-by-project approach that has been followed thus far is unsatisfactory – the nagging question continues to confront the champions of collaboration: What is the proper road?

Essentially, there are three basic forms that West European collaboration could take: specialization, transnational merger, and program collaboration. These forms, to be sure, are not mutually exclusive. Yet each denotes a major emphasis of approach and thus a reasonably discrete plan of attack.

## THE SPECIALIZATION MODE

As already indicated, escalating costs and efficiency criteria have combined to cast doubt on the viability of collaboration toward the multipurpose weapons system that can bridge a broad variety of perceived national requirements (e.g., the Tornado). The experience has caused analysts to ask whether it would make more sense to develop a series of simpler technological systems, each of which is optimized for a single role in the spectrum of requirements.(3) Since no individual West European country is in a position to embark on a program to meet the full range of European requirements, this implies specialization and a much more explicit division of labor among the European members of NATO. Specialization would entail national concentration in certain technological fields and services while relying on other members of NATO for technological products not produced indigenously. Already the Eurogroup has proposed the repartition of armaments production geared to national specialization.(4)

The benefits of specialization in defense procurement would accrue to both producer and customer. For the producer, specialization combines the benefits (theoretically, at least) of greater management efficiency than in multilateral enterprises, with the advantages of scale provided by sales of finished products to a larger market. Depending on security requirements, unit costs could be reduced further by exports beyond the NATO area.

The advantages afforded by specialization, however, are by no means limited to the producer. Customers would also benefit:

> They escape the early teething troubles inevitable in any equipment, and can avoid altogether a commitment to buy equipment whose performance does not live up to its promise; they do not have to make the longterm financial commitment; and they can often negotiate a favorable price, since the foreign manufacturer's first customer (usually his national armed forces) will have paid for most of his overhead.(5)

Although specialization would give the producer virtual monopoly over given sectors of technology, quality and price control theoretically would be guaranteed by the producer's need to sell his product to offset its high cost of development as well as by his dependence on other members of the Community for other essential items.

While specialization thus offers a rational and attractive road the practical obstacles are formidable. The biggest obstacle stems from abiding sovereignty preoccupations in Western Europe. Under specialization, each country would be dependent on others for the production of weapons systems and other equipment considered vital to its security. Until now, no country has shown any disposition to forfeit industrial opportunities or to relinquish control over any portion of its industry. The French, for example, have already expressed concern that the specialization proposed by the Eurogroup would lead to the disappearance of well-established segments of French industry.(6)

The "we can do it" syndrome of national pride in Western Europe, if anything, has been accentuated by mutual distrust on economic and political grounds. Given Great Britain's current economic travails, for example, can either the Federal Republic of Germany or France realistically be expected to place its faith in British production of a given system? Similarly, could Italy's NATO partners be expected to delegate to that country important segments in the common defense production in light of both Italian economic woes and the leftward drift of Italian politics?

Even if the principle of specialization were to be accepted by all European members of NATO, national pride would likely distort a rational implementation. No European government would support a specialization scheme that relegated it primarily to the production of subsystems or less sophisticated projects while other European states concentrated on the more advanced technologies. Any successful specialization plan, therefore, would somehow have to apportion to each European country a mix of both high- and low-technology production.

Notwithstanding current pressures for rationalization, governments will continue to be skeptical toward the concept of national specialization. Conceivably, some of the current misgivings could be scaled down through confidence-building measures; for example, the establishment of intra-Community inspection and quality control mechanisms as well as provisions for the unhampered exchange of all technological information, with the understanding that each nation reserves the right to withdraw from the specialization agreement and produce a particular system of its own. Such an escape clause, however, while it might lower initial reluctance toward participation in a given specialization arrangement, in the longer run could generate even deeper mutual distrust. Each country would tend to look apprehensively at its neighbor, anticipating that the latter was using the specialization agreement to build up a particular component of its industry, only to bail out when that purpose had been accomplished.

## THE MERGER MODE

Merging technological industries across national frontiers in Western Europe could offer significant advantages over the present project-by-project system of technological collaboration among nationally-based industries. The larger size of these new transnational industrial structures, for example, would potentially make them more competitive on the world market. In addition, by pooling resources, such larger companies could create a technical and financial base which would approximate more closely that of American firms. This, in turn, would open avenues for cooperation with the United States by lessening European fears of American domination. In addition, a reduction in the number of European firms competing in a particular technological field would not only curtail duplication of effort, but would allow each remaining firm to have a greater share of the market and in this way achieve greater economies of scale.

Shrinking markets and rising costs may prompt West European industries themselves to take initiatives toward more permanent links, possibly to the extent of transnational mergers. The Group of Six, Panavia's bid to extend its operations beyond the Tornado project, and the German-Dutch VFW-Fokker merger are examples of such initiatives. However, a considerable amount of consensus-building still needs to take place on the industrial level, especially concerning the timing of mergers. While accepting the concept in principle, officials in Britain's aircraft industry, for example, view transnational mergers as a long-term goal to be preceded by a transition period of transnational consortia. These consortia would be similar to, but more powerful than, Panavia, which has experienced problems at the sales and postsales level "due to its inability to build up a reputation of stability and reliability."(7) Aerospace officials on the Continent envision a shorter transitional phase than their British counterparts and appear more eager to move toward full-scale mergers.

Even with the wholehearted support of industry, however, transnational mergers of important technological industries within Western Europe will be difficult to implement without the consent and support of national governments. The political, economic and military importance attached by all nations to their publicly supported industries in most cases will tend to work against merger schemes in spite of national market pressure pushing in that direction. As in the case of specialization, the prospect of transnational mergers touches upon national feelings that are not easy for governments to deal with, irrespective of the economic logic of the argument. The establishment of viable transnational mergers, for example, could require further rationalization of specific national industries and perhaps even the phasing out of some less vital production facilities. Particularly in a period of recessionary economic trends, it would be difficult politically for a government to encourage consciously a move that might exacerbate short-term unemployment. Such a step most certainly would draw clamorous opposition from labor unions, especially in Britain.

Furthermore, the ultimate success of transnational mergers in the defense field is by no means certain and the risk of failure is very real. Even if mergers take place and management structures are streamlined, there is still no guarantee that such firms will be able to compete successfully on the world market. Despite its increased size and resource capabilities, VFW-Fokker, for example, has found it difficult "in the face of a worsening competitive situation, to develop new aircraft on its own."(8) There are indications that VFW-Fokker and Britain's Hawker-Siddeley may be seeking to rationalize their parallel individual efforts on the HS 146 and the Fokker Super F-28 or F-29 – both civil aircraft in the 100-seat category.(9)

More importantly, governments are likely to resist transnational mergers for fear of lessened control over industries considered vital to their national economies. Over the years, various merger schemes – centering primarily around the European aerospace industry – have been proposed. These proposals have called for the creation of one or two European airframe companies and/or a separate European missile company. The European firms most often cited as candidates for merger include Aerospatiale, BAC and MBB (for airframes), and Dassault, Breguet, Hawker-Siddeley and VFW-Fokker (for missiles). Difficulties arise, however, in trying to apportion control among the companies to be merged. As one analyst has noted:

> Would the French government, for instance, be willing to see its control of Aerospatiale reduced to a minority holding in a company whose other large stockholders were two of the largest British manufacturing concerns in the private sector, GEC and Vickers, and three powerful German families?
>
> Would the British and the Germans accept the French as the strongest partner in the new group with say, a 49 percent holding as against their 30 percent and 20 percent?(10)

Similarly, the virtually dominant position that Rolls Royce would muster in any European aerospace company inhibits mergers in this field.

Divergent national industrial and legal policies further obstruct the search for compatible companies and balanced shareholding arrangements for potential mergers. For example, earlier suggestions for merging Sud-Aviation with BAC-Weybridge had to be abandoned due to internal rationalization efforts in both Britain and France.(11) At present one also finds some concern on the Continent that Britain's plans to nationalize its aircraft industry could narrow further and perhaps even close Europe's options for transnational mergers in this field. While it is generally recognized throughout Europe that further rationalization of national aerospace industries is a prerequisite to more effective collaborative links among European countries and between Europe and the United States, aerospace officials on the Continent would prefer not to see one united British aircraft industry emerging from Britain's nationalization program. The net effect of such a development, they fear, "would be British dominance of the European aerospace scene, and an end to collaborative pacts with smaller companies, and the emergence in self-defense of equally big units on the continent."(12) Britain's aerospace industry and a continental European counterpart would thus be locked into a potentially disastrous rivalry.

In order to effect transnational industrial mergers, national governments must not only coordinate national industrial policies, but they must also take steps to harmonize their laws governing corporate management, operations and finance. The widespread incompatibility of national regulations currently makes it "virtually impossible to create. . . .the truly 'transnational' company into which all the participants. . .pour their entire resources and. . .work together as a single unit."(13)

## THE PROGRAM MODE

Project-by-project collaboration tends to magnify managerial inefficiencies and adds to total project costs. The difficulties of this approach arise from the fact that it "requires all the conflicting industrial and technological claims of the cooperating partners to be met within the project. . .while still adhering to a 50/50 financial balance, juste retour, and zero foreign exchange costs."(14) As a result, the assignment of R&D and production tasks tends not to be made according to criteria of efficiency and national capability, but, instead, by the need to give all participants an immediate and fair return on their investment.

By cooperating on a program basis, however, European members of NATO could be assured a just return on their investment over a series of collaborative efforts, thereby permitting greater flexibility in assigning national tasks in accordance with sound business practices. Project management could also be improved by awarding prime directorship of projects to single nations or national industries. Management responsibility would, of course, be rotated on an equitable basis over the life-span of the program.

This technique proved particularly successful in the joint Anglo-French helicopter program. Under the program launched in 1968, Britain and France agreed to develop three helicopters and produce them jointly: (1) the SA 330 Puma medium transport helicopter; (2) the WG Lynx general purpose helicopter; and (3) the SA 340 Gazelle light-weight helicopter. Two companies were involved in the package: France's Aerospatiale and Britain's Westland. Britain agreed to buy Puma and Gazelle helicopters built under the prime directorship of Aerospatiale with Westland as subcontractor, in return for the French purchase of the Lynx from Westland, in which Aerospatiale worked as a subcontractor.

An appealing characteristic of program collaboration is its relative political feasibility. Program collaboration demands less of a political and economic commitment on the part of participants than do the other modes of collaboration that have been discussed. National political, military, and economic sovereignty need not be compromised to the degree required for successful transnational industrial mergers or specialization. Yet this form of collaboration, too, bears shortcomings. For example, program collaboration in practice may be suited only for smaller projects. As one analyst noted, for program collaboration to work

> there must be a broad balance between the components of the package in their timing, their cost and their technological content. It is not easy to find a group of projects in a program which meets this criterion and the firm or industry which has to forge any share in the other part. The difficulty of balancing such a large project as the multi-role combat aircraft (MRCA) makes it virtually inevitable that projects on this scale will be carried out on a non-program collaborative basis.(15)

Thus, while program collaboration may be politically more practicable than other management options, it may not represent a long enough step forward. It is precisely in the area of high cost and sophisticated technology that the need for collaboration is most pressing. In addition, management techniques would be improved under program collaboration, but primarily within the framework of nationally based industries. Closer ties on a transnational basis could be impeded by the guarantee of contracts offered by the rotation of prime directorships. By maintaining a mix of prime directorships and subcontractual relationships over a series of collaborative efforts, national industries conceivably could forestall or avoid desirable transnational rationalization. Furthermore, unless program collaboration were combined with some type of specialization of function, the opportunities for avoiding duplication would be limited. Indeed, national industries would feel compelled to maintain duplicate R&D in order to be ready to serve as prime director when their turn came around.

In addition, while program collaboration would entail basic agreement among the participants on certain market questions, sufficiently long production runs would not necessarily be assured. As noted, the markets that have been created through present and past bilateral and multilateral collaboration may soon prove too weak to support highly sophisticated technological programs. At the same time, governments have demonstrated a marked reluctance to purchase systems in which they have not played some part in development or production. In order to widen the market, therefore, more nations may have to be brought into the collaborative program. Experience, however, has underscored the obvious fact that the most fruitful international cooperation in R&D tends to take place with the smallest number of partners.

## NOTES

(1) See Christian Science Monitor, September 15, 1975, p. 9.

(2) Felix Muller, "Second Western European Union Collaborating on a European Aeronautical Policy," Interavia, March 1976, p. 206.

(3) For a statement of this argument with respect to military aircraft, see Steven Canby, The Alliance and Europe, Part IV: Military Doctrine and Technology (London: International Institute for Strategic Studies, Adelphi Paper No. 109, Winter 1974/75), pp. 40-41.

(4) John H. Hoagland, "American and European Industry Relations in Military Exports to the Less Developed Countries," Paper prepared for the Conference on the Implications of the Military Build-Up in Non-Industrialized States, International Security Studies Program, The Fletcher School of Law and Diplomacy, Tufts University, May 6-8, 1976, p. 21.

(5) Roger Facer, The Alliance and Europe, Part III: Weapons Procurement in Europe -- Capabilities and Choices (London: International Institute for Strategic Studies, Adelphi Paper No. 108, 1975), p. 35.

(6) Hoagland, p. 21.

(7) American firms, on the other hand, are just accepting the need for national rationalization and have great difficulty contemplating even participating in consortia.

(8) Facer, p. 41.

(9) Aviation Week & Space Technology, December 20, 1976, p. 23.

(10) Facer, p. 41.

(11) See Christopher Layton, European Advanced Technology (London: Allen and Unwin, 1969).

(12) Financial Times (London), July 8, 1974.

(13) "Aerospace: The European Merger Debate," ibid., July 9, 1973.

(14) Thomas A. Callaghan, U.S./European Economic Cooperation in Military and Civil Technology (Washington, D.C.: Center for Strategic and International Studies, Georgetown University, 1975, revised edition), p. 54. All subsequent citations will be to this edition.

(15) Hugh Green, "Prospects for European Arms Co-operation," in John C. Garnett, editor, The Defense of Western Europe (London: St. Martin's Press, 1974), p. 103.

# 8 Defense Technology and the Atlantic Alliance—Beyond the Two-Way Street

Frank T. J. Bray
Michael Moodie

A strong argument can be made that the concept of a purely European approach to defense procurement is an idea whose time has passed. Even if the nations and/or industries of Western Europe were to take steps in any of the directions indicated in the previous chapter, they would soon encounter some formidable and durable obstacles.

Perhaps the most serious impediment to an exclusively European approach to defense procurement inheres in the size of the European market. It has been evident for some time that the domestic markets of those countries currently engaged in collaborative ventures are not large enough to sustain the economical production of sophisticated and high-cost, defense-related systems, and that this problem will not be resolved even if the markets of noncollaborating West European countries should be included. In order to aspire to minimum levels of cost-effectiveness, European industry would have to gain access to markets in the United States and non-Atlantic regions. As noted above, the American market has generally been closed to Western Europe's high-technology systems, with the notable exception of the Harrier and the Roland.(1) At the same time, "the rigidities of manpower allocations among industrial sectors, and the constraints of capital resources on new plant capacity, place some natural limits on the scope of European military exports."(2)

Other barriers to a purely European approach to defense industry issue from advances in the technological state-of-the art and their implications for military requirements. Pushing military technologies to the next plateau of development will demand levels of sophistication and resource allocation that may be beyond even the combined resources of Western Europe. Even if European firms were to overcome their problems of management and application, the low levels of R&D funding presently available would be likely to result in technologically outmoded, expensive, and unmarketable products.

Finally, the price for policies excluding the United States from collaborative ventures would be measurable not only in economic terms, but in potential political and security penalties as well. Europeans are sensitively mindful of the growing weight of the U.S. Congress in American economic and foreign policies, and they do not dismiss lightly the possibility of congressional retaliation for any European policy that excludes the United States. Politically, the effect would be a serious blow to an already weakened Alliance.

## THE ROLE OF THE UNITED STATES

Greater cooperation in defense procurement on a purely European-wide basis, therefore, may prove to be inadequate, necessitating collaboration within the broader Atlantic framework. The benefits to Western Europe of transatlantic collaboration are clear. Bringing U.S. industry into European projects could help Europe gain a foothold in the large American market, while reducing the prospects of fierce competition between European and American industries for exports to non-NATO countries. European industries would also benefit substantially from the input of U.S. technology. Additionally, U.S.-European collaboration would help to alter the Europeans' perception of standardization as a "buy American" policy.

The potential benefits of U.S.-European collaboration are by no means one-sided. For a number of compelling reasons collaboration will become increasingly attractive to the United States. In recent years even the American defense budget has come under increasing constraints as inflation and the skyrocketing cost of manpower have eroded its purchasing power. It is conceivable that the prohibitive price of future projects in defense technology may put them beyond the bounds of cost effectiveness even in the United States. One of the focal points of the debate over the B-1 bomber, for example, was its cost effectiveness.(3)

The problem in the United States is sharpened by shifting sociopolitical priorities that have clamped a tightening vise on defense and prestige projects. Indeed, after some three decades of military-industrial boom and liberal defense spending, the disconcerting recognition has dawned in official American circles that even the United States is resource-limited. This recognition animated the statement by President Ford at the NATO summit in 1975: "The pressures on defense budgets throughout the Alliance should by now have convinced each of us that we simply must rationalize our collective defense."(4)

In the coming years the promises of shared R&D costs, broader economies of scale, and elimination of wasteful duplication are likely to appear ever more attractive to the United States in its efforts to cut some corners in defense spending. In the next decade alone, the U.S. armed forces will require new conventional weapons systems costing billions of dollars. Technological collaboration may thus become a necessity rather than an indulgence for the United States – particularly for U.S. industry, which is barred by antitrust laws from full-scale mergers to cut costs and fill capacity and at the same time is subjected to sharpening uncertainties regarding the future level of government support. In this respect American industry, and to some extent the U.S. military, will be attracted to collaboration for the hedge it offers against governmental cancellation of projects. Doubts about sustained governmental support for a specific R&D project were first encountered with the cancellation of the supersonic transport (SST), which, although a civil aircraft, had many of the developmental characteristics of an advanced weapons system.

Finally, transatlantic collaboration would offer the United States subtle international political attractions. American participation in collaborative efforts would lock the United States into closer political association with its allies, not only as a result of the long lead-time of a collaborative project, but also because of the governmental, military and industrial interaction patterns that flow naturally from collaboration. Furthermore, transatlantic collaboration in weapons production would give the United States an opportunity to lobby for a common NATO policy toward exports of arms to non-NATO countries. European and American initiatives to seize export opportunities generated by the rush to arms in the Third World will further enfeeble the Alliance if a common policy is not developed.

There are indications that these considerations are already pushing American and European firms toward collaboration in civil technology. This is evident on the governmental level, as well as in the private industrial sectors, where both American and European firms seem more intent on expanding mutual ties than they have ever been in the past. A notable example is the domain of aerospace, which has witnessed a stepped-up flow of consultations between the two sides of the Atlantic. Collaboration certainly has been a subject of conversation in these meetings. Boeing and Aerospatiale, for example, reportedly have been working on a plan for the joint development of a shorter model of the Airbus. Aerospatiale might also join Boeing in the development of the latter's 7N7 – a derivative of the Boeing 737. In addition, Dassault has been negotiating with McDonnell Douglas to bring that company into its plans to develop a stretched version of the Mercure. French preoccupation with securing American participation in future aerospace ventures has led to speculation that France, at least, may be willing to reach a bilateral agreement with a U.S. firm at the expense of cooperation within Europe.(5)

The French, however, have not been alone in seeking American partners. Several joint U.S. and British aircraft projects have been under discussion, most notably between U.S.-based Pratt and Whitney and Britain's Rolls Royce concerning the development of the new JT10D engine. This engine is being designed to compete with the SNECMA-General Electric CFM56 being developed currently for the next generation of commercial airliners. The search for collaborative partners has not been generated only be Europeans. American firms seem to be responding favorably to European overtures and may even have initiated some discussions. As one analyst has stated, "even a casual observation of the tempo of negotiations abroad by U.S. aircraft and engine manufacturers . . . gives clear indication that no major future transport aircraft/engine program is possible without significant overseas involvement – not as subcontractors but as partners."(6) Boeing, for example, claims that it could raise the $1.4 billion required to launch both the 7X7 and 7N7 simultaneously. According to The Economist, however, Boeing is casting for European partners in order to reduce its individual burden, especially in light of the fact that "launching the 747 Jumbo almost killed the company."(7)

American policymakers, too, are beginning to take a fresh and hopefully more balanced look at the question of technological collaboration with their West European allies in the procurement of military systems. In May 1975, for example, then Secretary of Defense James Schlesinger endorsed, in principle, a British proposal to adopt "a much more vigorous approach to weapons standardization in NATO through military trade between the United States and Europe."(8) The preceding month at the NATO summit meeting, President Ford officially supported this concept and emphasized the need for agreement among the NATO allies "on a sensible division of weapons-development programs and production facilities."(9) The United States has also emphasized making cooperation in arms procurement within the Alliance a two-way street. Several arms procurement agreements have already been reached under this philosophy. The United States, for example, agreed to purchase the Aerospatiale/MBB Roland missile. The program is now moving into the pre-production testing phase following some initial technology transfer difficulties. According to Aviation Week & Space Technology, "the U.S. Army is getting an effective air defense missile system . . . at considerably less cost than if it had developed an entirely new system."(10)

While the two-way street concept must be welcomed as a positive development in NATO's arms procurement process, it cannot be considered the definitive and long-term formula for collaboration between the United States and its NATO allies. Improving the balance in the arms flow across the Atlantic will help to foster a cooperative spirit within the Alliance and possibly set the stage for necessary reforms in NATO procurement of major weapons systems. The two-way street as currently practiced, however, does little to promote the rationalization of, or to reduce the surplus capacity in, national defense industries. Without combining some form of specialization with the two-way street, individual nations will continue to attempt to produce a wide spectrum of sophisticated weapons systems, thereby compounding the duplication of R&D.

Witness, for example, the tank competition between the United States and West Germany. Very similar – and very expensive – tank prototypes were developed by Chrysler and General Motors to compete with a modified version of the West Germans' Leopard II. The initial upshot of the competition was the U.S. selection of the Chrysler prototype, modified to permit use of standard components developed for the West German tanks – in effect, creating a hybrid tank.(11) After lengthy consideration and debate, the United States agreed in early 1978 to fit its prototype tank with the West German 120mm gun instead of the 105mm type originally envisioned. West Germany had agreed earlier to modify the Leopard chassis to accommodate the Avco-Lycoming gas turbine engine used in one of the U.S. XM-1 designs. U.S. and European tanks will also feature a number of common components including the track, a range of standard screws, a U.S.-developed night vision device, and a German-designed gunner's telescope. Essentially, the tanks will be interoperable – a laudable achievement. An element of this kind of competition is, of course, healthy and desirable. Yet, had a hybrid tank been decided upon as the original goal, the development tasks could have been apportioned accordingly and much of the duplication of R&D and unnecessary expansion of capacity on both sides of the Atlantic could have been avoided.

If the Europeanization of defense procurement is an impractical objective because of an array of economic, technological and political factors, and if the two-way street is not the ideal form of cooperation within the Alliance, what technological role should the United States play in Western Europe? Economic, political and technological trends point to collaboration. The difficulty, however, lies in trying to achieve a consensus in Europe on when conditions are favorable for cooperation with the United States. In the past, disagreement on this question has blighted collaborative projects. The failure of Euratom, for example, stemmed in large part from the fact that five members of the Community chose the American line of technology, while France opted for a different one.(12) This same lack of consensus inhibited European space development: the British wanted to use American launchers and concentrate on the satellite package, while the Group of Four insisted that Western Europe should have its own launching capability.(13) Similarly, lack of European consensus over American participation plagued a prospective collaborative project for a new surface-to-air missile to replace the Nike, Hawk, Thunderbird and Bloodhound systems. Britain indicated that she would like "a purely European development based on her own expertise with this type of weapon" while Germany indicated that she would prefer U.S. participation since she would like "a link with the United States and access to American technology."(14)

Reluctance in Western Europe to consider the United States a collaborative partner is, in large part, a reflex conditioned by the fear of domination. This is the case, particularly in the aerospace industry, where American firms enjoy considerable advantage over their European counterparts with respect to government support and production runs. As a result, American firms have tended to outperform their counterparts in Europe. From 1960 to 1967, for example, annual output in the U.S. aircraft industry increased by 4.4 percent while that of Britain increased by only 1.7 percent. During the same period, per capita output in the British, French and other European aerospace industries was consistently lower than that of the United States.(15) Moreover, in 1967 constant prices, the American aerospace industry was able to outproduce in per capita output the total average EEC output by a ratio of approximately two to one.(16)

The vagaries of transatlantic technological collaboration cannot be blamed entirely on European attitudes. During the postwar decades, the position of the United States on defense collaboration with its NATO allies has been ambivalent at best. In the early years of NATO, the United States took the lead in advocating defense cooperation and collaboration, urging strongly the creation of balanced collective forces and the avoidance of duplication. In later years, when Europe's defense industries were again functioning, the United States initiated a program of cooperative development of defense equipment. A number of joint research and development projects were begun with Britain, France, West Germany and Italy. For the most part, however, the results were not successful, and American interest in cooperative projects waned considerably.

The reasons for this diminished American interest, however, went beyond the poor results of the projects undertaken. The United States itself had little need to participate in these projects since its own technological system was thought to be beyond reach. Congress could be counted on in most instances to appropriate the necessary funds, and industry proved capable of performing the task, no matter how complex. When collaboration was proposed, it was considered primarily to foster a more standardized NATO defense.

To Western Europe, however, standardization became synonymous with American domination. This impression was reinforced by protectionist American policies, offset regulations, and by the fact that in the first twenty years of the Alliance not one major European weapons system was adopted by the United States for use in NATO. U.S. corporate policies, which many Europeans felt were designed to perpetuate the fragmentation of European industry, also contributed to a generally negative environment for U.S.-European technological cooperation. In turn, European coolness toward U.S. standardization efforts was interpreted by Washington to have been motivated by British and French desires to develop national weapons systems so that they could compete for weapons sales opportunities coming to the fore in the late 1960s. Suspicions on both sides of the Atlantic will prove difficult to eradicate despite the aforementioned incentives that are pointing, ever more markedly, toward transatlantic collaboration.

## OPTIONS FOR PROMOTING TECHNOLOGICAL COLLABORATION

How can the nations of the Atlantic Community ease their mutual suspicions and encourage collaboration in the future? Options for promoting collaboration fall into three basic categories: (1) U.S. policies to set the stage for fruitful collaboration with its European allies; (2) measures European nations should pursue to enhance their attractiveness as collaborative partners; and (3) options for the entire Atlantic Community.

Breaking options down into such categories is necessary, for it is unrealistic to expect European and American industries or governments to adopt the same approach to reform. At least, European political and industrial figures seem willing to consider more comprehensive changes in present industrial structures than many of their counterparts in the United States who still have considerable difficulty in even thinking of reforms being undertaken beyond the national frontier. Differing American and European levels of tolerance toward reform can be tied to several factors:

1. Variations in basic business practices and philosophy (i.e., the American tradition of laissez faire vs. a general European propensity toward public ownership and heavy support of key industries).

2. Postwar situations and experiences (i.e., the American industrial giant vs. European industries desperately trying to compete with the United States while recovering from the devastation of the war).

3. Most importantly, the fact that European nations are about to

enter their second decade of technological collaboration while the United States has just begun to think in such terms.

### U.S. Options

To a large degree the initiative for resolving many of the problems relating to Community-wide collaboration rests with the United States. While Europeans are willing to consider technological cooperation with the United States, transatlantic collaboration is not likely to flourish if European industry is relegated to a subservient position to that of the United States. A European government official interviewed expressed the fear of U.S. technological dominance that still weighs heavily on European thinking on collaboration:

> If we become totally dependent on the United States for our defense and other technological needs without any significant development and procurement capability of our own, the United States will be able to take advantage of our situation and force on us any system at any price it wants. We would have no choice and no bargaining chips at all to strike a deal with Washington.

If American firms are to avoid the raising of exclusionary walls in Western Europe, they will have to offer European firms more than subcontractual roles in American-sponsored projects. Boeing's recent problems in persuading the Europeans to participate in the development of its 7X7 are illustrative of this point. A major stand in Boeing's negotiations with the Europeans appears to be its demand for project domination "in return for a stake in what, on past performance, will be the biggest selling aircraft of the next generation – and probably would mean more work for European aircraft factories than their own projects would bring. . . . This was too much for the French."(17) McDonnell Douglas, on the other hand, seems to be more attuned to European sensitivities about project management sharing. Consequently, it stands a much better chance of participating in collaborative ventures with the Europeans, particularly the French.

American firms will eventually also have to come to terms with the insistence by European firms that majority control over projects originating in Europe must be exercised on the eastern side of the Atlantic. Also, American companies should not be surprised if Europeans demand a quid pro quo for agreeing to include U.S. firms in a collaborative defense project. Such a demand could include the American company's agreement to refrain from producing competing systems in other sectors of the particular industry. Agreements of this nature would raise interesting questions relating to U.S. antitrust laws.

Initiatives toward wider defense collaboration in the Atlantic Community, however, should not be left entirely to industry – any more than responsibilities for national defense can be delegated to the market place. Furthermore, even if American and European industries can agree to collaborate on an equal basis, governments must assure that such collaboration is consonant with the long-range goals of the Alliance. The urge by industries to collaborate on a transatlantic level may be animated more by the quest for competitive advantage within their respective milieus than by the common goal of restructuring the Atlantic Community's technological resources along the most efficient lines possible.

The need for American governmental involvement in the casting of transatlantic collaboration is underscored by the fact that many of the major European firms are partially or even totally owned by their respective governments. Furthermore, in the final analysis only firm action on the part of the United States government can signal basic changes in policy and allay European reservations about collaborating with the United States.

Options at the American government's disposal for promoting collaboration on an Atlantic Community-wide basis include the following:

1. Moderation of American protectionist policies

American acquiescence in the unilateral West German decision to terminate offset agreements with the expiration of present arrangements would be a step in the direction of alleviating European resentment of forced American entry into the European defense market. The Buy American Act is also deserving of a detailed review. Not only are the Buy American Act and other protectionist measures invoked to justify retaliatory measures on the part of our West European allies, but the Act may very well cost America's industry more sales abroad in the high-technology areas than it creates for U.S. industries at home.(18) In 1974, during congressional debate over the Trade Act of 1974, for example, officials of the Aerospace Industries Association (AIA) testified that in the previous eight years U.S. aerospace firms had lost $2 billion in exports due to foreign government-directed procurement of indigenously produced goods. A 1971 report to Congress concerning the Buy America Act had found that:

> Policies and procedures implementing the buy-national procurement program generally permit Federal agencies to pay up to 50 percent more for domestic products over comparable foreign products, to protect domestic interests and to improve the U.S. balance of payments position.
>
> Although the buy-national procurement program has been in existence for a number of years information has not been accumulated to evaluate the effects of the program on the balance-of-payments or to determine what it had cost to obtain balance-of-payments deficits.(19)

To date, however, attempts to relax the Buy American Act have stumbled over the insistence by Congress on reciprocity on the part of our allies. The Trade Act of 1974, for example, permits the President, subject to congressional approval, to negotiate the relaxation or removal of the Buy American Act restrictions only on a reciprocal basis. While it may be justified in principle, American insistence on reciprocity poses some serious difficulties for West European industry. First, it is doubtful, given their generally small production runs, that national industries in Western Europe could effectively compete with U.S. industries in a completely open market. Perhaps even more important, as a senior EEC officer has admitted, "to suggest the reciprocal elimination of all restrictions would force our countries to face up to a problem they don't even want to face with the (European) community."(20)

Should the United States unilaterally reduce its protectionist regulations? This might be done on a trial basis with the clear message that a progressive phasing out of American restrictions will depend upon eventual reciprocation in Western Europe.

2. Modification of restrictions on the transfer of sophisticated technologies to members of the Atlantic Community

Consideration should also be given in Washington to easing restrictions on transfer of technology to members of the Atlantic Community. There is every reason for such restrictions to remain in force in such sensitive fields as nuclear weapons technology. Yet, in some less esoteric realms of conventional weapons systems an effort must be made to weight the costs of withholding them from our allies against the risk that their transfer may make them more vulnerable to the prying eyes of the adversary. Forcing European governments to copy our technology because we will not sell it to them not only takes contracts away from American business, but it leads to wasteful duplication of effort. The potential benefits of a broader technology transfer would not be one-sided: It is widely acknowledged that European firms are more advanced than American concerns in certain areas of weapons technology – for example, antitank and other light missile systems.(21) In this respect the 1975 Anglo-American Memorandum of Understanding on reciprocal prices is a positive step forward. The agreement stipulates that procurement bids "be evaluated without applying price differentials under 'Buy National' legislation . . . and . . . provide an alternative to the ad hoc and generally unsatisfactory offset arrangements which have been negotiated in the past to cover specific deals."(22)

3. Reemphasis on an American commitment to apply uniform standards to the competitive testing of American and European prototypes and a willigness to procure the winning system

The recent U.S.-West German tank competition is an example of how the United States should <u>not</u> implement this option. During the competition a joint American-British-West German study found the 120 mm. gun developed for the tank by West Germany to be the best suited to fulfill all performance requirements. The U.S. Army, however, disagreed, preferring the American-developed 105 mm. gun. This led to serious charges in Europe that the United States supported standardization only when American weapons were selected by NATO.(23)

Later the U.S. Army was accused by West German defense officials of trying to prejudice tank selection by persuading Congress to allocate funding for the development of the American tank before prototype competition had even taken place. Congress allocated $100 million for R&D for the American tank addition to an earlier R&D investment of $200 million. West German officials feared that by the time actual competition occurred the United States government would have invested so much in the development of its tank that it would have been financially and politically unable to select the West German model. The U.S. Army answered German criticism with the retort that American development programs "should not have to stop until the other guy can catch up."(24)

To many West Europeans the tank competition became "a test of whether the North Atlantic Treaty allies (could) achieve their often stated goal of standardization . . . and perhaps more importantly . . . whether the United States military services (were) willing to accept a European-developed weapon."(25) The American decision to procure a hybrid tank barely achieved a passing mark with respect to standardization, and was less than convincing as a demonstration of American commitment to more balanced procurement within the Alliance.

4. A commitment to fill a modest percentage of U.S. procurement needs from European sources

Even when competition between American and European systems is not involved, the United States should commit itself to filling a percentage of its equipment needs from European sources. Without such a commitment, it will be difficult, if not impossible, to ever progress beyond the concept of the two-way street in defense procurement.

It should be emphasized that American purchases of European systems would bring numerous benefits. As noted, European firms are more advanced in certain sectors of defense technology. American purchases from these European firms would not only enhance U.S. forces militarily and improve standardization throughout NATO, but they could help to encourage, at least in a small way, the acceptance of some form of specialization. Politically, American purchases of European systems could mitigate dissension within the Alliance, even to the point where the Europeans are more readily amenable to increased purchases of U.S. systems.

To be sure, creating the atmosphere for such U.S. concessions may not be a simple task. Conservative forces in the United States government, especially in the Defense Department, are likely to be skittish about leaving American industries less protected and placing faith in other nations for the supply of certain weapons systems. These trepidations will be particularly difficult to shake in the present economic environment. The Ford Administration itself did not accept even the two-way street concept without some reservations. Former Secretary of Defense Schlesinger, for example, is reported by one source to have advised Roy Mason, then Britain's Secretary of State for Defence, that "the United States has no intention of increasing its arms purchases just to keep British arms industries in business and to help Britain correct its balance of payments problems."(26)

Such conservative attitudes, however, are likely to come under increasing pressures from enlightened elements in the U.S. defense industry and in the labor movement. Heretofore, the large scope of U.S. international involvement has contributed to maintaining high production runs in the weapons industry, but the portents of the post-Vietnam era point to shrinking markets and declining production runs.

Moreover, U.S. weapons industries have been plagued by cost overruns at a time when government has become reluctant to increase its budget ceiling accordingly. The result has been cutbacks of original orders of weapons for the United States government, making American industry more dependent on arms sales abroad to fill capacity and amortize R&D expenditures. If the Carter Administration implements its stated goal of reducing U.S. arms sales to potentially unstable regions of the world, U.S. arms merchants are likely to look more intently at the NATO market, given the United States' long-term and firm commitment to the defense of Europe. Collaboration is the most important vehicle by which the potential abiding in the NATO market can be realized, since major European weapons-producing nations are unlikely to procure systems in whose development they have not had a part.

## European Options

The prospects for expanding collaboration from its essentially European orientation to a wider Atlantic Community framework rest on the coalescence of perceived interests on both sides of the Atlantic. Economic, technological and industrial forces are catalyzing American and West European attitudes in this direction. Firm governmental policies in Europe as well as in the United States, however, are necessary to channel these forces into an efficient and productive framework.

Options available to European governments to enhance the prospects of successful transatlantic collaboration include the following:

### 1. Measures to improve the European image as a collaborative partner

To date, the European record in satisfying American equipment needs in those few instances when the United States has purchased European systems has been less than stellar. The sale of British Harriers to the U.S. Marine Corps, for example, has been marred by the inadequate provision of spare parts and modification kits, service manuals that were incomprehensible to U.S. servicemen, and a lack of technical data to the point that some of the first Harriers delivered to the Marine Corps had to be cannibalized to keep the others operational. Hawker-Siddeley has proven unable to supply sufficient spare parts and technical data for the Marine Corps to meet its peacetime readiness goal of 60 percent of its tactical aircraft.(27) According to Aviation Week & Space Technology, the Marine Corps has found itself in competition with the Royal Air Force for necessary parts and regular maintenance activities to the extent that the Marines were "forced to send many components for repair to contractors in the United States and Britain and turnaround time has been as long as two years."(28)

The Roland missile, another two-way street purchase by the United

States, has also been plagued by problems, although not to the degree of the Harrier. The transfer of Roland technology has proven more difficult than envisioned originally, adding to increased development program costs and stretching procurement schedules. According to Brigadier General Frank Regano, the U.S. Army Roland Project manager, while the United States did not grasp fully the complexity of the Roland system, "the design was not stable in that the Europeans were trying to improve it while we were trying to duplicate it."(29) In addition, the American manufacturers of Roland – Hughes and Boeing – received technical data drawings from no fewer than thirteen companies in France, West Germany and Belgium, "so the U.S. partners have had to cope with some unique variations in the basically different European style."(30)

Given this less than satisfactory record, it is not surprising the U.S. government officials and businessmen are wary of purchases of European arms, not to mention collaboration with European countries in R&D – a far more complicated task than off-the-shelf purchases. In instances of off-the-shelf purchases, European armaments manufacturers must take immediate steps to ensure adequate provision for spare parts and maintenance. Governmental logistic support analyses of weapons exported to the United States might be helpful in this respect. To facilitate both direct arms sales and collaboration with the United States, European nations must streamline the procedures by which technical information is transferred to the United States.

### 2. Increased program collaboration

Despite the problems previously noted with program collaboration, it appears to be the most viable short-term alternative available to the West Europeans, particularly if it is combined with some moves in the direction of institutionalizing procurement policy coordination. Successful collaboration in this framework could prepare the ground for more sweeping changes in the future. Perhaps the defense sector that lends itself most readily to program collaboration in the immediate future is missile development, which is now carried on by several West European nations, often leading to duplication of effort. By engendering the habit of collaboration and teaching its benefits to recalcitrant nations, program collaboration on a substantial scale could be the first significant movement toward wresting a rational order out of the present chaos of policies and practices for the development and production of highly sophisticated weapons systems and equipment in the Atlantic Alliance.

## Community-wide Options

Many problems impeding collaboration between the United States and Western Europe transcend national, and even regional, boundaries. Options for dealing with these problems must be considered in a Community-wide framework. These options include:

1. The creation of task forces to analyze and make recommendations regarding a number of issues:

(a) rationalizing industrial practices;

(b) standardizing environmental and legal regulations and contractual procedures;

(c) clarifying further development and licensing rights;

(d) fostering agreement on Alliance military strategy and operational requirements;

(e) coordinating export policies.

Progress in all these areas must occur if collaboration on an Atlantic-wide basis is to flourish. As was noted earlier, differences in doctrine spell differences in operational requirements which, in turn, translate into diverse weapons systems and equipment. A basic consensus on tactical doctrine would help to dampen national incentives for systems specifically tailored to unique national military needs. It would also minimize the grist for debilitating disputes over weapons systems within NATO – such as the tank controversy that strained U.S.-West German relations in 1976.

Environmental requirements within the Atlantic Community must also be made more uniform so as to lessen controversies such as that which clouded the debut of the Concorde in the United States. In addition, legal questions regarding the ownership of patents and the right to the further development of joint technological projects must be clarified. For example, what would be the legal and political ramifications of a hypothetical West German or British unilateral decision to develop a new derivative of the Tornado or to continue on with the development of a Tornado family of aircraft? Problems could also emerge which are related to the further development of subsystems as well as to the development and marketing of civil products which are technological spinoffs of joint military research. The British avionics industry seems particularly worried with respect to industrial property rights to its components built for the Tornado. Confusion on these points is often built into collaborative contracts; as one British aviation executive stated, "no one knows who can be sued, much less where."(31)

The American experience with the Harrier and the Roland II demonstrates the problems in joint procurement efforts posed by dissonant industrial practices. Small, but nevertheless important, steps such as the standardization of maintenance manuals, could be taken immediately to enhance the joint procurement process. These steps would facilitate movement toward the longer-term goal of rationalizing industrial approaches to R&D.

2. The establishment of a standing committee on science and technology

Progress by the aforementioned task forces could spur movement toward the formulation of an Atlantic Community Science and Technology Program aimed at developing the necessary strategies and approaches for achieving the goals of the Community. Hopefully, an environment would have been created that would allow the present commitment of Eurogroup members to the strengthening of collaboration to be extended to include the United States. In time, certain nations within the Community might even be persuaded not to undertake the development of certain technological systems except on a collaborative basis.

Once these basic objectives had been achieved, the Community might consider forming a central procurement agency. Basically such an agency would have the same functions currently suggested for a European procurement agency, namely, defining specification for equipment; resolving differing national approaches to procurement; assigning contracts and management responsibilities; and maintaining cost and quality control.

The establishment of a central procurement agency, however, must be a <u>long-term</u> goal of the Community. Even if it were limited to a purely European level, at present such a scheme "for enforcing equipment collaboration (would) represent a leap forward beyond the capacity of the countries concerned to absorb fundamental changes in the way in which weapons are procured, even if some of the principles underlying these schemes were less questionable."(32) While such a move is ultimately necessary, including the United States in this kind of procurement agency would add additional biases that must be rationalized. This could prove quite difficult given the fact that, unlike European members of the Community, the United States is just beginning to seriously consider collaboration. It is important to emphasize that without an effective mechanism for balancing competition and cooperation among its European and American members, the Atlantic Community will find it difficult, if not impossible, to deal effectively with the technological problems it is likely to face in the future.

## BEYOND THE TWO-WAY STREET

Notwithstanding its potential benefits, collaboration in defense research, development and procurement in Western Europe promises to raise several problems for both Western Europe and the United States. While interrelated, these problems fall basically into two groups. The first set of questions relates to the collaborative process itself – i.e., how competing national interests and technological requirements can best be reconciled among themselves as well as with sound business practices and military logic. The second set concerns the proper relationship between the European members of NATO and the United States.

There is a growing understanding in Western Europe that constraints at the national and European levels inhibit the development and production of certain technological systems. These constraints protrude particularly in the fields of sophisticated defense and aircraft technology, where rising costs and surplus capacity have been compounded by growing public unwillingness to devote more resources to defense. European political and military leaders realize that something must be done to break defense production out of uneconomic and stultifying national compartments and that collaboration represents the answer. At the same time, however, the record of collaborative projects thus far is hardly an impressive one.

The shortcomings of present collaborative modes as well as the urgent need for improved methods are being driven home vividly by the Tornado project. While the Tornado is one of many collaborative efforts now underway in Europe, the impact of the project's success or failure on political, military and industrial thinking about defense procurement will be considerable. This project represents the first time that Britain, West Germany and Italy have cooperated in defense technology. Moreover, each of these countries has placed faith in the aircraft's ability to fulfill its national military needs. Yet, the project already has entailed excessive costs and wasteful duplication of effort and the indications are that the final product will not meet the expectations of the participants.(33)

Should cooperative technological efforts be carried on within the Atlantic Community as a whole or on an intra-European basis? The question of the American role in the procurement of advanced defense technologies promises to loom larger in American-European relations as Europeans strive to improve the efficiency of their cooperative efforts and as the United States begins to realize that in some sectors, at least, technological cooperation with Europe may be in its interest.

Excluding the United States from collaborative procurement efforts would seem only to perpetuate many of the divisive tendencies that currently threaten the Alliance. These surfaced, for example, during the tank competition between the United States and West Germany when several European countries drew linkages between an objective assessment on the part of the United States of the German Leopard II and their own willingness to purchase the American-made Airborne Warning and Control System (AWACS). Linkages of this nature, in the long run, can only be detrimental to standardization within NATO as well as to political amity within the Atlantic Community.

Failure to collaborate on an Atlantic Community basis will also lead to heightened competition for arms markets in the Third World, thus straining further the already weakened political bonds of the Alliance. West European countries have already begun to exploit the possiblity of linking arms transfers to guarantees from OPEC nations on future oil supplies. Saudi Arabia, for example, signed an agreement with France to supply the French with 27 million tons of oil over the next three years in exchange for weapons, machinery and technical assistance.(34) Similar agreements between OPEC nations and other members of the Atlantic Community may be expected.

Finally, a competitive environment that has been sharpened by disparate American and West European approaches to defense procurement can be exploited by the Soviet Union and others to their own advantage. Rolls Royce, for example, has negotiated an agreement with the Soviet Union for jet engines to pump natural gas from Siberia. The engine being sold is the Avon, in previous years the workhorse for a whole generation of British military aircraft.(35) In light of Rolls Royce's leadership in aeroengine design and the

Soviets' traditional difficulties in developing jet engines for military aircraft, this agreement has potentially significant implications. Similarly, the Chinese have agreed to purchase large quantities of Rolls Royce Spey engines for use in their new combat plane – "an inexpensive one but with supersonic performance similar to America's latest F-16."(36) Moreover, the Soviets or others could exacerbate the competitive environment between the United States and Western Europe by enticing European firms with the blandishments of Soviet and East European civil markets and perhaps even participation in joint nonmilitary technological ventures on terms favorable to European needs and in tune with European sensitivities.

American participation in collaborative defense procurement ventures offers clear benefits. For Western Europe, closer cooperation will provide access to crucial American markets and technological know-how. Reciprocally, defense-related industry in the United States, facing dwindling government contracts and surplus capacity, could benefit from broader inroads into the West European market. Greater cooperation in defense procurement on a mutually acceptable basis can strengthen substantially the sinews of alliance interdependence beneath the caprices of national policies.

The very concept of Europeanizing defense procurement attests to the divisive forces within the Alliance. Much of the incentive for technological collaboration within Western Europe has been spurred by the fear of American technological dominance. Attempts to limit collaboration to Western Europe reached an apex in 1972 with the publication of the Spinelli plan for the reorganization of the European aerospace industry, which had as one rallying point the exclusion of the United States from the European market.

The exclusionary aspects of the Europeanization campaign have developed not only from deep-seated resentments of U.S. technological overlordship, but also from what might be characterized as the billiard ball theory of European unification. This is the concept, drawn from physics, that objects achieve density in the clash with other objects. Inasmuch as the will toward political unity in Western Europe has faltered in the face of an apparently lowered threat from the east – so the argument runs – it can be rekindled only in the competitive clash with other forces. And in the economic-technological sphere the logical competitor for Western Europe is the United States.

Even if there is theoretical plausibility to the concept, it breaks down in practical application in the defense R&D and procurement realms. As this study has endeavored to show, not only is meaningful and efficient collaboration on a West European level blocked by national and particularist restraining walls, but its economic feasibility is highly questionable. Even under the most optimistic assumptions, European collaborative efforts could not aspire to the level where they could meet crucial West European requirements for sophisticated weaponry. Under the same best assumptions, a European defense R&D and procurement community, even if it overcame problems of management, could not find the scope of market that would lend cost-effectiveness to production runs, let alone make it truly competitive with U.S. industry.

The solution to NATO's defense procurement problems must be sought in an Atlantic framework. This is not to say that greater collaboration on a

European level is not fruitful or that it is necessarily inimical to the larger Atlantic framework. Yet much depends on the basic approach that is charted at the outset of the process; an exclusionary approach, once embarked upon, tends to become self-perpetuating. The United States must point the way toward an Atlantic framework through initiatives and concessions. It must do so, not so much from a sense of alliance altruism (although there is room for that, too), but rather from an enlightened appreciation of the problems that are beginning to assert themselves in broad sectors of American armament industries and, last but not least, the need to maintain in the Atlantic Community adequate defense capabilities.

## NOTES

(1) The United States, however, will probably be the country to take the Harrier to the next level of development.

(2) John H. Hoagland, "American and European Industry Relations in Military Exports to the Less Developed Countries," Paper prepared for the Conference on the Implications of the Military Build-Up in Non-Industrialized States, International Security Studies Program, The Fletcher School of Law and Diplomacy, Tufts University, May 6-8, 1976, p. 2.

(3) This problem is not limited to the defense sector, however. According to The Economist, "Lockheed simply cannot afford to go ahead with the shortened 200-seat version of its TriStar." September 11, 1976, p. 80.

(4) New York Times, April 29. 1975, p. 1.

(5) See Robert Prinsky, "Atlantic Alliance: Discussions of Joint Projects Are Pressed by French and U.S. Plane Manufacturers," Wall Street Journal, May 14, 1976, p. 38.

(6) Hoagland, p. 9.

(7) The Economist, September 11, 1976, p. 81.

(8) Thomas A. Callaghan, U.S./European Economic Cooperation in Military and Civil Technology (Washington, D.C.: Center for Strategic and International Studies, Georgetown University, 1975, revised edition), p. 1. All subsequent citations will be to this edition.

(9) New York Times, April 29, 1975, p. 1.

(10) Aviation Week & Space Technology, January 17, 1977, p. 58.

(11) According to the New York Times (November 13, 1976, p. 1), however, it was generally agreed on both sides that, largely for nationalistic reasons, it would be impossible to standardize on the same tank. See also, "Tanks: U.S. and FRG Reach Key Agreement," Defense & Foreign Affairs Digest,No. 8-9. 1976, p. 90.

(12) René Foch, Europe and Technology: A Political View (Paris: The Atlantic Institute, Atlantic Papers No. 2, 1970), p. 40.

(13) Ibid.

(14) Roger Facer, The Alliance and Europe, Part III: Weapons Procurement in Europe -- Capabilities and Choices (London: International Institute for Strategic Studies, Adelphi Paper No. 108, 1975), p. 38.

(15) Commission of the European Communities, Studies on the Aeronautical and Space Industries of the Community Compared with Those of the United Kingdom and the United States, Vol. 4 (Turin, Italy: SORIS, 1971), p. 448.

(16) Commission of the European Communities, The European Aerospace Industry -- Position and Figures, Document 111/956/74-E, February 1975, p. 17.

(17) The Economist, September 11, 1976, p. 81. A primary reason for Boeing's position is its fear that, unless it dominates the project, it could lose its leadership in the American market.

(18) Callaghan, p. 95.

(19) The Comptroller General, "Coordinated Consideration Needed of Buy-National Procurement Program Policies," A Report to Congress, December 1971; cited in Callaghan, p. 97.

(20) Callaghan, p. 94.

(21) Serious thought might also be given in American industrial and governmental areas to extending the concept of the "two-way street" beyond its present military orientation since European firms are ahead of American firms in some sectors of civilian technology. For example, several European countries – France in particular – are well advanced in technologies relating to the energy transfer, solar heating and the utilization of the oceans as a source of energy.

(22) G.H. Green, "British Policy for Defence Procurement," a lecture given at the Royal United Services Institute for Defence Studies, February 16, 1976,

published in Royal United Service Institute Journal, September 1976, p. 24.

(23) John W. Finney, "Bonn Charges Bias in Selection of Tank," The New York Times, December 18, 1975, p. 11.

(24) Ibid.

(25) Ibid.

(26) As reported by John W. Finney, "U.S. Urged to Buy Arms in Europe," The New York Times, September 27, 1975, p. 6.

(27) The average readiness rate for the Harrier from January 1974 to March 1976 was 42 percent, with a low of 22 percent and a high of 55 percent. Aviation Week & Space Technology, January 17, 1977, p. 23.

(28) Ibid.

(29) Ibid., pp. 57-58.

(30) Ibid.

(31) "U.K. Avionics Industry Fears Further Decline," Aviation Week & Space Technology, May 29, 1972, p. 48.

(32) Green, P. 102.

(33) Frankfurter Rundschau, November 7, 1974.

(34) "Saudis Purchase French Magic Missile," Aviation Week & Space Technology, June 2, 1975.

(35) The Guardian, December 10, 1976, p. 15.

(36) The Daily Telegraph, November 30, 1976, p. 5.

# IV

# The Political Challenge of Finlandization— The External and Internal Processes

# 9 The Soviet Strategy of Finlandization of Western Europe— The External Process

James E. Dougherty

The Soviet Union's preferred strategy for extending its influence over Western Europe during the last quarter of this century will be through a process of Finlandization rather than by overt military attack – although the latter option will beome an ever more palpable contingency (and therefore an ever more plausible threat overhanging the political arena) as the military disparities between NATO and the Warsaw Pact continue to widen. Factors rooted in both the Russian historical tradition and in Marxist-Leninist ideology combine to produce a predilection for the patient, indirect, attritional approach to the accomplishment of foreign policy goals. Until recent years, the Soviets have had to operate from a position of decidedly strategic military-technological inferiority vis-a-vis the West. Even when in a decisively inferior position, they often adopted a militant, aggressive stance; psychologically, rhetorically, and politically, but not militarily. They were ever ready to test the mettle of the capitalist adversary to probe outward and to take advantage of whatever opportunities might open – in Czechoslovakia, Berlin, Greece, Turkey, Iran, Korea, the Middle East, Vietnam and elsewhere. But they were constantly prepared to ease the pressure and back away from military embroilment rather than risk provoking a decisive response by the West against the heartland of Socialism – Soviet territory.

Ostensibly, the steady growth of Soviet military capabilities relative to those of the West have made the leaders in the Kremlin more relaxed, more confident and more patient than ever. Khrushchev's grave miscalculation in Cuba in 1962, by starkly posing the risks inherent in any critical and direct confrontation between the superpowers, heightened the conviction of his successors that the decisive offensive against the capitalist world had to await the amassment of a margin of Soviet military superiority across the full spectrum of capabilities that would be sufficient to inhibit any concerted Western responses to the march of Socialism. A Soviet priority, in other words, has been the fashioning of an overwhelming counterdeterrent. Yet, this counterdeterrent is not being cast in the U.S. model of mutual destruction or doomsday. All of their theoretical pronouncements, as well as operational programs (including their heavy emphasis on civil defense), attest to the Soviet belief that if war should be triggered – e.g., by the desperate throes of the capitalist system – it must be waged and it must be won.

In the meantime, the Soviets can review the evolution of the last five years with satisfaction. It was their arms policy in the Middle East, after all, which made it possible for Egypt to launch the October War of 1973, and Soviet encouragement, backed by proximate power, played a not insignificant role in the Arab oil embargo in the wake of that conflict. That crisis sent repercussive waves throughout Europe, and put Europeans on unambiguous notice that future decisions made in Moscow with respect to the Middle East could affect vitally their political and economic destinies. The Greek-Turkish crisis of 1974-1975, and Portugal's internal turmoil in the same period, transmitted the message to knowledgeable Europeans that the Soviets, in the words of Shakespeare, had to be counted among "those who have the power to hurt and do none." Events in Southeast Asia in the spring of 1975 and in Angola late in that same year (fraught with implications for Europe's dependence on raw materials from distant sources) suggested that the United States was no longer able and/or willing to conduct a foreign policy backed by military force in Asia and Africa. Small wonder that the West Europeans went with relatively little optimism to the Finland station to initial the Helsinki Accords.

For three decades, Europe has been the most stable of all the areas of superpower competition in the world, because of the political astuteness of the Europeans themselves and the awareness of the superpowers that direct confrontation in that region would pose the gravest dangers. Other areas of the world, however important they are strategically – the Middle East, Southeast Asia, the Indian Ocean and the coasts of Africa – have been less critically sensitive than Europe, and thus safer for competitive game-playing in the eyes of Soviet strategists. These strategists are determined to remain cautious, and to eschew leaps into the unknown with incalculable consequences. If at any point they decide to back away from a situation because of some unexpected development, they will portray their action as being in the best interests of world peace. As they grow stronger, both strategically and conventionally, they will probably become willing to probe farther and to press harder. If they should become confident that the correlation of forces has shifted decisively in their favor – and that the West perceives this as clearly as they do – they may become tempted to commit Soviet forces in support of a fraternal government or communist revolutionary force even if this should involve the risk of a possible confrontation with U.S. forces. But they are most likely to place themselves in such a situation unless they enjoy a high degree of certitude that their move will be interdictive; that it will constitute, as a result of careful planning and timing, the last safe move that a superpower can make under the circumstances; and that it will be the United States that must back away from the confrontation – as the Soviets did in Cuba.

## THE CONCEPT OF FINLANDIZATION

As the Conference on Security and Cooperation in Europe (CSCE) was drawing toward a conclusion preparatory to the signing of the Helsinki Accords in July-August 1975, the Soviet Union went out of its way to pay tribute to Finland and to the Soviet-Finnish relationship "as a model for the development of relations between states with different social systems and as a concrete example of a constructive approach to urgent questions of modern international life."(1) The suggestion that the behavior of Helsinki should become a paragon of the behavior of other European capitals strengthened apprehension that Moscow might henceforth seek to reduce the freedom of maneuver of West European states to a level comparable to that enjoyed by Finland.

The term "Finlandization," which apparently was first used by Professor Richard Loewenthal of the Free University of Berlin in 1962,(2) refers to a somewhat inchoate and subtle process whereby the countries of Western Europe would be weakened gradually from a political, economic, sociological and military standpoint; separated from the overarching protectve power of the United States; and slowly transformed into a set of isolated, neutralized states which would find the needles on their political compasses oriented increasingly toward Moscow as the single magnetic center of power capable of shaping the outcome of events in Europe.

The concept of Finlandization grows out of a plausible presumption that in politics the evaluation of long-term trends is often more important to policy formulation than the precise calculus of quantitative balance at any precise moment. West Europeans are a highly sophisticated political people, sensitive to the winds of power. They have understood balance of power politics much longer and much better than their American counterparts.

The concept of Finlandization presupposes that power casts its shadow before it in the unmistakable form of attitude formation and influence. Implicit in the concept of Finlandization, then, is the notion that the Soviets, under favorable circumstances, could extend their hegemonic sway westward over the Continent, over Scandinavia and over Great Britain without resorting either to war or to military occupation – merely by dint of the iron fist in the velvet glove (to borrow the Bismarckian image) which would be implicit in Moscow's possession of overwhelming power unmatched in Western Europe. In such a scenario, there would be no need for sabre-rattling, or the uttering of threats, or the issuance of orders and ultimata. Knowledgeable West European politicians and diplomats would know through political intelligence and instinct what constituted acceptable or unacceptable behavior on their part in the eyes of the Soviets. They would know in advance what was expected of them, adjust their policies accordingly, and furnish their own domestically plausible justifications and explanations for doing so.

Finlandization denotes a gradual process; it is by no means an established phenomenon at the present time. On the Soviet side it is a preferred strategy; on the West European side, a feared fate. The U.S. commitment to Western Europe remains a key variable. Western Europe cannot easily be Finlandized so long as the United States maintains credible commitment in NATO, as well as a military presence sufficient to support that political credibility. Without such a commitment and presence, it is almost inevitable that the process of Finlandization would be completed. Yet, it is important in this analysis that we recognize a fundamental difference between the existing situation of Western Europe and that of Finland. To gain an appreciation of both the present differences and the potential future danger, it will be instructive to examine briefly the model of Soviet-Finnish relations, and then consider how the Soviets would like to draw analogies between the pattern of Soviet-Finnish relations in recent decades and the pattern of Soviet-European relations in the future.

Although many commentators have used the term "Finlandization" during the past decade, relatively few have subjected the concept to careful analysis – and even then only briefly.(3) Perhaps we take for granted a widespread intuitive comprehension of Finland's plight. Few can fail to see that a powerful state will exercise a sphere of influence over a relatively weak neighbor when there is no prospect of constraint as the result of the countering presence of another correspondingly powerful intervenor. The Soviet Red Army need not occupy Finland in order to establish Soviet domination. The Soviet military presence is a basic and permanent factor underlying the USSR's ability to intervene at will in the political life of the East European people's democracies and to preserve the political, ideological and military status quo within the zone that those countries comprise.

In contrast to Eastern Europe, which constitutes a hard sphere of influence, Finland is a soft sphere, in which the weak state defers voluntarily to the stronger and the stronger refrains from behaving as highhandedly as it might.(4) The Soviet Union could have converted Finland into a full-fledged satellite after World War II if it had wished to do so. Both the Soviets and the Finns know this, and the knowledge underpins the soft sphere of influence relationship. Helsinki avoids pursuing policies which would be displeasing to Moscow, and accepts a series of political accommodations in order to preserve a situation which, however humiliating and hard to bear, is less intolerable than outright military occupation would be. Moscow, for its part, is content with less than the absolute control which it is capable of obtaining, because it recognizes that, even without direct military pressure, Finland is unlikely to act contrary to Soviet interests, and that the wider costs of converting Finland into a hard sphere of influence would probably be high in comparison to the additional benefits that might be gained.

If the Soviets had blatantly violated Finland's neutrality in recent decades, it would have to pay a price throughout the Scandinavian region and beyond. Under those circumstances, Denmark and Norway would have been much less disposed to pursue a course of nuclear neutralism in NATO, and much more ready to allow the emplacement of U.S. atomic weapons on their soil, as well as the passage of American nuclear submarines in their territorial waters. Furthermore, there had long been a tacit understanding in Northern Europe that the Western-oriented neutrality of Sweden is a quid pro quo for the Soviet-imposed neutrality of Finland.(5) If the Soviet Union had applied overt pressure against Finland, Sweden would have been motivated to reassess its foreign policy posture and at least to consider, for national security reasons, full-fledged entrance into the Atlantic Alliance, and not merely tacit cooperation with it for defense planning purposes.

The superpower in the Soviet-Finnish type of relationship is able to extract concessions or to force adjustments in the situation whenever conditions make a change necessary. In a crisis, the threat of actual military occupation is always there; the mere announcement that the Soviet Union intended to carry out maneuvers near the Finnish border would be sufficient to send shivers up and down the Finnish Peninsula. The weaker state, by sharp contrast, can bring about favorable changes in the relationship only by resorting to its most persuasive diplomacy. The superpower need not always be inflexibly adamant. If its leaders are intelligent, they will display occasionally a benign countenance and grant the supplicant's request for permission to follow a certain course of action. Both parties, then, for quite different reasons, prefer the more subtle to the harsher mode of sphere-of-influence relationship. But in the final analysis, the relationship works because both parties proceed according to the assumption which an Athenian ambassador long ago announced to the magistrates of Melos: "the powerful exact what they can, and the weak grant what they must."(6)

In what ways have the leaders of Finland, reading the political weather reports and signals emanating from their neighbor, felt constrained to defer to Soviet wishes – by anticipation if not by actual direction? Finland has not been free to associate politically or economically with any other state or group of states in the absence of Soviet permission. Its desire to participate in the Marshall Plan for European recovery was aborted when the Soviet Union declared officially that it would view this as a hostile act.(7) The USSR vetoed Finland's application for admission to the United Nations, and between 1952 and 1955 withheld approval for Finland's joining the other Scandinavian states in the Nordic Council.(8) Because of the importance of Finland's trade ties with Western Europe, Premier Khruschev grudgingly permitted the Passikivi Government to take part, on a limited basis, in the European Free Trade Association – no doubt because Moscow viewed that grouping as a competitor of the politically more dangerous European Economic Community. Not until 1973, after Britain joined the EEC, had the climate of detente improved to a point where Moscow was willing to authorize a closer association between Helsinki and Brussels – and then only after Finland had made significant political and economic concessions to the Soviet Union and to Comecon. Even though Finland would prefer to carry on the great bulk of its foreign trade with the West, it is obliged for political reasons to strike a balance of trade between East and West, lest the nation's neutrality be compromised.(9)

Moreover, Finland has no choice but to permit the Soviet Union – to the extent that it wishes to do so – to define the ground rules whereby domestic politics is conducted, by setting the margins of political acceptability for parties and personalities. In 1974, as part of the Finnish-EEC understanding, the Soviets secured an extension in the term of office of their protegé Kekkonen without the uncertainty and possible embarrassment of an election. Also, on occasion, Moscow has made clear its displeasure with and opposition to Finnish political parties or coalitions – especially the Social Democrats and the Honka Centrist Front – causing them either to trim their sails or to collapse. The Finnish government, quite understandably, feels compelled to support or at least pay lip-service to the Soviet position on most international issues and refrains from opposing Moscow on fundamental issues, such as NATO, Chile and the Middle East. Even the Finnish press, while inclined at times to be moderately critical, engages in a mode of self-censorship calculated to avoid irritating the Russians.

Finally, the Soviet Union, by putting threatened or actual pressure upon Finland, is able to send repercussions through a larger region. This was demonstrated in the Note Crisis of late 1961, when the USSR suddenly presented in Helsinki a demand for military consultations, just as President Kekkonen was completing a friendly visit to the United States. The Soviets apparently sought to warn Finland not to become too friendly with the leader of the Western Alliance and also to show concern over what their propagandists were then roundly scoring as German "revanchist militarism." Moscow was interested in conveying to Denmark and Norway its opposition to any military cooperation on their part with the Federal Republic which might alter the status quo in the Baltic. In this respect, the USSR was not successful: Denmark, although not enthusiastic about defense cooperation with Bonn, refused to be dissuaded from negotiating for the establishment of a joint Danish-German Baltic Approaches Command in NATO.(10) Kekkonen finally managed to put off the Soviet demand for military consultations, but Finland had been compelled to pay a price in the form of domestic political adjustments – rescheduling parliamentary elections and withdrawing a presidential candidate unacceptable to Moscow. The fiction of Finnish neutrality was preserved, but few failed to see that the Soviets had made their point.

Whether or not Moscow will be able to Finlandize the countries of Western Europe will depend not only on the shifting global and regional balances and on the effectiveness of Soviet diplomacy, but also on the political intelligence, determination and shrewdness of Western political leaders. Will these leaders show voluntary and anticipatory deference to the Kremlin's wishes merely because they perceive the military power of the USSR to be steadily increasing compared to that of the United States? George F. Kennan has said: "It takes two to make a successful act of intimidation in international life, just as it takes two to make a successful act of blackmail among individuals."(11) If one party is resolved to overcome or eliminate the fear that renders him vulnerable to blackmail, then the blackmailer cannot practice his art because there is no psychological weakness to be exploited.

## THE TRAJECTORY OF THE SOVIET STRATEGY

A central point made earlier deserves to be reiterated: So long as the United States continues to provide a credible military-political counterweight to Soviet power in Europe, West Europeans need not seriously fear Finlandization, for that fate befalls those who lack a genuine protector. But Moscow can be expected to employ some of the assumptions and techniques of Finlandization in order to remove the major obstacles – especially NATO – to achieving the results of the Finlandizing process. Efforts will continue to condition the West Europeans into believing that the American military presence in Europe has become an anachronism, now that the territorial status quo has been ratified by the Helsinki pact; that the retention of thousands of tactical nuclear weapons in NATO Europe will pose an increasing yet unnecessary danger of catastrophe; that the gradual scaling down of forces by the two alliance systems in Central Europe will be an inevitable, even though slowly-emerging, outcome of the MBFR talks in Vienna; and that the security of Europe will be better served not by developing or purchasing new, costly weapons systems but by institutionalizing detente and by promoting economic-technological cooperation, as well as friendly contacts, between the two halves of Europe, within the framework of all-European security.

The Soviets are engaged in an extremely delicate operation vis-a-vis Western Europe. They seek to promote a form of pan-European detente – Lenin's "peaceful coexistence" in its latest phase – which will help to accomplish a number of objectives: (1) widen the sense of political distance between the United States and its European allies, and persuade the latter that the former, although maintaining a physical presence, is becoming so unreliable a guarantor that the West Europeans should begin thinking of security in nonmilitary terms, as the Finns have done; (2) arrest permanently the movement of the European Community toward any forms of political and military unity unfavorable to the USSR; (3) enhance among the Western democracies a political climate conducive to the growth of pacifism and antimilitarism, and a steady decline of public support of those countries for defense expenditures; (4) bring about the phased withdrawal of the U.S. military presence from Western Europe without stimulating Britain, France and Germany into the compensatory action of moving toward European military cooperation, especially in the nuclear realm; (5) foster the notion that socialist and nonsocialist systems can coexist and cooperate peacefully even at a time when a variety of political, psychological and socioeconomic forces (e.g., national particularism, alienation, corruption, revolutionary discontent, energy and materials shortages, unemployment, inflation, monetary and trade problems, strikes and governmental instability) indicate that the capitalist democracies are passing through what the Marxists expect is their gravest crisis.

Undoubtedly Soviet strategic analysts have devoted the greatest attention to the question of timing and phasing the severance of the U.S.-European military linkage. For nearly two decades, the Soviets frequently demanded, in uncompromising language, the withdrawal of all U.S. forces and the liquidation of all U.S. bases and facilities in Europe. That was a natural line to pursue in the Cold War era, when no one expected anything of the sort to happen. But in the era of detente and arms negotiations, politics and diplomacy in Europe have become much more complex and ambiguous. The Kremlin's long-range goal is still to bring about the withdrawal of American military power from the continent, and to reorient Western Europe toward the Soviet socialist system. But Moscow must worry, and be extremely careful, about how it approaches its goal, for it is determined to minimize the possible undesirable consequences of U.S. retrenchment.

The principal contingency to be avoided would be a strengthening of the conviction among West European political leaders that if the U.S. pledge to protect Europe becomes unreliable, the European Community will have no choice but to forge a common foreign and defense policy, based on the coordination of British and French strategic nuclear weapons programs, and including some form of West German support, cooperation and participation. The Europeans themselves have always recognized that serious difficulties inhere in the concept of European nuclear deterrence. The political problem of the role to be played by West Germany is seen as the thorniest of all. If British and French submarine-launched ballistic missiles were to become the nucleus of a European deterrent force, the Federal Republic would certainly want a voice in their management, and this would prove more unacceptable to the Soviets than the prolongation of the U.S. military presence.(12)

During the early 1970s, as British entry into the Community drew near and the transatlantic dialogue over the future shape of NATO spurred Europe's efforts to define its own identity, there was increasing discussion of the technical, strategic, economic and political aspects of European deterrence.(13) In late 1973, when NATO was passing through a period of intense strain as a result of the consequences of the Yom Kippur War and anti-Kissinger sentiment in Western Europe was running high, the Soviets expressed concern over, and opposition to, the idea of closer West European cooperation and unity in defense and political matters.(14) In all probability, what the Soviets perceived as a critical juncture in the history of the European unity movement had already passed. The oil/energy crisis had set in motion a chain of economic developments – balance of payments deficits, inflation, unemployment, shortages and strikes – which, while heightening the sense of vulnerability of Community members to the operation of forces beyond their control, also led to squabbling within the EEC and brought to a halt the movement toward European unity which had seemed to have such a favorable prospect only a few months earlier. Many Europeans, long suspicious that the United States was unenthusiastic over the potential emergence of a politically, economically and militarily united Europe, began to fear that the United States, in an attempt to placate the Soviets for the sake of fostering detente, would actively oppose European unity.(15)

There seems to be general agreement that the European unity movement has become stalled during the last three years.(16) Not even the direct election of a European Parliament will mark a genuine forward surge on the part of the Community, because the powers of the Strasbourg Assembly probably will be strictly limited. Nevertheless, the idea of European defense cooperation in a form that will allow the French to participate with the members of Eurogroup outside the formal structure of NATO(17) will continue to attract European policymakers in the future – more or less depending upon the perception of the threat in the minds of Europeans – and the Soviets will seek to minimize the lure of such an alternative as the U.S. defense commitment to Europe undergoes steady erosion. (For the assumptions under which the Soviets might support a "benign" European unity movement, see the next chapter.)

## MBFR AND FINLANDIZATION

It is at this point that the MBFR negotiations in Vienna must be examined briefly in the light of the Soviet strategy of Finlandization. West European policymakers, despite an oft-professed desire to achieve a military balance at a lower level of forces in Central Europe, are far from enthusiastic about the prospect of troop reduction, and accept MBFR only grudgingly as preferable to the kind of unilateral U.S. withdrawals which seemed imminent in the early 1970s, when the protracted U.S. balance of payments deficit made the Mansfield Amendment popular enough in the Congress to appear as a real threat to NATO.(18) West European defense analysts are worried deeply about the maintenance of a military equilibrium in Europe, recognizing that the replacement of the assumption of U.S. strategic superiority by the assumption of superpower parity has made the regional situation more dangerous than ever. In their view, the balance of power in Europe, seen as a political-psychological function of the military balance, has been slowly but inexorably tilting against NATO because of Soviet quantitative superiority in armor and tactical air forces, substantial Soviet reinforcement advantages in the initial phase of hostilities, and expanding Soviet naval deployments in the Mediterranean, in the northern waters off Norway, and around the coasts of Africa. Moreover, whereas it was assumed five years ago that NATO possessed an unquestioned superiority in tactical nuclear weapons with which to counter the Warsaw Pact's greater conventional power, the Soviet Union has been steadily expanding its theater nuclear capabilities and now, with its SS-20 missiles, Backfire Bombers, and improved tactical air systems, can strike with nuclear weapons much farther westward than NATO can eastward. The West Europeans are aware that it will be difficult to negotiate any force reductions in Europe which will enhance their own security, given the immutable military advantages bestowed by geography upon the Soviet position in Europe.

MBFR negotiations provide a mechanism whereby the USSR can exercise leverage over the direction and rate of change in the European political-military environment. Those negotiations have helped to relieve pressures for precipitate unilateral U.S. troop withdrawals, with potentially unsettling and unpredictable consequences. They also furnish the Soviets with opportunities to test and exacerbate potential political fissures in the negotiating position of the NATO allies – differences between Europe and the United States, differences among the British, Germans and other Europeans, differences between incumbent and opposition political parties, differences among the military services of NATO countries. The longer and more frustratingly the Vienna talks drag on, the more welcome will Soviet concessions be. No matter what precise agreement might issue from MBFR, it is likely that the West Europeans will accept it as inevitable with the political rhetoric of high hopes but with deep underlying misgivings. Any MBFR agreement is certain to produce a much more rapid acceleration of pressures for cuts in the military budgets of NATO countries and to create a slippery slope for American force withdrawals from Western Europe – yet, phased withdrawals that will enable the Soviets to cope with, or even exploit, any destabilizing consequences.

For the last ten years, the Soviets have seemed determined – except for their invasion of Czechoslovakia in August 1968 – to reduce tensions in Europe as a prelude to the deterioration of the Atlantic Alliance and the Finlandization of Western Europe. The Soviets are well aware that whenever they intervene to clamp down upon liberalizing tendencies in Eastern Europe or to exacerbate conflicts in Western Europe, they are likely to provoke counterproductive reactions in the West – stepped-up political criticism of Moscow, calls for a reassessment of detente, the growth of NATO or EEC cohesion, and increases in Western vigilance and defense spending. Moscow has learned how to assess the costs of its past hardline policies vis-a-vis Berlin, Hungary, Czechoslovakia and, to a lesser extent, Portugal. In fact, the Soviets have demonstrated that they know exactly how to produce an adverse reaction in the West any time they see a need to do so in order to establish what they regard as optimal control over changes in the total European political-military environment.

The Soviets can be expected from time to time to press for Western acceptance of proposals often made and rejected in the past – e.g., mutual pledges to refrain from the first use of nuclear weapons, and the creation of nuclear-free zones in Central Europe and the Mediterranean. The Soviets realize that NATO is more dependent than the Warsaw Pact upon the public espousal of a nuclear strategy. As former Inspector General of the Bundeswehr Ulrich de Maiziere has pointed out, strategic nuclear weapons – which are primarily political weapons – constitute the decisive backbone of deterrence, while tactical nuclear weapons provide the essential linkup between strategic nuclear and conventional forces. NATO's entire strategy of flexible response, said de Maiziere, "is based on the fact that it is flexible to whatever action is taken by whatever aggressor, ready to come up with the appropriate military response, without a programmed reaction, without a predetermined series of responses, and without reassociation of the nuclear option."(19) Tensions persist between European and American perspectives of tactical nuclear weapons. Whereas European strategists prefer to regard them as an escalation link between NATO Conventional forces and U.S. strategic forces (and thus a powerful strengthener of deterrence), American strategists see them as a backstop in case of conventional Soviet breakthrough, with the hope of keeping the nuclear battlefield limited to Europe – and mainly Western Europe. The Soviets will find it advantageous, therefore, to keep offering proposals which provoke debate in Western Europe about the advisability of retaining tactical nuclear weapons within European NATO. Such a debate will, in itself, help to undermine the credibility of NATO's current strategy.

## SOME OF THE LIKELY IMPLEMENTS OF FINLANDIZATION

It is not possible to inventory all the ways in which the Soviet Union will pursue its strategy of Finlandization and of gradually accumulating leverage with which to influence political, economic and military developments in Western Europe. Yet, several of the more salient possibilities must be considered:

1. If and when communist parties should come to power in any West European countries (whether members of NATO or EEC or not), the Soviets will seek to exercise whatever influence they have over such parties to

compound rather than to ameliorate the planning difficulties that confront the Atlantic Alliance and the European unity movement. (The subject of Eurocommunism and the Alliance is dealt with in the chapter that follows.)

2. The USSR will continue to strive to persuade the Europeans that the hosting of U.S. and NATO bases and facilities involves great dangers; that European countries which make such assets available should extract a higher price for them; and that, in the long run, the European countries will be better off after they have phased out such foreign military bases and facilities.

3. The USSR will express its opposition, both through public criticism and more confidential diplomatic communication, to all significant efforts by the West Europeans to improve NATO defense capabilities (e.g., by purchasing U.S. weapons systems, or by reorganizing, re-equipping, and upgrading the training of forces), or to make progress toward closer NATO or European defense cooperation (e.g., through standardization, joint exercises, collaboration on weapons production, etc.). They will characterize any such moves as provocative to the Soviet Union and inimical to the processes of peaceful coexistence.

4. Soviet leaders will probably try to develop closer personal contacts with the leaders of West European governments comparable to those once enjoyed with De Gaulle and Brandt, and to promote a greater variety of contacts between Soviet officials and prominent personalities within Western political parties. These contacts will enhance the Soviets' ability to intervene more effectively and less offensively in the domestic politics of democratic countries by giving advice, exploiting domestic partisan conflicts to Moscow's advantage, and making timely concessions or threats calculated to help or hinder the electoral prospects of a particular party or leader.

5. Soviet leaders may seek future opportunities to intervene dramatically in the internal affairs of selected West European countries – as they did by furnishing financial and political support to the Portuguese Communist Party during 1974 and 1975 – if for no other purpose than to demonstrate their ability to do so with relative impunity. The West Europeans are keenly aware that the Soviets are more able and ready to intervene in West European affairs than the Western allies in East European affairs (see the discussion below on the Conference on Security and Cooperation in Europe and the Helsinki Pact). The lesson is not entirely without effect. To be sure, the Portuguese crisis did not lead to the catastrophic consequences that some Western observers feared: the U.S. base complex in the Azores was not lost, nor did the USSR gain clear access to new facilities in the Portuguese Atlantic. Yet there was an unmistakable change in the political climate of the Atlantic Community – one which probably helped to prepare for a subsequent outcome in Angola that was decidedly disadvantageous to NATO and Western Europe.

6. The West will have to be prepared to see the Soviets try, from time to time, to exacerbate conflicts between two NATO allies (e.g., Greece and Turkey over Cyprus or Aegean oil) which are certain to weaken the Atlantic Alliance and to compound its problems of military planning and cooperation, and to poison relationships between one or more allies and Washington.(20) The Soviets might also be tempted on occasion to lend covert token support

or overt rhetorical support to subnational separatist groups (e.g., Scottish, Welsh, anti-Ulster Irish, Walloon and Basque) merely to remind Western capitals of Moscow's ability to bring about a worsening of their internal rigors if they prove uncooperative or pursue too pronounced an anti-Soviet line on key issues. Obviously the Soviets must tread warily in this area, for such intervention could prove counterproductive if it were to become too blatant. But abundant opportunities for Soviet mischief-making exist in Western Europe, and the Soviets can be counted upon to look for subtle ways of exploiting them to their own needs.

7. Undoubtedly, the Soviet Union will seek to make use of economic resources, policies and instruments to advance its strategy of Finlandization, but will probably find its potential for extending political influence through the projection of economic power much more limited than its potential for extending political influence by projecting an image of military power. The USSR still possesses a surplus of energy (which may or may not give way to the shortage which U.S. intelligence sources recently forecast for the early 1980s) and abundant raw material resources, and these may become important levers in the future. At the present time, however, the Soviets need Western technological transfers more than the Europeans need Soviet energy and raw materials. This will remain the case so long as Western Europe can be assured of access to supply sources in the Middle East and Africa. But even though the Europeans are breathing more easily over the improvement in their relations with the Arabs since 1974, and over the reduction of overt Soviet influence in the Arab world, they are aware that the USSR is a power with a growing potential for intervening disruptively in the Middle East as it did in 1955-1957, in 1967 and in the early 1970s, prior to and at the climax of the 1973 war. The Europeans more recently have watched uneasily as the Soviets have extended their influence deep into Africa and expanded their capabilities for applying pressure upon Western Europe's sources of supply and sea lines of communication. As they look to the future, the Europeans realize that the Soviets' power to hurt the economies of Western Europe may for a long time be more important than the power to help. In order to hedge their bets, therefore, the Europeans may feel constrained to buy a certain amount of Soviet good will by entering into economic arrangements with the Soviet Union and the Eastern bloc on terms which may not make economic sense unless the larger political framework, and the Europeans' longer-range apprehensions, are taken into account.

8. At the present time the countries of Western Europe do not depend to any great extent upon imports from the East. The Comecon area generally runs a deficit with the EEC. Comecon members will continue to seek agreements with the Economic Community in Brussels, but more on a bilateral rather than on a multilateral basis, as the EEC would prefer. The extent to which the EEC is willing to accommodate Comecon on less than a basis of economic quid pro quo will be a measure of Western Europe's desire for political reasons both to placate the Soviet Union and to ameliorate the economic conditions under which the peoples of Eastern Europe live. The latter purpose is not entirely altruistic. To be sure, there has always been a strong feeling in the West that the populations of Poland, East Germany, Czechoslovakia, Hungary, Romania and Bulgaria are a part of Europe and

should not be excluded from the concept of a united Europe. But there is also a strong element of enlightened self-interest at work here. West Europeans, remembering 1953, 1956 and 1968, realize that the potentially explosive situation obtaining in the people's democracies poses grave dangers to the preservation of a stable peace in Europe as a whole, and they will be interested in making a contribution toward keeping that situation under control.

9. The Soviets in the years to come will probably step up their demands for closer ties between EEC and Comecon and for all-European conferences on energy, technological cooperation, traffic and environmental protection. They are likely to use their oil, natural gas and raw materials resources to extract from Western Europe the most favorable concessions possible in long-term trade agreements that will bring to the USSR needed technology. As in the past, so in the future, the ability to bring to bear the bargaining power of a state trading monopoly will prove an advantage in exploiting the particular interests of private profit-seeking corporations. The Soviets may attempt to employ their limited economic leverage initially against some of the smaller members of NATO (e.g., Denmark and Norway) to induce them to put more distance between themselves and the Alliance, and eventually to pry them loose from it. They will also apply whatever pressure they can to negotiate favorable deals with European maritime neighbors (e.g., Norway) on the division and development of oceanic and seabed resources (fishing, oil and other mineral deposits). Through a wide variety of political-economic policy instruments, they will try to make progress toward a number of important objectives simultaneously:

(a) weakening the West European integration movement as it has developed up to the present time, and reorienting it toward the accomplishment of Soviet policy objectives by distinguishing sharply between what they will portray as genuinely European and American imperialist interests;

(b) fostering a climate increasingly hostile to the operation of American-dominated multinational enterprises in Europe;

(c) gradually lending credence to the assumption that all-European economic undertakings and business cooperation between socialist and nonsocialist countries is to be achieved under the tutelage of the USSR, with the United States playing a diminishing role;

(d) building European support for Soviet positions on international political and economic issues in the United States, and in conferences on the law of the seas, energy, environment, and relations between the industrial countries and the producers of primary raw materials;

(e) obtaining West European assistance that would enable the Soviet leadership to narrow the technological gap between the USSR and the West in nondefense sectors, and thus to remedy the glaring deficiencies of their socioeconomic system without having to pass through domestic reforms that could be painful and perhaps dangerous.

10. The Soviets, despite their own dismal record of economic dealings with developing countries, will continue to support the disadvantaged countries in the North-South negotiations over raw materials. These countries have been the hardest hit by the economic dislocations of the post-1973 energy and payments crises. Whereas the more resilient, free economies of Western Europe, despite continuing inflationary and unemployment problems, have at least partially recovered from the shock, the most severely affected poorer countries find themselves in a worsening deficit situation. The only way in which they will have any reasonable prospect of improving their economic condition will be to work out a long series of pragmatic compromises on prices and trade policy with the industrialized importers of their products. Generally, it will be to the Soviets' advantage to encourage the poorer countries to adopt a hard ideological line; to demand the whole loaf, not half, and to resist all West European efforts to negotiate practical, mutually beneficial agreements except for those which Moscow, for reasons of its own, may be willing to condone or promote. Thus the Soviets can be expected to make full use of their growing power, prestige and ability to intervene in the Third and Fourth Worlds in order to advance the success of their strategy of Finlandizing Europe.

## CSCE, FINLANDIZATION, AND ALL-EUROPEAN COLLECTIVE SECURITY

The contrast between the political-ideological systems of Western Europe and the East European communist states (including the USSR) is fraught with the gravest implications for the ultimate success of the Soviet strategy of Finlandization. Political and intellectual elites in all Western democratic countries have long been appalled at the political quality of life in Soviet Russia and under the regimes propped up by Soviet power in Eastern Europe. Those elites are well aware that, despite all the talk about detente for more than two decades and despite repeated references to the processes of mellowing, liberalization and convergence, vast differences continue to mark the human political condition in Western and Eastern Europe. Given a pure freedom of choice, far more Europeans would vote with their feet by moving westward than eastward – a powerful reason why communist governments cannot permit freedom of choice.

For the Soviets, peaceful coexistence has always implied the channeling of international conflict into relatively safe and controllable arenas where Moscow's strictly limited advantages might be optimized. Muscovite leaders, whether in the Czarist or the Communist dispensation, realize that they must be extremely clever in their efforts to project from an essentially unattractive, even ugly, political system an image of an enlightened regime endowed with a universal, salvific mission.

Several years before the Helsinki Conference on Security and Cooperation got under way, the Warsaw Pact's "Declaration on Strengthening Peace and Security in Europe," issued from Bucharest in July 1966, and the European communist parties' "Statement on European Security," issued from Karlovy Vary in April 1967, laid the groundwork for the strategy of Finlandization.

These statements also contained in embryo the programs which, if implemented, would lead to Soviet political-military domination of the European Continent. The Soviets were anxious to convene an all-European security conference in order to secure the ratification of the postwar territorial status quo and the establishment of a new collective security system in Europe following the dissolution of the two military alliances.

These appeals looked fair at a superficial first glance. In reality the dissolution of NATO and the Warsaw Pact would work clearly to the advantage of the Soviet Union, which could rely upon sheer proximate power to continue enforcing its writ in Eastern Europe while pressing sharpened wedges of political influence into an unprotected and disorganized Western Europe. Knowledgeable Western political leaders understood these dangers, yet were unable to resist the popular appeal of the summons to Helsinki.

For a year, prior to the fall of 1973, West Europeans displayed a remarkable degree of self-confidence concerning their ability, even while remaining dependent upon the United States for military defense, to hold their own in the economic sphere and to progress ultimately toward the formulation of a common European foreign policy. Their optimism was rudely dispelled, however, by the Arab oil embargo and OPEC's fourfold increase in the price of oil. Suddenly Europeans realized that they were still at the mercy of international forces beyond their control and much less able than they had thought to be masters of their own destiny. Preoccupied with domestic problems of economic retrenchment and the conflicts which accompanied them, the Europeans slowed their march toward unification. Faced with the acrimonious strife of organized interests at home, and perplexed at events in the United States during the Watergate period, more than a few thoughtful European observers began to wonder ominously whether democratic institutions within the Atlantic Community could survive the last quarter of the twentieth century.

It was against this background that the Soviets pressed their demands for the Helsinki Accords. The United States was never enthusiastic about going to Helsinki. Originally the Soviets called for an all-European conference, but they realized that there were no prospects for a meeting until they dropped their initial opposition to U.S. and Canadian participation. Also, they had to consent to a quadripartite Berlin Accord as a precondition to Western acquiescence in CSCE. As a further concession to the United States, they agreed to enter into MBFR negotiations. In the Nixon-Brezhnev meeting of June 1973, they dropped their earlier demand that CSCE must be brought to a successful conclusion before MBFR could even begin. (As subsequent developments demonstrated, CSCE was concluded and the Helsinki Pact was signed long before there was any hope of progress in the MBFR talks in Vienna).

With varying degrees, West Europeans have been willing, for the sake of peace, to give some recognition to the postwar territorial status quo on the Continent, but they have not been willing to place their blessing upon the political-ideological status quo in Eastern Europe. This attitude is not merely a matter of liberal humanitarian sentiment on behalf of oppressed peoples. Even deeper lies the fear mentioned earlier – fear that the situation in Eastern Europe contains the seeds of political upheaval with ominous consequences for the stability of Europe as a whole. West European leaders have reiterated that if detente is to become genuine and lead to justified mutual confidence between East and West, then political conditions in Eastern Europe and even in the Soviet Union must become more tolerable for individuals in terms of basic human rights, including freedom of movement.

Soviet leaders have always been preoccupied, almost pathologically, with the nationalities problem. Virtually every dissident who protests the denial of basic human freedoms is seen as a potential catalyst of ethnic revolt. The Soviets, therefore, perceive the dangers which prolonged detente poses to the internal order of their empire. For years their subject peoples have been continually warned that the West, compelled by the shifting correlation of forces to relax its aggressive military pressure against the communist countries, is stepping up efforts to subvert these countries and to wage psychological and political warfare on their territory under the guise of the free exchange of ideas. The peoples of Eastern Europe are told over and over that the West seeks to use the Helsinki Accords to penetrate their societies, misinform the working classes, implant a nonsocialist model of man and of individualistic morals, and promote counterrevolutionary discontent and agitation. The socialist regimes insist that the expansion of East-West cultural relations, human contacts and information exchanges must be based on the principles of noninterference in the internal affairs of states and respect for the laws and customs of all countries. This means, in effect, that the communist world should be free to propagate its ideas in the Western democratic countries, whose laws permit unrestricted expression, but the Western countries must not try to propagate their ideas within the communist states, because the laws of the latter prohibit such activity. Only one side, then, is to be given the opportunity to advocate political change within the domain of the other. Any other arrangement would fail to meet the definition of fair ideological struggle and would be certain to jeopardize peaceful coexistence and detente.

Prior to the signing of the Helsinki Pact on August 1, 1975, West European diplomats pressed much harder than the U.S. delegation for political change in the East, especially on the score of human rights, as a sign of good faith on detente. They evinced the view that their American counterparts had not importuned the Soviets as insistently as they might have on Basket III issues pertaining to human contacts and the freer flow of ideas across East-West boundaries. They were inclined to believe that Secretary Kissinger was more deferential to the Soviets than he really had to be under the circumstances, because he was more interested in nurturing detente and the multipolar balance than he was in the moral dimensions of the problems of Europe's division. Yet, in the final analysis, the West Europeans realized that there were definite limits to which they could press the issue. They certainly were not willing to advocate a return to the tensions of the Cold War period.

Since the early 1970s, in the preliminaries to the CSCE and in the CSCE itself, the Soviets have come close to obtaining a formal treaty of settlement more than a quarter century after the end of World War II. The most important aspect of this settliment in Soviet eyes has been a recognition of postwar realities by the West. Thus, the Red Army's end-of-war conquests in

Eastern Europe have, for all practical purposes, been legitimated by the Western nations. The Soviets have been able to extricate themselves from the political onus of the Moscow-managed invasion of Czechoslovakia, while the West Europeans have discreetly put aside their earlier demands for a formal renunciation by USSR of the right to apply the Brezhnev Doctrine.

The Soviet Union can be expected to interpret the Final Act of CSCE signed at Helsinki in 1975 as a means not only of discouraging Western intervention into the eastern communist empire but even of inhibiting Western initiatives against developments within the West favorable to Moscow. We should not forget that when EEC governments sought to use their economic leverage to reduce the radical role of communists in the Lisbon government during 1975, Moscow went beyond merely hinting – it bluntly asserted – that such activity constituted a violation of the spirit of Helsinki. The same type of accusation was leveled against Secretary Kissinger's warning in early 1976 that the coming to power of Eurocommunist parties would have an adverse effect upon the Atlantic Alliance.

The West Europeans are aware that the Soviets, despite the prohibitions in the Helsinki Final Act against intervention in the internal affairs of other states, are stepping up their espionage and infiltration activities in the Federal Republic and in other Western countries. Since the signing of the Helsinki Accord, the Soviets have displayed a growing and even arrogant self-confidence by adopting a tougher line on Berlin, where the degree of tension or relaxation has long been a barometer of East-West relations in Europe from cold war to warm detente. During 1976 and 1977 the Soviets contended that the 1971 Quadripartite Agreement applied only to West Berlin; that the three Western Allied Powers retained no rights whatsoever in East Berlin, and that the West Germans would be well advised to stop questioning Moscow's interpretation of the Berlin Agreement and give up trying to forge symbolic links between the FRG and West Berlin. Unless the Western allies can persuade the Soviets to attenuate their toughened stand on the status of the former German capital, the feeling is likely to grow among many Germans that they had better resign themselves to what fate holds in store.

The West Europeans, ever sensitive to shifts in the power balance and the political climate, are growing increasingly fearful that they will have little choice in the decade ahead but to adjust and defer to the accumulating strength – essentially military strength – of the collosus to the east. What causes particular apprehension is the thought that the process of Finlandization will compel them to pay political and economic tribute to Moscow, thereby augmenting the Soviets' ability to pursue their foreign policy objectives in non-military dimensions more effectively than they have hitherto been able to do. Before we look at the requirements of a Western counter-Finlandization strategy, we should acquaint ourselves with the Finlandizing Syndrome in its internal manifestation – i.e., Eurocommunism.

## NOTES

(1) Pravda, April 5, 1975.

(2) Richard Loewenthal, "After Cuba, Berlin?," Encounter, December 1962.

(3) See, e.g., George F. Kennan, "Europe's Problems, Europe's Choices," Foreign Policy, Spring 1974.

(4) See John Vloyantes, Silk Glove Hegemony: Finnish-Soviet Relations 1944-1974 (Kent, Ohio: Kent State University Press, 1975), pp. 1-32.

(5) See Samuel Abrahamsen, Sweden's Foreign Policy (Washington: Public Affairs Press, 1957), pp. 90-91.

(6) Thucydides, History of the Peloponnesian War.

(7) Arthur Spenser, "Finland Maintains Democracy," Foreign Affairs, January 1953; and Allen Kunisto, "The Passikivi Line in Finland's Foreign Policy," Western Political Quarterly, March 1959.

(8) Isvestia, as late as September 19, 1954, asserted that the effort to bring Finland into the Nordic Council was inspired by Western reactionary and imperialist circles.

(9) Arvo Rytkonew, "Finland's Talks on the Reciprocal Removal of Obstacles to Trade with European Socialist Countries," Yearbook of Finnish Foreign Policy, 1974 (Helsinki, 1975), p. 10.

(10) See The Times (London), November 15 and 25, 1961; Richard P. Stebbins, The United States in World Affairs, 1961 (New York: Harper and Brothers, For the Council on Foreign Relations, 1961), pp. 159-160; and Kalevi Holsti, "Strategy and Techniques of Influence in Soviet-Finnish Relations," Western Political Quarterly, March 1964.

(11) Kennan, p. 15.

(12) Even worse from the Soviet standpoint would be the possibility that West Germany, confronted by U.S. troop withdrawals, the gradual breakup of NATO, and the failure of France and Britain to cooperate toward credible European deterrence will conclude that she must henceforth take whatever steps are necessary to assure her own defense. In the most extreme case, this could mean repudiating the Nonproliferation Treaty and acquiring a nuclear weapons capability. Such a specter has prompted Soviet writers in the past to issue such vague but ominous warnings as the following: "The appearance of nuclear weapons in the FRG would indeed compel the Soviet Union and other European socialist countries to take serious countermeasures." Ia. Aboltin, Politika Gosudarsty i Razoruzhenie (Policies of States and Disarmament)

(Moscow: Izdatel'stvo "Nauda," 1967), Vol. I, p. 73; quoted in W.W. Kulski, The Soviet Union in World Affairs: A Documented Analysis 1964-1972 (Syracuse, N.Y.: Syracuse University Press, 1973), p. 131.

(13) The fear that West German participation in a European nuclear force might merely be the first step toward ultimate nuclear independence for Bonn in large part prompts Moscow's hostility to the creation of a European force. See Andrew J. Pierre, "Nuclear Diplomacy: Britain, France and America," Foreign Affairs, January 1971, and "Can Europe's Security be 'Decoupled' from America?," ibid., July 1973; Francois Duchene, "A New European Defense Community," ibid., October 1971, and "The Strategic Consequences of an Enlarged European Community," Atlantic Community Quarterly, Summer 1973; Wynfred Joshua and Walter F. Hahn, Nuclear Politics: America, France and Britain (Beverly Hills, Calif.: Sage Publications, for the Center for Strategic and International Studies, Georgetown University, 1973); Paul C. Davis, "A European Nuclear Force: Utility and Prospects," Orbis, Spring 1973.

(14) New York Times, November 22, 1973.

(15) See the editorial, "The Hostile Friendship of the Two Giants," The Times (London), June 21, 1974.

(16) See the following samples of West German press comment: "EEC Foreign Policy Cooperation Leaves Much to be Desired," Frankfurter Rundschau, September 15, 1975; "Europe Enthusiasm Cools," Frankfurter Neue Presse, December 18, 1975; "EEC Lacks Political Clout, Schmidt and Giscard Agree," Kolner-Stadt Anzeiger, February 16, 1976; "EEC's Repeated Failure to Reach Agreement on Key Issues Engenders Despondency in Brussels," Frankfurter Allgemeine Zeitung, May 6, 1976.

(17) See the Eurogroup Communique, November 5, 1975; text in Survival, January/February 1976, pp. 31-32.

(18) The economic, as distinguished from the neoisolationist, case for unilateral U.S. troop cuts was substantially altered by the fact that after the Middle East War of late 1973 and the ensuing energy crisis, the U.S. balance of payments had improved while that of the European allies had worsened dramatically. New York Times, January 26, 1974. The neoisolationist case was weakened, at least temporarily, after the collapse of the U.S. position in Southeast Asia. On June 2, 1975, Senator Mansfield announced that he would not reintroduce his amendment because, following the Indochina debate, it was the wrong time to withdraw troops from Europe. Congressional Quarterly Weekly Report, June 7, 1975, p. 1162.

(19) Ulrich de Maiziere, "No Feasible Alternative Exists to 'Flexible Response' Strategy," Die Zeit, December 1975; reprinted in The German Tribune, January 4, 1976.

(20) In the Eastern Mediterranean, the Greek-Turkish dispute over Cyprus and Aegean oil continues to smolder when it is not flaring. The two erstwhile loyal allies of the United States have become progressively alienated from the leader of the Alliance. NATO's operational effectiveness in a pivotal segment of the Southern Flank continues to be seriously impaired by decisions on the part of Athens and Ankara to curtail U.S. and Alliance basing rights. Throughout the earlier history of NATO and the Cyprus dispute, Turkey had appeared to enjoy U.S. favor as militarily the more important of the two countries. That condition began to change in 1965, when President Johnson issued a stern warning against any military action over Cyprus. In more recent years, Secretary Kissinger's apparent bias toward Turkey aroused Greek voter constituencies in the United States to organize for the purpose of advancing Greece's cause in the Congress. Resentment over the Congressional policy of curbing arms transfers has led to a fundamental reassessment by the Turks of their relationship with the United States. This factor, combined with growing interaction between Turkey and the Soviet Union and a left-nationalist trend in Turkish politics, has moved Turkey toward a more neutral posture. NATO planners will probably find it increasingly necessary to question their ability to count upon Turkish cooperation with regard to assuring Western security interests in the Strait in time of crisis.

# 10 The Internal Process of Finlandization

Diane K. Pfaltzgraff

Previous chapters of this study have traced the Soviet strategy of Finlandization in its military and political dimensions – as a function of the application of Soviet power. In the Atlantic Community at-large there is an internal side to the Finlandization process, reflected in the multiplicity of trends that have disrupted economies, weakened governments and generally undermined democratic institutions. These trends have issued largely from complex factors and circumstances in the evolution of industrialized society. Through Soviet ideological prisms, they represent the inherent capitalist contradictions that ordain the final triumph of Socialism as well as, in the strategic context, the dialectical counterpoint of growing Soviet power and the changing correlation of forces.

The trends are manifold and variegated, but they find discrete political expression in the growth – both in momentum and respectability – of leftwing forces in Western Europe. Salient in this respect has been the phenomenon of Eurocommunism – West European communism in its latest manifestation.

In the 1974-75 period, there appeared in Portugal – a country weary of protracted guerrilla warfare in Angola, where a substantial portion of the Portuguese Army had undergone radicalization – a threat of governmental takeover by hardline, pro-Soviet communists. NATO policymakers, worried about the most serious communist breach of political-strategic solidarity in the history of the Western alliance, took steps to quarantine Portugal within the military organization in order to safeguard common security interests. The United States, aware of the importance of the Azores for its own ability to exercise leverage in the Eastern Mediterranean, issued warnings to the Soviet Union that a communist takeover in Portugal would be regarded as a blatant violation of the ground rules for European detente which were then being negotiated in Helsinki. West European governments, especially those that were members of the EEC, made it clear that they would not cooperate economically with any government which strong-armed its way to power in Lisbon and posed a threat to the security of NATO's southern flank. A serious communist challenge was for the time being turned back – at least in Western

Europe, if not in Southern Africa and along the South Atlantic lines of communication on which Western Europe depended for raw materials.

But almost as soon as the Portuguese crisis subsided, a new political specter began to haunt Western Europe – Eurocommunism. The term was coined not by the West European communist parties but by a Yugoslav journalist in 1975.(1) It was picked up by the Western press and, at first, was repudiated by some of the more orthodox and hardline communists, especially in Paris. Eventually, however, it was embraced for its public relations value by many Spanish, Italian and French communists despite or because of Moscow's condemnation of the word as a capitalist invention. Ever since early 1976, European and American political observers have been trying to analyze the phenomenon and assess its potential consequences, while to the East theoreticians and propagandists have acted as if Eurocommunism were the worst of all heresies.

## THE FRENCH ELECTIONS OF MARCH 1978

It was obvious from the results of the Italian national election in June 1976, and from voting trends in France as early as 1974, that communist parties might come to power in those countries not by way of violent revolution, but rather through the ballot box.(2) There was prolonged speculation over where Eurocommunism would first triumph – whether in Italy, as the result of an "historic compromise" between the Italian Communist Party (PCI) and the Christian Democrats (DC), or in France through a victory of the Communist-Socialist union de la gauche in the 1978 National Assembly elections. Either development would pose serious implications for the survival of parliamentary institutions and the maintenance of economic stability in Italy and/or France, as well as for the political health of the Atlantic Alliance, the preservation of military security throughout Western Europe as a whole, and the political-economic future of the European Community.(3)

French municipal elections held in March 1977 reflected the continued success of the Left in France. At the same time that Jacques Chirac, who had resigned the previous August from President Giscard d'Estaing's cabinet, was easily defeating the President's handpicked candidate for the mayorship of Paris, the French Socialists won control of 23 municipal councils previously held by the Center-Right while the French Communists gained 10. For its part, the Center-Right parties gained control of only three councils previously held by the Left.(4) Communists now enjoyed seats in the governments of 147 cities, including 25 previously run by the Socialist Party alone or by Socialist-centrist coalitions.

Electoral trends in France during 1977 seemed to indicate that the prospects for a victory of the Left in the March 1978 elections to the National Assembly were great. That events did not transpire exactly as hoped by the Left nor as predicted by the polls is explained, in large measure, by the split among the parties of the Left in September 1977.(5) Thus, on the first ballot in March 1978, the Socialists drew a total of only 22.5 percent of the votes, the Left Radicals 2.1 percent, and the Communists 20.5 percent. Given

Table 1 French National Election – 1978

| Parties linked to the Joint Program: | Number of Seats in Parliament | | Percentage of votes | Total Votes Cast |
|---|---|---|---|---|
| | 1978 | 1973 | 1978 | 1978 |
| Communist Party | 86 | 72 | 18.61 | 4,744,868 |
| Socialist Party | 103 | 88 | 28.31 | 7,212,916 |
| Left Radicals Movement | 10 | 12 | 2.33 | 595,478 |
| TOTAL: | 199 | 172 | | |
| Far Left | 1 | 3 | | |
| TOTAL FOR THE OPPOSITION | 200 | 175 | 49.26 | 12,553,262 |
| For the majority | | | | |
| RPR (Rally for the Republic) | 148 | 184 | 26.11 | 6,651,756 |
| UDF (Union for French Democracy) | 137 | 115 | 23.18 | 5,907,603 |
| Allied Candidates supporting the President of Republic | 4 | 12 | | 305,763 |
| Various others | 2 | | | 57,418 |
| TOTAL FOR THE MAJORITY: | 291 | 311 | 50.71 | 12,922,540 |

* These figures were released by the French Ministry of the Interior

the slim margin between the Socialists and Communists (which cast into doubt Mitterand's contention that he would be able to control the PCF in a government coalition), the French electorate reverted to its traditional pattern of shifting toward the Right in the runoff election. Because under the French electoral system urban areas where the Left tends to be strongest are underrepresented in comparison with the more conservative rural areas, the Left needed a popular vote majority of more than 52 percent in order to be sure of gaining a majority of the seats in the Parliament.

After the first ballot, the PCF announced that it would renew the electoral pact with the Socialists despite the fact that they had been unable to agree upon a revision of the Common Program.(6) On the second ballot on March 19, the parties of the pro-Government majority polled 50.71 percent of the total vote, winning 291 seats in the National Assembly, while the Left won 49.26 percent of the vote and 200 seats. Still, while the Center-Right "won," the results were not without contradiction. Of the total votes cast, the majority parties received 12,922,540 as compared to 12,553,262 for the opposition. Moreover, in comparison to 1973, the parties of the majority actually lost seats while those of the opposition gained seats, thus narrowing the gap between the two. The Socialists won 103 seats and 28.31 percent of the vote (compared to 88 seats and 20.36 percent in 1973); the Communists won 86 seats and 18.61 percent of the vote (compared to 72 seats and 21.25 percent in 1973); the Left Radicals won 10 seats and 2.33 percent (compared to 3 seats and 3.3 percent in 1973).(7)

Despite its apparent defeat, the Left could interpret the augmentation of its legislative strength as a successful stage in its inexorable march to power. At the same time, the PCF and the PS could castigate one another for the failure of their bid to form a government in 1978.(8) On balance, the electoral victory of Giscard d'Estaing and his supporters represents a temporary setback in the electoral fortunes of the French Left. With the Left in disarray, the Government had proven able to attract votes by several means: by raising fears about having communist ministers in key cabinet posts, by posing the possibility of a constitutional crisis should the Left win, and by describing the prospects for economic and social chaos should the opposition's proposals be initiated.(9) With his electoral victory, Giscard and the Center-Right have gained added time in which to institute those economic and political reforms upon which the future prospects of the Left and French democratic institutions will largely depend.

## POLITICAL TURMOIL AND TERRORISM IN ITALY

While the Left in France encountered significant obstacles during 1977 and early 1978 in its quest for political power, the fortunes of the Italian Communist Party prospered. In June 1977, the PCI moved closer to positions of formal governmental power with the conclusion of an agreement between it and the Christian Democratic Party to consult on the government's future proposals to parliament and the shape of the government to carry out future plans. The agreement, labeled by some a mini-accord, signified the first time cooperation between the two parties was formalized at the national level.(10)

Originally intended as a limited emergency program, the agreement became instead an elaborate statement intended to please everyone. As an all-purpose program, little effort was expended in resolving its obvious contradictions. Assessing the program, Claire Sterling commented:

> Actually, nobody in the Byzantine world of Italian politics expects it to be carried out as written. . . .Its purpose was to buy time for the Christian Democrats. . . .They've paid for the time by giving the Communists important political recognition as co-signers of a razzle-dazzle program that neither could take seriously, without demanding many real concessions from the Communists in return. . . .As a sweetener, they have thrown in a conspicuous share of patronage, the transfer of control over welfare funds, substantial tax-collecting items and credit institutions from the national government to regional and local governments. Since the Communists happen to be installed in regional and local governments representing two-thirds of the electorate, while they themselves represent only one-third, the benefits are evident.
>
> Communist leaders are delighted to get the political recogniton, a useful first step to eventually joining the national government. The patronage is singularly useful to them too because, as the top communist hardliner Armando Cossutta once told me, they mean to use their local and regional alliances to converge upon and eventually encircle the capital. "The historic compromise . . . begins at the periphery and advances toward the center," is the way Cossutta put it. "That . . . is how it is going to happen."(11)

Other observers, as well, commented on the possible negative implications of the mini-accord for the prospects of the Italian democratic process. By all but eliminating the opposition, it restricted the normal give-and-take between a majority and an opposition, one of the touchstones of the democratic process. From the perspective of the Christian Democratic Party the agreement was justified on the grounds that it would make the PCI accept more direct responsibility for what might prove to be unpopular economic and social measures.

For the PCI the arrangements worked out during the summer of 1977 proved unsatisfactory for several reasons. Most important, the continued inability of the government to solve Italy's unemployment and inflation problems risked the traditional communist support among the working class. Thus, Berlinguer's own brother publicly expressed concern that the Party was in danger of losing its working class character as more members of the middle class joined its ranks and assumed positions of leadership.(12) Increasingly, it appeared to the PCI that its agreement with the DC compromised its support among such groups as students and younger workers, many of whom were hardest hit by continuing high levels of unemployment. Instead of viewing the PCI as their natural defender, these groups now saw the PCI as one of the parties of the establishment. In short, dissatisfaction over the relative costs and benefits accruing to the party from its increased support of the government contributed to its demands in January 1978 for increased recognition in return for the party's support of needed economic and social reforms.(13)

In addition to the formidable economic and political issues confronting Italy's government during 1977 and early 1978, there was a rising tide of violence and terrorist activity which threatened the stability of Italian political institutions. Not only did the violence promote a climate of fear which might generate support for authoritarian solutions, but some were concerned that eventually it might deflect the PCI from its moderate course – although until now it has had the effect of drawing the PCI closer to the DC.(14) Speaking to the party's Central Committee in January 1978, Berlinguer appealed to PCI members to fight against political violence and terrorism. He argued that democracy and socialism are inseparable and sought to further the image of the PCI as a responsible political movement anxious to avoid the disruption of Italian society caused by terrorist activities.(15) Thus, in its effort to obtain cabinet posts the PCI utilized the argument that the increase in political violence warranted an emergency government. The irony in the situation did not pass unnoticed:

> The irony is that in our latest round of troubles the extreme left has started armed attacks on members of the Communist Party, and the Communist press is calling for police protection. And while this is going on, Berlinguer continues to demand power for his party on the grounds that "without the Communist Party it is impossible to govern Italy."(16)

The kidnaping on March 16, 1978 of former Premier Aldo Moro and the murder of his five bodyguards represented the most serious terrorist challenge to date to the Italian government. Moro's kidnaping and subsequent murder demonstrated to many not only the powerlessness of the government, but suggested also a comparison between the increase in violence during the past year and the widespread chaos in Italy prior to Benito Mussolini's fascist takeover in 1922.

From the perspective of the PCI, the terrorist activities of the Red Brigades, which claimed responsibility for the kidnaping of Moro, have proven a mixed blessing. On the one hand, the identification of some of the band's members as disillusioned, former PCI members may damage the party's efforts to dissociate itself from its identification as a party for whom violence is an acceptable revolutionary tool. It may thus detract from the PCI's ability to create a new image for itself as a party committed solely to the use of peaceful means to achieve political power. On the other hand, the terrorism associated with the activities of the Red Brigades has also redounded to the PCI's immediate benefit by strengthening its bargaining position with the DC on the terms for participation in government. Since both the PCI and the Red Brigades remain committed to the same ultimate objective, namely, the creation of a communist society, the differences between them pertain primarily to the appropriate tactics to achieve that goal. At the very least, by contributing to the sense of crisis in Italy the Red Brigades have demonstrated the growing paralysis of government, making more probable a scenario from which the PCI stands to gain the most.(17)

Continuing economic problems and increasing violence thus contributed to the PCI's claim in January 1978 that the problems were serious enough to warrant the creation of an emergency government.(18) After seven weeks of political negotiations, five of Italy's six major parties agreed to form a new government which would have formal communist support. The agreement was a significant victory for the PCI as it obtained explicit and recognized participation in a voting majority, enhancing its role as a legitimate party in the Italian political process. Thus, the latest crisis marked yet another step forward in the march of the PCI toward achieving formal cabinet status. With the new agreement, ostensibly the government could count on a majority of 569 seats out of the 630-member lower house, and 299 out of 322 seats in the Senate. Only the Neo-Fascists, the National Right, the Liberals, the Radicals and the Democratic Proletarians remained in the opposition.(19)

For the United States, the March 1978 agreement represented a setback in its efforts to prevent a wider role for communists in West European governments. On January 12, concerned at the prospect that the Christian Democrats might be forced to accede to formal cabinet status for the PCI, the U.S. State Department had issued a statement aimed at preventing that step.(20)

## EUROCOMMUNISM AND DEMOCRACY

Recent events in France and Italy seem to challenge the assumptions, once prevalent in the West, that communism is incompatible with Western values and institutions; that it is hostile to the security interests of the United States and its allies; and that communist parties must be excluded from any governing role in parliamentary democracies. Although the importance of the changes taking place on the European political scene is widely recognized, there is considerable disagreement as to whether the United States and Western Europe should look upon the phenomenon of Eurocommunism as, on balance, more an opportunity to deepen a schism in the world communist movement than a grave threat to democratic systems and the Atlantic Alliance. Do the changes that have been publicly professed by the leaders of the West European communist parties warrant treating those parties henceforth as basically no different from other political parties? What are the realistic prospects that the communists will become cooperative participants in the pluralistic political systems of Western Europe? What are the assurances that countries such as Italy and France can be governed more effectively with communist participation in a ruling coalition?

Those who view with equanimity the accession to power of Eurocommunist parties argue that the circumstances under which this is expected to occur would reduce the justification for fear. The communists would not form a government by themselves as a majority party; instead, they would enter as relatively inexperienced members of a coalition. In Italy they would be aligned with a larger Christian Democratic Party; in France they would govern with a larger Socialist Party. In neither case, so the argument runs, would the coalition experiment lead to the destruction of parliamentary institutions because the Communist Party would be the junior partner.(21)

Yet the notion of a democratic apprenticeship under the tutelage of senior partners in Italy and France ignores the dynamic nature of the interrelationships between the junior and senior members in any coalition. It is difficult to imagine that an unreformed Italian DC, in a coalition with the PCI, would long be able to retain its predominant position in such a partnership. Indeed, so long as the PCI holds objectives at variance with those of the DC, competition between the two parties will focus not only on which objectives should have priority in governmental programs, but also on the issue of which party should enjoy the major role and possible credit for their enactment.

In France, even prior to the falling out of the Communists and the Socialists in September 1977, largely over the issue of how many industries were to be nationalized,(22) it was recognized that a left-of-center coalition was not a predictable partnership.

Perhaps most important, the split between the PS and the PCF illustrates a fundamental distrust between the two parties. As the campaign for the National Assembly progressed, the PCF directed a growing tirade against the PS, accusing it of reverting to class collaboration. Such charges lend credence to the view that the PCF may have concluded already that their policy of compromise with the Socialists had eroded support among the working class. Hence, the party could ill afford to be a junior partner in a leftwing government with a weakened power base and without the means to impose revolutionary change in economic policy. Indeed, communist leaders may well have doubted their ability – any more than that of the Center-Right – to deal effectively with France's pressing economic and social problems. For these reasons, the French Communists may have preferred to remain in opposition rather than to occupy a subservient position to the PS, especially given Mitterand's frequent assurances that his party would control the PCF. The PCF may even have feared that Mitterand, having achieved an electoral victory with the support of the PCF, would abandon his leftist partners to form a left-center coalition with Giscard. The PS, in turn, may have harbored fears that the PCF might mount a grassroots effort to seize power as had the Portuguese Communists.(23)

The split at the national level also brought increased dissension at the local level. In municipalities where the PS and the PCF ruled in coalition, disagreements occurred increasingly along party lines. Labor conflicts also reflected differences, with the Communist-dominated labor federation adopting more militant positions against management than the Socialist-dominated labor federations.(24) Finally, the indirect elections to the Senate held on September 25 reflected the disarray of the Left. While polls had predicted confidently that the Left would gain more than twenty seats, they actually gained only ten seats.(25)

By their increasingly hardline attacks on their former Socialist partners, the PCF signified rejection of its willingness to assume power through parliamentary coalitions, at least those in which it would be a junior partner. Hence, the split undermined the credibility of one of the claims of Eurocommunism, namely, that West European communists were becoming a less sectarian force and were more willing to join other parties under parliamentary democracy.

Doubts about Mitterand's ability to control the Communists were also raised by the continuing rift within the PS over the question of relations with the PCF. The leftwing CERES group, including approximately 25 percent of the party's members, called for closer ties with the PCF at the Nantes Congress held in early June 1977. While Mitterand was able to maintain party unity on this occasion and throughout the period prior to the March 1978 elections to the National Assembly, disappointment with the party's performance in that election may make it more difficult for him to hold together the disparate tendencies within PS ranks.(26) If the union had won in 1978, it would have been extremely difficult for Francois Mitterand to succeed in denying to the PCF for an indefinite time all of the major ministries – foreign affairs, defense and interior.(27) Once having established positions of strength within the government, PCF leaders could be expected to rely on superior organizational discipline to extend their control. They would be aided in this quest by some obvious Socialist weaknesses.

While the Socialist Party leadership may please its more militant supporters by moving toward closer cooperation with the Communists, it also risks alienating moderate voters, who may drift to the Center or even to the anticommunist Right.(28) When European communist parties expand their influence and their voting strength, they often do so at the expense of the noncommunist Left, as they have done in Italy. That is precisely what the PCF seemed determined to do during the attacks upon Mitterand, the PCF certainly was not playing the role of a deferential junior partner.

Early in 1978, Marchais issued an ultimatum: The PCF would promise to maintain leftist union discipline by supporting Socialist candidates on the second ballot on March 19 only if the PCF itself had won 21 percent of the vote in the first round on March 12. This condition was announced at a time when the polls were predicting a 20 percent vote for the PCF and as much as 30 percent for Mitterand's Socialist Party. The meaning of the message was clear: If the Socialists' initial margin of electoral strength over the Communists' was too wide, the PCF would not cooperate on the second ballot. Presumably Mitterand was expected to make sure that some normally Socialist votes would be cast for Communist candidates on the first ballot. Throughout most of the election campaign, the PCF refused to deal respectfully with Mitterand. It accused him of justifying rather than condemning President Carter's remarks during his January 1978 visit to France, warning against Communists in government – remarks which to the PCF and others constituted an American intervention in France's domestic affairs. The PCF accused the Socialist leader of duplicity and treachery and of withdrawing from the struggle against capitalism in his desire to manage the economic crisis instead of working to bring the French people out of the crisis.(29)

If the French Socialist Party becomes divided internally and weakened electorally, the prospects that it would prove a qualified tutor to its Communist coalition partners would not be bright. In fact, some Socialist leaders might be even more willing to accede to Communist demands for revision of their Common Program following an electoral victory than to allow the breakup of a coalition deemed essential for gaining and retaining political power. If in the past the Socialists were zealous guardians of constitutionalism, they may now be ready to assign a higher priority to controlling the government than to preserving democratic procedures. The French Socialist leaders, in the words of one observer, were compelled as early as 1976 to play down the question of commitment to constitutional government and to suggest that it should not be regarded as very decisive after all.(30)

In Italy, the Socialists have suffered most from the increase in electoral support for the PCI. Historically, the Italian Socialists have held diverse views on whether or not to cooperate with the Communists. In 1947, internal dissension on this question led to a split within the party; even today leftwing and rightwing factions are divided in their opinions on the issue. In January 1976, the PSI precipitated a governmental crisis by withdrawing its support from the DC government of Prime Minister Aldo Moro and demanding that the Communists be brought into a more direct role in the government.(31) The motives behind this move were both complex and paradoxical. In recent years, the PSI had become increasingly disenchanted with the center-left formula, i.e., Socialist participation in coalition with the Christian Democrats and other parties, which had enabled them to play a major role in most Italian governments since 1963. As their own electoral fortunes declined in each successive election, the PSI saw itself squeezed between the two larger parties, the DC and the PCI. Yet, because the PSI comprises a smaller part of the electorate in comparison with these two parties, if the Socialists are to share political power, it must be as a partner of one of the larger parties. In short, behind the PSI decision to bring down the Italian government in January 1976 was its growing concern that already the PCI and the DC had effected a de facto historic compromise.(32) These circumstances led to the decision taken at the March 1976 Congress of the Italian Socialist Party to adopt a strategy of the left alternative or the socialist alternative, i.e., a PSI-PCI coalition. Yet, this strategy is fraught with uncertainties. Not the least is the ability of the PSI to win sufficient electoral support to warrant consideration by the PCI as a coalition partner and to overcome PCI concern about being politically isolated on the left – a concern which has underlain the latter's search for the historic compromise with the Christian Democrats.

For a strategy of the socialist alternative to be successful, the PSI would have to draw more support from voters who have heretofore opted for the Christian Democrats or the Communists. In the June 1976 election, however, the PSI attracted only 9.6 percent of the vote, with some of its former supporters swinging to either the PCI or the DC. In light of current trends, the socialist alternative, were it to come about in Italy, would find a smaller, weaker Socialist Party in a coalition with a much stronger PCI. The PSI position, therefore, would probably be no better than it has been as the junior member of center-left governments with the DC: saddled with the onus of responsibility as a member of the government, yet unable to exercise much influence in the determination of policy. In coalition with the Communists the PSI would not be able to tutor or put a rein on its Communist partners. It is more likely that the leftist alternative would find the PSI swallowed by the larger, more powerful PCI.

## The Eurocommunist Parties and Acceptance of Democratic Ground Rules

During the past few years, both the Italian and French communist parties have sought to broaden their respective electoral appeals by championing freedom of speech, press, religion and association. They have expressed toleration of a pluralistic party system and have declared that if brought into the government they would abide by democratic principles and relinquish power when so directed by the voters, notwithstanding the fact that such toleration is clearly contrary to Marxist-Leninist ideology and to communist practice.(33)

Santiago Carrillo, the leader of the Spanish Communist Party (PCE), posed new problems for relations between the Soviet Union and West European communist parties when, in February 1977, the PCE added its name to the list of other West European communist parties critical of East European governments for their mistreatment of dissidents. He has also declared that in Western Europe there could be no socialism not founded on the democratic consent of the majority. The Madrid Summit, held on March 2-3, 1977, attended by the three communist secretaries-general of Spain, Italy and France – Carrillo, Berlinguer and Marchais – represented yet another challenge to Soviet authority and appeared to contribute to a widening rift between the Soviet bloc parties and nonruling communist parties in Western Europe. At Madrid, the three communist party leaders stressed their support for national roads to socialism, the parliamentary route to power, and political pluralism. Yet, they also sought to avoid the appearance of creating a new center of communism to rival the model of the Soviet Union.(34)

Madrid was soon followed by the publication of Carrillo's Eurocommunism and the State, in which Carrillo noted explicitly the challenge of Eurocommunism in Western Europe as well as in Eastern Europe by rejecting the model of socialism practiced there. Carrillo alleged that the Soviet model does not constitute a genuine workers' democracy and that it harbors many coercive traits in its relations with other Eastern socialist states, as demonstrated by the military occupation of Czechoslovakia in 1968.

Replying to Carrillo's charges in a review of his book published in New Times, the Soviet Union charged him with anti-Sovietism and with contributing to a split in the world communist movement. The Soviet response met with varying reactions from East and West European communist parties. PCI leaders, for example, were careful to deny the possibility of a break in relations between them and Moscow over the issues raised by Carrillo. In Eastern Europe, reaction ranged from full support of the Soviet position by Bulgaria, Czechoslovakia and East Germany, to opposition by Romania and Yugoslavia. In sum, this exchange between Moscow and its supporters, on the one hand, and the more independent parties, on the other, reflect the continuing ideological struggle within the world communist movement which bears important implications for the future of Eurocommunism and its claims to autonomy from Moscow.

Although the Soviet Union subsequently appeared to retreat from its initially harsh attack on Carrillo in other articles in New Times by reaffirming its respect for the independence of fraternal parties, it maintained its critical view of Carrillo. It is possible that these more recent pronouncements may illustrate that the Soviet leadership is in search of more indirect and sophisticated means to control rebellious members of the communist movement. Thus, articles have extolled the merits of the real socialism, i.e., socialism as first implemented in the Soviet Union, and have called for the urgent need to coordinate actions among all in the communist movement.

Carrillo's criticisms have struck at the heart of the legitimacy upon which the Communist Party of the Soviet Union and other East European communist parties have based their rule. For by contending that communism is not incompatible with constitutional democracy he appears to acknowledge the existence of a higher law than that of any particular communist party. The existence of human and political rights beyond those derived from a communist party call into question the legitimacy of the totalitarian governments of Eastern Europe and the Soviet Union. Moreover, such an assertion, if believed, brings into question the differences between the communist and socialist parties of Europe.(35)

Having given assurances of loyalty to democracy, some in the West contend, the communists should no longer be denied an opportunity to demonstrate concretely their adherence to democratic processes in responsible governing positions. Short of putting them to the test, it is not possible, of course, either to prove or to disprove with confidence that communist parties, despite their half century or more of implacable opposition to constitutional government, are now suddenly willing to change their ways. How sincere are Marchais, Berlinguer and Carrillo in their utterances about national independence, pluralism of parties and "profoundly democratic socialism"? Even if we were to give them the benefit of the doubt, once their parties had achieved power how secure would be their leadership positions against Leninist-Stalinist hardliners, who have already criticized them for selling their souls in return for electoral popularity within a bourgeois sytem? Moscow has sought to strengthen the hand of the militant elements within the Western parties by urging all communists to adhere to their revolutionary tradition and resist the lure of the parliamentary path to power. It is all right, say Soviet theoreticians, for the Western parties to master all the tactics of bourgeois democratic politics, but they must remain ready to resort to violence at the decisive moment, for ultimate questions of power cannot be resolved through voting. As Lenin realized, the great historical issues are decided only by force.(36)

Leaving aside the question of leadership personalities and their sincerity, can it be assumed that the commitment to constitutional democracy will be maintained by their respective parties as a whole? It is quite possible – even likely – that the communists will want to come to power in the image of good democrats who are ready to step down when they have lost at the polls. Yet, depending upon which ministries and government facilities the communists manage eventually to control (formally or informally), it is also quite likely that elections which hitherto had been free would become prey to manipulation. It is also possible that the communists, once in power, will exceed the bounds of fair play rules in their efforts to discredit and undermine the other political parties which may have to be tolerated during the period of transition to socialism.

In control of economic ministries, the communists could lay the foundations for a Marxist state by pursuing policies that lead to greater inflation, an increase in capital flight from France and Italy, shortages, the collapse or expropriation of business, and other dislocations which could contribute to a general atmosphere of strikes, demonstrations, civil disorders and perhaps terrorist activities – a critical situation that would seemingly justify a communist demand for drastic emergency measures in defense of the state.(37) Under such circumstances, it is not difficult to imagine a communist decision, acquiesced in reluctantly by others in the government coalition, to suspend civil liberties and to postpone elections until order has been restored.(38)

Despite verbal assurances, there is as yet no proof that Eurocommunists have become convinced democrats. Such proof certainly cannot be inferred from internal party processes: Democratic centralism in hierarchically controlled decision-making remains largely unaffected by recent communist pledges to respect the institutions and practices of pluralistic political systems. To be sure, the principle of democratic centralism has been challenged by dissidents within both the French and Italian communist parties at various times in the past generation. To such threats to central control, party leaders have responded in a variety of ways, including trials and purges. As Neil McInnes observes:

> If . . . examples of disunity dispose of the myth of the monolithic CP, they are not intended to bolster the other myth about progressive liberalization of the Leninist party. There is no secular trend towards de-Leninization of the western parties. Demands for "more democracy" inside the parties are put forward by Leftist dissidents, dissatisfied with their leaders' compromises with social democracy. This is the Stalinist paradox of western communism. Leninist rigidity is defended by party bureaucrats anxious to stay on good terms with Moscow while they seek local office in alliance with socialists. On the other hand, "more democracy" is demanded by Leftists who refuse that sort of integration into western democracy and who are disdainful of socialist leaders. For them "liberalization" of the party would not mean its "social-democratization" but its radicalization. In short, Stanlinism within the party goes with a penchant for reformist alliances; the cry for more democracy within the party comes from Leftist revolutionaries.(39)

According to McInnes, the demands for reform in communist parties are largely tactical. So, too, are apparent concessions granted by the leadership closely attuned to the requirements of successful electoral politics and the interest of the press in such matters.(40) For communist parties to de-Leninize or democratize themselves might unleash within their ranks fissiparous tendencies which their leaderships would find difficult, if not impossible, to control. As McInnes suggests:

> There are forces pressing for relaxation of Leninist discipline but there are contrary forces too. The men who control the party

> apparatus know that by "democratizing" it they would risk losing the support of Moscow without any certainty of gaining new electoral support or new members. After all, democratic socialism is already organized as a party in most West European countries, and the communist movement has always sought to mark itself off from it. To that end, the discipline of the Leninist party and the myth of its monolithic unity are a positive advantage.(41)

Thus, the very limited steps taken thus far do not warrant support for the contention that the French and Italian communist parties should be accepted as equals to the parties that participate fully in pluralistic political systems. Arthur Schlesinger, Jr., while taking issue with Henry Kissinger's denial that the Western communist parties are genuine national parties that have thrown off their historic allegiance to the Soviet Union, agreed with the former Secretary of State in deriding the theory that those parties have undergone a metamorphosis into democratic socialism.

> A Communist party that ignores Moscow is not uncommon in this polycentrist world. A Communist party that regards the democratic process as anything more than a convenience in the road to monopoly power is a phenomenon the world has yet to see. . . . Communist leaders like Berlinguer in Italy and Carrillo in Spain may well be personally honest in their democratic professions. But, under pressure, they would have no antecedent traditions of . . . pluralism to fall back on – only the Leninist tradition of the monolithic state, with a single party and no legal opposition.(42)

## THE SHIFT OF WEST EUROPEAN COMMUNIST PARTIES IN PERSPECTIVE

Historically, Moscow has sought to maintain a monolithically united world communist movement under Soviet leadership. The Western parties were once regarded as little more than fifth columns, ready to execute whatever directives the Soviet party might issue. Now it seems to be taken for granted by many in the West that within a matter of years those parties have become autonomous to the extent that they have turned into thorns in the side of the Kremlin leadership.(43)

The latest rift, which is being compared to the defections of Tito's Yugoslavia in 1948 and China in the 1960s,(44) came to the West's attention in the fall of 1975 during a debate over revolutionary directives addressed to French and Italian comrades in a Pravda article which was reported to have aroused resentment among Western communist leaders.(45) In a meeting at Rome in November 1975, Italian and French party leaders Berlinguer and Marchais issued their joint declaration of independence from Moscow and pledged to seek power by democratic means. The two parties agreed on the basic principles of defending democracy and liberty. "In this spirit, all liberties, whether they are the fruit of the great democratic bourgeois revolutions, or of the great popular struggles of this century, headed by the working class, must be guaranteed and developed."(46) A primary objective of the joint statement was to promote closer cooperation among democratic and leftwing forces.

As early as 1969 at the World Communist Conference, Berlinguer had rejected the idea that the same brand of socialism was valid for every situation. The French party, historically much more Stalinist than its Italian counterpart, was for a long time reluctant to deviate from loyalty to Moscow. But early in 1976, some weeks before the opening of the 25th Soviet Party Congress, Georges Marchais – speaking at the French Party Congress in the presence of Andre Kirilenko, top deputy of Soviet leader Brezhnev – publicly declared himself in favor of dropping all reference to the "dictatorship of the proletariat" in the party's constitution because it evoked the memory of "the fascist regimes of Hitler, Mussolini, Salazar and Franco."(47) Marchais made no direct reference to dictatorship in the Soviet Union, but he criticized that country for "unjust and unjustifiable acts" of repression against its citizens – acts, he added, which are not a necessary consequence of socialism. "It is natural," said Marchais, "that we express our disagreement with repressive measures that infringe on freedom of opinion, expression or creativity wherever they occur."(48)

Marchais pledged that French communism would henceforth travel the road to socialism under the French colors. Considering the fact that the French party throughout its history had been undeviatingly loyal in adhering to the zigs and zags of the Moscow line, and had refused for years to subscribe to the Italian communist doctrine of polycentrism, the new PCF spirit of '76 was interpreted as a major development on the European political scene.

PCF historian Jean Elleinstein published a radical critique of Stalinism. Without denying that the USSR might someday evolve in a more liberal direction, the deputy director of the party's research center contended that there have never been any democratic structures or habits in that country, and that the Soviets have not in fact made any real progress in liberal development up to the present time. Elleinstein traced the origins of the Stalinist system right back to Lenin (something that Khrushchev had never done). He concluded that the Revolution which had stormed the Winter Palace in 1917 was now completely outdated. He declared further that the PCF had become unreservedly committed to a pluralistic political system. Within the PCF itself, however, the historian defended the principle of democratic centralism, and argued that pluralism there would constitute a great danger for the party's internal life.(49) Not surprisingly, Moscow directed some of its most vehement blasts at Elleinstein's historical scholarship.

## The Limits of Autonomy

Such apparent declaratory changes of direction on the part of Marchais must be kept in perspective, and their significance should not be exaggerated. Marchais pointedly reiterated the support of French Communists for the principle of proletarian internationalism, which one student of the PCF has called one of the "flying buttresses" of all communist parties, along with democratic centralism and the dictatorship of the proletariat.(50)

Furthermore, as Alexander Solzhenitsyn has pointed out, within recent years both French and Italian Communist leaders have continued to attend not only open party congress meetings in Moscow but also closed meetings presided over by Soviet leaders.(51) Even after condemning roundly Santiago Carrillo for writing a book in which he criticized Stalin and Soviet policies (such as the 1968 invasion of Czechoslovakia), and after accusing the Spanish leader of endorsing the reactionary imperialist policy of arming Western Europe against world socialism, the Kremlin nevertheless invited Carrillo to take part in the festivities in Moscow celebrating the 60th anniversary of the October Revolution in late 1977.

On many occasions as well, the PCI has addressed the issue of PCI independence from the Soviet Union. Berlinguer, for example, has refuted the charge the PCI autonomy implies that the party has become less internationalist than it once was:

> But our independence of political action and theoretical research, our organizational independence, our rejection of the idea of any kind of leading party or leading state and our constructive relationship with the socialists – none of these things means either that we wish to become social democrats, or that we cease to be internationalists (even though the Italian Communist Party does not belong to any International).
>
> We oppose common directives and constraints on our organization. On the other hand, we welcome opportunities for cooperation and joint research. Our initiative, in conjunction with the Polish party, in calling for a pan-European conference of communist parties to discuss the development of detente and cooperation between all European countries, has that aim in view.(52)

At other times, PCI leaders, questioned about the implications of their continued ties to the Soviet Union for the ability of the European Left to cooperate in the task of building a united Europe, have repeatedly denied any contradiction or that their ties would hamper cooperation among socialist and communist parties in Western Europe. Indeed, party officials are not unaware that the party, if it were to reject its ties with the Soviet Union, might create dangers for itself by unleashing divisive tendencies within the party's ranks. One official explained it this way:

> . . . as the line of differentiation from the USSR's experience and that of other Eastern countries becomes more accentuated, this must be accompanied by a strong development in the party's study and commitment in the search for an original road to progress toward socialism in Italy. I believe that we could face negative repercussions in our ranks if our critical differentiation from the USSR's reality seemed to transform itself into an abandonment of internationalism and of the aim of socialism . . . If the abandonment of the formula of the dictatorship fo the proletariat seemed to signify the renunciation

> of the assertion of the working class role in the leadership and transformation of Italian society, we could suffer backlashes. The abandonment of that formula must not signify a renunciation of the aim of working class hegemony. We are not witnessing the historical decline of the old ruling classes. The present crisis will not be left behind without the participation of the working class in the decisions affecting the country's future – a participation which is still being resolutely opposed.(53)

Thus, the PCI continues to recognize that the Soviet Union provides for its members a myth in which to believe. "In hard times, for communist party members the Soviet Union was proof that socialism is not an unrealistic ideal. The existence of the USSR allows you to say: Socialism is a reality, a 'shining' reality."(54)

Such views lend support to the idea that the PCI is unlikely ever to renounce its fundamental loyalty to the USSR and to the concept of socialist solidarity. Even if one maintains that this feature becomes less distinctive as the PCI finesses its rhetoric in a search for a broader political base, it nevertheless cannot be completely separated from other ideas held about the nature of the party. As Blackmer observes:

> The PCI would find it difficult to maintain the viability of its self-image as a Leninist party – that is, as a disciplined, centralized party able to maintain unity and effectiveness while taking difficult decisions – if it were to cut itself off from the Soviet party that best represents the continuity and force of this political tradition. Too severe a break with the USSR and with the traditions of proletarian internationalism would not merely arouse the substantive opposition of many in the party, but would also tend to legitimize the very principle of opposition by weakening belief in the basic concept of democratic centralism.(55)

There exist certain other limitations to the independence of the PCI from the Soviet Union. Among the most important of these is the party's financial support from the bloc countries. In early 1976, the PCI took particular delight in embarassing the Christian Democrats and other parties in the wake of revelations about CIA contributions to Italian political parties. Such revelations, together with allegations of Lockheed payments to DC party officials, provided the PCI ammunition for questioning the autonomy of Italian political leaders.(56)

But, at the same time it was charging other parties with financial irregularities, the PCI itself was under scrutiny regarding its own sources of financial support – raising questions about its own clean hands and independence from outside sources. Thanks to its numerous relationships with Italian export-import companies engaged in trade with East European countries, the PCI serves as a broker for trade between Italy and these countries, receiving commissions for its services. In addition, the PCI's involvement in the National Cooperative League places the communists in a strategic position to influence decisions affecting the Italian economy.

While funds derived from East-West trade have been important to the financial well-being of the PCI, a far more important source has been cash payments from the Soviet Union.(57) How important are these funds to the prosperity of the PCI? The answer to this question could provide an important indicator to the credibility of the party's claim to independence from Moscow. On the one hand, some have seen in the evolution of PCI attitudes toward a more independent position an indication that it is less dependent upon Soviet beneficence today than in the past – perhaps due to the increased prosperity of its commercial enterprises.(58) Others note, however, that an opposite conclusion might be drawn:

> . . . the growth of the Communists' economic strength has taken place only to the extent that Italy has become increasingly involved in commercial relations with the Soviet bloc, and that this only confirms the intimate and unbreakable links that bind the PCI to the Russians. Supporters of this view cite the substantial shift in the pattern of Italian exports toward the Soviet bloc and OPEC and other developing countries in the past few years. In fact, whereas in 1973 Italian exports to "countries with planned economies" constituted only 4.9 percent of total exports, by the first half of 1975 they amounted to more than seven percent. Moreover, government-insured exports to the Soviet Union went from nine percent of the total in 1969 . . . to a whopping 19 percent in 1975.
>
> . . . The PCI has taken the lead in stimulating Italian commerce with Third World and Comecon countries. . . . In other words, the party is promoting a pattern of foreign trade that would shift Italy's commercial ties away from the West and toward the Soviet bloc and the developing countries.(59)

In light of this, the practicable extent of the PCI's avowed independence from the Soviet Union becomes all the more questionable. Even if the PCI were able to reduce its dependence on direct financial support from Moscow and rely more on income from its affiliation with cooperatives or its relationships with export-import companies having extensive trade dealings with Eastern Europe, Soviet good will toward the PCI remains essential to this middleman role. Thus, if the Soviet Union were to become sufficiently displeased with PCI attitudes or policies to cut off direct financial assistance, it could also discourage other members of Comecon from concluding commercial agreements favorable to the Italian party. In sum, if the PCI wishes to maintain its financial solvency, its autonomy will continue to be hostage to the Soviet Union.

## Discord at the East Berlin Conference of June 1976

Western observers who have long believed that the world communist movement is disintegrating found sustenance for their views in the speeches at the June 1976 conference of the twenty-eight European communist parties held in East Berlin. If appearances were to be believed, the Soviet leaders, recalling with bitterness the loss of their influence over Yugoslavia and China, now faced the prospect that the international organization of fraternal communist parties was about to enter upon its final dissolution.

The conference declaration affirmed "the principles of equality and sovereign independence of each party, noninterference in internal affairs and respect for their free choice of different roads in their struggle for social change of a progressive nature and for socialism."(60) On the basis of such passages, the conference was interpreted as having put an end to Soviet domination of the West European communist movement.(61) Spanish party leader Carrillo fervently denied that the world communist movement was still a church in which Moscow filled the place of Rome. "We, the Communists, have no center that gives us directives, have no international discipline imposed upon us."(62)

In East Berlin, Berlinguer, seeking accreditation of his role as a spokesman for an independent Eurocommunism, attempted to portray Eurocommunism as the best means to transform Western societies from capitalism to socialism. This would be accomplished, according to Berlinguer, by maintaining the framework of existing international alliances as the best guarantee against foreign interference. Berlinguer denied the right of the Soviet Union to play the leading role in the communist movement.(63) Indeed, at one point in his address, Berlinguer noted: "This free debate of ideas is one way to increase the attraction of socialism."(64) Perhaps this reflected a wish to exploit the internal debate within the communist movement as a means of convincing Italian voters of the sincerity of the party's independence from Moscow and to accentuate to Italian voters the idea of equality and independence allegedly belonging to each communist party.(65)

To place Berlinguer's remarks in perspective, one slould also read those of Brezhnev who, at the same conference, cautioned Western communist parties to remain "true revolutionaries, convinced opponents of replacing the capitalist with the socialist system," and to beware of the dangers posed by cooperation with other democratic forces. Brezhnev observed that it is in its identity as a working class movement that communist parties find their purpose. "And it is responsible for its actions first of all before the working people of its own country, whose interests it expresses and defends. but it is precisely this that provides the basis for the Communists' international solidarity."(66)

Thus, Brezhnev appeared to recognize diversity within the communist camp, but he also called for unity. Recognizing the importance of internationalism because of the similarity of working class interests, Brezhnev observed, "it is clear . . . that the more influential the communist party is in its own country, the larger can be its contribution to the struggle for the common aims of communists on the international scene."(67) The Soviet leader also warned of the need for the socialist camp to coordinate its efforts in face of the danger posed by reactionary circles in NATO. Notwithstanding Brezhnev's apparent recognition of the autonomy of communist parties, the final document of the East Berlin conference merely expresses the consensus of those in attendance and does not necessarily preclude the possibility of another Czechoslovakia in the interest of socialist solidarity.(68)

## Other Criteria of "Independence"

The statements uttered in East Berlin, and embodied in the final document of that conclave, illustrated the serious stresses and strains within the world communist movement. But the subtleties of rhetoric do not really attest to the independence of West European communist parties from Moscow. Other indicators must be consulted. One of them is a comparison of the parties' positions on important foreign policy and national security issues with those of the Soviet union. If one uses this criterion, the PCF could not warrant identification as an independent party for most of its existence. Only since 1975 has the PCF criticized tentatively the Soviet Union on such matters as the treatment of political prisoners and a tendency to be soft on capitalism. While the French Communists initially condemned the Soviet invasion of Czechoslovakia in 1968, in successive years they quietly acceded to Soviet actions there. The PCF has supported the Soviet position on other issues as well.(69) At the very least, application of this criterion casts doubt on the alleged determination of the French Communist Party to travel under the colors of France and to increase its independence from the foreign policy of the Soviet Union.

In the case of the PCI, the party has had a longer history of publicly opposing the Soviet Union on certain issues. It has displayed particular adeptness at reconciling its role as a national political party with the requirements of its international responsibilities as a Marxist party. Whether under the leadership of Antonio Gramsci, Palmiro Togliatti, or Enrico Berlinguer, the PCI has sought to straddle these two roles. Supporters of the view that the PCI is indeed an independent party cite such examples as PCI criticism of Soviet intervention in Hungary in 1956, Togliatti's Yalta testament in 1964 which criticized Stalinism and expressed Togliatti's faith in national paths to socialism, PCI criticism of Soviet intervention in Czechoslovakia in 1968 and, more recently, Berlinguer's statements at the Twenty-fifth Congress of the Soviet Communist Party in February 1976 and at East Berlin in June 1976. But this kind of recitation ignores other important issues on which the PCI's views have clearly paralleled those of Moscow: conspicuous recent examples are the PCI condemnation of Israel in 1973, and support for the MPLA in Angola in 1976.

A strong case can be made that the continuation of an international atmosphere of detente within which they can pursue their national objectives is in the mutual interest of the Soviet Union and the West European communist parties. Berlinguer's comments, both at East Berlin in June and earlier in February 1976 (at the 25th CPSU Congress), acknowledged the contribution of detente to the achievement of communist objectives. He asserted that the PCI supported a "foreign policy which within the framework of our country's international alliances will actively contribute to detente and firmly defend our sovereignty against any foreign interference in internal affairs."(70)

It seems premature to believe that communist leaders in Moscow had been compelled at East Berlin to preside over the liquidation of their international Leninist empire. George Marchais, the PCF leader, noted that the conference showed two things: each communist party is independent and sovereign, and this fact does not prevent either friendship or international solidarity. "Our party, which is very attached to these ideas, is pleased to note that they emerged strengthened from the conference . . . . Everything is moving and in the right direction."(71) Thus, Brezhnev was not merely trying to put the best face on a bad situation when he said that "the vigorous activity of communists in Western Europe is yielding fruit."(72) In fact, there was no doctrinal revolution at East Berlin; no heresy arose to overturn orthodoxy. Little was said at East Berlin in June 1976 that had not been said at the World Communist Conference of June 1969 in Moscow. The final document of the 1969 conference did not condemn Maoism or China, nor did it proclaim the international tutorial primacy of Moscow. But it did say that all communist parties enjoy equal rights, and that "there is no leading center of international communism . . . . Each party . . . works out its own policy in full independence, determines the directions, forms and methods of struggle."(73) Berlinguer had spoken in 1969 about the need to take special national conditions into account, including the characteristics of democratic and pluralist political systems.

There is perhaps a tendency to oversimplify the highly complex and subtle relationship that links Moscow with the Western parties. Even though they are united in their unswerving dedication to the goal of bringing about the complete triumph of the communist revolution throughout Europe, and of severing the political-military connection between Europe and the United States, there may still exist some genuine and deeply felt differences over strategy and tactics, timing and methods, priorities and the distribution of costs, just as there have always been throughout the history of the Leninist movement. The Soviet and Western parties are fully agreed in their determination to take advantage of what they perceive to be the present profound crisis of Western capitalist society and the shifting correlation of global strategic forces. But during the last few years communist parties in Moscow, Rome, Paris and elsewhere have been split over the most efficacious strategy for exploiting that crisis. Some members of the Soviet Politburo have undoubtedly suffered misgivings over the electoral tactics recently adopted by the Italian and French parties. Hard liners suspect that any close association of Communists with democratic socialists of bourgeois parties will cause an erosion of Marxist-Leninist ideological purity. They may have feared that the Eurocommunist parties might move too fast, frighten the West, and thereby jeopardize the United States-Soviet detente in a crucial phase of the military technological competition between the superpowers. By being openly critical of the Eurocommunists before the latter should come to power, Moscow may have thought to put itself in a better position to disclaim responsibility later for Eurocommunist policies that might jeopardize detente. Probably most serious of all were Soviet fears lest the spirit of national autonomy being flaunted by communists in Western Europe, where it is a sign of self-confidence, vigor and health, spread to the regimes of Eastern Europe, and even to the Soviet Union itself, where it would in the Kremlin's eyes be a virulent disease.

The Soviets ostensibly regard the impact of Eurocommunist ideas upon their East European satellites to be of considerable potential danger. Reformers in these countries "increasingly point to the Eurocommunists."(74)

Moscow is afraid that the human rights implications of the Helsinki Accord, combined with growing discontent over economic conditions, could give rise to mounting problems of political control within Eastern Europe. Soviet dominance in that region has always depended heavily upon the presence of Soviet military power. Moscow always feels apprehensive about its ability to control communist parties that lie beyond the reach of the Soviet Army,(75) and the thought that Eurocommunist Parties in Rome and Paris, determined to prove themselves nationalist and democratic, might begin to provide models of political behaivor to disgruntled communists and other nationalists in Eastern Europe who want more independence themselves is bound to send shivers down the spines of Soviet leaders.

It is quite plausible to interpret developments among the European communist parties as a movement from close order to open order drill. When the Soviet leaders score the Western parties, they do so for mixed motives: They do not begrudge the newfound success of Western disciples, and they are not adverse to helping make those parties look more respectable to Western publics, but they are also under pressure to placate domestic hardliners. They know, too, that the communist movement is now executing what may well be the most difficult and delicate political maneuver in history, one bound to give rise to serious strains and dangers, as well as unprecedented opportunities. Moscow, quite naturally, wants to see the Leninist-Marxist ideology and organization thrive in the West. It also wants to make sure that the fortunes of Eurocommunism do not advance in such a way as to get out of phase with, or even interfere with, the pursuit of other Soviet goals which are of equal or greater importance.

All good communists know that they have much more in common with each other than with Western bourgeois democrats, and that they have no choice but to remain implacably and uncompromisingly opposed to the latter. They realize that the policies of communism must evolve from a dialectical process over the most effective techniques of overcoming the West. The dialectical clash itself, embodied in national parties, factions of parties and individual personalities, heightens the ability of the movement to exert maximum control over this delicate process, to respond with pragmatic flexibility as circumstances permit, and to cope with the complicated challenges and problems bound to appear as byproducts of the process.

The key fact remains that the West European communist parties are still committed to an international movement in which the Soviet party retains an undeniable leadership role. This does not mean that the Western parties want to be dominated or dictated to by Moscow. But they are realistic enough to understand that Moscow's leadership is a function of its power and that their own future political fortunes will depend to a considerable extent upon the continued growth of that power, as well as upon a continuation of various forms of support (financial, political, psychological, and other) which only Moscow can supply.

In short, those in the West who argue for the acceptance of the inevitability of communist accession to West European governments and who look for silver linings in that cloud can point legitimately to differences between Moscow and West European communist parties. But do such differences point to truly independent West European parties, converted to parliamentary democracy, let alone to a conclusive split in the communist movement? Such differences as do seem to exist revolve more around tactics (and varying domestic-political requirements) than fundamental goals. Indeed it can be argued that Moscow's ostensible tolerance of these differences reflects not weakness on the part of the Kremlin, but rather a confident recognition of strength. At an historic stage when, from the Soviet vantagepoint, the correlation of forces is decisively changing in Moscow's favor, ideological orthodoxy and the close-order drill can easily (and profitably) be loosened in the interest of expediency.

## THE LIMITS OF "INFECTION" IN EASTERN EUROPE

One of the benefits that allegedly would accrue to the West from the accession of communist parties to power in Western Europe is the impact on the people's democracies of Eastern Europe. Supposedly, the East European communist regimes, attempting to emulate their West European comrades, will strive to increase their own independence from Moscow. The Titoist doctrine of national communism, which met the clenched Soviet fist in Poland and Hungary (1956) and in Czechoslovakia (1968), will beckon the East European parties westward from Moscow and toward liberalization. There will be an opportunity to reverse the processes whereby the economic integration of Europe has developed according to two mutually exclusive regional patterns. With communists helping to formulate policies for EEC governments, an intensification of economic links and the easing of restrictions on the movement of people and ideas between the two parts of Europe allegedly can be expected.

Such hopes are not well founded. Relations between Moscow and the people's democracies would be complicated by the communists' accession to power in Western Europe, just as they were by the negotiations leading to the Helsinki Accords of 1975. Yet, to assume that Eurocommunism will help to ease life in Eastern Europe – any more than has the CSCE and the Helsinki Accords – may prove to be little more than wishful thinking. Indeed, the opposite may occur. If the Soviet Union fears the kind of demonstration effect in Eastern Europe that many Western observers profess to foresee, both the Soviet leaders and their hardline colleagues in East European capitals might simply impose more rigid controls. The latter are likely to undertake such immunization measures irrespective of their penchant for relative independence from Moscow.

Throughout the preparatory talks leading to the East Berlin conference, the communist parties of Poland, Czechoslovakia, Hungary, Bulgaria and East Germany supported the Soviet Union staunchly and stressed their loyalty to Moscow.(76) Because of the presence of Soviet armed forces within or near their borders, and because of their heavy economic dependence upon the Soviet Union, none of the members of the Warsaw Pact is in a position to stray far from Moscow-prescribed orthodoxy.

The East Berlin Statement was by no means a triumph for Titoist doctrine. But whereas Yugoslavia had stayed away from the 1969 Moscow communist summit, Yugoslavia was present at the East Berlin meeting.

"Whatever the substantive deficiencies of the 1976 document from Moscow's standpoint, it had the advantage of being agreed to by every European communist party except the Albanian."(77) This might be interpreted as evidence that the security of the communist movement is being reforged at a more sophisticated level – one that features a reconciliation of approaches with respect to the vastly different scenarios that confront communist forces in Eastern and Western Europe. Perhaps the Yugoslavs, bearing in mind the willingness of some Western communists to critize Soviet military intervention in Eastern Europe, are seeking to insure their country's security by helping to strengthen the Western parties and thus to build a political deterrent against any Soviet attempt in the post-Tito era to reestablish influence over Yugoslavia. If so, this could prove to be a dangerous gamble, for the rise of Eurocommunism might very well – as we shall see subsequently – bring about a weakening of the Atlantic Alliance and an undermining of the European military-political equilibrium on which the independence of Yugoslavia has crucially hinged since 1948.

## EUROCOMMUNISM AND THE EUROPEAN ECONOMIC COMMUNITY

It is difficult to imagine how the investing of West European communist parties with a voice in the making of EEC policies will serve the cause of European unity. Originally both the PCI and the PCF opposed the establishment of the European Economic Community, and each did its best, until quite recently, to obstruct the economic integration of Western Europe. The PCI was the first to accept the Common Market as a fact of life and to realize that continued stubborn hostility to the EEC would hinder severely the party's efforts to broaden its popular appeal.

Berlinguer, speaking at East Berlin, restated PCI strategy in Europe:

> . . . we will continue to develop our European initiative in many and various directions: on the all-European level, in order to help promote detente and cooperation; on the West European level, in order to find the broadest meeting points with other leftwing, democratic and progressive forces; and on the level of the EC, in order to make our contribution toward ensuring that the process of integration is democratic and consistent with the interests of the working classes.(78)

As part of its international strategy, therefore, the PCI has pursued an active campaign to enhance its image with other groups in Western Europe. Seeking to take advantage of what it perceived as new trends in Europe's social democracies as well as a new sense of militancy in West European trade unions, the PCI wishes to assume the role of an active protagonist in building socialism. Berlinguer has decried repeatedly what he has called attempts by a conservative counteroffensive in Europe to offset the growing convergence of leftwing forces on the continent.

In pursuit of its goal to speed the advance of socialism, the PCI has sent its leaders abroad for meetings with their counterparts in other European states. Such visits serve to promote PCI relationships with democratic forces abroad and, in turn, enhance the respectability of the PCI in domestic politics. In late 1977, the PCI began to broaden its efforts among European parties to include greater attention to Communist-Socialist party contacts and meetings. The PCI intended to create an Institute for Foreign Policy Research to promote the development of united workers and democratic forces. In part, the greater attention paid to relations with socialist parties may reflect disappointment at the prospects for cooperation among Eurocommunist parties in light of the differences among them which had become more apparent in 1977. Thus, the failures of the Left in France and differences with Carrillo over his harsh views about the Soviet Union have necessitated a change in tactics by the PCI to enhance its international and domestic image. Moreover, the meetings with officials and party leaders in other West European countries have had as one of their objectives to encourage a neutral stance toward the prospect of the PCI gaining a governmental role – and PCI leaders hope that this development would lead to a change in the current hostile U.S. attitude toward PCI participation in the government.(79)

A recurrent theme in PCI views toward the EEC is the need to democratize the institution in order to make it less susceptible to the pressures of Western monopolist interests. According to Pietro Ingrao, the first step to democratization of the EEC would be through universal suffrage.(80) It was the objective of the PCI, according to Ingrao, to promote "a greater influence on the people's part to reduce the influence of monopolist groups, to direct Europe toward a policy which will protect workers' interests and provide valid answers to the economic crisis."(81)

This antimonopolist position was reiterated by Giorgio Amendola, a PCI member of the European Parliament, who admitted that earlier the PCI had misunderstood the Common Market as an enemy. But the party now realized "that it was a windmill, that a European community did not exist and had to be created."(82) Europe had been endangered by the recent economic crisis, by competition from the United States, and had not controlled adequately multinational corporations. Thus, according to Amendola, Europe must overcome its internal divisions to create an economic unity as a premise for a political unity. Moreover, he stressed the need to develop a European policy aimed at European autonomy. In short, the communists want to build a European community "because the multinational companies can only be fought with multinational powers and these powers can be efficacious only if they have a democratic basis by means of elections by universal suffrage to the European Parliament."(83)

Reading the views of various PCI officials makes it clear that the European Community they envisage would be one autonomous from the United States. In a report of his meeting with Belgian Prime Minister Leo Tindemans, Berlinguer commented:

> Great democratic potential exists in our countries, and we Italian Communists will continue to work with increasing commitment to insure that the EC countries' leftwing and popular forces achieve the necessary rapprochement and implement all possible agreements in

> order to be able to support together action aimed at building a Europe which is community-minded, democratic and advanced, which is a factor for peace and cooperation, which will establish relations of friendship on the basis of autonomy and equality with both the United States and the Soviet Union and all the other socialist countries, and which will build relations of a new, mutually advantageous type with the developing countries.(84)

The announcement by the PCI in September 1977 that it was about to initiate a major campaign to gain seats in the European Parliament brought renewed speculation about their motives. At the very least, the PCI appeared to hope that its role in regional organizations such as WEU and the EEC would enhance its image as a respectable political party. Parallels were drawn, for example, to the party's experience in the WEU where, by voting in support of such measures as the standardization of equipment in NATO, the PCI encourages perceptions that it is a legitimate, national party. But, given the purely consultative status of WEU, such votes carry no practical effect on national decisions in the field of defense. It has also been observed that the PCI's WEU experience has not been without contradiction. In one instance, a PCI member of the Political Committee, drafting a West European position on human rights for the Belgrade conference, included a passage stating that work is a civil right and that unemployment constitutes a violation of that right. This action, which was decried by other members of the Committee, served to illustrate how the party might have served as an instrument of Soviet viewpoints – a situation which might be repeated in the EC.(85)

While the Italian Communist Party has long supported direct elections to the European Parliament in the interest of democratizing the institutions of the EEC, PCF leader Georges Marchais had long held that this would be a "crime against France."(86) It was with surprise, therefore, that the French public learned in April 1977 that the PCF would support a National Assembly bill for the direction election of the European Parliament. Such support, however, was not without conditions. To obtain the needed parliamentary support for direct elections in the EC, Giscard had to include within the text of the government's bill an assurance that there would be no extention of the powers of the European Parliament beyond those already set forth in the Treaty of Rome.(87)

Early in 1978, the PCF election program statement favored France's participation in the Common Market with the aim of freeing the EEC from domination by the multinational trusts and the United States.(88) If past attitudes and policies serve as valid indicators of future positions, the PCF still might be expected to pursue policies toward the EEC that are more hostile than those of the PCI. But the fact that the PCI appears more receptive to using the institutional approach to democratize the EEC need not be read as support for the organization's goals, nor does it mean that the PCI would abstain from seeking to promote socialism within that institution.

In sum, West European communist parties in France and Italy will work for trans-European cooperation, but strictly on communist terms – using the EEC where possible to weaken West European economic integration as well as to prevent political and defense unity. The communists will either bend the EEC to their revolutionary purposes or – what amounts to the same thing – they will strive to paralyze it. The Europe envisaged by Eurocommunist parties would be increasingly neutralist and anti-American.

## ATTITUDES IN THE ITALIAN COMMUNIST PARTY TOWARD NATO

Perhaps the most dangerous of the myths surrounding Eurocommunism is the belief that, as Eurocommunists draw closer to the seats of power, they become more responsible guardians of their respective countries' fundamental interests, prominently the interest of preserving the military balance in Europe. Corollary assumptions are that as members of a ruling coalition they will be loyal to NATO, and that there is therefore little cause to worry about serious efforts by the communists to take such countries as Italy and France out of the Atlantic Alliance.

The recent reassurances by the PCI of the party's new tolerance of NATO and Italy's membership in the pact must be balanced by other statements of party leaders which cast considerable doubt on this avowed commitment. First, it is well to recall that the turnabout in the party's declared policy toward NATO is both recent and sudden. As late as in 1972, for example, Berlinguer, addressing the 13th Congress of the PCI, called for "the struggle against the Atlantic Pact," and urged Italy to free itself from its bonds of subordination to NATO. At that time – and, indeed, since then – the PCI perspective on NATO was linked clearly to a broader struggle to liberate Europe from American hegemony,(89) as well as to the Soviet summons for the eventual dissolution of the two opposing blocs in Europe. The PCI thus holds the view that greater European independence, i.e., a changed framework for European-U.S. relations, would present a greater opportunity to develop more amicable East-West European relations. A loosened NATO, or a democratized NATO is but a stage toward the eventual dissolution of the alliance.

The equivocal nature of PCI views toward NATO is illustrated in the contradictory statements of party leaders. It appeared that, as the electoral prospects of the PCI seemed to improve, the party moderated its earlier hostility toward the Atlantic Alliance. In March 1975 Berlinguer expressed the opinion that the party would no longer raise the question of Italy's withdrawal from NATO.(90) Justifying their changed position, party officials noted that a unilateral change in alliance structures would be upsetting to detente.(91) Even though the PCI is willing to accept Italian membership in NATO as a fact of life, its presence is viewed as a negative fact and a danger to peace and national security. Luciano Radice, a member of the Central Committee, also raised doubts about the PCI commitment to NATO. Questioned about the response of the PCI in the event of a world crisis, Radice replied that "We would choose the Soviet side, of course." Later, qualifying this blanket statement, Radice observed:

> It depends. If there is an imperialist aggression with the avowed objective of rolling back socialism, we would feel entirely absolved of

> any obligation of "loyalty" to the "defensive" character of NATO and take the side of the Soviet Union. But we would, in such an extreme emergency, also do our utmost to restore peace.(92)

Clearly, if the PCI entertains such views it could hardly be expected to be a stalwart supporter of the Alliance. Indeed, denying the validity of the assumption that the Warsaw Pact might attack NATO, the party seeks to avoid the difficult choice between its responsibilities as a national political party and its role as a member of the international communist movement.(93)

In an interview published in Corriere della Sera on June 15, 1976, immediately prior to the election on June 21-22, Berlinguer went so far as to suggest that he viewed NATO as a shield to protect the individualism of the Italian way to socialism. The PCI could pursue its own course without fear of Soviet intervention. "I do not want Italy to quit the Atlantic Pact 'also' for that reason, and not only because our exit wouild upset the international balance. I feel more secure being here. . . ."(94) Such an admission demonstrated the lengths to which the PCI was willing to go to emphasize its autonomy from the Soviet Union and reflected the extent to which Berlinguer was willing to exploit electoral opportunities. Yet, in the same interview, Berlinguer also expressed concern about the difficulties Italy faces as a member of NATO in pursuing its own destiny:

> I feel that, since Italy does not belong to the Warsaw Pact, from that viewpoint there is absolute certainty that we can proceed along the Italian path to socialism without any conditioning. But that does not mean that problems do not exist within the Western bloc. It is equally true that we feel constrained to claim within the Atlantic Pact – a pact which we do not, however, question – Italy's right to decide its own destiny autonomously.(95)

As a NATO member, it appears that the thrust of Italy's efforts to prevent foreign interference is to be against other Alliance members.

In general, the PCI has not been precise regarding any specific proposals it may have for Italy's defense policy should it gain office. One exception, however, was provided by an interview with PCI Board Member Ugo Pecchioli in November 1975, in which he noted communist disagreement with the efforts of extra parliamentary groups wishing to bring the parties into the barracks and unionize soldiers. Still, Pecchioli observed that other forms of representation for members of the armed forces should be achieved on matters such as the use of leisure time, living conditions, and military regulations. He also called for more direct contacts between defense officials and the parliament, rather than through the ministerial bureaucracy.

PCI attitudes toward NATO nuclear bases were bared in December 1975 by a PCI deputy during the course of a debate on the defense budget. Arrigo Boldrini posed the question whether the Italian government should not consider the issue of assuming greater national control over NATO bases located in Italy. He pointed to Turkey's success in obtaining revisions in agreements on NATO facilities located on its territory.(97)

At the very least, such statements hardly suggest clear sailing in NATO-Italian relations should the PCI obtain a more active role in governmental decision-making. Even if the PCI were excluded from a direct role in security matters, the very fact that it would give overwhelming priority to domestic matters would further inhibit Italy's ability to meet its defense commitments within NATO. Even while tolerating Italian links with NATO, the PCI's adherence to the long-term objective of a dissolution of the blocs would act as a constant qualifier of even this declaratory posture. While party leaders may exercise restraint for a time on the question of NATO, they can be expected to press for various disarmament and denuclearization schemes and to engage in harassment of NATO activities and American forces and bases in Italy. They may be willing to retain nominal membership in NATO so long as this imposes few burdens on Italy and provides an opportunity to obstruct planning in the Alliance. But if they should prove only minimally successful in keeping the Atlantic Alliance from achieving its goals, they will probably concentrate their anti-NATO strategy where the prospects for effective action are best – i.e., in Italy itself – by working to disengage Italy from the NATO integrated command and to eliminate the presence of U.S. forces and bases in Italy.

## FRENCH COMMUNIST ATTITUDES TOWARD NATO

The French Communist Party has always been hostile toward the Atlantic Alliance; even during recent years it has shown less disposition than the PCI to disguise this hostility. The PCF has pushed vigorously for nonrenewal of the Atlantic Treaty in 1969, when it became possible for any member to withdraw upon giving one year's notice. During negotiations with the Socialists over the drafting of the 1972 Common Program, the PCF continued to demand the withdrawal of France from the alliance but finally accepted a vague commitment to respect France's existing alliance commitments. The phrase actually means very little, especially in view of the evolution of the foreign and defense policy thinking of the Socialists, who had insisted on the inclusion of the phrase in the Common Program.

The two parties comprising the Union of the Left hoped to capitalize on the fact that Gaullist sentiment for an independent France is deeply held by large segments of the French population. One of the very few occasions when the PCF wholeheartedly supported de Gaulle was in his withdrawal of French forces from the NATO integrated military command in 1966. Even at the East Berlin Conference in late June 1976, France sought a denunciation of Western imperialism and the Atlantic Alliance but the final statement of the conference carried no such sentiment – only a provision advocating the dissolution of both alliances in Europe. Then, too, PCF leaders know that the Socialists, who once favored the alliance, have undergone a profound change of attitude in recent years. Even though the Socialists insist that they are more realistic than the PCF about the need for maintaining French membership in the Atlantic Alliance during a period of delicate equilibrium in Europe, they have resisted any suggestion that France should return to NATO military integration. Both the PCF and the PS, which for many years have denounced national nuclear forces, have moved toward acceptance of the idea of retaining the force de dissuasion. Still, both look forward to the eventual dissolution of the two military blocs, which they profess to see as the instruments by which the two superpowers dominate Europe. The Socialists champion the idea of West European independence from the United States, but they do not support moves toward European defense cooperation (which is sharply opposed by both the PCF and the Soviet Union). What is most disturbing, perhaps, to advocates of Western defense – most pleasing, of course, to the PCF – is the growing tendency of the Socialist leaders in France to regard the United States as a greater menace than the Soviet Union to the models of national, regional and global systems which they would like to see evolve.(98)

Marchais has exuded confidence that the tide of history in Europe is shifting in favor of communism. The West has been forced to accept peaceful coexistence and detente; the prospects for disarmament are improving; French workers should take hope from "the new correlation of forces in the world." Marchais condemned Giscard d'Estaing's decision to place French armed forces along side the "imperialist" West German Bundeswehr in a forward battle posture facing the borders of the socialist countries. The PCF leader called for "a policy of initiatives favoring the transcendence and then the dissolution of antagonistic blocs."

> Until this prospect is attained France, respecting its alliances, will remain a member of the Atlantic Treaty. It will not display less willingness to embark upon the path of independence with regard to any political and military bloc whatsoever.(99)

Marchais did not utter a word of criticism of Soviet military policy. Were it to gain office, a government of the Left in France could be expected to support Soviet positions in negotiations on SALT, MBFR and the creation of nuclear-free zones in Central Europe and the Mediterranean. The PCF would be certain to condemn any effort to reorient France gradually toward closer cooperation with the Alliance and to demand instead that emphasis be given to the strategy of tous azimuts or omnidirectional defense – i.e., a strategy not aimed primarily at the threat of attack from the East but capable of dealing with any threat of aggression from whatever source.(100)

Whether communist parties in governing coalitions prefer to subvert the Alliance by remaining in it or to weaken it politically by advocating withdrawal, it is virtually certain that they will place high priority on domestic economic programs, disparage the need for defense spending, cut military budgets as much as possible (except insofar as this would hurt local communist interests and alienate the military services), and oppose every form of European defense cooperation. They will strive to move their countries toward an anti-U.S. neutralism. They will espouse schemes of disarmament and a dissolution of blocs – and if these schemes ever materialize, they would redound to the great disadvantage of the United States whose military presence and contribution to equilibrium in Europe depend upon a treaty commitment and a security guarantee backed by forces stationed in Europe, but to the great advantage of the Soviet Union as a superpower whose ever-present shadow in Europe is an immutable geographical fact.

Chapter 10. NOTES

(1) Jean-Francois Revel credits Deutschland-Arkiv (April 1977) with tracing the origins of the term to Frane Barbieri. See Revel's article, "The Myths of Eurocommunism," Foreign Affairs, January 1978, p. 293.

(2) In the election for the Chamber of Deputies the PCI received 34.4 percent of the vote as compared to 27.2 percent in 1972. The Christian Democratic Party percentages were 38.7 in 1976 and 38.8 in 1972. Thus, the PCI gained in electoral strength while the DC was barely able to maintain its 1972 voting strength. The shift of votes to the Communists was at the expense of the smaller parties. The net effect has been a polarization of Italian politics. In the last French presidential election in April 1974, a coalition of the PCF and the Socialists, put together for the presidential runoff ballot, came within one percentage point of achieving victory.

(3) In Spain, the Communist Party (PCE) won only 9 percent ot the popular vote and 19 out of 350 seats in the June 1977 election for a post-Franco Cortes. The PCE appeared to have no chance of coming to power, but it was determined to play a significant role in shaping the New Spain. During 1977, PCE leader Santiago Carrillo emerged as a major figure in the Eurocommunist movement with the publication of his book, Eurocommunism and the State.

(4) James F. Clarity, "Advance by Leftists is Conceded in France," New York Times, March 15, 1977; see also Flora Lewis, "French Look Ahead to Next Elections," ibid., March 24, 1977.

(5) Events surrounding the PCE-PS split will be described more fully below. For an evaluation on why the polls were wrong, see Jim Browning, "French Asking How Did Polls Miss Their Mark," Christian Science Monitor, March 29, 1978.

(6) This meant that 245 Socialist candidates who had led on the Left in their districts were supposed to receive Communist votes on the second ballot, and 147 Communist candidates were supposed to be supported by Socialist voters. Opinion polls taken shortly before the runoff showed that many Socialist voters, especially white-collar workers, had become alienated by the alliance with the PCF.

(7) See Table 1.

(8) J.P., "Mr. Robert Fabre Wants to Give up the Chairmanship of the Left Radicals Movement," Le Monde, March 23, 1978; see also, "Socialist Party: Georges Marchais Helped the Right," ibid., March 22, 1978. For the PCF view of the election, see "PCF Politburo Statement," L'Humanité, March 21, 1978, as well as Rene Andrieu, "Rejected," ibid.

(9) Jim Browning, "Giscard Takes to the Hustings," Christian Science Monitor, January 31, 1978. See also Paul Lewis, "Two Studies See French Economic Chaos if Left Rules," New York Times, September 15, 1977, and his "Socialists in France Minimize the Costs of Economic Plans," ibid., February 15, 1978.

(10) Paul Betts, "Italy: High Hopes for the Mini-Accord," Financial Times (London), June 22, 1977.

(11) Claire Sterling, "Italy: 'Something' For Everyone," International Herald Tribune, July 6, 1977. Another correspondent, David Willey, writing in the Christian Science Monitor, expressed similar views regarding concern about the effect of decentralization on the fortunes of the PCI and DC. Moreover, Willey also observed that the real power of the country was seen to be wielded by the respective party secretaries rather than by the Prime Minister or by Parliament in the negotiations over the agreement. See his "Italian Parliament Debates Economic Program," ibid., July 14, 1977.

(12) "Berlinguer Brother Attacks Party's 'Change of Class,' " The Times (London), June 21, 1977.

(13) Joseph C. Harsch, "The Italian Nightmare," Christian Science Monitor, January 17, 1978. See also, Jonathan Spivak, "Resignation of Andreotti's Government Plunges Italy into Political Uncertainty," Wall Street Journal, January 17, 1978; and Claire Sterling, Why The Communists Junked the Italian Government," Washington Post, February 2, 1978.

Spivak noted that Berlinguer was under pressure from the unions to gain greater political concessions from the Christian Democratic Party. By edging to the right on economic policies designed to combat Italy's inflation, the PCI has spurred the growth of a more radical left-wing movement. Yet, according to Spivak, the PCI retained at least some hope of maintaining discipline among the youth and workers.

Sterling disagrees on the latter point, arguing that events surrounding the call for a general strike proved that the PCI could not restrain Italian workers.

(14) "Candle For a Birthday," The Economist, August 6, 1977.

(15) Henry Tanner, "Italian Reds Hold Parley and Insist on a Cabinet Role," New York Times, January 27, 1978. See also "Berlinguer Calls for Emergency Government of Broad Unity," L'Unità, January 19, 1978.

(16) Rosario Romeo and George Urban, in an interview which originated with Radio Free Europe and was excerpted in The Washington Review of Strategic and International Studies. This appeared as an editorial entitled "Troubled Italy," New York Times, January 2, 1978. See also, Henry Tanner, "Italy's Outcast Population," ibid., November 13, 1977.

Flora Lewis has also commented upon this fact: "The rise of violence in Italy, which has links to extremists on both ends of the political spectrum in other countries, is largely based on the development of a new proletariat, outside the unions and the official economy. The Communists neither represent nor control these groups and their growth is spreading the doctrines of anarchy, nihiliam and destruction." "Sharing Italy's Anxieties," ibid., January 22, 1978.

(17) For an analysis of the Red Brigades and their goals, see Michael Ledeen, "Violence is the Catalyst in Italy," Philadelphia Inquirer, April 23, 1978. Ledeen contends that the Red Brigades are bent on provoking the government into emergency antiterrorist acts which will be interpreted as fascist by the working class. They will then rise to overthrow the government, creating a new one in which the PCI will have a dominant role. The latter, in turn, would thus be forced to return to its Leninist traditions.

(18) Peter Nichols, "Italian Communists Renew Coalition Demand," The Times (London), December 16, 1977, and "Berlinguer Calls for Emergency Government of Broad Unity," L'Unità, January 19, 1978.

The Italian Socialist Party also participated in the demand for a coalition including communists. See Peter Nichols, "Italian Call for Coalition including Communists," The Times (London), December 12, 1977. "Italian Communist Chief Renews Demand for Role in Government," New York Times, January 19, 1978.

(19) Sari Gilbert, "Italians Agree on Cabinet," Washington Post, March 9, 1978.

(20) For the text of the U.S. Statement on Italy, see the New York Times, January13, 1978. The statement declared, in part: "We do not favor such participation and would like to see Communist influence in any Western European country reduced. As we have said in the past, we believe the best way to achieve these goals rests with the efforts of democratic parties to meet the aspirations of their people for effective, just, and compassionate government.

"The United States and Italy share profound democratic values and interests, and we do not believe that the Communists share those values and interests.

"As the President said in Paris last week: 'It is precisely where democracy is up against difficult challenges that its leaders must show firmness in resisting the temptation of finding solutions in nondemocratic forces.' "

Predictably, the statment drew a negative response from the PCI and the PS. Sari Gilbert, "Italian Communists Score U.S., Charge Internal Interference," Washington Post, January 14, 1978. L'Unità charged that President Carter was trying to influence the political situation in Italy and observed that the American policy statement was in conflict with the President's earlier promise of noninterference. See "Was U.S. Interference in Italian Crisis Requested by Sectors of DC?," L'Unità, January 14, 1978. See also, Gian Carlo Pajetta, "Rumors of American Interference: What Reply Does the DC Intend to Give?," ibid., January 10, 1978.

(21) See, e.g., Robert J. Lieber, "United States Foreign Policy and the West European Left," New York Times, August 19, 1975. Lieber described Mitterand's achievement as follows: "Mr. Mitterand's electoral and programmatic alliance with the Communists has been a striking success for the Socialists. By creating an attractive rejuvenated party, not least by his willingness to propose substantial and occasionally radical measures of domestic reform, Mr. Mitterand has succeeded in making the Socialists the senior partner. Clearly, it is Mr. Mitterand who has exploited the Communists, thereby contradicting the conventional wisdom – borrowed from the Eastern European context of 1944-47 – 'that if you sit down to dine with the Communists, it is they who will devour you rather than vice versa'."

(22) In their effort to update the 1972 Common Program, the Socialists and the numerically small Left Radical Party could not reconcile their differences with the PCF over nuclear defense policy, minimum wages and the number of industrial firms to be nationalized. The union had earlier agreed to nationalize nine large private industrial groups, plus most of the banking, financial and insurance sectors. According to the Socialist formula of nationalizing only 100 percent owned subsidiaries of the nine, about 300 or 400 companies would be covered; the PCF insisted that all subsidiaries as much as 51 percent owned would be taken over – this would mean about 1450 companies; but the PCF later reduced its demands to fewer than 800. Given the dominance of the Communists in the Confederation Generales du Travail (CGT), the larger nationalization program would ensure Communist control of France's leading industries and the principal economic ministries of the government. Victor Zorza, "Why Nationalization Matters to French Communists," Manchester Guardian Weekly, October 9, 1977. By the beginning of 1978, Mitterand made a gesture of reconciliation to the PCF by offering a commitment to increase the national minimum wage level by more than a third. The Economist, January 7, 1978, p. 37. Differences over defense policy will be discussed below.

The split was precipitated by the walk-out of Robert Fabre, leader of the Left Radicals, in protest against the communist proposals for sweeping nationalizations. While controversy surrounds the reasons for his action, the most likely explanation is that he wished to avoid being presented with a fait accompli on the issue by the two major parties. Alternatively, he may have sought to strengthen the stand of the Socialists in their negotiations with the Communists on the Joint Program. See "The Disunion of the Left," The Times (London), September 16, 1977. See also, Flora Lewis, "Left Wing in France Fails to End Discord," New York Times, September 15, 1977. See also her "French Socialists Reject Demands by Communists," ibid., September 11, 1977; "French Leftist Negotiations Fail, Jarring Red Hopes of Sharing Rule," ibid., September 24, 1977; and "French Socialists and Communists Issue Rival Appeals to the Voters, ibid., September 29, 1977.

Whether or not the Soviet Union directly influenced the decision of the PCF to adopt a tougher stance in its negotiations on the Common Program has been the subject of much speculation. According to one expert on these issues, Annie Kriegel, Professor of Political Sociology at the University of Paris, Nanterre, Moscow was likely to be just as happy if Giscard's government remained in office in light of its having maintained a certain distance from the United States. Moscow may have been concerned that, had the Socialists gained office, they may have encouraged closer relations between Bonn and Paris, an event which runs counter to Moscow's objective to break the Franco-German alliance. More simply, Marchais may not have wished to come to power unless the PCF were the dominant party. See her interview with Robert Prinsky, "Communist-Socialist Discord in France Confuses '78 Election and Irks, or Maybe Pleases, Moscow," Wall Street Journal, October 25, 1977.

President Giscard d'Estaing also alluded to Moscow's concerns when he noted during the campaign that Moscow fears a left-wing government because it might contaminate some regimes responsive to Moscow and that it was behind the hardened position of the PCF regarding the revision of the Common Program. See Jim Browning, "Do Soviets want French Communists to Lose?," Christian Science Monitor, September 20, 1977.

(23) Jim Browning, "Walkout Splits France's Leftists," Christian Science Monitor, September 18, 1977.

(24) Jonathan Kandell, "French Left's Fight Reaches Grass Roots," New York Times, November 13, 1977. See also his "French Leftists' Quarrels Spreading across Nation," ibid., February 16, 1978.

For a revealing account of the difficulties encountered at the local level in trying to rule together, see Ronald Koven, "France's Left Can't Get Together – In Paris or in Reims," Washington Post, March 1, 1978. In particular, the Socialists in Reims charged that they had been shut out of city affairs under a communist mayor.

(25) Jim Browning, "French Leftist Coalition Cracking," Christian Science Monitor, September 27, 1977. See also, Ian Murray "Union of Left Makes Only Small Gains in French Senate Poll," The Times (London), September 27, 1977. Of the 113 contested, the Union of the Left won 46, a gain of ten. In an enlarged Senate (from the previous 99 seats), this represented 40.68 percent of the seats, compared with 30 out of 99 previously held or 30.30 percent.

(26) Julian Mundy, "French Socialists Still Split," Christian Science Monitor, July 19, 1977. See also, "Conference Tests Unity of Mitterand Party," The Times (London), June 28, 1977.

(27) The PCF would undoubtedly like one of the three major posts, but might compromise by asking for Labor, Social Services, Civil Service, Youth, Nationalized Industries, Planning and a new Secretariat for Disarmament. Prior to the March 1978 elections, the PCF proposed, in fact, the split of the Ministry of the Interior. They would be given responsibility for local government while the PS would retain control of the police. They also proposed the merging of economic ministries to give them control over the economy.

(28) In February 1978, Le Nouvel Observateur surveyed Socialist voters on the

type of government they preferred to see after a Left victory. Nearly two-thirds favored a Socialist government without Communists, 32 percent expressed a willingness to accept an alliance with the Center Right, and only 28 percent favored a coalition with the PCF.

(29) Jonathan Kandell, "Carter's Visit to France Coincides with a High Point in Relations," New York Times, January 8, 1978; "Carter Warns Chief of French Socialists on Tie to Communists," ibid., January 7, 1978; and "French Socialist Leader Denies Carter Expressed Concern Over Red Links," ibid., January 10, 1978.

(30) Hadley Arkes, "Democracy and European Communism," Commentary, May 1976, p. 42.

(31) See Lamberto Furno, "The Socialists Are Not Giving An Ultimatum," La Stampa (Turin), January 10, 1976. In this report on a press conference with Secretary De Martino, the Socialist Party leader noted that Italy confronted an emergency situation and that the Center-Left formula was no longer adequate. Rather a strong government, with the support of the PCI, was essential. In describing the kind of Communist support needed, De Martino spoke of "external support or communist abstention" or possibly other forms of cooperation. See also "PCI Participation in the Country's Leadership Needed for Effective Political Swing," L'Unità, January 10, 1976.

(32) See Antonio Padellaro, "Statistical Document Drawn Up by PCI; Parliamentary Group Secretary asserts: 'All Most Important Laws Supported by Communist Vote,' " Corriere della Sera, January14, 1976. The article cites a report prepared by Mario Pochetti, the Secretary of the PCI Parliamentary Group, which showed that all important legislative measures approved in the Chamber had the support of Communist deputies. In particular, he noted Communist support for the 18-year-old vote and the abortion law. It was this situation to which the PSI objected when it decided to withdraw its support in January 1976.

(33) George Marchais, speaking at the Conference of West European Parties in East Berlin on June 30, 1976, declared his allegiance to "profoundly democratic socialism," including "freedom of opinion and expression, freedom of creation and publication, freedom to demonstrate, freedom of assembly and association, free circulation of persons inside the country and abroad, religious freedom and the right to strike." It also applies, he said, "to respect for universal suffrage with the attendant possibility of democratic alternation, the right of political parties including opposition parties to exist and operate, the independence and freedom of activity of the trade union; the independence and justice and the rejection of any official philosophy. . . ." Text of speech in L'Humanité, July 1, 1976.

Similarly, Enrico Berlinguer, speaking at the same conference, spoke of "struggling for a socialist society based on the assertion of the importance of personal and collective freedom and of guaranteeing them; of the principle of the secular and not ideological nature of the state and its democratic articulation; of a multi-party system and of the possibility of the government majorities alternating; of the autonomy of the trade unions, of religious freedoms, of freedom of expression, culture, art and science. . . ." Text of speech in L'Unità, July 1, 1976.

It might be noted that Marchais' attacks upon President Giscard d'Estaing's policies as reactionary, imperialistic, adventurist, anti-social and anti-democratic illustrate that he is by no means ready to give Giscard's party the benefit of the doubt as a legitimate democratic opposition party within the scope of democratic terms as defined by the PCF.

(34) New York Times, March 4, 1977.

(35) "Eurocommunism: Don't Touch," International Herald Tribune, July 2-3, 1977.

(36) Victor Zorza, "Soviets Tell Eurocommunists Violence is Inevitable," Christian Science Monitor, September 26, 1977. The Pravda article by Konstantin Zarodov reminding Marxists of the ultimate necessity of violence was ignored by L'Humanité in Paris and by L'Unità in Rome.

(37) Even before the March 1978 elections, the prospect of a Leftist victory caused capital investment in France to come to a virtual standstill for several months. Capital was being exported, the value of the franc was fluctuating markedly as a result of political uncertainty, and gold was being hoarded. Peter Jenkins contended that, regardless of whether the PCF has cut its ties to Moscow, it would nevertheless wreck French democracy with its economic programs of nationalization and inflationary policies. "Eurocommunist Sheep and Goats," Manchester Guardian Weekly, November 20, 1977.

(38) Marchais, in his East Berlin speech of June 30, 1976, seemed to anticipate such a contingency when he warned that struggle is necessary "to paralyze the attempts of reaction to resort to illegality and violence." Text in L'Humanité, July 1, 1976.

The advent of communism to power in any West European country is likely to usher in a polarization of politics and to generate extreme reactions on the authoritarian Right – particularly when the Communists start acting "true to form" in the eyes of conservatives. The Communists undoubtedly learned from what happened in Chile and Portugal that there are limits to what they can accomplish without a broad base of political support within the nation at large and within the armed forces. Still, they may miscalculate their support and overplay their hand, inducing attempts at a right-wing coup. But regardless of whether leftist or rightist extremism wins, constitutional democracy will be endangered.

(39) Neil McInnes, The Communist Parties of Western Europe (London: Oxford University Press, 1975), p. 137.

(40) Ibid., p. 139.

(41) Ibid.

(42) Arthur Schlesinger, Jr., "Eurocommunism and Detente," Wall Street Journal, August 25, 1977.

(43) According to one writer, the Kremlin is chagrined because the course being pursued by the Eurocommunists might "sour Mr. Brezhnev's detente plans for reviving the old Western fears about Soviet intentions." Christopher S. Wren, "West Europe's Communists Irk Soviet, Too," New York Times, May 2, 1976. A Japanese correspondent was moved to speculate that once West European communists had broken with Moscow, they might become "the fiercest proponents of national independence within the Western camp." Takashi Oka, "Stalinist Curtain Divides Communists," Christian Science Monitor, February 25, 1976.

(44) See Joseph Fromm, "Revolt of West Europe's Reds: Alarm for Russia – and U.S. Too," U.S. News and World Report, March 22, 1976.

(45) In the Pravda article, Konstantin Zarodov chided the Western parties for pursuing a moderate line at a time when the "crisis of capitalism" was producing conditions highly favorable to an upsurge of the world revolutionary movement. See Victor Zorza, "Western Comrades Resent Kremlin Directives," Manchester Guardian Weekly, September 27, 1975; and "Watching the West Slide," ibid., October 4, 1975. See also Boris Ponomarev, "The World Situation and the Revolutionary Process," World Marxist Review, June 1974, pp. 3-15.

(46) In Paris it was reported that the statement was described by one PCF official as a major effort by the French Communist Party to be viewed in the same light as the Italian Communists. The statement might also be viewed in the context of maneuvering with regard to the European Communist Party Congress. See The Times (London), November 19, 1975, especially Peter Nichols, "Communists of Italy and France Review Their Stand on Europe." See also Alvin Shuster, "French and Italian Reds Concur on Aims," New York Times, November 18, 1975; and Hella Pick, "Communists Call for Broad Front to Gain Democratic Power," The Guardian, November 23, 1975.

(47) James F. Clarity, "Paris Red Charges Soviet Repression," New York Times, February 5, 1976.

(48) Ibid. See also the earlier accounts: Richard Wigg, "M. Marchais Explains Why French Communists Issued Challenge to Moscow over Forced Labor Camps," The Times (London), December 15, 1975; and Charles Hargrove, "French Communists Refuse to Toe Soviet Line on Labour Camps," ibid., December 22, 1975.

(49) Jean Elleinstein, Histore du phénomène stalinien (Paris: Editions sociales, 1975). See also his interview with the Lisbon journal Expresso, November 26, 1976, as reported in Kevin Devlin, "Jean Elleinstein, PCF's Anti-Stalinist

Outrider," Radio Free Europe Research, RAD Background Report/21, January 17, 1977.

(50) Annie Kriegel, Les communistes francais (Paris: Seuil, 1970, second edition), p. 256. This is worth keeping in mind, since that particular phrase, "proletarian internationalism," was deleted from the final statement issuing from the East Berlin Conference of European Communist Parties in late June 1976.

Illustrative of the skill displayed by communist spokesmen in tailoring their messages to their audiences, Plissonier, in Moscow to attend the Soviet Party Congress, remained discreetly silent on the question of abandoning the "dictatorship of the proletariat."

(51) "What would people in France say," asks Solzhenitsyn, "if a high government official were to attend a secret meeting of high officials of Chile or South Africa – and then said he didn't agree with Chilean or South African policies but had simply come to listen to their opinions?" Quoted in C.L. Sulzberger, "Does National Marxism Exist?", New York Times, March 10, 1976.

(52) Carlo Casalegno, Interview with Enrico Berlinguer, "Onward March of a Western Communist Party," EUROPEA, supplement of The Times (London), February 3, 1976.

(53) Alfredo Rodisco, Interview with Enrico Berlinguer, "Onward March of a Western Communist Party," EUROPEA, supplement of The Times (London), February 3, 1976.

(54) Ibid.

(55) Donald L.M. Blackmer, "Continuity and Change in Postwar Italian Communism," in Donald L.M. Blackmer and Sidney Tarrow, editors, Communism in Italy and France (Princeton, N.J.: Princeton University Press, 1975), pp. 66-67.

(56) Gian Carlo Pajetta, "CIA Funds," L'Unità, January 9, 1976. Pajetta called for the investigation of possible CIA funding to Italian political leaders because of its implications for Italy's independence.

(57) See Michael Ledeen and Claire Sterling, "Italy's Russian Sugar Daddies," The New Republic, April 3, 1976. See also McInnes, op. cit., pp. 126-130, for a description of the finances of European communist parties.

(58) Ibid., p. 21.

(59) Ibid., p. 21. PCI Secretariat Member Gianni Cervetti and Central Administration Section Chief Guido Capelloni denied the New Republic charges that the PCI received funds either from export companies or cooperatives. Moreover, they defended PCI financial assistance to such

concerns as an effort to improve Italian exchanges with socialist countries and to help small and medium-sized firms in Italy. See "PCI Money: Where It Comes from and How It is Spent," L'Unità, April 11, 1976.

(60) "Excerpts from Statement and Speeches at Communist Meeting in East Berlin," New York Times, July 1, 1976.

(61) "Soviet Union Bows to the Tito Doctrine," Manchester Guardian Weekly, July 11, 1976. See also Charles W. Yost, "Communism: No Longer one Man's Family," Christian Science Monitor, July 8, 1976.

(62) The question of "international discipline" versus "national independence" has special significance for Spain. The legalization of the Spanish Communist Party poses important implications for the delicate experiment in post-Franco liberalization now under way in Madrid. See "Spanish Parliament Liberalizes Penal Code, Making Political Activity Legal," New York Times, July 15, 1976.

(63) Text of Berlinguer's June 30 address to the East Berlin Conference of Communist and Workers Parties, "We are Fighting to Open up New Roads Toward Socialism in Italy and Europe," L'Unità, July 1, 1976.

(64) Ibid.

(65) In his efforts to project an image of the PCI as an independent party, Berlinguer has gone so far as to suggest that Italian membership in NATO provides a useful shield to prevent the Soviet Union from interference in the creation of the Italian way to socialism. This rather extreme statement apparently did not enjoy unanimous agreement within the party since it was omitted when L'Unità reported on this interview. See Corriere della Sera, June 15, 1976.

(66) "Excerpts from Statements and Speeches at Communist Meeting in East Berlin," New York Times, July 1, 1976.

(67) Ibid.

(68) Christian Science Monitor, July 1, 1976.

(69) Ibid., February 25, 1976. January 1977, for example, the PCF condemned the French government for its support of Zaire by transporting Moroccan troops on French aircraft.

(70) The Times (London), February 28, 1976.

(71) "A Satisfactory Balance Sheet," L'Humanité, July 2, 1976.

(72) "Three Ways to European Communism," Manchester Guardian Weekly, July 11, 1976.

(73) Peter Osnos, "Communist Summit Broke Little New Ideological Ground," Washington Post, July 12, 1976.

(74) Heinz Timmermann, "Eurocommunism: Moscow's Reaction and the Implications for Eastern Europe," World Today, October 1977, p. 379.

(75) Edward Crankshaw, "Europe's Reds: Trouble for Moscow," New York Times Magazine, February 12, 1978, p. 19.

(76) "Europe's New Renegade Reds," Time, December 8, 1975.

(77) "Moscow and the European Communist Conference," Soviet World Outlook (Center for Advanced International Studies, University of Miami), July 15, 1976.

(78) See Berlinguer's East Berlin speech, L'Unità, July 1, 1976.

(79) The Times (London), March 3, 1976. See also Flora Lewis, "Italian Reds Seek Europe-Wide Alliance of Leftist Parties," New York Times, December 1, 1977, and Eric Bourne, "Eurocommunism's Momentum Runs Down," Christian Science Monitor, March 29, 1978.

(80) Vera Vegetti, "Exceptional Interest in the Hague in the Italian Communists," L'Unità, May 8, 1976.

(81) Ibid.

(82) Peter Nichols, "Communists of Italy and France Revise their Stand on Europe," The Times (London), November 19, 1975.

(83) Ibid.

(84) "Berlinguer Discusses EC Problems with Tindemans," L'Unità, October 7, 1975.

(85) "Italian Reds Seeking Wider Role in Europe," New York Times, September 18, 1977.

(86) New York Times, June 4, 1976.

(87) "French Cabinet Agrees European Poll Bill," The Times (London), May 19, 1977. See also, Charles Hargrove, "M. Marchais Drops Party Objection to EEC Poll," ibid., April 19, 1977; "Adjustment of Debate on Direct Elections Demanded by Gaullists," ibid., June 13, 1977; and "French Direct Elections Bill Becomes Law," ibid., July 2, 1977.

(88) L'Humanité, January 10, 1978.

(89) L'Unità, March 14, 1972.

(90) Ibid., March 19, 1975.

(91) Ibid., December 12, 1975. Report on "Television Interview with Enrico Berlinguer."

(92) Ina Selden, "Views of Reds Arouse Debate in Italy Again," New York Times, April 17, 1977.

(93) Giampaolo Pansa, "PCI and USSR: Deputy Pajetta, Can We Trust You?," Corriere della Sera, May 30, 1976.

(94) Giampaolo Pansa, Interview with PCI Secretary General Enrico Berlinguer, ibid., June 15, 1976.

(95) Ibid.

(96) L'Expresso, November 16, 1975.

(97) "PCI for a Military Policy to Meet National Needs," L'Unità, December 4, 1975.

(98) The themes summarized in this paragraph are elaborated by Michael M. Harrison, "A Socialist Foreign Policy for France," Orbis, Winter 1976, pp. 1485-1491.

(99) L'Humanité, July 1, 1976.

(100) George Marchais has said: "France must have a national defense which really ensures the country's independence. This defense must be all round. Finally, the country must give itself the political means (of defending itself), for instance by conclusion of non-aggression treaties." "Communists 'Evolving' on French Nuclear Arms," The Times (London), May 1, 1976. The defense platform of the 1972 Common Program called for "renunciation of the nuclear force in any form whatsoever," but in April 1976 M. Louis Baillot, a Communist member of the National Assembly who is regarded as the party's defense expert, was quoted as saying that 'nuclear weaponry can be considered as an element of political independence," and that "the nuclear force presents itself as a fact, and it is impossible not to recognize this." James F. Clarity, "French Reds Shift Stand on Defense," New York Times, April 25, 1976.

The PCF election program statement of January 1978 declared that national independence must be preserved, the two alliances must be dissolved and replaced by a European collective security treaty. "In all circumstances, France must possess the military resources to insure its security and independence. As things stand at present, this implies retaining nuclear weapons at the minimum level required for this purpose within the framework of an omnidirectional (tous azimuts) strategy of deterrence. . . ." L'Humanité, January 10, 1978.

# 11 A Western Counter-Finlandization Strategy

James E. Dougherty

Finlandization appears to be the strategy which the Soviets would prefer to apply to Western Europe. Evidence has been accumulating for several years that Moscow is actually trying to put such a strategy into operation, with at least some success. As the Soviets view it, the process is essentially dialectical. Therefore it is fraught with ambiguities and the tension of opposites, as conflict always is. The movement is by no means unilinear. Temporary setbacks and reverses have to be expected. But is only the net long-term outcome that matters.

## SOVIET STRATEGY, TIMETABLE AND FLEXIBILITY

We do not contend that the Soviets have a precise timetable for extending effective hegemony over Western Europe. What they do possess is an intelligent and sophisticated strategic plan for accomplishing their foreign policy objectives as the correlation of forces between rival social-power systems shifts in their favor. The plan helps them to impose some kind of rational order upon a variety of disparate events, developments and trends in the international milieu, to understand what is happening, to avoid catastrophic mistakes, and to establish priorities and phase their policy efforts in a sequence best calculated to produce advantageous results.

Soviet strategic planners may find it useful to attach time parameters to the various phases of the process through which their relationship with the United States and Western Europe is evolving. They engage in something comparable to what Western business executives and other organizational administrators call management by objective. The setting of a target or goal to be achieved by a specific deadline does not necessarily entail a prediction that it will be successfully achieved on schedule, but it provides an aiming point which facilitates a more effective galvanizing of energies. With the experience of several five-year plans behind them, the Soviets realize quite well that plans often go awry, that unforeseen factors may intervene, and that the attainment of goals or other outcomes may have to be postponed. It makes sense for Soviet planners to fix their sights on the neutralization and Finlandization of Western Europe by the mid or latter-1980s. If the objective is not fully reached by that time, they can always identify the factors which will explain why the plan was derailed, and they can then face the next five or ten-year period with renewed confidence that they are closer than ever to the final triumph.

As Soviet strategists see it, the period of discontent, disarray, and discord within the capitalist world reached its climax during the period from the mid-1960s to the mid-1970s – from the social-political turmoil generated by the Vietnam War to the economic-political chaos resulting from the Middle East War of late 1973 and the ensuing energy-financial crisis which nearly ripped the Atlantic Alliance apart. The Soviets have watched with keen interest the efforts of Western governments since 1974 to reverse their toboggan slide, regroup their forces and stabilize the situation. Not all the economic and political changes of the last three years have necessarily been favorable to Soviet ambitions.

In Greece, Portugal and Spain, dictatorial governments whose policies had been a source of constant embarrassment to the United States because of its security ties with them have disappeared from the scene. Those countries have begun moving haltingly toward constitutionalism. In all three, communist parties have acquired a new operational freedom, but on balance the democratic West looks more democratic than it did before, and communist propagandists have had a few well-worn strings removed from their bow. Indeed, although several West European countries governed by fragile coalitions continue to feel the heavy strain which severe economic conditions place upon their political institutions, the cause of democracy throughout the region as a whole does not appear quite so desparate as it did in 1974 – when the Europeans' loss of confidence in their own systems was exacerbated by the appalling spectacle of what was happening in the United States during the Watergate crisis. But, in view of the recurring terrorism against politicians, diplomats and businessmen, the question whether democratic institutions will be able to survive the last quarter of the twentieth century still gnaws at the minds of many thoughtful Europeans.

To be sure, serious economic and social problems persist – unemployment, inflation, industrial strife, energy shortages, payments deficits, the petro-dollar glut, severe monetary fluctuations, and conflicts over trade both among the industrialized states and between the industrialized and developing countries. Nevertheless, the pace at which Europeans and Americans seemed to be rushing headlong toward internecine economic conflict four years ago has been somewhat moderated. Allied governments have tried to approach their disputes over economic policy more maturely and intelligently, and they have blunted, at least for the moment, the cutting edge of Suslov's gleeful prophecy of impending doom for the Western capitalist system. The process could be reversed, of course, and rapid deterioration of interallied relations could once again set in as the result of an international economic crisis due to forces over which the vulnerable economies of Europe can exercise little or no control. The Soviets are well aware of Europe's economic vulnerabilities and of the opportunities to which they give rise for the acquisition of future strategic leverage. Even in the absence of an economic crisis brought on by another oil price rise, 1978 witnessed serious strains in the trade and monetary relations of the United States with West Germany and Japan. Because of huge U.S. deficits, the dollar continued its long term decline against the deutsche mark and the yen.

When the long-range trends are analyzed, the Soviets can find ample cause for optimism. Viewed through their Marxist prism, the West is currently passing through a period of dynamic social change in conformity with the forecast made by scientific socialism. Within Western society, because of the laws of intrinsic and inexorable social development, and also because of decades of communist intervention into the process (through propaganda, infiltration, manipulation, diplomacy, crisis stimulation, psychological warfare, and persistent efforts to bring about a decisive shift in the world correlation of forces), the dangerous values of what they characterize as an arrogant, activist, aggressive and unpredictable bourgeois culture are being replaced by the values of a more benign, passive, pacifist and more easily manageable (and predictable) quasi-socialist culture. Throughout the West, the interest of elites and public alike in the imperatives of military security is in long-range decline, despite occasional impulses to the contrary. Annual increases in Western defense budgets seldom keep pace with the rate of inflation.

Western societies experience swelling guilt complexes over their own deficiencies and injustices, and over such new weapons systems as they continue to develop, in spite of mounting evidence that the Soviet momentum in the military production sector has been much greater during the last decade. NATO, notwithstanding a good deal of public rhetoric on the need for weapons standardization and interoperability of components to simplify the logistics problem in wartime, has made progress in this direction at no more than a glacial pace. In fact, German-American rivalry over a future NATO main battle tank and the efforts of the two allies to work out a compromise between the claims of the Leopard II and the XM-1 produced embittered relations between Bonn and Washington, as well as between the military and industrial establishments of the two countries. The tensions were reduced considerably when the U.S. Army decided in January 1978 to outfit its new XM-1 tank with a German 120mm gun, but controversies over issues of standardization and interoperability, as well as over the meaning of the transatlantic two-way street in arms purchasing, were expected to recur.

Most West European governments, even though now managing tenuously to muddle through a period of eased external pressures, still suffer from fundamental structural weaknesses which make responsible elites apprehensive over what may lie ahead. The Europeans realize the dangers of national particularism, yet the movement toward closer economic, political and defense cooperation has been virtually stalled at dead center since late 1973, when Moscow sounded an ominous warning against European unification as then conceived. Prospects exist for the further expansion of the EEC to encompass new members at each end of the Mediterranean – Portugal and Spain, Greece and Turkey – but every proposal along these lines involves problems and potential conflicts which threaten to dilute whatever cohesiveness remains. Community members are already experiencing difficulty in planning to carry out the all-European parliamentary elections to which they have formally committed themselves. In all member states, competition among political parties and between national legislators and European parliamentarians will complicate the task.

Meanwhile, as shown in Chapter 10, the fortunes of several West European communist parties continue to improve perceptibly. Their political evolution toward ostensible autonomy and their advent to positions of power in governing coalitions might conceivably, as some observers argue, erode the principle of international proletarian solidarity so dear to communist hardliners in Moscow and also compound the problems faced by the USSR in Eastern Europe by nourishing the desire for liberalization. But these are debatable and reversible hypotheses. Regardless of how the Soviets might view it, a growth of political influence by Eurocommunism is certain to pose serious dangers to the viability of NATO and of the European Community as we have hitherto known these organizations.

A plausible case can be made that the phenomenon of dissidence in Eastern Europe and in the USSR in recent years has been the function not only of resentment against communist oppression but also of the attraction and psychological support of a Western democratic alliance nearby, militarily and politically strong enough to apply pressure upon the Soviet Union to loosen its grip in the interest of promoting detente. In other words, the proximity of the NATO presence has been a factor encouraging individuals in the Eastern bloc to aspire to greater freedom. If the anti-American policies of the Eurocommunist parties – protestations of approval for NATO notwithstanding – lead to a weakening of the Alliance, a reduction of the security linkage between Western Europe and the United States, and the neutralization of Europe, communist regimes will encounter much less difficulty in dealing with dissidents, for they will be fewer and farther between, as well as less bold and much more resigned to their fate. The authors of this study are convinced that Eurocommunism, on balance, will endanger more than benefit the cause of human freedom throughout Europe as a whole.

There is one set of assumptions under which the Soviet Union might come around to favoring a certain mode of limited and carefully circumscribed European unity. Such a contingency could arise out of circumstances in which Eurocommunist, Gaullist, and other anti-American forces would be sufficiently powerful to revamp the European Community into an organization that would be economically cooperative with the communist states to the East, bent on phasing out the U.S. military presence in Europe, and unlikely to contemplate forms of European defense cooperation that would give rise to serious misgivings in Moscow. The USSR would probably discern distinct advantages in a West European unity organization that was militarily separatist vis-a-vis the United States, militarily weak in its own right, and politically and economically obsequious to a communist bloc more monolithic than it is today. Such a European organization, of course, would be the antithesis of the West European unity movement of the last three decades. It would be compelled to seek its security in an all-European framework. It would be politically neutralist in much the same sense as is Finland today. And the prospects for the survival of its democratic institutions and its tradition of liberal civilization would be dim indeed.

Many experienced European observers, assessing the steady shift in the global and regional political-military balance, as well as the growing Soviet capabilities in land, sea and air forces to threaten West European oil and raw materials sources in the Middle East and Africa, project an increasingly bleak future in which Europe will have little choice but to accommodate to the realities of Soviet power as the countervailing U.S. guarantee becomes less credible. In the realm of international politics, perceptions of long-range trends and emerging outlines of the future count for more than the precise numerical calculus of the military power balance at any given point in time.

It is against probable futures that politicians hedge their bets. European politicians are still inclined to think – with good reason – that Europe is politically, economically, culturally and strategically more important than Asia is to the United States. Yet they cannot help wondering when the general phenomenon of U.S. reversion to isolationism and retrenchment from global strategic responsibilities will affect Europe. Even while working consciously to prevent an unattractive future from coming to pass, or to postpone it as long as possible, they often cannot avoid tailoring unconsciously their policies to what they regard as inevitable in the long run. Perhaps they hope thereby to build up with the erstwhile foe and ascending hegemonic power a certain amount of political credit which will make the future relationship less intolerable than it might otherwise be if they should adamantly oppose to the bitter end what seems to be inevitable.

Not only the governing capitals of Western Europe are nervous. Within recent years it has often been suggested that even the Vatican, which for a century has been implacably hostile to Marxist ideology, now feels compelled to bow to the inevitable and to seek a pragmatic accommodation with the Marxist regimes to the East. The Church, in order to advance her institutional interests and win a minimal freedom of religion in the people's democracies, has hosted a parade of communist officials from Eastern Europe and the USSR, done favors for communist governments (e.g., by arranging the removal of Cardinal Mindszenty from Hungary), muted her criticism of communist violations of religious and political rights, recognized postwar territorial realities in regard to the German-Polish border, and acquiesced in the appointment of pro-Marxist bishops in Eastern Europe. This was a far cry from the anticommunist stance of Pope Pius XII, who had virtually called for a just war of liberation on behalf of the Christian states of Eastern Europe following the Soviet suppression of the Hungarian uprising in 1956. But that posture seemed counterproductive to Pope John XXIII and Pope Paul VI, especially after it became clear that the West was determined to pursue a policy of detente.

The Vatican, with its vast fund of diplomatic experience, has been assessing carefully the East-West struggle for a long time. Persistent reports emanating from Rome reflect a growing concern among Church officials concerning the strength and durability of Western democratic institutions. For a decade there have been recurring indications that Pope Paul VI, who once warmly championed the European unity movement (as Pope Pius XII had done earlier), has been forced to conclude that it has failed and that Western Europe is now destined to lose its political and economic autonomy during the

1980s. The rising fortunes of the Eurocommunist parties within the heartland of Western Christendom serve as an additional harbinger of the dissolution of the Atlantic Alliance. If Western Europe should undergo Finlandization, the Vatican would be increasingly expected to throw its weight behind the movement for Marxist democratic socialism in Latin America – behind Allende-type regimes and behind those theologians of revolutionary liberation who already characterize Christ as a Palestinian Ché Guevara.

## SOURCES OF EUROPEAN STRENGTH

Despite these pessimistic signs, it is far from certain that the Soviets can apply to the whole of Western Europe a strategy of political domination which has worked so effectively in the case of a small, weak neighboring state such as Finland. The population of the Soviet union is more than fifty times that of Finland; its margin of economic-technological-military power is much greater. Possessing an overwhelming power superiority in relation to Finland, the USSR has managed quite successfully to achieve its foreign policy objectives vis-a-vis that unfortunately situated country.

In assessing the larger regional scene, it should not be forgotten that the total population of the European members of NATO is greater than that of the Soviet Union, and so is their total political-economic-technological-cultural potential. Only in the military power dimension can the Soviet Union be said to possess an insuperable margin of superiority over Western Europe. In that dimension – psychologically frightening and politically impressive but not always readily usable to achieve specific policy objectives in a predictable manner – the West Europeans cannot possibly approach the capabilities of the Russians within this century. The West Europeans are for the most part resigned to this condition, and do not expect to alter it substantially. But in the realms of diplomacy, politics, economics, science and technology, and all those other areas of creative social and cultural intelligence in which free peoples shall always be superior to dismal totalitarian ideologues and their bungling bureaucrats, the West Europeans can, if they concert their efforts, prove more than a match for the Soviets, with all the vulnerabilities peculiar to their own system.

Raymond Aron has chided Europeans and Americans for having become so critically hostile toward their own culture as to lose perspective:

> In matters of productivity, technical innovation, living standards, scientific progress and human freedom, it is the West, the United States and Europe combined, which has taken the lead over the last 10 years. . . . (O)ne must recognize that it is from the European-American centre of the world economy that the Third World now seeks aid, and not from the so-called socialist countries; it is the West, and it alone, which possesses the means to reduce, little by little, the gap separating the rich and poor countries. The spokesmen of the Third World take some satisfaction in railing against American or Western imperialism. Yet when a Latin American intellectual is forced out of his country by some military coup, where does he take refuge – in Moscow?(1)

The International Institute for Strategic Studies has called attention to the fact that military strength looms so large in the thinking of Soviet leaders because in a country as "economically uncompetitive, culturally repressive and ideologically increasingly barren," the primary instrument for achieving global power and influence has to be military might.(2) The Soviets cannot but realize that the whole of humanity is moving toward a universal social order marked by technology, creative invention and problem-solving, the mobility of people and ideas, and the development of a humanist, pluralist culture which enables people not only to satisfy their basic needs (something that the Soviets can at least hope to achieve for their own people) but also to fulfill their aspirations for a life that is free and filled with self-actualizing and socially worthwhile experiences (something that the Soviets cannot do even for their own people, much less help others to obtain.)

The Soviets lag behind in nonmilitary technology. In many technological areas all they can do is imitate and borrow from the West. In the realms of politics, economics, art and social behavior they are afraid to imitate or borrow, lest the pace of change escape the ability of central planners to control it. Thus, aside from the military, diplomatic and trade sectors, and a few scientific and cultural areas where their accomplishments cannot be ignored, the Soviet Union simply does not make interesting news in a volume comparable to that of Western societies. The individuals who command attention outside are the dissidents and the defectors. For the most part, Soviet life remains dull and uninspiring, and the Communist Party of the USSR – utterly opposed to the pluralism and permissiveness of Western culture – wants to keep it that way.

It need not be taken as a given, then, that Finlandization (as the term is understood here) will be the inevitable fate of Europe. What is required urgently within the Atlantic Community is a revived confidence that Europe can remain the master of its own political destiny; that ways can be found to reverse the incipient process of Finlandization which has been under way for several years; and that policies can be formulated within NATO and within European institutions calculated gradually to produce over a period of from five to ten years a heightened sense of self-confidence on the part of the Europeans themselves. We need not assume, merely because some important trends are running in the Soviets' favor, that all of them do so, or even that all those now running in their favor will continue to do so. If the underlying assumptions on which Western elites base their interpretations of contemporary historical movements are essentially pessimistic, this will undoubtedly reinforce the tendency toward the working out of the self-fulfilling prophecy. The individual or the society whose view of history is excessively gloomy – in the Spenglerian sense of awaiting the inexorable Untergang des Abendlandes – is quite likely to place the most unfavorable interpretation upon unfolding events, to accept them with an attitude of stoic resignation, and to miss opportunities for improving the situation simply because efforts toward improvement are looked upon as futile.

If the Western Alliance is to fend off the danger of Europe's being Finlandized, this will require neither a naive nor a Pollyannish approach to international relations in the nuclear age, but rather an intellectually healthy, well-balanced political-military-economic-socio-cultural analysis of the problems which will confront NATO and Europe between now and 1990. Whatever policies the Atlantic Community adopts will have to be based upon a frank recognition that the Soviets will always enjoy a natural military advantage in the European theater. This is a simple matter of sheer power-in-being multiplied by the additional leverage provided by geographic proximity. It is likely that, barring major domestic upheavals and fundamental internal changes within the USSR – which are not being predicted – the Soviets will continue for an indefinitely long time to allocate a larger relative and absolute amount of resources to the production of military capabilities than will the United States, particularly in regard to capabilities earmarked for Europe. Unless the United States and its European allies take steps to reverse the post-Vietnam decline in defense-mindedness on the part of publics and governments, the Soviets appear certain to be able to look forward to a widening margin of superiority across the total spectrum of military prowess, even though in some segments the West will retain a quantitative and/or qualitative edge. This will be even more true if the United States, instead of keeping pace with the Soviets in the development of military capabilities, pursues policies of unilateral disarmament, decoupling and retrenchment from Europe, and unreciprocated self-restraint in the realm of arms control.

"Mutual uncertainty about the nature of the central strategic balance," wrote Alastair Buchan shortly before his death, "is more probable than a simple transference of strategic superiority from the United States to the Soviet Union."(3) He was undoubtedly hinting that uncertainty of the precise character of the strategic balance, based on the compensating and fluctuating asymmetries involved in contemporary military-technological developments within a context of differing geostrategic requirements, might itself exert a stabilizing effect upon the relationship between the two superpowers by making the utmost strategic caution an imperative demand. Buchan's view was better taken than that of those strategic analysts who have always attributed destabilizing consequences to uncertainty. All through the period of crude strategic parity, which is presumed to have prevailed throughout the era of SALT – from the late 1960s to the present time – the situation has been marked by uncertainties which have had a more stabilizing than destabilizing effect, because the uncertainties on each side were kept within the limits of a tolerably stable psychopolitical balance. Even if one side or the other happened to think that it possessed a significant margin of superiority in a particular dimension of military-technological power, neither superpower has worried seriously until recently about the possibility of a surprise attack, deliberately planned and executed by its adversary. Military strategists have continued to worry, as they are supposed to, about the numbers game, the possibility of decisive technological breakthroughs, and the worst possible case. But until recently it has been taken for granted, especially by Western strategic analysts, that political leaders in Washington and Moscow could not possibly, under the circumstances of strategic parity, conceive of any rational purpose to be served by a deliberately planned first strike, because the risks of retaliation would be too frightful.

The governments of the superpowers have therefore been compelled, willingly or not, to pursue policies based upon a realistic understanding of the politico-military environment, and to accommodate themselves, however grudgingly, to each other's vital, irreducible national interests in spite of their ongoing political, ideological and economic rivalry. The most dangerous aspect of the strategic balance during the last three years has been that the uncertainties which formerly made for stability have been superseded by a new certainty which is destabilizing – the certainty that Soviet momentum with regard to the development, production, and deployment of significant weapons systems has been much greater than American momentum since 1970, and that the balance has been shifting steadily toward the communist bloc. There is a growing recognition among strategists that while the U.S. doctrine of strategic deterrence calls for each side to restrain its ability to undermine the retaliatory capability of the other, Soviet doctrine requires maximizing the ability to blunt the nuclear striking power of the adversary in the case of war.(4)

## THE MILITARY REQUIREMENTS OF COUNTER-FINLANDIZATION

It will be of the utmost importance for the United States to keep a credible strategic deterrent umbrella extended over Europe. The peoples of Europe must remain convinced that their security remains inextricably bound up with that of the American people. The first prerequisite for stalemating the Soviets in their strategy of Finlandization will be the ability of the United States to affirm convincingly that it intends to provide for the peace, stability and defense of Europe. The United States should encourage the Europeans to move toward closer cooperation among themselves in the area of defense – but only to improve the West's overall defense position, not to pave the way for the decoupling of European defense from the U.S. strategic deterrent.

The United States may be able to allow the size of its strategic nuclear arsenal to drop below that of the Soviets, but not by very much. Certainly there can be no consideration of finite deterrence in the sense that the United States needs only a limited number of strategic missiles and other weapons systems to provide for the common defense regardless of what the Soviets build. If the gap between Soviet and U.S. strategic military capabilities becomes too wide, there will be adverse political repercussions and the Europeans will become increasingly apprehensive about the global (and even more about the regional) balance between the superpowers.

Thoughtful European observers realize that even when the United States was regarded as strategically stronger, the two superpowers were in a condition of general political-military equilibrium in Europe. The most salient strategic fact of the current decade, so far as Europeans are concerned, is that the basic assumption on which the security of the NATO area was founded during the first twenty years of the Atlantic Alliance no longer obtains. Ever since the SALT negotiations got under way in late 1969, it has become increasingly clear that the former condition of U.S. strategic superiority has been replaced by the condition of strategic parity between the superpowers and that the relative position of the United States, far from improving, has steadily become weaker. U.S. defense officials make no effort to deny that the landbased ICBM force will be highly vulnerable to Soviet missiles in the early 1980s. Although the Soviets, given their preferred strategy of avoiding nuclear war and of pursuing a strategy of Finlandization, may never come to look upon their strategic superiority as militarily usable, nevertheless they can be counted upon to seek ways of projecting a putative superiority for the purpose of reaping political gain. In the final analysis, therefore, the measure of strategic superiority will consist not in any mere comparison of numbers of weapons held by the two superpowers, but rather in the way in which such a comparison is perceived and interpreted for its political significance.

As the global strategic balance has changed, Europeans have worried more about the balance in their own region, which, in political-psychological as well as military terms, has been tilting slowly against NATO because of the inequality of NATO and Warsaw Pact conventional ground forces (especially since the 1968 invasion of Czechoslovakia); Soviet quantitative superiority in armor and tactical air forces; substantial Soviet reinforcement advantages during the first sixty days of hostilities; and expanding Soviet naval deployments in the Mediterranean, in the northern waters off the coast of Norway, and along the eastern and western coasts of Africa (a region vital to Europe as a source of raw materials).

In its arms negotiations with the Soviet, particularly in SALT and MBFR, the United States should always bear in mind the sensitivities of its European allies, and either consult with them or keep them as fully informed as possible.

1. The United States should strive to negotiate in SALT an agreement or agreements which will appear equitable to Europeans and which will not arouse misgivings on the grounds that European interests are adversely affected.

2. More specifically, the United States should not negotiate with the USSR agreements (a) which would ignore the legitimate concerns of Europeans, for example, over the deployment of weapons systems such as MR-IRBMs, including the new SS-20 missiles or Backfire bombers, which pose a more immediate threat to Western Europe than to the United States; (b) which would eliminate weapons systems – the so-called forward-based systems, such as carrier-based aircraft in the Mediterranean or F-111Es in Britain – which are deemed necessary for the maintenance of an adequate NATO defense capability; or (c) which would asymmetrically inhibit the future technological upgrading of military forces in Europe to the disadvantage of NATO, for instance, as a result of a ban, or the acceptance of short-range limits, on cruise missiles.

3. Outside of formal negotiations, the United States should be careful not to make ostentatious arms concessions to the Soviet Union which rightly or wrongly appear in the eyes of Europeans as unilateral disarmament measures. Neither President Carter's 1977 decision to cancel the B-1 bomber program nor his 1978 decision to delay the development of the neutron bomb (enhanced radiation weapon) served to improve the confidence of the European allies in the ability of the United States to provide steady, firm and intelligent leadership fo the Alliance. The first was regarded as either a strategic-military mistake, a case of poor planning, or a sign of dangerous discontinuity, unpredictability and partisanship in U.S. security policy. The second was

looked upon as an instance of inept public relations and gross diplomatic mishandling by the Carter Administration. The Europeans are quite sophisticated enough to realize that contemporary defense decisions are a complicated business, fraught with technological-economic, political-diplomatic, military-strategic and moral-ethical subtleties. Nevertheless, the Europeans believe that the leader of the Alliance must also keep growing in sophistication, commensurately with the challenges of the situation, and not demonstrate an increasing lack of sureness and competence which can only make the world more unstable than it has been.

4. While seeking to negotiate in MBFR a lower level military balance in Central Europe, without enhancing reinforcement advantages the Soviets already enjoy by virtue of geography, the United States should formally reassure its allies that it will not withdraw unilaterally its military presence from Europe. The decision of the Carter Administration in early 1978 to budget an increase for U.S.-NATO forces was a definite move in the right direction.

5. The United States should exercise the greatest care when it comes to negotiating a modification in the deployment of tactical nuclear weapons on NATO territory. Even though NATO had earlier offered to trade some tactical nuclear weapons for some Soviet armor, it would not be wise for the Alliance to maintain this negotiating position without major modifications. It seemed like a logical tradeoff when MBFR began, but the situation has changed drastically in the last five years. The United States can no longer think of placing a ceiling on its own nuclear capabilities in the European theater (in return for a relatively minor reduction of Soviet armor) under a plan which places no limits on those expanding Soviet nuclear forces (SS-20s and Backfires) that are of growing concern to the European allies. In fact the time has come for NATO to develop a wholly new approach to negotiating a theater balance – one that will permit appropriate linkages to be drawn between the superpower strategic equation and the European regional equation by dealing with the widening spectrum of nuclear weapons that are not being covered satisfactorily either in SALT or MBFR.

The nations of the Atlantic Alliance must do whatever is feasible politically to maintain and improve their deterrence/defense capabilities. Unless they receive the kind of provocative stimulus which the Soviets are determined to avoid giving, however, Western governments will probably continue to lag behind the Soviets in military expenditures. This is the inescapable fate of democracies engaged in protracted strategic competition with communist states. It is incumbent upon pro-NATO elites within the West to work tirelessly to instill in their countrymen an abiding concern for adequate defense preparedness, without expecting miracles to happen. Soviet policymakers may make mistakes and behave unwisely at times, even from the standpoint of what is in their own best interest. Their lapses may contribute temporarily to NATO alertness and willingness to step up defense programs – but only temporarily, so long as a decisive frontal challenge to the West is eschewed, consistent with their preferred strategy.

If we preclude a major, dramatic Soviet military threat or move that would shock the West into a behavioral change, Western societies will have to find ways of overcoming a mounting skepticism with regard to the utility of military force and defense expenditures – force used by, and funds appropriated by, Western governments. If Western governments fail on this score, they will have to face the more hopeless task of compensating for a widening margin of Soviet military superiority. In this worst case, the peoples and governments of the Atlantic Community would then have to be convinced that if military force is not really available for use by Western governments as an instrument in support of diplomacy, it is even less available for use by the Soviets in view of their preferred strategy. If they could be convinced of this, the West Europeans would be able to free themselves of the self-paralyzing pessimism and malaise that has begun to grip them in the present decade, and begin to devise creative political, economic and other initiatives in which they are more than a match for the Soviets – and in which they can reverse the assumptions concerning the tide of history, forcing the Soviets gradually (and in a carefully controlled manner) into a more reactive, defensive posture in European diplomacy. But while we can conclude safely that the Europeans would readily regain self-confidence if their perceived slide of the West into an inferior military position could be reversed, it is highly doubtful that any purely political-psychological substitute for adequate military power would ever work in Europe. The Europeans, after all, have been weaned for centuries on balance of power politics. They cannot blithely jump over their own shadow.

## NONMILITARY REQUIREMENTS OF COUNTER-FINLANDIZATION: THE ECONOMIC DIMENSION

The international system of the last quarter of the twentieth century is filled with political, economic-technological and sociological complexities and subtleties. It is the sort of system in which the Atlantic Community ought to be able to operate much more effectively than the Soviets, for in order to be comprehended, managed and played most successfully, it requires an open, quick-reacting, creative, enterprising intelligence. This is not the sort of contest in which the Soviets perform at their best when pitted against a Western adversary in full command of a panoply of nonmilitary instruments of foreign policy. The Soviets are capable of consummate subtlety every now or then, when they enjoy the leadtime advantage of planning a well-executed performance on a stage of their own choice, as when they planned the "great grain robbery" of 1972. But their policymaking apparatus is over-bureaucratized and forced to operate according to an uninspiring, self-paralyzing rationality couched in outmoded Marxist mental constructs and terminology. When the international system changes too rapidly, or when too many different things are happening simultaneously, the Soviet leadership becomes uncertain, divided and unwilling to react quickly. Soviet communists like to move with certainty, and to achieve this they need time to absorb and analyze what is going on. Their very ideology, reinforced by psychological traits in the Russian modal national character, predisposes them to respond slowly and cautiously to external challenges. They are much less ready than Western leaders to undertake great gambles or risks. They may build some risks into their planning process, but only after they have performed what they regard as a carefully thought out and prudently evaluated probability analysis of the outcome. By and large they are extremely reluctant to embark upon leaps into the unknown, especially when they face the possibility of decisive, frontal encounters the consequences of which are unpredictable. This holds not only in the military realm, but in the political and economic as well.

During 1975, the Western countries showed some signs of beginning to emerge from the political and economic doldrums in which they had been stalled in 1974, when the strains on the Atlantic Alliance were greatest as a result of disillusionment, economic dislocation and inflation, sense of betrayal among allies, nationalistic particularism, and uncertainty about the future. At least a modest amount of political self-confidence began to be restored. The impression grew that the eye of the storm had passed and that, despite the persistence of unemployment and inflation problems, the political leaders of the Atlantic nations were making some modest progress at the economic summit meetings in Rambouillet (1975), Puerto Rico (1976) and London (1977) toward muting the rhetoric of strident nationalist protectionism which characterized much of their discourse in 1974. The Bonn Summit Meeting of 1978 showed that there is still a sizable gap between the public profession by the leaders concerning their awareness of interdependence and the policy performance of lower echelon decisionmakers who are subject to intensive pressures from domestic vested interest groups. Nevertheless the rhetoric of international economic cooperation is vastly preferable to that of recrimination, for it reflects a mode of diplomacy more suitable to an alliance. Even though it may seem to be a matter of atmospherics more than of substance, it is of the utmost importance that allies continue to act in public like allies, despite personality clashes between leaders (as reported, for example, between President Carter and Chancellor Schmidt) and despite occasional temptations to shift blame or to criticize each other for failing to take decisions which all are agreed are very difficult for elected leaders to take.

Basic structural differences in the allies' national economies persisted, however, and these gave rise to conflicts of interest and disagreements over economic policy during the 1977-1978 period. There are fundamental policy differences, for example, between the strong economies (the United States, West Germany and Japan) and the weaker economies of Western Europe (Italy, Britain, France and others). The latter, generally speaking, look for the solution to their own economic problems in the governmental stimulation of rapid productive expansion within the strong economies – an expansion that will lift the levels of international trade as a result of increased importing by the Americans, the Germans and the Japanese.

The stronger economies, while anxious to reduce unemployment, are wary of pursuing policies that will again unleash the inflationary forces only recently brought under control. Among the stronger economies, the United States is obliged by virtue of both its leadership position within the Alliance and its own economic interests to lean toward a centrist position. It cannot but be deeply concerned over the economic future of Britain, France, Italy and the smaller countries of Western Europe which depend so heavily on what the larger allies decide to do. Furthermore, the United States has been interested for several years in the achievement of a better balance in the international trade patterns among Japan, Western Europe and itself. The stronger economies are at odds among themselves concerning the best trade and monetary policies to be pursued.

The United States wants Western Europe to assume a larger share of the burden of keeping Japan an economically satisfied power by importing more Japanese products, and it also wants protectionist-minded Japan to reduce its own tariff barriers, import more U.S. goods, and place voluntary curbs on its exports to the American market. As for Europe itself, the United States would like to see West Germany buy more from its West European neighbors. The Bonn government has resented frequent U.S. references to the Federal Republic's trade surplus as a major cause of international economic disequilibrium and U.S. demands for German inflation (i.e., revaluation of the DM) as the solution.(5) In the long run, both Japan and West Germany will have to be encouraged to increase their imports, but the United States must realize that they will be willing to do this only within a framework of stable economic growth without runaway inflation.

The most serious economic problem confronting the West in the first half of 1978 was that of the dollar decline. The value of the world's principal reserve currency had been slipping steadily for more than a year in relation to the deutsche mark, the Japanese yen and the Swiss franc. Americans were spending more dollars abroad than foreign markets could readily absorb. Within a few short years the United States had gone from a sizable balance of payments surplus to a twenty billion dollar deficit. International economists were not fully agreed on the causes of the dollar's fall, but the factors most usually cited were an increase in U.S. dependence on foreign oil imports, the failure of Congress to enact an energy program, and the U.S. inflation rate, attributed to deficit budgeting and a reluctance to institute wage and price controls.

The Germans and the Japanese resented what they regarded as the self-indulgence and mismanagement of the American economy, which seemed unable to bring inflation and energy consumption under control. In effect they were saying: We have disciplined ourselves and curbed inflation, but now we are being punished for our efficiency. Both Bonn and Tokyo feared that the continued drop in the value of the dollar would help U.S. exports, weaken the foreign trade and balance of payments positions of other OECD nations, and further slow an already sluggish growth rate among those nations. Many economic analysts and policymakers throughout the Atlantic Community were worried that the export of U.S. inflation might set off a chain reaction of retaliatory protectionism which would stifle world trade and usher in a prolonged recession. Nearly all agreed that if the dollar could not be stabilized, and if confidence in it could not soon be restored (despite the basic vigor and strength of the American economy), the long-range adverse economic and political consequences would be incalculable.

U.S. policymakers are entitled to try to persuade the strong economy allies to pursue policies thought most likely to redound to the general advantage of the Alliance and of the international system as a whole. And they cannot be denied the right to set forth their ideas concerning the best ways of dealing with such problems as unemployment through reflation and trade stimulation or preventing the spread of nuclear weapons by de-emphasizing plutonium technology. But U.S. policymakers have to realize that political leaders in other friendly countries may have very different ideas on optimum solutions to common problems, and often may be faced with serious domestic constraints (in the form of party coalition imperatives or financial-industrial-labor interests) when it comes to following the U.S. lead.

Americans should be willing to adopt a healthy skepticism toward the self-righteous tone of morality and enlightened idealism in which they seem forever destined to couch their foreign policy pronouncements and justifications. They ought not to be surprised when Europeans attribute to them less exalted motives than Americans do to themselves. Europeans, for example, perceived more national self-interest than altruism in the Carter Administration's decision to cut off international atomic assistance in the form of plutonium and breeder reactor technology. The avowed purpose of the decision announced in April 1977 was to minimize the risks that peaceful materials would be diverted toward nuclear weapons production by non-nuclear-weapon states. Europeans hastened to point out that the United States can readily afford to renounce plutonium technology and focus its attention upon the easier-to-control supply of uranium fuel because it possesses oil, coal and uranium reserves adequate to meet the bulk of its energy needs, at least until the end of the present century. West Germany, France and Japan, on the other hand, lacking such resources and much more heavily dependent upon forces beyond their choice and control cannot afford to forfeit plutonium and breeder reactor technology.

In fact, when the United States increases its dependence upon imports of Arab oil from 22 percent of its total needs in 1973 to 38 percent in 1977, the Europeans became worried – despite the current glut on the world oil market – about the availability of oil supplies in the 1980s, as well as the possibility of another devastating oil price hike. North Sea oil has been a help, but the Europeans are convinced that nuclear energy, and especially breeder reactor technology, will become more urgently necessary with the passage of time, particularly if the Americans do not curtail their oil-guzzling habits.

The West Europeans and the Japanese insist that they are no less interested than the United States in reducing the risks of nuclear materials diversion into weapons production by developing countries anxious to acquire a nuclear power industry. But they also contend that the American way need not be the only or the best way of discouraging proliferation. Admitting the dangers which inhere in plutonium reactor and nuclear fuel reprocessing technology, the West Europeans and the Japanese take the position that the solution lies not in opting for a mode of technology which concedes the advantage to the United States and puts Europe out of the nuclear export business, but rather in developing a more effective system of materials control and safeguards against diversion through the International Atomic Energy Agency and other mechanisms. Even so ardent an exponent of arms control and opponent of proliferation as Senator Frank Church has sounded a warning against President Carter's policy on plutonium: "President Carter's determined antiproliferation policy and his abandonment of plutonium as a nuclear energy source for the United States leads the Germans to suspect that he wants to throttle their infant nuclear industry and export capability."(6)

Despite differences among Atlantic nations on economic policies, there is general agreement on the general economic goals toward which the Western nations must work cooperatively:

1. Overcoming their present inhibitions concerning economic growth and technological development so that they will be able to expand employment and production, within a framework of controlled inflation, in order to progress toward a solution of the pressing problems confronting their own societies, the less developed countries and the international system as a whole.

2. Dealing with the petrodollar surpluses that are now straining the world's financial structures and processes.

3. Continuing to liberalize international trade by dismantling tariff and quota barriers that cannot be rationally justified on economic grounds.

4. Reducing international monetary fluctuations to manageable proportions through the creation of a monetary system that will be stable, flexible enough to accommodate expansion and change, and fair enough to command widespread support.

5. Discovering and developing alternative sources of energy so that the industrialized nations can reduce their relative dependence upon oil and avoid the kind of cutthroat competition that could lead to chaos in world oil market prices during the 1980s, or to another major economic crisis if oil prices are again employed as a political weapon.

6. Working steadily toward the diplomatic cultivation of a rationality of interdependence between the industrialized nations of the West and the economically disadvantaged countries of the Southern Hemisphere and Asia, especially through agreements on trade and tariff preferences and commodity price stabilization. This will be a task of extreme difficulty and will require careful planning and coordination of foreign aid and international development policies by national governments and international financial institutions. The purpose must be to foster the greatest possible degree of comparative advantage and complementarity in producing to meet the world's growing economic needs, while minimizing harmful disruptions. Even when Western governments wish to help the less advantaged nations with trade preferences, they find that importing cheap manufactured goods from Asia or Latin America hurts their own industries and compounds their unemployment problem. The Western nations must bring themselves to realize that they cannot stifle competition from the Third World. In the long run this would be inefficient. But the countries which export cheap goods must also be aware that excessive competitiveness may cause severe economic dislocations and unfavorable political reactions within the West. Both the industrialized and the less advantaged nations will be called upon to exhibit intelligence and mutual forebearance while working out long-range policies that permit the optimal phasing of adjustments. The poorer countries will not stand to gain if, by assigning a higher priority to the redistribution of the world's wealth rather than to its sustained expansion, they place demands upon Western economies which would, if met, stunt their overall growth.

7. Accepting confidently the challenge of applying their political-diplomatic, intellectual, scientific, technological, economic and cultural resources to move toward a carefully planned and integrated solution of the most serious problems confronting both industrialized and poor countries – in

the areas of world hunger and food production; protection of our air and water environments against pollution and dangerous climate changes; a guaranteed supply of energy and raw materials to sustain the development of a more humane civilization; transportation and urban congestion; the export of reactor technology for peaceful purposes of power production without increasing the dangers of uncontrolled nuclear weapons diffusion (an objective that can be attained either through the expansion of enriched-uranium supplies or the establishment of regional nuclear fuel reprocessing plants under adequate international safeguards); promoting within the Atlantic Community and among other like-minded states agreements for collaboration in regard to scientific-technological research, development, transfers and productive efficiency; the control of those forms of terroristic violence which exacerbate international tensions; and the creation of an equitable international legal regime to govern the uses of the sea and the exploitation of the sea's vast living and nonliving and life-sustaining resources.

What we are saying here, in effect, is that the Atlantic Community will have its best chance of meeting successfully, and overcoming, the Soviet strategy of Finlandization by being faithful to its own authentic tradition, by regaining confidence in its ability to become once again the master of its own destiny, by throwing off the reactive, negative, fearful siege mentality (living in the shadow of Soviet power) into which the Soviet psychological strategists would like more than anything else to thrust it. What is required, first and foremost, is not so much a policy panacea as a new attitude, a new mood, a new vision within the West, articulated by leaders who have about them an air of credibility when they sound the call to constructive action. The Atlantic Community must become inspired with the compelling idea that it has before it, on the international conference table, an agenda of great and humanly useful tasks to perform.

Western leaders deserve to be faulted for ever having allowed the Soviets to pose as avant-garde solvers of the real problems besetting contemporary societies. What do the Soviets know about the control of environmental pollution? Virtually nothing. What can they contribute toward a solution of the world's hunger problem through the creation of international food reserves when, after sixty years of their style of planning, they still must occasionally depend upon U.S. grain imports and the prayers of the *muzhiks* for good weather and bountiful crop years? In the North-South negotiations, the poorer countries must be persuaded that their future well-being depends not upon a form of bureaucratic planning which flows from an outmoded nineteenth-century Marxist ideology, but upon the application of creative scientific intelligence and the allocation of economic and technological resources which are most abundantly available in the Atlantic Community. Increased Soviet intervention in Africa in recent years has made the underdeveloped world more wary of Moscow's global military mobility. In this connection, it is worth noting that the foreign ministers of more than a hundred nonaligned countries, meeting at Belgrade in July 1978, gave some signs that Soviet expansion is replacing Western imperialism as the object of their concern. As it becomes clearer that the Soviets have more power to hurt than to help the Third World, perhaps the latter will gradually grow more willing to work out mutually beneficial economic arrangements with a post-imperialist West.

It is not our purpose here to lay out a complete blueprint for the solution of all the major problems confronting the Atlantic Community today. The life of an alliance is not lived exclusively in accordance with detailed blueprints. More important is the prior requirement for a sense of commitment to the values underlying the Alliance. The political leaders of the Western democratic states must continue to work steadfastly, as they have begun, to strengthen their mutual convictions concerning their ability and their determination to engage in a quest for cooperative problem-solving. Communication among the leadership groups of Atlantic Community countries should be further intensified, both bilaterally and multilaterally. If Western summit conferences are to be well prepared and productive, contacts and exchanges among lower level policy advisers, planners and decision-makers must become more frequent and routine. There is a need for institutionalizing more effectively the joint planning processes of Atlantic Community governments in order to make progress in the areas inventoried above.

As a crucial first step to galvanize the problem-solving energies latent within the Atlantic Community, we propose specifically that the North Atlantic allies form a Priorities Task Force, composed of distinguished policymakers and nongovernmental consultants. Meeting either in one alliance capital or in several over a period of weeks or months, this Priorities Task Force would be expected to: 1. identify the most urgent shorter-term and longer-term challenges confronting the Atlantic Community and the international system as a whole; 2. analyze in a general manner the way in which these challenges and problems are interrelated; 3. suggest, with a view to both desirability and practicality, the optimal order in which the various tasks ought to be undertaken, with regard to such factors as the likelihood that progress in one problem area will have a beneficial multiplier effect in the quest for subsequent solutions to other problems; the total cost of making substantial headway; the availability of resources; the technical, economic and political obstacles to be overcome; and the probability that governments can be induced to negotiate fair and constructive agreements; 4. indicate those areas in which, even if all allied governments are not yet prepared to act in concert, cooperative action might be organized by some governments without producing adverse consequences for others; 5. formulate a practicable problem-solving agenda for the Atlantic Community, with specific goals and objectives to be accomplished during the time period 1980-1990.

It may well be that the world is tired of task forces and international conferences which seek to identify urgent problems, define goals, and formulate strategies for getting us from here to there. The highly touted meetings of the past decade – designed to come to grips with the problems of food and population; arms control and disarmament, energy and environmental pollution; trade and money, international development and the law of the sea – have not accomplished much. They have often begun with a rhetorical fanfare that aroused unrealistic expectations; they have usually ended with bland communiques which papered over fundamental differences of approach, ignored serious obstacles, and called for benevolent initiatives that would take unique regional, national and local circumstances into account. Yet despite the uninspiring experience of the past, the nations of the Atlantic Community cannot escape the future. That is simply not the way of

Western civilization. The problem-solving record of the Atlantic Community in the last three decades has been better than that of the world as a whole. The entire international community depends upon the ability of the Atlantic societies to keep on learning, experimenting and trying – hoping and dreaming, daring and succeeding.

## THE POLITICAL REQUIREMENTS OF COUNTER-FINLANDIZATION: HUMAN RIGHTS AND EAST-WEST RELATIONS

It was inevitable that American intellectuals and political and religious activists of various types would, during the Bicentennial period, rediscover their own revolutionary tradition and reemphasize their own commitment to human freedom and human rights. The United States, under the leadership of President Carter, has mounted an ideological offensive against governments which violate human rights, including the Soviet Union. Although the President has said several times that he has no intention of singling out the Soviet Union for special opprobrium, and although he has criticized other governments, Moscow has regarded itself as the prime target.

Actually, during the last year of the Ford Administration the human rights issue first surfaced in the context of the post-Vietnam, post-Watergate struggle between Congress and the Executive. Several groups that were anxious to call attention to the suppression of human rights in foreign countries took the position that the United States could not do too much about the situation in communist states, but should try to take action where it could realistically exercise leverage – for example, by cutting off the flow of arms and other assistance to the governments of such countries as Brazil, Chile, Uruguay, Iran, South Korea and the Philippines. Conservatives and other pro-defense groups argued that if the United States were to erect the human rights issue into a punitive criterion to be applied exclusively against countries that were a part of the U.S. international security system, the net effect would be to weaken that system and harm the cause of human rights in the long run.

Upon taking office, President Carter placed emphasis upon the human rights issue in his policy pronouncements. He took the position that no member of the United Nations can look upon the mistreatment of its citizens as solely its own business, and that no member can avoid the responsibility to speak out when torture or unwarranted deprivation of rights occurs in any part of the world. "The basic thrust of human affairs points toward a more universal demand for fundamental human rights. The United States has a historical birthright to be associated with this process."(7) Admitting that the United States often fell far short of its own professed ideals in the human rights area, he expressed a determination to work for the elimination of those deficiencies, quickly and openly. This was bold rhetoric. President Carter seemed buoyed by the conviction that he had struck a chord on which he could help to build a new national consensus.

Earlier, many West Europeans had criticized Kissinger for failing to press the human rights issue (Basket III) with sufficient vigor in CSCE. Now, many think that President Carter has been espousing the cause too vigorously, not merely by affirming the principles and goals to which the United States is committed, but also by writing to, or receiving, prominent Soviet dissidents, and by calling for substantially larger appropriations from Congress for Radio Liberty and Radio Free Europe.(8) The Europeans were not opposed to a resumption of the political-ideological offensive by the United States after having been on the defensive for so long, but they were apprehensive lest the new Carter thrust, and some of the specific means associated with it, so antagonized the Kremlin leadership as to be counterproductive. In particular, they feared that the human rights campaign would break down the climate of trust on which detente and strategic arms negotiations depended; that it might provoke the Soviets to crack down on dissidents in Eastern Europe (even more heavily than they had already begun to do so in the wake of the Helsinki Pact), and seal off Eastern Europe from human contacts with the West; and that it might set in motion an action-reaction process culminating in an explosion in East Europe (say, in Poland, Czechoslovakia or East Germany) which would be dangerous for regional stability and world peace.(9) Thus, during 1977 the West Europeans tried to impress upon the United States that the Belgrade Conference should not be made an occasion for pillorying the Soviet Union.(10)

The Soviets face the problem of keeping under control, during a prolonged period of detente, an empire which contains many discontented individuals and frustrated ethnic and religious groups. Dissidents have been emboldened by detente, by the provisions of the Final Act of Helsinki (the text of which has been widely publicized), and by the rise of Eurocommunism. As the dissidents view the situation, this is the favorable time for them to put forth their claims to freedom and to appeal to the West for support in the form of pressure on Moscow. Several groups in Eastern Europe busied themselves for two years gathering documentation to substantiate their charges of official repression at the Belgrade review conference in late 1977. A senior analyst for Radio Free Europe, after surveying the protest movement of workers, intellectuals and Catholic leaders in Poland, the widespread support for Charter 77 in Czechoslovakia, and the applications for exit visas by more than 100,000 persons in East Germany, summed it up in this way:

> Instead of calling for an end to the present system of government or a radical overhaul of policy . . . the petitioners are now making the apparently modest request that their countries' laws be enforced. . . . Carefully shunning any direct political statements, the petitioners document and publicize actions which they consider violations of these laws. The legalistic focus of these protests presents special problems to the authorities, since it all but excludes the possibility of bringing direct criminal charges against their authors.(11)

It is not surprising that the Soviets have reacted with such sensitivity to President Carter's stress upon human rights. Undoubtedly, they resented the fact that Carter seized the ideological initiative and threw them onto the defensive. The dissident movement in the communist block is not yet of such magnitude as to pose serious problems of control for the Soviets. The situation is still quite manageable. But the Soviets are probably genuinely concerned about what the human rights campaign might portend for the longer future, especially within the socialist states of Eastern Europe. In any event, the Soviets apparently regard Basket III and the human rights issue as Western instruments of psychopolitical warfare, and Brezhnev has declared that the USSR will not tolerate U.S. interference in its internal affairs.

West Europeans do not take exception to the affirmation of human rights in principle and to the profession of greater political freedom as a goal to be worked toward on a global basis. Many are inclined to agree that the pendulum ought to swing back from a period in which the notion that nothing should be done to disturb detente was oversold to the American public. Moreover, as we have seen previously, thoughtful West Europeans are convinced that if detente in Europe is to be made solid and permanent, the human rights situation in Eastern Europe must be ameliorated. But they worry about some of the specific means by which President Carter may choose to manifest his concern in this area – means which might, unnecessarily, frighten or irritate Soviet leaders.

Many Europeans are inclined to think that, for reasons of geographical proximity and historical experience, they are in a better position than Americans are to gauge the texture of the East-West dialogue about human rights and human contacts in Europe. They believe that they have a better intuitive understanding of how far the West should press the issue in concrete sets of circumstances. Also, they are aware that the human rights issue may boomerang, more upon the United States than upon Western Europe, despite the fact that when the Soviets mount their own offensive against Western societies for violating human rights they cite some particular charges (e.g., high unemployment rates and rents, restriction of higher educational opportunities, and exploitation of foreign workers) which are addressed to alleged abuses on both sides of the Atlantic.

The United States did not wish to abandon its human rights posture at the Belgrade Conference. But it did not wish to alienate the Soviet Union and make it veer toward an even more intransigent policy, with possible adverse repercussions on the SALT II negotiations. Moreover, the United States could not ignore the cautionary advice proferred by its NATO allies, with whom it had worked out agreed positions in evaluating Soviet compliance with the Helsinki Final Act. The Common Market group, by effectively coordinating their own approaches, succeeded in its efforts to tone down Western accusations against the Soviet bloc. After nearly six months of discussion, the Belgrade Conference ended with a declaration that made no mention of the human rights issue. The Helsinki signatories accomplished little more than to agree that they would meet again in Madrid in 1980.(12) That West Europeans should counsel the United States to be prudent is understandable, but it will not be a good sign if they become too zealous in urging the United States to tone down its stand on human rights in order to placate the leadership in Moscow.

U.S.-Soviet relations seemed to deteriorate to a low point in the summer of 1978, when Pravda declared that "changes dangerous to the cause of peace are taking place" in American policy and accused the United States of trying to undermine detente and return to the Cold War.(13) A few weeks later, the trial of dissident Anatoli Shcharansky was widely portrayed as a calculated

Soviet affront to Carter, inasmuch as the Soviets linked the accused to the CIA in spite of the President's denial. In Europe there were misgivings that the Soviets might be getting ready to blame the whole dissident movement on U.S. instigation.(14) Tension was exacerbated by an increasing tendency on the part of the Soviets to mete out severe treatment to American journalists, businessmen and diplomats. When President Carter retaliated against Soviet suppression of dissidents by cancelling the sale of computers and oil exploitation technology, and also by curtailing the exchange of high-level governmental officials, no one doubted that as the rhetoric got warmer the foreign policies of the superpowers grew cooler. Some observers thought it was merely a case of both sides adopting a posture of tough talking in order to demonstrate firmness before signing a SALT II treaty. Others took hostility to be real and not contrived, and thought that it might have adverse effects upon the chances for a new SALT agreement.

The United States, instead of trying to conduct an ideological-political campaign from a posture of strategic parity, the validity of whose assumptions becomes increasingly dubious, would probably be better advised to pursue measures in the areas of military-technological and other defense policies calculated to inspire confidence in the credibility of the U.S. deterrent, while at the same time encouraging the West Europeans to formulate their own human rights strategies tailored to the exigencies of the European scene. This is not to suggest that the United States should once again mute its commitment to human rights. With fidelity to its own authentic political tradition, it should continue to provide a general inspirational leadership in this dimension of international humanitarianism, and let the Europeans know that it welcomes their partnership in this endeavor and will furnish diplomatic endorsement of their efforts.

The Europeans should be encouraged to develop their own initiatives on the improvement of the human political condition in Europe as a whole. They can then proceed with confidence to work out approaches which will not wreck detente and the climate of trust needed for successful arms negotiations of symmetrical effect, nor arouse false hopes and provoke further oppression in Eastern Europe, but which will promote beneficial results and help to facilitate the benign evolution of communist societies toward more enduringly humane and democratic forms. It is important that the United States and its West European allies coordinate their policies in this area and work out common strategies that will command broad support throughout the Atlantic Alliance.

One of the crucial tasks facing the Western allies will be to devise a long-range political strategy on human rights which will put pressure on the Soviets to liberalize without at the same time penalizing friendly developing countries, and without arousing the ire of the People's Republic of China, where the rights of individuals and groups are violated even more flagrantly than they are in the USSR, and where all contacts with the outside world are more rigidly controlled.(15) It is possible to draw a plausible distinction – one which would make sense around the globe – between the exigencies of maintaining social order in countries still in the relatively early stages of the nation-building process and the requirements of domestic tranquility in an industrially advanced society such as the USSR.

It is understandable that the governments of countries just emerging from feudalism and beginning the transition to modernization may deem it necessary to impose severe discipline upon individuals and social groups uprooted from traditional folkways, fragmented and disoriented by rapid change, and rendered unruly by prematurely rising expectations which end only in frustration. But a technologically modernized society like the Soviet Union, so richly endowed with natural resources as to enjoy a unique self-sufficiency, populated by an intelligent, energetic, and skillful citizenry, proud of its achievements in education, science, economic production and the arts, and possessing abundant military capabilities for ensuring against all threats to national security, ought to be able to preserve internal peace and order without constantly resorting to the devices of political repression. Within recent decades, West Germany and Japan have furnished striking examples of how technologically advanced nations can carry out profound changes in internal and external political behavior – from totalitarian to democratic systems – and become stronger and more stable in the process. The fact that the Soviet Union has made such little progress toward genuinely democratic procedures during the sixty years since a revolution which was supposed to be for the people is a failure for which the communist leaders in Moscow should be made to pay before the bar of enlightened world opinion.

Western diplomatic strategy, therefore, should aim at making justifiable allowances in those cases of countries not long removed from the colonial-imperial experience or not far along the path to economic development, where governments are trying to carry out needed social reforms but find their efforts hampered or obstructed by terrorists, guerrilla rebels, agitators, violent demonstrators and strikers or extremist organizations, whether radical or reactionary, bent upon their overthrow. The strategy should also be designed to motivate the Soviets – through a combination of guilt-induction, political coercion and a system of rewards for positive encouragement – to modify their behavior by moving closer to Western democratic civilization, adopting methods of social control that are less stifling and less bureaucratically tyrannical (reflecting a shift from pathological insecurity to greater self-confidence, more open and more conducive to loyalty, freely given, in a system which respects individual dignity and rights). In sum, the objective should be to convince the Soviets that, despite the remarkable gains they have made in education, the sciences and the arts, technology and economic production, they remain politically the most backward of all the industrially advanced nations in the world and most in need of political development. Given their vast power and the powderkeg nature of the ethnically diverse empire over which they hold sway, such political development will be imperative for the sake of European regional stability and world peace.

## NOTES

(1) Raymond Aron, "My Defence of Our Decadent Europe," *Encounter*, September 1977, p. 8.

(2) *Strategic Survey 1976* (London: International Institute for Strategic Studies, n.d.), p. 2.

(3) Alastair Buchan, "Tomorrow's America," *Orbis*, Spring 1976, p. 31.

(4) See Stanley Sienkiewicz, "SALT and Soviet Nuclear Doctrine," *International Security*, Spring 1978, pp. 65-83.

(5) Horst A. Siebert, "Pressure by the West on Bonn for Economic Sacrifices," *Die Welt*, March 9, 1977; reprinted in *The German Tribune*, March 20, 1977.

(6) Cf. Edward Cowan, "Senator Church Urges President to Reverse Position on Plutonium," *New York Times*, May 3, 1977. Senator Church called the Administration's nuclear energy policy "a formula for nuclear isolationism" more likely to reduce rather than enhance the influence of the United States in shaping the world's nuclear future. Cf. also John W. Finney, "Not Exporting the Atom Also Has Some Risks," *ibid.*, June 5, 1977, and R.G. Livingston, "The Souring of U.S. Relations with Bonn," *Baltimore Sun*, May 2, 1977.

(7) President Carter's Address to the Permanent Representatives of the United Nations, Department of State News Release, March 17, 1977.

(8) *New York Times*, March 23, 1977.

(9) Karl E. Birnbaum, "Human Rights and East-West Relations," *Foreign Affairs*, July 1977, pp. 783-799. The author singled out the misgivings of observers in West Germany: ". . . always most sensitive to changes in Washington that might affect its precarious security, as well as being the West European country with the most immediate interest in a low-tension relationship with the East." (pp. 793-794.)

(10) See Jonathan Kandell, "Some Allies in Europe Now Worry Over Detente," *New York Times*, July 17, 1977.

(11) Thomas E. Heneghan, "Human Rights Protests in Eastern Europe," *The World Today*, March 1977, pp. 90-91.

(12) See David A. Andelman, "Accord in Belgrade: To Meet Again, Period," *New York Times*, March 12, 1978.

(13) *New York Times*, June 18, 1978.

(14) "Now Carter is in the dock with Shcharansky," *Manchester Guardian Weekly*, July 16, 1968.

(15) Robert W. Barnett, former U. S. Deputy Assistant Secretary of State for East Asian Affairs, has warned against the temptation to make human rights a criterion for further improvement in U.S.-PRC relations. "We should want to seek better understanding of the moral content in how and why Peking has sustained the legitimacy of its authority through means alien to the political experience of the Western World." Barnett suggests that the acceptance of the age-old Confucian tradition of subordinating individual liberty to collective obligation may be the moral equivalent to what Americans understand by human rights. "Make an Issue of Human Rights in China? No," ibid., April 2, 1978.

# V

# The Arena of Resources and Economics— Energy, Monetary and Trade Problems Within the Community

# 12 Monetary Policies in the Atlantic Community

Brian Griffiths

The past decade has been a period of monetary turbulence in the Atlantic Community. After years of monetary stability, inflation has emerged as one of the most serious and intractable problems facing most countries. Not only has the pace of inflation increased dramatically during the past decade, but rates of inflation between countries have also diverged significantly. Largely as a consequence of this, the postwar international monetary system, established at Bretton Woods in 1945, has in effect been abandoned. The gold exchange standard system, characterized by fixed exchange rates with the dollar as the dominant currency, has given way to the present system of managed or "dirty" floating, in which exchange rates are essentially market-determined but subject to a good deal of intervention from central banks.

## THE NEW SIGNIFICANCE OF MONETARY POLICY

At the same time as the rate of inflation has increased and much of the edifice of the Bretton Woods system has been dismantled, increasing emphasis has been given, in both the realm of ideas and among policymakers, to the role of monetary policy as part of overall domestic economic policy. As a result of the Keynesian revolution, the major emphasis during the postwar years of most, if not all, governments in their attempts at demand management was on fiscal policy and changes in the public sector budget effected through changed taxation and expenditure policies. Monetary policy was allotted an essentially subsidiary role, and the emphasis in many countries was not so much on controlling the growth of the money supply as on managing interest rates and controlling bank credit. With the growth of monetarism, however, and especially the success of the monetary approach in explaining and predicting the recent global inflation and individual countries' balance of payments, increasing weight has been given to monetary policy and, in particular, if inflation and balance of payments deficits are to be avoided, to the need for central banks to exercise firm control over money supply growth.

In view of the increasing importance which has come to be placed on monetary policy, and the poor record of many countries within the Atlantic Community in this sphere, we shall examine the monetary policies within the Community, placing particular emphasis on ways in which the problems they give rise to might be remedied.

## DOMESTIC MONETARY POLICIES

The source of the monetary instability of Atlantic Community countries in recent years lies in their domestic monetary policies. In each country monetary policy is the responsibility of the central bank and the ministry of finance or treasury, and it is to the actions of these authorities that we must look if we are to understand what has gone wrong. Since the late 1960s monetary policies in all countries have been characterized by (1) a more rapid rate of growth of the money supply than at any other time during the postwar years, and (2) large short-term fluctuations in money supply growth about a higher average rate.

The major thrust for the recent global monetary expansion resulted from the fact that the world was on a dollar standard and that the United States, as a consequence of the way in which it chose to finance the Vietnam War, created an excess of dollars. In the mid-1960s the Johnson Administration decided both to escalate the scale of the Vietnam War and to finance the increased costs associated with the war by borrowing rather than raising taxes. Between 1957 and 1965 government expenditure rose at an annual rate of just about 6 percent per annum. But between 1965 and 1968 it increased by no less than 15 percent per annum. Taxes, however, were not raised. As a result, the government deficit rose and the money supply was allowed to expand to help finance the deficit.

As the monetary authorities allowed excess money to be pumped into the economy, the effect on the balance of payments and hence the transfer of dollars to other countries was soon evident. Between 1945 and 1965 the United States trade balance was in surplus. For example, between 1960 and 1964 it averaged over $5 billion annually; but soon the surplus was whittled away. In 1965 it was $4.9 billion, in 1966 and in 1967 $3.9 billion, in 1968 $600 million, and in 1969 $700 million. Although in 1970 it rose dramatically as a result of the recession to $2.1 billion, in 1971 – the crisis year – it moved into deficit to the tune of $2.9 billion. This was the first time the United States had been in deficit on its external payments in more than a hundred years.

As the United States created excess dollars and as these were transferred to the international economy through the trading account and the Euro-dollar markets, so other governments found themselves under intense pressure to expand their domestic money supplies in line with the United States. If they did not, they built up balance of payments surpluses, induced massive speculative capital inflows, and so were forced to revalue their currencies against the dollar. The 1970 Annual Report of the International Monetary Fund states clearly the dilemma facing many countries such as West Germany, Japan and Switzerland:

> Perhaps the most important implications of the increased mobility of capital permitted and facilitated by the Euro-currency market and the international bond market are to be found in the challenges that they present to both the effectiveness and the independence of national monetary policies, except perhaps in the United States, where resort to the Euro-dollar market by the domestic banking system or other domestic borrowers does not ordinarily expand the monetary base.

Despite the obvious interdependence of the system, the United States continued to create dollars and treat its balance of payments with "benign neglect." In addition, "surplus countries" stubbornly refused to revalue their currencies, so that the net result was a dramatic growth in the money supplies of individual countries and in the world money stock. If we measure the increase in the money stock of the major developed economies apart from the United States (Belgium, Canada, France, Germany, Italy, Japan, Netherlands, Switzerland and the United Kingdom), we find that (using quarterly figures adjusted to an annual rate) it increased between the first quarter of 1966 and the third quarter of 1970, and by the third quarter of 1972 it had risen to an average of 18 percent. The inflationary implications of these policies have been all too apparent, not only in the United States but throughout the Atlantic Community. In the first half of the 1960s the rate of inflation for the Group of Ten countries averaged between 2 and 3 percent per annum, while between 1970 and 1975 it averaged nearly 8 percent and in 1974 reached 13 percent.

As we examine the evidence of the past decade, there are a number of lessons that can be learned. In the first place, the evidence suggests that the rate of growth of the money supply is an extremely important factor in explaining the behavior of monetary magnitudes – namely, the growth of money income, nominal interest rates, the rate of inflation and the exchange rate. As a result of the Keynesian view of aggregate economic behavior, money income has been explained frequently by fiscal policy, the wage demands of trade unions, and the value of the exchange rate, while the rate of inflation has been accounted for by cost pressures such as higher import prices, rising interest rates, and the conflict between labor and capital over the share of the gross national product. As a result of the magnitude of money supply increases over recent years, and particularly as a result of the examining periods and in which fiscal and monetary policy have been moving in different directions, the evidence has tended to undermine certain basic Keynesian relationships and to confirm monetarist predictions.

In particular, the following propositions tend to be associated with the growth of monetarism:

1. The growth of money income is related systematically to the growth of the money stock; fiscal policy has a short-term but not a long-term impact.

2. The greater the rate of growth of the stock of money, the higher interest rates will be.

3. The balance of payments is a monetary phenomenon: Deficits are the result of countries expanding monetary growth more rapidly than the rest of the world, and surpluses are the function of slower expansion than the rest of the world.

4. Inflation results from the creation of excess money.

The last of these propositions – namely, that inflation is a monetary problem – needs to be emphasized. It means that ceteris paribus a permanent increase in the rate of growth of the money supply will result in a permanent increase in the rate of growth of the price level. For the world economy as a whole, the rate of inflation in the 1970s has been two to three times as great as it was in the 1960s, which follows a correspondingly dramatic increase in the rate of growth of the world's money supply. Similarly, if we examine the experiences of industrial countries we find that the same is true: a significant and lasting increase in money supply growth results in a significant and lasting increase in the rate of inflation. As a corollary, those countries which have pursued relatively restrictive money supply growth policies (for example, over the last few years, West Germany and Switzerland) have a rate of inflation less than those which have pursued more liberal policies (such as the United States and Canada), and less still than those which have pursued extremely liberal policies (such as Italy, Japan and the United Kingdom).

A dramatic example of the inflationary consequences of a monetary expansion – an example that, because of the large magnitudes involved, comes about as close as any economist could desire to being a controlled experiment – is afforded by the recent evidence of the United Kingdom. As a result of indebtedness to the International Monetary Fund in the late 1960s the rate of growth of the U.K. money supply was brought under strict control. Throughout most of 1969 it grew between 2 to 3 percent. Then, starting in the last quarter of 1969 and continuing until the first quarter of 1971, it increased to a rate of about 10 percent. In the first half of 1971, largely in response to enormous pressure from the media, the trade union movement and the national employers federation, as well as to the growth in the number of people unemployed, the Heath Government decided to abandon a fairly cautious anti-inflationary monetary policy and set out on a bold gamble to raise the rate of growth to a permanent new level of 5 percent per annum. As part of the policy, interest rates were to be kept down in order to stimulate investment. The immediate effect of this policy was that the money supply started to grow at an alarmingly rapid rate. By the third quarter of the year it had climbed to 15 percent, and by the end of 1971 to 22 percent per annum. Despite growing concern and criticism from certain academic economists and independent financial commentators, the process accelerated. By mid-1972 it was growing at between 28 and 30 percent and remained at that level for no less than a year, after which it was reduced in an equally dramatic fashion.

The results of this experience are a dramatic confirmation of monetarism. The initial effects of the money supply being out of control were a stock market boom and rapidly falling interest rates. Though there soon were pressures on rates to rise, these were resisted by the government, thus accelerating monetary growth and exacerbating the problem. Partly as a result of the monetary expansion and partly in view of its inflationary consequences, property prices spiraled. Within a year there was an equally dramatic increase in the growth of real output. Industrial production had remained roughly constant between the second quarter of 1970 and the end of 1971. But in 1972 it rose by no less than 10 percent, and over the same period real gross national product grew by nearly 9 percent. Despite the effect of price and wage controls introduced in 1972, which were still in force until the February 1974 general election, price indices showed a dramatic inflation, but, as always, after a considerable time lag.

In 1972 the United Kingdom's rate of inflation, measured by the retail price index, was only 7.7 percent. In 1973 it was 10.6 percent and in 1974 nearly 20 percent. Because of the existence of price controls and food subsidies, this last figure is an underestimate of the true rate of inflation. These two factors must account to some degree for the discrepancy between the retail and wholesale indices for this period: Judged by the behavior of the wholesale prices, the rate of inflation in 1974 was 28 percent. There can be little doubt that it was this more than any other single issue that led to the downfall of the Heath Government. Perhaps the most beneficial, if only, long-term effect has been to establish the credibility of monetarism as a serious approach to monoeconomic policy.

To suggest, however, that inflation is a monetary phenomenon does not mean that nonmonetary factors have no part to play in its explanation. All too frequently monetarists suggest that the money supply can be controlled like water, by turning the tap on and off, as if the whole process took place in a political and social vacuum. As all central banks in the Atlantic Community are either directly or indirectly controlled by their governments, central bank decisions to increase money supply will be influenced by all sorts of factors: the desire to keep down the mortgage rate for housing finance, the number of people unemployed, the short-term rate of growth of real consumption, and the like.

The importance of nonmonetary factors in accounting for inflation is not that they exert a direct effect on the price level, but rather that by influencing central bank behavior in controlling money supply growth they exert an indirect influence. Hence, although the oil price rise of 1973 had a small direct effect on the absolute price level in the countries of the Atlantic Community, its major effect was to change relative prices (i.e., the price of oil in terms of other goods) quite dramatically. The extent to which this might be considered inflationary, however, depended on the response of monetary policy to such an event, something which differed noticeably between countries.

The second lesson which emerges from the experience of these years is that the pursuit of inconsistent objectives causes permissive money supply growth which, in turn, results in inflation. It is not that the governments of the Atlantic Community purposely set out over the last decade to create inflation. Rather, this was the unintended consequence of their pursuit of other policies. From a political point of view, therefore, if money supply growth is to be reduced and kept low so as to ensure a return to price stability, it is critical that policymakers should be confronted with the appropriate range of choices. All too often in the past, and largely as a result of the Keynesian legacy, the monetary implications of economic policy in such diverse fields as employment and housing have been neglected. It is particularly important to emphasize that an increase in the rate of monetary expansion, while it may have a short-term effect in reducing unemployment and interest rates, will in the longer term have precisely the opposite effect. Increasing inflation will lead to less employment and rising, not falling, interest rates. Whatever, therefore, the immediate effects of policy may be, no government is able to increase output, buy more employment or achieve lower interest rates.

The third lesson that emerges from the past decade and one that should not need emphasis – but that, regrettably, in view of the writings of numerous academic economists, still does – is that inflation still remains one of the most important economic problems facing the Atlantic Community. Various academic economists have argued that if all those who participate in economic life fully anticipated the rate of inflation, then, because contracts could be suitably adjusted, inflation would have very little impact on our societies. It is true that attempts to measure the resource costs of inflation have not shown any dramatic results – unlike, for example, the resource costs of unemployment which are all too obvious. The effect of inflation in our societies, however, is more like a cancer – insidiously destroying the very fabric of the market economy. First, not all inflation is anticipated; second, even if it were, many are constrained from adjusting contracts because of various government regulations and laws. As a result, the greatest effect of inflation is to redistribute capriciously income and wealth and so undermine the efficiency of the market economy and the viability of representative democracy. It remains, at present, one of the most important threats facing Western democracies.

## FLOATING EXCHANGES RATES AND THE END OF THE BRETTON WOODS SYSTEM

The increasing monetary instability of the past decade and the important changes which have taken place in the international monetary system can be understood adequately only when seen against the background of the past century. The forty or so years in the period preceding the First World War stand out as a period of great monetary stability, with monetary growth in the world as a whole being restricted by the growth of the gold stock. The world as a whole was on a gold standard, with each central bank committed to maintaining the gold convertibility of its currency. This was a period of price stability, with the balance of payments surplus or deficits of individual countries being removed through monetary policies. As a whole, the system possessed a certain automaticity in that an emerging surplus or deficit in a particular country would trigger action by central banks which led to an outflow or inflow of gold bullion. The situation changed, however, with the coming of war.

As a result of the First World War and the enormous increase in government spending, unaccompanied by increased taxation, which produced rapid money supply increases, most countries were subjected to considerably higher rates of inflation. In many countries the inflation continued after the war – and in some, such as Austria, Germany, Hungary, Poland and Russia, it accelerated into hyperinflation. In face of widespread economic and political uncertainty and monetary instability, it was not surprising that the gold standard could not easily be reestablished.

As a result, currencies were allowed to float against each other. By the mid-1920s, however, a number of the most important and most stable countries were determined to go back to gold, but at rates which (with the advantage of hindsight) were clearly unrealistic and so imparted a deflationary bias to the whole system. With the onset of the Great Depression in the United States and the attempts of other countries to resist importing unemployment, the system was placed under intolerable strain and collapsed finally in the early 1930s. The absence of any clearly defined rules within which monetary relations and economic transactions were conducted meant that the situation became chaotic. Countries pursued "beggar-my-neighbor" policies, imposed tariffs and import quotas against one another, and engaged in "offensive devaluations," with a consequent reduction in international trade and investment. What is important to note about this period is that the collapse of the gold standard system and the rise in protectionism were inextricably bound up with each other. In other words, the problems in accommodating various countries' monetary policies were not restricted to the monetary field but affected the whole of international trade as well.

When the architects of the postwar international monetary system met in Bretton Woods in 1944, it was with the intent of designing a system which would ensure considerable freedom of trade and investment in a world economy characterized by full employment. Certainly the twin evils of the 1930s – protectionism and recession – had to be avoided or else the very political stability of Western capitalist democracies would be threatened. As a result, two important new international institutions, the General Agreement on Tariffs and Trade (GATT) and the International Monetary Fund (IMF), were established – the object of the former being the reduction of trade barriers between countries and of the latter the orderly adjustment of balance of payments. As a condition for membership in the IMF, countries were required to peg their currencies to the dollar, and the U.S. dollar to gold at a price of $32 an ounce. Countries could change the par value of their currencies but only under conditions of fundamental disequilibrium. If countries found themselves in balance of payments difficulties, they could borrow small amounts for short periods from the Fund. After a certain amount of borrowing, however, the terms were very strictly laid down and administered by the Fund.

Apart from some initial changes in the late 1940s, the system seemed to work reasonably well in the 1950s and into the early 1960s. However, by the second half of the 1960s and the early 1970s the system ran into serious trouble and was abandoned finally in 1973 when one country after another decided to float currrency. All of the problems of this period had been apparent earlier, but not nearly as acutely. The major problem that arose in the mid-1960s was that countries began to pursue noticeably divergent monetary policies. In particular, as described above, President Johnson found himself under great pressure, given his commitment both to escalate the

Vietnam War and to press on with the task of building the Great Society. Both of these ventures involved considerably increased government expenditures which the President did not wish, for political reasons, to match with higher taxation. As a result, in the second half of the decade monetary growth in the United States increased relatively rapidly – especially in contrast to countries such as West Germany and Switzerland.

Largely because of the experience of inflation and the devastation it caused in the 1920s, one of the major objectives of economic policy in certain European countries was to prevent inflation from increasing at the rate it attained in the United States and the United Kingdom. As a result, the American balance of payments moved into deficit and the European balance of payments into increasing surplus, so that the dollar was clearly overvalued in terms of European currencies. The United States was unprepared to devalue the dollar in terms of gold, and the surplus countries were reluctant to revalue their currencies in relation to the dollar. The United States was reluctant to raise the dollar price of gold as this would give gold a more important role in the international monetary system – something that ran counter to the whole thrust of American policy. On the other hand, the surplus countries were reluctant to revalue their currencies because of the implied tax on exporters and subsidy to importers – a combination strongly opposed by certain pressure groups. As a result, surplus countries accumulated dollars, there were massive speculative capital flows, and the whole system came under great pressure. One indication of the pressure on the dollar was the "gold rush" of March 1968, which resulted in the effective abandonment of gold as the basis of the gold exchange standard. Another was the pressure on the German mark in 1968 and 1969. The decision to allow the mark to float and the acceptance, however reluctant, of this by the IMF augured ill for the future of the fixed exchange rate system.

In the following year, the Canadians floated the dollar, and by mid-1971 the pressure was so great (in terms of the accumulation of dollars in various countries) that the mark and the guilder were allowed to float and other currencies were revalued; and then, in August 1971, when President Nixon formally abandoned the gold convertibility of the dollar, a period of general floating began, contrary to the whole intention of Bretton Woods. Although the Smithsonian agreement of December 1971 established a new set of parities, within the following two years one country after another opted out of the system and in favor of floating – the system we have at present. Rather than take part in general floating, a number of EEC countries decided to float their currencies jointly against the dollar and allow a limited range for floating against each other – the so-called snake within the tunnel. However, this solution soon came under great pressure. The present system of floating, which is a contravention of the original IMF Articles of Agreement, was recognized formally at the Jamaica conference in January 1976.

As we examine the evidence of the past decade, we can draw a number of specific conclusions. In the first place, a greater degree of flexibility in exchange rates was both inevitable and desirable in the late 1960s and early 1970s in view of the different monetary policies being pursued by different countries. Similarly, the emergence of generalized floating after 1972 was also inevitable in view of the differential rates of inflation which opened up between countries (see Table 1). The system of fixed exchange rates collapsed, therefore, simply because different governments within the Atlantic Community wished to pursue different economic policies.

Table 1 Inflation in Major Industrial Countries (Consumer Prices)

| | 1972 | 1973 | 1974 | 1975 |
|---|---|---|---|---|
| United States | 3.3 | 6.2 | 11.0 | 9.4 |
| Canada | 4.8 | 7.6 | 10.9 | 10.8 |
| Japan | 4.5 | 11.7 | 24.5 | 11.8 |
| France | 5.9 | 7.3 | 13.7 | 11.7 |
| West Germany | 5.5 | 6.9 | 7.0 | 6.0 |
| Italy | 5.7 | 10.8 | 19.4 | 17.0 |
| U.K. | 7.1 | 9.2 | 16.0 | 24.0 |

Source: OECD Main Economic Indicators; Quarterly Review, August 1977, National Institute of Economic and Social Research.

No government can pursue an autonomous monetary policy under a regime of rigidly fixed exchange rates. Under a fixed exchange rate system, if any government wishes to pursue a rate of monetary expansion significantly different from the rest of the world, it will be forced either to devalue or to revalue the price of its currency relative to the others. Put differently, if a fixed exchange rate regime is to be crisis-free, or reasonably so, then a necessary condition to achieve this is for the individual governments that are part of the community to pursue, broadly speaking, similar money supply growth targets. During the 1960s this was precisely the problem that arose in the Atlantic Community as a result of the divergent policies of the United States and the Federal Republic of Germany. Such divergent preferences could not be accommodated within a fixed exchange rate system. The result was the realignment of exchange rates. What happened between West Germany and the United States is not an isolated episode, but rather one endemic to an international monetary system which contains within it countries of widely differing preferences.

A second conclusion is that the system of generalized floating has worked tolerably well. In view of the exigencies to which the international economy has been subjected over the past few years – widely divergent rates of inflation, the worst recession since the Great Depression, the uncertainties created by the oil crises – there can be no doubt that the system has worked much better than one with fixed exchange rates. Not even the staunchest supporter of fixed exchange rates would have desired anything other than floating exchange rates at the outset of the oil crisis.

Nevertheless, a number of criticisms of the present system have been made: namely, that exchange rate changes have been excessive, that they disrupt trade and investment, that forward exchange markets have not developed sufficiently, and that the system is inflationary because it is so permissive. The argument that exchange rate changes have been excessive, which has been put forward by a number of central bankers, means, presumably, that the movements in rates which have occurred are in excess of what could be justified on the basis of changes in the underlying financial and economic conditions. The major problem, however, with attempting to determine the force of such an assertion is in trying to determine what precisely are the changes in the underlying financial and economic conditions. Investors are not interested in those changes which have already taken place, as all past information will have influenced existing market prices. They are interested in the expected changes in financial and economic conditions. In view of the uncertainties in the economic outlook of, for example, Italy and the United Kingdom over the past few years – both being countries which have seen large movements in their exchange rates – it would be very difficult to conclude that rates have moved excessively. In addition, a certain amount of the movement arises because of the intervention of governments, namely, by attempting to maintain rates at unrealistic levels and so inviting speculation by the private sector. If we examine the movements of exchange rates of various European, Canadian, and Japanese, currencies, it is difficult to believe that they are in any sense excessive. The greatest downward movements in rates have occurred in those countries whose governments have created excess domestic money balances.

The other major criticism that has been leveled at the present system is that it is permissive and inflationary. It must be stressed that a system of floating exchange rates is neither inflationary nor deflationary. The source of inflation can be traced to the domestic fiscal and monetary policies of governments. In a period of inflation, movements in the exchange rate are a reflection of the relative policies of different countries, but this is different from the system itself containing an inflationary bias. In fact, after generalized floating was adopted in 1972, the world rate of inflation increased initially but has since fallen, and quite as dramatically. Over the past decade one of the major arguments put forward for floating, especially by countries such as Switzerland and West Germany, has been that floating permits them to pursue a less inflationary policy than other countries.

## SOME ISSUES FOR THE ATLANTIC COMMUNITY

In thinking of the future of monetary policies in the Atlantic Community and of ways in which they might be accommodated, it is important to make certain assumptions regarding the whole framework within which such policies will be carried out – the role of gold, the probability of attempts at a European monetary union, and the likely degree of exchange rate flexibility which will persist.

Since the breakup of the Bretton Woods international monetary system and the adoption by countries of floating exchange rates, a new kind of international monetary system has begun to evolve. The process was begun by the Committee of Twenty's Outline of Reform and has been furthered by the Interim Committee of Governors. By contrast to the previous system, the most noticeable feature is floating, rather than fixed, exchange rates. It is true, however, that most countries' currencies have not been allowed to float cleanly, but rather have been subject to active intervention on the part of central banks.

Another major feature has been the attempt to demonetize gold. The official price of gold has been abolished; one-sixth of the IMF's gold holdings are to be sold for the benefit of developing countries; another sixth is to be returned to member countries; the remaining two-thirds will be kept by the Fund until, on the basis of an 85 percent majority of the total voting strength, member countries decide to dispose of it. The total gold stock held by the IMF and the Group of Ten was not to be increased for the two-year period mid-1975 to mid-1977; and over the same period there was to be no attempt by countries to peg the price of gold.

Alongside the desire to demonetize gold has also been the wish to see Special Drawing-Rights (SDRs) become the principal reserve asset in the system, so that in the future central banks would hold a large part of their foreign exchange reserves in the form of SDRs. On the basis, therefore, of the current decisions being taken by the trading members of the Fund, the kind of Atlantic Community which will emerge over the next decade is one in which "dirty-floating" countries' gold has been demonetized and SDRs have become the major important asset held by central banks.

While certain governments, especially the United States, will continue to press for reform along the lines that we have seen over the past few years, one cannot help but be somewhat skeptical of the extent of any possible reform route. In the first place, there will certainly be pressures angling for a return to fixed exchange rates. The late Professor Harry G. Johnson of the University of Chicago observed that on each occasion on which we had generalized floating, a return to fixed exchange rates invariably ensued: after the Napoleonic Wars, in the mid-1920s, after the Second World War, and in Canada in 1962 after a decade of floating. The main pressure for such a return will come from those who believe that the system of floating is permissive, hence inflationary; from the officials of the IMF who need employment; and from central bank and treasury officials who prefer to place the responsibility for their own domestic mismanagement on foreigners.

Because a balance of payments deficit no longer imposes discipline on government's monetary and fiscal policies, there are many who feel that the present system of floating not only accommodates, but actually initiates inflation. Certainly, compared with the gold standard era, floating exchange rates are permissive. However, it would be naive to suggest that a return to fixed rates would solve the problem of inflation. Ultimately this problem is related to the preferences of governments for overfull employment, their failure to control government expenditure, and their attempts to deal with pressure groups through certain interest rate and wage policies. As far as the IMF is concerned, it already appears that an agreement is close at hand, under which the Fund would have powers to police world exchange rates and to recommend that countries change their exchange rate policies under certain circumstances, such as protracted large-scale intervention in one direction in the exchange market, an unsustaining level of official or quasi-official borrowing, or excessive and prolonged short-term official or quasi-official lending for balance of payments purposes. In addition to this, members would be expected to intervene to correct short-term disorderly market conditions. The sentiment which underlies such an approach as this is that private capital markets are inherently unstable, hence, require government intervention. At the very least, the regime will be one of dirty floating, and the present changes could easily pave the way for a return to fixed rates.

With respect to the role of gold, the pressure has come very much from the United States. However, it is not clear that the pressure has had the intended effect of demonetizing the metal. Gold is now far more valuable than previously at an official price to central banks. The restrictions which IMF member governments undertook were only for a period of two years, which in itself is a reflection of the unwillingness of nations to abandon the metal. Governments may, as a matter of practice, peg the price simply by their decisions to buy and sell, and the fact that governments may now engage with each other in gold transactions gives gold a liquidity which previously it was denied. If in the future a group of central banks decided to form a gold bloc-control by fixing a range within which the rate would be allowed to move, it is difficult to see what could be done about it. Therefore, far from diminishing the role of gold, the changes that have taken place over the past two years may well enhance it.

The other possibility is that once again the EEC countries may attempt to form some kind of monetary union. Certainly this is still the intention in Brussels, but the discrepancy between the overall economic policy of countries such as West Germany on the one hand and Italy and the United Kingdom on the other would make such a union an impossibility at present and for the foreseeable future. Some countries are committed to living with very different rates of inflation than others, and as long as this persists a monetary union is impractical.

Even if a European currency came into existence, it would not, in itself, create a major problem for the Atlantic Community: by implication, the rates would be fixed within the EEC and the currency, presumably, would still float against the dollar. Whether rates are fixed or flexible within the EEC is not a key issue. What would be important, however, about moves toward monetary union would be the additional weight it would give to European pressure to reform the international monetary system in the direction of greater rigidity in exchange rates and possibly favoring gold alongside or, in the French case, in place of SDRs as the principal reserve asset in the system. Since it is necessary to secure 85 percent of the voting power within the Fund in order to undo the reforms of the past few years, it is likely that the international monetary system as a whole will be dominated by the United States for the foreseeable future.

The general drift suggests (1) a continuation of the present system of dirty floating, but with successive challenges to move back to fixed rates; (2) the demonetization of gold in general, but the prospect of a gold bloc developing in which monetary growth is tied to gold; and (3) probably more skepticism about the role of SDRs than the present architects of change would feel desirable.

## THE DESIGN OF DOMESTIC MONETARY POLICIES

If the Atlantic Community is to achieve greater monetary stability, the starting point must be appropriate domestic monetary policies in each of the countries concerned. The design and implementation of monetary policy in many of these countries still leaves a good deal to be desired. Several aspects of this problem need special emphasis. In the first place, monetary policy proper should be concerned with the control of the money supply. Although there is no unique definition of money, and hence no unique collection of assets which we can label "money," nevertheless there are in most countries a narrow and a broad measure of money – the former attempting to include especially those assets used to facilitate transactions, and the latter those conveniently used as a temporary abode of purchasing power. Monetary policy, therefore, should be concerned with determining the appropriate rate of growth of both of these particular magnitudes. One finds frequently, however, that monetary policy for many central bankers and private bankers really means credit policy, i.e., control of interest rate levels and rate of growth of credit extended to the private sector by the banking system.

In many countries central bankers are more concerned with the appropriate level of interest rates than with money supply growth, and with controlling part of the asset side of the commercial banks' balance sheets than with the growth of their liabilities. This confusion between monetary and credit policy is nothing new. It is, however, disconcerting to find central bankers continuing to pursue credit policy at the cost of neglecting monetary policy. Frequently, when money supply growth in a particular country becomes excessive, it is not that the government of the day sets out as a matter of policy to pursue such a course of action; rather, it is usually the unintended consequence of the central bank pursuing some form of credit policy – such as trying to keep interest rates low artificially or to accommodate the government financial requirements within the banking system.

The major reasons a central bank should pursue a monetary rather than a credit policy are that it is able to control the money supply effectively, while it is not able to control the total of credit, and it is capable of pegging interest rates only over a very short time period. It can control the money supply because, as we shall see later, it is able to control the amount of high-powered money (notes and coin plus bank cash reserves) with a high degree of accuracy. By contrast, the price and volume of credit are things that are determined by the demand for credit from consumers, corporations and the public sector, and by the supply of loanable funds, which is influenced but by no means controlled by the monetary authorities. In addition, the relationships between the rate of growth of the money stock and the rate of growth of money income, the balance of payments and exchange rate, the level of interest rates and the rate of inflation, are reasonably clear in theory and seem to be increasingly confirmed in numerous studies drawn from various countries. By contrast, there is no emerging consensus in the economic literature of clear relationships between credit, even if it can be measured appropriately, and other economic variables in whose behavior we are interested. Finally, as an indicator of the monetary intentions of the government, the rate of growth of the money stock, though not entirely independent of the decisions of the private sector, is still predominantly so; whereas the price and quantity of credit are determined within the economic system, and so reflect market pressures rather than the control policies of the central bank.

Not only should monetary policy be concerned with controlling the money supply rather than credit, but, second, the monetary authorities should pursue a policy of stable monetary growth. While it would be very difficult for any government to follow, let us say, a money supply growth target of 5 percent on a day-to-day or a week-to-week basis, it should be possible on a month-to-month basis to pursue such a target. This means that the monetary authorities should make stable monetary growth the overriding objective of monetary policy. To facilitate this, it would be useful if all central banks publicly set themselves specific targets for monetary growth for periods of one year ahead and revise them as little as possible. It is important that they should be targets and not ceilings, as monetary growth below a certain target can have just as serious consequences for the economy as growth too far above the target figure.

Pursuing a policy of stable monetary growth has one very important implication for monetary authorities: they must, as a consequence, give up control of interest rates and the exchange rate as objectives of policy. One general principle in this field is that it is impossible for a central bank either to peg interest rates and control the money supply or to fix the exchange rates and retain control over monetary expansion. If a central bank attempts to peg interest rates, it must sell stock to the private sector if they wish to buy, or be ready to buy stock if they wish to sell. But settlements for both of these transactions will change bank liabilities and so the money supply. Similarly, if a central bank attempts to peg the exchange rate, it then has to buy or sell its currencies, depending on the preferences of currency holders. But such transactions will once again mean that it forfeits control over the money supply.

The implication, therefore, of the monetary authorities pursuing a policy of stable monetary growth is that they must be prepared to tolerate small day-to-day fluctuations of prices, both in the securities and the foreign exchange markets. But greater freedom for rates to move on a daily basis will almost certainly mean smaller long-term fluctuations in these rates.

The classic case of a central bank pursuing interest rate and exchange rate objectives with a concomitantly erratic money supply growth is that of the Bank of England since mid-1971, when it introduced a new framework of control with the intention of enabling it to exercise greater control over monetary growth. As a result of pursuing an interest-rate and exchange-rate policy, but not a stable money-supply-growth policy, the Bank of England has allowed the rate of growth of the money supply to be effectively a residual. The most glaring example of this was in 1972-1973 when the major objective of policy was to bring interest rates considerably below a market-determined level, with the consequence that money supply growth rose to 25 to 30 percent a year. Even over a twelve-month period between 1976 and 1977, the growth of the money stock (annualized on a three-monthly basis) reached a growth rate over 20 percent in the autumn of 1976, but by the spring of 1977 the money stock was actually falling at a rate of 10 percent a year. The attempt to peg rates on a day-to-day basis has resulted in large fluctuations on a quarter-to-quarter basis in both interest rates and the exchange rate. Such instability creates serious problems for the economy.

A third principle in designing a suitable monetary policy is that the monetary authorities should set out to control the money supply through control of the monetary base. The concept of the monetary base (or stock of high-powered money as it is sometimes referred to) is derived from consolidating the monetary balance sheets of the monetary authorities, and can be thought of either in terms of liabilities (notes and coin held by the public and the commercial banks' cash reserves) or assets (gold and foreign exchange reserves, the central banks' holding of government stock plus loans to the private sector). Thought of in terms of liabilities, the monetary base is an essential input in the money supply process. Regardless of the demands on the banks – to make additional loans to the private or public sector – the money supply cannot be expanded when the banking system is able to augment its holding of reserves. If we assume that the public's demand for notes and coins is automatically provided for, this typically means an increase in the monetary base. If we examine empirical studies of money supply determination, we find that, while in principle the money supply may change because of changes in the public's desire to hold notes and coin relative to bank deposits, and in the commercial banks' desire to change the proportion of assets which it holds as cash (in other words, changes in the demand for the base), by far the most important factor affecting the change in the money supply is the change in the base itself, which comes about as a result of net government transactions, open market policies, and net movements across the exchanges.

From the point of view of the monetary authorities, the monetary base is a magnitude over which they have complete control. They are, in fact, in a monopoly situation with respect to its production. Hence, from their point of view it is a far more efficient method of monetary control than the alternative of trying to guess what the demand for money is at a certain interest rate and then supplying it to the market at that rate. As a method of operating, this is a hit-and-miss procedure, yet it is one that is all too prevalent among central bankers.

One added advantage of the monetary base approach to monetary control is that it indicates more accurately than any other variable – such as short-term interest rates, bank credit, the public sector deficit, or even the money supply itself – the monetary behavior of the monetary authorities. Regardless of what the central bank or finance ministry says it is doing, its actions must ultimately be judged by what is done. And in order to find this out the monetary base is unrivaled. If the central bank buys stock or extends credit to the private sector or sells foreign exchange, the monetary base will fall. In this sense it is a far better indicator of the monetary behavior of the monetary authorities than interest rates, bank credit or even the money supply.

# 13 Resource Issues and the Atlantic Community

Robert L. Pfaltzgraff, Jr.

Before the end of this century, and perhaps even within the next decade, the West's major industrialized powers – the United States, the states of Western Europe, and Japan – face increasing danger as a result of high, and especially in the case of the United States growing, dependence on imports of natural resources, and oil in particular. Although industrialized states have always been dependent upon imports for some raw materials and resources, they have traditionally had greater control over producers either by virtue of political hegemony in vitally important Third World regions, or as a result of military capabilities with which they could secure such access, or because of supply-demand relationships favorable to consumers, especially abundant supplies and relatively low prices. None of these conditions is present in the late twentieth century, even though the level of dependence of industrialized states upon resource and raw material imports has grown dramatically.

The reasons for the decline in such capacity by industrialized states are numerous. Suffice it to say, however, that the diffusion of power (economic and military) that characterizes our age has begun to give rise to a series of state and nonstate actors whose possession of mineral wealth, together with growing military and economic capabilities, provides leverage of unprecedented dimensions in relationships with industrialized, resource-consuming countries. Such states often seek modernization and aspire to regional influence by means of Western industrial techniques. Many are acquiring advanced generation military capabilities, and in the process providing lucrative markets for the sale of new-technology weapons by industrialized states, notably the United States, Britain and France.

Weapons systems of unprecedented destructiveness, greater accuracies, and in some cases lower unit cost, are becoming increasingly available to states with the means to buy them. Although the advent of new technologies has enhanced the need for resources, and for the extractive capacity of resource-producing states (the latter has not kept pace with the former), it has not given to consuming states the technological means for the protection of resources, especially in transit, to match the destructive potential of other groups, state and nonstate, bent upon interdiction. One widely held view is that the growth in economic and military power in the hands of oil-producer states increases the volatility of the Middle East. Another view, also espoused, strongly is that the sale of advanced technology weapons to oil-producer states provides for the West, and the United States in particular, increased political influence with their governing elites, as well as leverage over their military establishments by virtue of the supply of spare parts and the servicing of military equipment.

Moreover, the growth of Soviet military power at all levels – strategic and conventional, in land forces and naval capabilities – relative to the United States confronts noncommunist industrialized states, including the United States, with additional problems in the utilization of military power for the protection of vitally important resources. The capacity of the Soviet Union for the global projection of naval power is increasing at a time when the dependence of industrialized noncommunist states upon sea lines of communication is growing. Soviet strategy is designed, so it appears, to gain positions of strength to the east and west of the Persian Gulf and its oil-producing states. Soviet support first for Somalia, and then for Ethiopia, together with the coup d'etat of April 1978 in Afghanistan, are illustrative of this Soviet strategy. These ominous trends in the growth of Soviet capabilities for the projection of military power, including the deployment of nearly 50,000 Cuban proxy forces to Africa, contrast sharply with the retrenchment first of West European power from the Third World, and more recently the inability or unwillingness of the United States to take steps effectively to counter Soviet power.

Resource and raw material needs have given increased importance to the role of geopolitical factors in defining the security interests of the United States, its European allies, and Japan, in the late 1970s. Such factors impinge on the security interests of the United States and of its allies at several levels:

1. Resource issues are contributing to, and are affected by (as noted above), a diffusion of military and economic power of unprecedented dimensions. While Soviet military power grows, the world of the next generation will probably contain a series of regional powers, whose status, in some instances at least, will have been attained by the transfer of wealth from resources and raw materials for which demand is outpacing supply.

2. Resource issues are contributing not only to the transfer of nonnuclear defense technologies (weapons of unprecedented accuracy and ease of operation) but also the prospects for nuclear proliferation by virtue of the greater competitiveness of nuclear power, which increases the possibility of developing weapons-grade plutonium from certain kinds of reactors.

3. Resource issues are increasing greatly the importance of the oceans as a source of food and minerals and as the means for the transit of vital resources and raw materials to consumer states. This is evidenced by the growth of exclusive economic zones (200 miles in the case of several powers, including the United States) and the capability of states, by virtue of new technologies, to extract resources from traditionally hostile maritime environments (e.g., North Sea oil) and to make use of maritime technologies (e.g., supertankers) to move large quantities of resources from their point of

origin to their destination for consumption.

Resource issues provide evidence of the inherent limits of globalism, regionalism and international organizations in the resolution of "global" issues in an "interdependent" international system. Instead, we have witnessed a growing "politicization"(1) of international economic relations at the state-to-state level and increased potential for conflict as a result of resource issues. Although resource issues affect the economic and political well-being of noncommunist industrialized countries, whose economies are closely intertwined, and have crucially important implications for relationships between the United States and its principal allies, solutions have been sought, for the most part, by means of national rather than multilateral frameworks. National solutions, in themselves, will prove inadequate, and perhaps even self-defeating, in coping with the problems of energy supply in the remaining years of this century.

## RESOURCE ISSUES AND ALLIANCE RELATIONS BEFORE THE 1970s

As early as the 1950s, resource issues had affected Alliance relationships, with Britain and Iceland locked in confrontation over fisheries when the Icelandic government attempted to restrict British trawlers operating in nearby waters. In 1956 Britain and France faced the prospect of an interruption in oil supply as a result of the Anglo-French invasion of the Suez Canal Zone. By the late 1960s, increasing dependence on Middle East oil had contributed to a growing pro-Arab stance by West European governments. In particular, French policy underwent a dramatic change from its earlier pro-Israeli orientation during De Gaulle's tenure, and especially at the time of the Six Day War in 1967.

The end of the Algerian war in 1962 made it possible for De Gaulle to seek to reestablish for France a role in the Arab world. De Gaulle set out to strengthen France's position, to limit the influence of the "Anglo-Saxon" powers and the Soviet Union, and to capture for French industry lucrative arms markets in the Middle East. At the same time, France and Western Europe were becoming increasingly dependent on Arab oil as most European economies experienced unprecedented growth rates and consumed ever rising amounts of energy. From 1950 to 1970, global production and consumption of energy grew at an average annual rate of 4.2 percent, from 31 million barrels per day in 1950 to 73 million barrels per day of oil equivalent in 1970. Oil and natural gas accounted for virtually all of the growth in production in this period, with the greatest increase occurring in the 1960-1970 decade.(2)

In the 1960s, imports of energy from outside the European Community increased during each year of the decade. The growth in energy consumption and in energy imports proceeded more rapidly than the increase in energy value. Despite sharp increases in energy dependence, the share of energy imports in the value of total European Community imports remained stable, with an increase from 14 percent in 1960 to 17 percent in 1970.(3) In short, Western Europe, like other energy consumers, had easy access to growing supplies of relatively cheap energy at a time of rapid and sustained economic growth. On the eve of the October 1973 war, Western Europe imported 70 percent of its energy from the Middle East and, hence, the potential economic and political leverage available against Western Europe by oil-producing states was of unprecedented dimensions.

## THE OCTOBER WAR AND ENERGY DEPENDENCE

It is evident, even to the casual observer, that this growing West European energy dependence on the Middle East provided both the basis for the dislocations confronting Western Europe during and after the October War and the catalyst for the response of the European Community and its members to the Middle East. That conflict confronted industrialized states with two distinct but related issues: how to cope with the curtailment of oil in the short-term; and how to deal with the longer term issue of a sharp rise in the price of oil. These problems may be stated in more detailed form as follows:

1. how to assure stability of supply in light of production cutbacks instituted by the Organization of Petroleum Exporting States (OPEC);
2. how to respond to a selective embargo against states, in particular the Netherlands, singled out by the Arab oil producers;
3. how to cope with the problem of sharply increased oil prices (from $2.59 to $11.65 per barrel as posted at Saudi Arabian ports;
4. how to reconcile immediate national concerns (i.e., the need to minimize economic dislocations) with broader interests both in the European Community and, in the case of Western Europe, Canada, the United States and Japan, in relationships with allies; and
5. how to reconcile relationships with other industrialized, energy-importing states with relationships with oil-producer states.

Differences in approach to each of these policy issues emerged within the European Community, within the Atlantic Alliance, and in relations between Japan and the United States, as individual states, in most instances, took unilateral action to assure adequacy of energy supply. The United States and its major West European allies engaged in a transatlantic verbal exchange unprecedented in the Alliance. The dispute revolved about contrasting approaches to the Middle East crisis based on differing levels of dependence upon Middle East oil, with Western Europe perceiving the prospect of economic disaster as a result of the curtailment of energy supplies, although in retrospect it is apparent that several factors, including a mild winter and the rapid increase in the price of oil, had the effect of reducing the demand for oil in Europe. In fact, between October 1973 and April 1974, the European Community countries maintained oil reserves of an 80-day equivalent of consumption.(4) Thus, in retrospect – although this was less apparent at the time of the October War and its immediate aftermath – the industrialized, oil consuming states coped effectively with the immediate problems posed by curtailment of energy supply.

Reciprocal recriminations arose over the lack of consultation on Middle East issues – Western Europe accusing the United States of developing a condominium relationship with the Soviet Union, and the United States expressing displeasure with the lack of consultation by the European

Community in the formulation of a European approach to the Middle East. Widely divergent approaches were addressed to the energy crisis, with the United States objecting strenuously to European efforts to conclude bilateral agreements with oil-producing states, and the Europeans voicing displeasure over the lack of American sympathy with the European need to obtain oil wherever possible in order to ensure an adequate supply. Above all, the unilateral efforts of many import-dependent industrial states provided evidence, especially in the case of Western Europe and perhaps less so in Japan, of a lack of confidence in the resiliency of economies and political systems in advanced industrial, or post-industrial, societies to cope with the energy crisis. What this augurs for their political will in the event of a military crisis in Europe can only be the object of conjecture.

These differences came as only the most recent manifestations of issues long dividing the United States and Western Europe as a result of divergent and in some cases competitive economic relationships, fear in Western Europe that the United States would reach agreements with the Soviet Union without adequate consultation with Western Europe, and evolving European policies which have progressively favored the Arab world as Europe's dependence on Middle East oil has grown. The evolution of the European Community, with its cumbersome, decision-making structure, has created for European-American relations new problems related as much to the process by which policy is formed as to the substance of policy itself. However, the Middle East crisis of October 1973 brought each of these issues in the transatlantic relationship into sharper focus as Western Europe strove for an identity measured, so it seemed, by the distance of the European policy from the United States.

In the autumn of 1973, Western Europe's vulnerability to forces over which it had little or no control became more evident than at any time in the past generation. Europe appeared helpless against the threats of Arab oil-producing states wielding the oil weapons, even though, for the short-term at least, Western Europe had reserves of oil, as noted above, adequate to withstand pressures from oil-producing states. In singling out the Netherlands for a total oil embargo, the oil-producing states created for the European Community a challenge, to which the European members, notably Britain and France, responded by agreeing, in effect, to enforce the oil embargo against the Netherlands, which not only had manifested pro-Israeli proclivities, but also had served as the point of transit and refining of oil for Western Europe and for shipment to the United States. In any event, such an embargo proved ineffective because it was short-lived and the Netherlands could draw upon existing stocks of oil.

Within the European Community, there were important differences in approach and in manifestations of hostility to United States policy. France adopted a policy even more sympathetic to producer states than the Federal Republic. French policy was designed both to assure access to energy and, under the arch-Gaullist Foreign Minister Michel Jobert, to establish a European policy stance as widely different and divergent as possible and necessary from the United States. Under the Heath Government, with its own Gaullist orientation, Britain aligned herself with France during the October War and its immediate aftermath. The German Federal Republic, torn, as almost always, between its West European and Atlantic connections, sought to maintain a form of neutrality.(5)

The weakness evidenced by Europe during the crisis, together with the longer-range potential implications of the increase in oil prices for the West European economies, cast doubt upon one of the fundamental premises of American foreign policy in the early 1970s, namely, the development of partnerships with emerging centers of power. Europe constituted neither a partner nor an emerging center of power, but a weak collection of states attempting to make deals with oil-producing states to secure adequate supplies of oil. Perceptions of national interest, of economic nationalism, and of European economic interest differing sharply from that of the United States transcended perceptijons of transnational interest, of multilateralism, and of solidarity in face of challenges posed by producer states.(6)

## THE BROADENED CONCEPTION OF ALLIANCE SECURITY

In the 1970s, as noted elsewhere in this volume, the security of Western Europe remains crucially dependent on the preservation, or the restoration, of a political-military balance between NATO and the Warsaw Pact in the face of a massive and sustained build-up of Soviet military power. However, the problem of European security, almost from the founding of NATO, has included threats from regions outside Europe and the North Atlantic area. At successive points in its history, members of NATO have disagreed on the nature of extra-Alliance challenges to the Alliance and the appropriate responses to them. In 1956, the United States opposed British and French military intervention in the Middle East and, earlier in the 1950s, was not prepared to give large-scale direct support to France in Indochina. In the 1960s and early 1970s, the West Europeans looked with disdain upon U.S. policies in the Third World, including Southeast Asia and the Middle East.

In the 1970s, the principal extra-Atlantic problems affecting the Alliance have included resource issues, especially the threat to, or the actual interruption of, oil supplies, increases in price, and the vulnerability of the sea lines of communication upon which Western Europe and the United States, as well as Japan, are dependent. The problems for the industrialized world posed by such threats increased as the military-political influence of Western Europe in regions outside the Atlantic area – notably that of Britain (in the Persian Gulf) and France (in Algeria) – waned. The withdrawal of West European power occurred at a time when industrialized states were becoming dependent to an unprecedented extent on imports of vital resources and raw materials and oil, especially from the Middle East and Persian Gulf.

Thus the conception of security for which the Atlantic Alliance was formed remains central, but it is by no means adequate in itself to the challenges facing Western Europe in the late 1970s and beyond. As a result of the salience of resources, the security of NATO depends upon developments beyond the North Atlantic area. Yet Western Europe has been unable tor unwilling to take steps that would have safeguarded oil supplies located in regions where, less than a generation earlier, European powers had exercised major influence. The United States has had the task of protecting vital sea lanes, although military power has not been sufficient in itself to prevent the interruption in oil supply and the rapid increase in the cost of energy; and the capacity of the United States, relative to the Soviet Union, to protect important sea lines of communication appears to be declining.

Particularly at the time of the MIddle East War in October 1973, the Atlantic Alliance was inadequate in light of the type of security threat facing Western Europe from the curtailment of supply and the quintupling of oil prices. Western Europe risked the destruction of its economies at the hands of Arab oil producers – if Western Europe did not adopt policies at variance with the pro-Israeli stance of the United States. In short, differing levels of dependence upon external resources by the United States and Western Europe, and also the United States and Japan, led to divergent security and foreign policies as resource-dependent Alliance members took separate action to obtain access to resources. In the October War and its immediate aftermath, major emphasis was placed on national rather than transnational solutions, especially in the early stages of the crisis. Multilateral frameworks were considered in order to deal with the longer-range issues such as conservation, stockpiles and research.

## ENERGY PROJECTIONS

Political and economic projections are fraught with considerable potential for error. In order to assess the implications of resource issues for relations among industrialized states, it is necessary to develop assumptions based on alternative projectons of resource dependence and energy demand and supply. For example, they must contain a series of assumptions about economic growth and demand for oil in consuming countries, as well as availability of oil supplies. These are dependent on levels of resources and the extractive capacity of oil producers within a specified time period – say, between 1977 and 1985, or between that year and 2000. The adequacy of energy supply relative to demand is related to the ability of consumers to increase energy production, to find alternative sources of energy, and to engage in effective conservation measures.

To what extent, and during what time span, we should ask, will Western Europe, Japan and the United States remain dependent on what types of energy imports? Do similar patterns of dependence extend to other resources for which industrialized countries rely heavily on imports? What analogies, if any, can be drawn from energy as a resource issue for alliance relationships among industrialized countries faced with possible shortages of other critically important raw materials? The likelihood exists that Japan and Western Europe as a whole (excepting, of course, Norway and the United Kingdom) will remain dependent upon oil imports in the 1980s at levels comparable to the late 1970s. Will indigenous sources of energy and programs of conservation be adequate to reduce drastically existing levels of dependence on imports within the next decade?

At best, the exploitation of major new discoveries of oil and natural gas lies in the more distant future beyond 1985. Although Western Europe and Japan may increase the allocation of funds for research for alternative sources of energy, technological breakthroughs, even if they were to come about, would not affect greatly the availability of energy in the next decade.

Therefore, noncommunist industrialized countries will have within their frontiers only a relatively small part of the energy they will need to maintain even modest rates of economic growth.(7) We may summarize such trends as follows:

1. Oil will account for about one-half of Western Europe's energy consumption in the 1980-1985 period. Despite British and Norwegian North Sea production, the European Community will depend on imports for between 70 and 85 percent of its energy needs in the 1980-1985 time period.

For Japan, the pattern of oil dependence will remain comparable to the European Community as a whole: 70-75 percent in 1980, and 65-70 percent in 1985. European Community levels of energy import dependence are based upon the assumption of a modest real economic growth of about 2.5-3 percent per year. In the case of Japan, a growth rate of about 6 percent is projected. For Western Europe (OECD), energy needs have been projected to increase more slowly (2.9 percent)(8) on an annual basis between 1975 and 1985 than was the case between 1960 and 1974.

2. The level of dependence of the United States on oil imports has increased substantially since the October 1973 period, even though the United States is both the principal energy consuming country of the world and is considered to have the greatest potential for reducing its consumption and oil import needs by means of stringent conservation policies.

Despite Alaskan oil and offshore resources, the United States will be dependent in 1985 upon imports for at least 40 percent of its oil. With an annual real growth rate of about 4 percent (4.4 percent between 1975 and 1980, and 3.5 percent between 1980 and 1985), the United States would reach an oil consumption level of 18.4 million barrels a day in 1985, of which 9.7 million would be imported.(9) An increasing percentage of U.S. oil imports will come fron the Persian Gulf area. The increase in U.S. dependence on Persian Gulf oil can be expected to enhance competition for resources vital to Western Europe's economic recovery and growth.

It has been estimated that, in order to keep pace with world demand for oil in the next decade, one North Sea- or Alaskan-size oil deposit should have been discovered every three years over the past decade – since it takes at least a decade to bring new oil discoveries into production. There are uncertain prospects, at best, for the discovery of major new oil deposits. It has been suggested, therefore that substantial increases in established reserves in the next generation will come principally from increases in the recovery rate from existing proven reserves. Such recovery methods include thermal processes and chemical flooding which together might raise the recovery rate from its existing level of 25-30 percent to as high as 40 percent by the end of this century.(10) As the Commission of the European Community, in a judiciously worded statement, put it:

> Whereas during the period 1960-70 there was a relative surplus of energy, the market in the future will be subject to more difficult conditions which would lead to major problems of supply at certain times and in certain areas . . . . The energy market – both in the Community and worldwide – will, therefore, become more insecure than it has been in the past. The most difficult period may well be the

> next 10-15 years. In particular, additional petroleum imports required by the three great consumers – the USA, Japan, and Western Europe – will in 1980 run to 1,300 million tons compared with 1970; this figure is so high that the question inevitably arises as to whether and how the available geological reserves can be discovered and exploited in time.(11)

According to this and the official estimates upon which the Carter Administration has based its quest for an energy policy, world demand for energy, by 1985, will have increased to the point where production increases no longer will match demand growth. Such trends would put severe upward pressure on the price of oil, perhaps to a level substantially higher than the current price of just under $12 per barrel, provided world reserves of oil and natural gas remain at approximate existing levels and major reserves beyond those already known to exist cannot be tapped before 1985.

The future of world oil demand and supply relationships is further complicated by consumption and production trends in the Soviet Union. Although estimated to contain vast deposits of oil and natural gas, production from existing fields in the Soviet Union is declining relative to demand. By the mid-1980s, the Soviet Union may have been transformed from a net exporter to a net importer of oil. To remain self-sufficient in oil, the Soviet Union would have to develop new fields located for the most part in the Siberian region. Because of climatic and other conditions, large-scale investment, including the use of some of the most advanced extraction technologies available only in the West, would be needed. In the early 1970s, the United States and Japan expressed interest in providing such assistance. The obstacles to such assistance included severe Soviet restrictions on prospecting to determine amounts of oil and natural gas contained in Siberian reserves. The Japanese were reluctant to contemplate such a joint venture with the Soviet Union without American participation. The failure of the Trade Expansion Act of the Nixon-Ford Administration made large-scale United States and Japanese investment in the Soviet Union in effect impossible. The Trade Expansion Act foundered on the Jackson Amendment on Soviet emigration since guarantees by the United States government of American investment in Siberia became impossible in the absence of legislation contained in the proposed Act.

Even if a decision were to be made now to develop Soviet Siberian oil and natural gas, the effect on Soviet demand for energy imports in the next decade would be minuscule because of the leadtime needed to bring new oil and natural gas fields into production. Therefore, we face the prospect that the Soviet Union and East European communist states, which themselves have been dependent on Soviet energy imports, will enter the world market. The effect of major oil import bills upon East European economies is likely to be profound indeed. To what extent, for example, will balance of payments problems, together with internationally induced inflation, result in substantially lower growth rates, with possible domestic political consequences destablizing for communist regimes, with what effects on Soviet propensity to use coercion, and with what effects in turn on Western Europe and the Atlantic Alliance?

Whatever the effects upon East European economies and political systems, together with relations among communist states, the growing dependence of Warsaw Pact countries on oil imports from outside the communist world will coincide with increased, or at least continuing high levels of dependence by the United States, Western Europe and Japan upon oil imports and, in particular, increasing imports from the Persian Gulf. Saudi Arabia may be unable, or unwilling, both for political and economic reasons, to increase production well above existing capacity: 10-11 million barrels per day, and projected 1985 levels of 18 million barrels per day. With its excess production capacity reduced, or eliminated altogether, Saudi Arabia would be unable to act as a price moderator in OPEC.(12) It is beyond the scope of this chapter to examine in great detail the implications of the entry of the Soviet Union and other Warsaw Pact members into the Middle East oil-supplier markets. Would the Soviet Union, for example, seek to assure preferential access to Persian Gulf oil by assisting forces bent upon replacing existing conservative governments with revolutionary regimes? Or would the Soviet Union compete with other oil purchasers to provide goods and services in demand in oil-producing states, thus reducing the supply of oil and increasing further the price of energy for the United States and its allies?

## MAJOR RESOURCE ISSUES AND ALLIANCES

As the Middle East War and the energy crisis of 1973-1974 showed, resource issues have profound implications for alliance relationships among the world's major industrialized powers. Resource issues add to the vulnerability of some alliance members to resource blackmail, either by the Soviet Union or by producer states, or by both, acting either independently or in concert. Resource issues increase the potential for conflict between members of opposing alliances – for example, between Norway and the Soviet Union as a result of conflicting claims to oil and natural gas located in the Barents Sea, or between Japan and the Soviet Union over fisheries. Resource issues give rise to security problems, including the protection of offshore oil installations and the safeguarding of sea lines of communication vital to the transport of important resources. Resource issues have potentially far-reaching effects upon relations among Alliance members resulting from competition for resources and disputes arising from claims to offshore resources. Examples include the dispute between Greece and Turkey over Aegean oil, and friction between the United States and Japan over the exploitation of fisheries, especially as a result of the 200-mile economic zone instituted by the United States on February 28, 1977.

Other intra-alliance issues include competition for weapons exports resulting form the need for arms-for-oil deals to ensure adequate energy supplies; the effect of the growth of national arms exports on the prospects for NATO weapons standardization and technological collaboration; increased competition, as well as friction between the United States and other Alliance members resulting from divergent policies on the export of nuclear reactor technology (for example, the controversy between the United States and the Federal Republic over Bonn's decision to sell reactor technology to Brazil);

and the implications of externally generated inflation resulting from the sharp increases in oil prices upon the West European and American economies and their defense budgets. In Western Europe, the United States interest in the sale of arms to oil-producing states has been viewed as a means of strengthening the American grip on oil. Last but not least, resource issues have potentially profound implications for the internal cohesiveness of states.

The precise effects of high rates of inflation upon democracies are difficult to determine. Could democratic political, social, and economic systems survive an increase of several-fold in oil prices – an increase that is conceivable if one engages in worst case analysis of energy demand-supply trends in the next decade? Radical groups of the far right and far left are likely to gain electoral strength in democratic systems in times of economic crisis. High rates of inflation, together with declining investment and productivity, may deepen balance of payments problems in Western Europe, together with a weakening of currencies under conditions of a floating exchange rate. Since the price of oil is pegged in United States dollar units, the depreciation of the French franc or the Italian lira relative to the United States dollar produces an increase in the foreign exchange cost of oil.

Moreover, the effect of resource issues is to increase centrifugal tendencies within existing states, especially if those resources are located in close proximity to, or within, a region that has developed, or is developing, its own sense of separateness. Thus, Scottish nationalism has been enhanced by North Sea oil. The discovery of offshore resources near Spain might have similar consequences, given that country's historic internal cleavages. In the case of an independent Scotland in control of oil revenues, the economic problems confronting a truncated Britain would place even greater constraints than in the recent past on defense spending. Britain would probably be compelled by economic circumstances to reduce substantially her defense capabilities, including those assigned to NATO.

## NUCLEAR POWER

A substantial portion of world energy needs, especially the generation of large amounts of electricity could, and perhaps must, be met by nuclear power. Nuclear power may prove a more efficient substitute for coal, as well as for oil, in producing electricity. It may account for as much as 10 percent of the primary energy consumption of the European Community by 1985, and could rise to 20-25 percent by the year 2000. By the end of the century, nuclear power stations may be producing between 50 and 70 percent of the electricity consumed by the European Community. Nuclear energy could provide as much as 21 percent of the primary energy consumed on a worldwide basis by the year 2000 – equivalent to the oil consumption of noncommunist countries in 1975.(13)

Early in the post-World War II period, the United States initiated programs to make use of the atom as an energy source. However, by the time of the 1973-1974 energy crisis the United States was generating less than 5 percent of its electricity by nuclear power.(14) This was far below the projections made a decade earlier of what would have been technologically feasible.

After World War II, Britain and France built nuclear reactors for electrical power generation. The Federal Republic of Germany began research on nuclear power in 1954, and in 1957 the European Community organization, Euratom, was founded to provide a framework for a European atomic power industry. Euratom failed in its objectives, however, when its member states continued to give priority to national atomic energy programs, in preference to a multilateral European effort.

Yet during this period, the national reactor programs of West European states, especially Britain(15) and France, were based upon the relatively unsophisticated technology of natural uranium, together with uncoordinated transnational engineering and marketing arrangements. With the technological lead in light water reactors that used enriched uranium, the United States established a dominant position in world export markets. In the mid-1970s, U.S.-designed reactors of this kind accounted for 85 percent of nuclear power in OECD countries. Westinghouse and General Electric, the two principal U.S. producers of light water reactors, were dominant in world markets outside the North Atlantic area, by virtue of direct exports and licensing agreements. The United States was the principal supplier of enriched uranium to nuclear reactors located in Europe and elsewhere. In order to reduce long-term dependence upon the United States, even before the 1973 energy crisis, two uranium enrichment consortia, Eurodif and Urenco, were established in Western Europe; and R&D, within a European collaborative framework, was undertaken on the gas centrifuge.

The rapid rise in oil prices increased the competitiveness of nuclear-generated electricity and enhanced the attractiveness of nuclear power, including the fast breeder reactor, as a source of energy. The present generation reactors based on enrichment technologies use a scarce resource, uranium, in which shortages could become apparent within the next decade even if additional reserves are discovered. Unlike the United States, Western Europe and Japan are heavily dependent upon imports of natural uranium, since the principal uranium reserves are located in Australia, Canada, South Africa, and the United States. With the use of the breeder reactor, which produces more fissionable materials than it uses, scarce uranium would be replenished.

The fast breeder reactor issue holds potential for discord between the United States and its industrialized allies, including members of the European Community and Japan, for several reasons: the possible implications of the breeder reactor for nuclear proliferation and the closely related interest manifested in recent years in Western Europe in exporting breeder reactor technology, or the full fuel cycle, to Third World and other states. Other opposition to the fast breeder reactor has arisen from apprehension that nuclear materials might be seized by terrorists for threatened, or actual, use against public authorities, and from the problems associated with the disposal of highly radioactive waste, and the possibility of an accident in a nuclear power plant resulting in the release of radioactivity.(16)

Although breeder research continues in the United States, President Carter, in 1977, vetoed appropriations for the construction of a demonstration breeder reactor on the Clinch River in Tennessee. The Administration held that, because present breeder technologies are not sufficiently advanced, the plutonium they produce might be converted to nuclear weapons. Carter contended that "a viable and adequate economic nuclear program can be maintained without . . . reprocessing and recycling of plutonium."(17) The United States position appeared to be based upon the assumption that the reprocessing and recycling of nuclear fuels would not be necessary to assure the adequacy of supply.

This position contrasted sharply with that of the European Community and its member states. According to the Commission of the European Community: "natural uranium sources are finite and supplies are by no means assured. The Community reserve amounts only to about 3.5 percent of world reserves, which are estimated to total about 3.5 million tons. Reprocessing and fast breeders would make significant contributions to reducing dependence."(18) In contrast to the United States, the European Community regards the breeder reactor as an essential link in the Community strategy of reducing dependence on outside sources of energy. Therefore, in order to reduce dependence on energy imports and to diversify energy sources, the European Community proposes to press the development of fast breeder reactors and the reprocessing of spent nuclear fuel.

Already, West European governments have given emphasis to breeder reactors in their energy policies. In the past generation, European Community members have spent more than $25 billion on fast breeder reactor research and development. Present levels of expenditures account for about 30 percent of total R&D energy. Since 1973, several breeder reactors have come into operation in Western Europe. These include the French Phoenix, with a 250 MWe capacity and the British PFR. Several West European collaborative advanced reactor projects have been initiated. With the Benelux countries, the German Federal Republic is working on a 200 MWe SNR reactor, scheduled for completion in 1980. In the same year, France, Italy and the Federal Republic plan to have an industrial version of the Phoenix, known as the Superphoenix, ready for operation. France and West Germany are engaged in collaboration on advanced reactors.

Thus, there is growing interest in Western Europe in technological collaboration in the development and production of fast breeder reactors, hence the potential for discord at the transatlantic level between the United States and its European allies. For this reason, there is a strong possibility that the Atlantic Nations will make less than optimum use of the time available to utilize nuclear power effectively as an energy source in the remaining years of this century. The result will be to help to perpetuate the dependence of the United States and Western Europe upon oil imports, with the prospect of increasing competition for this scarce resource.

## CONCLUSION

Resources are likely to have an even more profound effect on Alliance relationships in the next decade, and in the remaining years of this century, than in the recent past. This conclusion is based upon two principal sets of factors: First, the projection of existing trends in energy production and consumption for the next decade, with the potential for additional price increases and possible interruptions in supply as a result of the inability of supply to keep pace with demand. Second, the likelihood that Alliance members will remain dependent, or perhaps even increase their dependence, on resources vital to their economic well-being. These include raw materials other than oil such as iron ore, coal, uranium, bauxite, chrome, and, especially in the case of Japan, agricultural products. For some of these resources, conditions analogous to those of energy may exist. If so, other resource issues will post formidable problems for members at a time when industrialized states will continue to confront the problem of energy supply, perhaps in competition not only with each other, but also with the Soviet Union and other emerging consumer states.

The trends in resource import-dependence that confront the United States, Western Europe and Japan contain ominous implications for industrialized countries. If the United States and its major allies are to avert potential economic disaster, they must take steps to reduce dependence on oil imports, especially from the Persian Gulf. There is no dearth of proposals to reduce energy import-dependence. This means continued efforts to increase the efficiency of automobiles and other products which consume oil; the decontrol of prices for domestically produced energy in order to encourage conservation in the short run and the development of alternative energy sources in the longer term. Steps such as the insulation of buildings, and especially homes, and the substitution of more abundant, domestically produced energy such as coal have been proposed both officially and by nongovernmental studies.

Industrialized countries have adopted policies designed to share oil in the event of energy shortages. Even before the energy crisis of 1973-1974, many consumer states had begun to build stockpiles of oil supplies for 60-90 days. In the aftermath of the crisis, assistance was provided to states facing massive balance of payments problems as a result of energy imports. Similarly, there has been discussion of longer-term policies that states should adopt. These include increased funding for the development of energy sources as an alternative to oil, as well as the exploitation of technologies for the extraction of oil under difficult geological conditions. Increased emphasis on nuclear power, solar energy, the extraction of oil from shale, and the more efficient exploitation of resources on the seabed have been proposed. Although the prospects for its realization are not bright, especially in the absence of comprehensive national energy policies and discord among industrialized states on such issues as nuclear power, a comprehensive energy strategy for the United States and its allies, notably Western Europe and Japan, is needed. Such a strategy would have as its essential components: (1) the development of policies for the industrialized countries as a whole designed to reduce energy import-dependence over the next decade and; (2) the creation of longer-term policies with the objective of creating alternative sources of energy.

Central to the future of the Atlantic Community is the development of a more adequate framework providing for concerted action especially on the longer-term problems of research and development for alternative sources of energy, the exchange of information about ongoing R&D, efforts to reduce the emerging divergence between the United States and its principal allies on nuclear power and especially the fast breeder reactor, and common efforts to diversify energy supply, especially to draw more heavily upon regions beyond the Persian Gulf. Such proposals do not form the basis for a common Atlantic Community policy in energy. To an even greater extent than other issues examined in this volume, an energy policy embracing the United States and its NATO allies appears impossible to achieve. Not the least of the obstacles to such a policy lies in the inability of member states, and especially the United States, to evolve their own comprehensive national energy policies. Therefore, the industrialized, energy-importing states are cast back upon piecemeal efforts to achieve consensus, policy harmonization, and occasionally policies within a multilateral framework on pressing energy issues.

While the linkages between energy policy and economic and military security issues are numerous, there remain fundamentally important relationships between the vulnerability of the West to the interruption and curtailment of energy supply and the continued erosion of their political-military power in comparison to other states, notably the Soviet Union. Although political-military power in itself will not be adequate to safeguard energy supplies, the economic well-being of the industrialized, noncommunist world will be placed in even greater jeopardy if the strategic-military balance shifts decisively toward the Soviet Union. Hence, the inextricable relationship between the political-military capabilities of the Atlantic Alliance – considered in other chapters in this volume – and the quest of the United States and its allies for energy policies at the national and international level adequate to provide for their economic growth and well-being in an era of increasing resource constraints.

## NOTES

(1) See, for example, Robert J. Lieber, Oil and the Middle East War: Europe and the Energy Crisis (Cambridge: Center for International Affairs, Harvard University, 1976), p. 53.

(2) World Supplies of Primary Energy: 1976-1980 (London: Energy Economics Information Services Ltd., 1976), p. 1.

(3) According to a European Community study: "Altogether the degree of energy dependence, which expresses in percentage terms the share of supplies originating in countries outside the Community in the total requirements, has grown in the years (between 1960 and 1970) from 39% to 66%, the actual energy imports of the Community rising from 200 million tce (tons coal

equivalent) to 650 million tce. The Community thus appears in the first rank of buyers on the world energy market, accounting for approximately 30% of the whole of the world's imports. For crude oil alone, it leads with 406 million tons in 1970, ahead of Japan (142 million tons), EFTA (130 million tons, 94 of which for Great Britain), and the United States (87 million tons). Commission of the European Communities, Prospects of Primary Energy Demand in the Community, 1975-1980-1985 (Luxembourg: Office for Official Publications of the European Communities), p. 31.

(4) Romano Prodi and Alberto Clo, "Europe," in Raymond Vernon's, The Oil Crisis (New York: W.W. Norton, 1976), p. 101.

(5) For a good analysis of French and West German perspectives and policies, see Horst Mendershausen, Coping with the Oil Crisis: French and German Experiences (Baltimore, Md.: The Johns Hopkins Press, 1976), esp. Chapter 4.

(6) The events of late 1973 pointed up the need, however, for the United States and other major noncommunist industrialized states ot work more closely together to develop a framework for common action on energy issues. In December 1973, Secretary of State Kissinger had called for the creation of a Trilateral Energy Action Group to strengthen cooperation among both oil-consuming and oil-producing nations in order to conserve existing energy supplies, develop new resources, and evolve an international collaborative research program for technologies to exploit existing energy sources, such as shale oil, and to find new sources, such as solar energy.

From this, together with other initiatives, including the Washington Energy Conference of oil-consuming states (members of the European Community, Norway, Japan and the United States), held in February 1974, came impetus for the formation of the International Energy Agency established on November 15, 1974, within OECD to develop a program of cooperation in emergencies and for the longer term. The new organization included a Governing Board consisting of ministers or their delegates from member countries, and a Management Committee, composed of senior representatives of each state and four Standing Groups, each with one or more representatives of each participating country to deal with (a) emergency questions; (b) the oil market; (c) long term cooperations; and (d) relations with producer and other consumer countries. The original twelve members of IEA were Belgium, Canada, Denmark, the German Federal Republic, Ireland, Italy, Japan, Luxembourg, the Netherlands, Norway, United Kingdom and the United States. Austria, Spain, Sweden and Turkey joined in 1975. See U.S. Energy Policy, October 1973-November 1975, Selected Documents, The Department of State, Bureau of Public Affairs, Office of Media Services, No. 3, December 1975.

(7) See, for example, Melvin A. Conant and Fred R. Gold, Geopolitics of Energy, a Report to the Committee on Interior and Insular Affairs, U.S. Senate, Energy Publication No. 95-1 (Washington, D.C.: GPO, January 1977), esp. Chapter 11.

(8) See World Energy Outlook (Paris: Organization for Economic Cooperation and Development, 1977), p. 55. See also Dankwart A. Rustow, "US-Saudi Relations and the Oil Crisis of the 1980s," Foreign Affairs, April 1977, pp. 494-516.

(9) OECD, World Energy Outlook, 1977, p. 37.

(10) "How Much Oil in the World?," Petroleum Economist, March, 1978, p. 86.

(11) Commission of the European Communities, Problems, Resources and Necessary Progress in Community Energy Policy 1975-1985 (Luxembourg: Office for Official Publications of the European Community), p. 35.

(12) See The International Energy Situation: Outlook to 1985, Central Intelligence Agency, April 1977.

(13) Report of the Workshop on Alternative Energy Strategies, Energy: Global Prospects, 1985-2000, (New York: McGraw Hill, 1977), p. 215.

(14) Exploring Energy Choices, a Preliminary Report of the Ford Foundation Energy Policy Project (Washington, D.C.: 1974), p. 7.

(15) Britain did not join Euratom until her accession to the Rome Treaties in January 1973.

(16) The problem of nuclear reactor safety has been hotly debated between the advocates and opponents of nuclear power. Those who favor nuclear power base their case on the impressive record of the nuclear power industry in establishing effective safety procedures. The opponents contend that it may not be possible to preserve such high levels of safety as the number of nuclear power plants increases. For a balanced discussion of such arguments, see Energy: Global Prospects 1985-2000, pp. 190-196.

(17) Quoted, in Tom Alexander's, "Why the Breeder Reactor is Inevitable," Fortune, September 1977, p. 124.

(18) European Community Background Information, No. 22/1977, July 29, 1977.

# 14 Trade and the Atlantic Community— The Major Issues

Lawrence Bell

In the volatile zero-sum game of world balances of payments, each new year holds the chance of dramatic changes in the relative standings of the players. The events of 1977 provided one more illustration. The United States had a trade deficit of $26.72 billion. For the same period of time, immense worldwide trade surpluses emerged in Japan ($15 billion), West Germany ($18 billion) and Saudi Arabia ($25 billion).(1)

These astonishingly diverse trade outcomes, coupled with significant unemployment in the major trading nations, have generated intense pressures upon these nations to alter the behavior of their economies and their trade postures and, in the case of Japan, even the fundamental structure of its economy. These same pressures have dramatically changed attitudes in the developed nations toward the Third World. "The industrial development of the third world was (formerly) proclaimed a case for public sympathy; now it is privately cursed as a bloody nuisance."(2)

In the closing days of 1977, the Organization for Economic Cooperation and Development (OECD) predicted slow growth (3 percent for all member nations combined by the second half of 1978) and a rise in unemployment to 17 million from the current 16.3 million.(3) Accordingly, OECD summoned West Germany and Japan to accept greater responsibility for world trade growth by stimulating their own economies to higher growth rates. The United States has also pressed its rich opposite numbers to risk faster internal growth for the sake of other nations with much less possibility of autonomous growth. West German Chancellor Helmut Schmidt has stated that West Germany will not risk accelerated domestic inflation to oblige those who ask it to be an economic locomotive to haul the world out of its present unemployment situation.(4) He has also defended West Germany's 1977 growth rate of 2.4 percent as respectable, albeit less than expected, and has pointed to the fallen dollar as a threat to the world economy and a hindrance to West German exports.

For its part, the United States has defended vigorously its trade account posture as a service to the world economy. Treasury Secretary Blumenthal has asserted that the United States has made a major contribution to the stability of the international monetary system and has challenged the surplus nations (Japan, West Germany, Switzerland and the Netherlands) to join us in public-spirited deficit.(5) Washington remains firm in the view that the dollar's troubles stem both from huge oil imports here and from the inadequate growth of the West German and Japanese economies. Conversely, in Europe it is widely suspected that the United States prefers to have a cheap dollar as a competitive trade weapon, and would rather have a dollar-devaluing trade deficit than endure the pain of a major reduction in energy imports.(6)

It is possible, but far from certain, that 1978 has brought an historic accommodation between the United States and Japan after a year of dispute that, for a while, threatened to produce a major trade war between the two nations.(7) Both pledged support for the final stage of the worldwide trade discussions that began in Geneva in the latter half of January 1978. Japan agreed to the following measures to increase its imports: reducing tarriffs on $2 billion worth of imports, effective April 1, 1978; removing quotas on twelve products, eleven of them agricultural; making an effort to raise its imports of high quality beef for the next fiscal year by 9,000 tons; tripling its orange imports and quadrupling its citrus juice imports; sending a variety of trade missions to the United States to discuss increased imports of forest products, machinery, citrus fruits and juices; taking various measures to increase opportunities for foreign suppliers to penetrate Japan, ranging from changes in procedures and simplified import inspection requirements to expanded credit for imports. Japan further promised to undertake a comprehensive review of its foreign exchange control system and to reduce the surplus in its current international payments account by $4 billion in the next fiscal year. Looking beyond the coming year, Japan promised to continue reasonable efforts to eliminate the current account surplus and even to accept a deficit if such should occur.

On behalf of the United States, Robert Strauss, the special trade representative, expressed confidence that Congress would pass an effective energy bill in the next few months and that the United States would then improve its trade position by reducing American dependence on foreign oil and by increasing exports. It remains to be seen how much of the promised agenda on both sides will in fact come to pass.

Much less hopeful for the future state of trade policy is the drift of recent events within the European Economic Community. The prospect is one of great dissension within the EEC and with nations outside it, particularly with Japan. Three striking developments in the EEC occurred in 1977: a sharp rise in unemployment in the nine-nation area; the adoption of semi-protectionist policies in textiles and steel; and the full integration of Britain, Ireland and Denmark with the six original Common Market members, creating a market of 270 million people, with very great potential bargaining power in the final stage of the world trade negotiations at Geneva in 1978. Ironically, it is precisely at the time that unprecedented economic integration has been achieved in Europe – with the removal in July 1977 of the last customs duties on industrial goods among fifteen European nations – that one notices among European leaders a great uncertainty whether economic integration will really help them to cope with the twin specters of inflation and unemployment that plague so much of the Free World.

One need not be the ultimate pessimist to sense the danger in these growing doubts about the evolving regime of interdependence, which has been one of the most striking developments on the world scene after World War II. The extraordinary rise of integration among international markets, once seen as the yellow brick road to growing wealth among the participating nations, is now increasingly viewed as exacting an appalling price in terms of national autonomy, as individual economies appear increasingly at the mercy of events originating elsewhere and so beyond their control. In the present atmosphere, it is an effort to recall the attitudes and events of the Kennedy Round with its falling tariffs for industrial goods. Since then, we have seen the proliferation of nontariff barriers to trade as major instruments of policy, and a growing disposition to question the adequacy of the General Agreement on Tariffs and Trade (GATT). In the realm of rhetoric, lip service is paid to the principles and rules of GATT. In practice, Europe, the United States and Japan oscillate between protectionism and free trade, with the ebb and flow of domestic pressures on behalf of special interests. There is no lack of dark clouds over the final stage multilateral trade negotiations at Geneva. Nonetheless, there have been hopeful signs as well. Knowledgeable observers have been encouraged by the extent to which the system of open world trading came through the most severe recession of the postwar era.

## ATLANTIC TRADE PATTERNS

### Trends in U.S. Trade

The U.S. economy has long been known for its modest dependence on foreign trade – considered in relation to its GNP. The U.S. trade balance was positive every year from 1950 to 1970, though the size of the surplus declined in the latter 1960s, falling prey to accelerating inflation and an overvalued dollar. Substantial deficits appeared in 1971, 1972 and 1974 with Canada, Japan and OPEC in particular. Aside from 1972, the United States has enjoyed a trade surplus with the EEC in every postwar year. Future prospects appear to turn on success in high-technology products, on developing expanding markets for agricultural output, and on the character of the investment milieu in both developed and less developed nations.

Differentially favorable inflation rates in the United States and the depreciation of the dollar have fostered exports to the EEC, Canada and Japan. Among other influences, the exchange rate for the dollar may encourage multinational firms to expand exports from the United States rather than to expand plants in foreign countries. Both as supplier and market, OPEC has soared in importance. Trade with communist countries remains a very small percentage of U.S. foreign trade, despite its rapid growth until recently.

### Trends in EEC Trade

Intra-European trade grew rapidly after the formation of the EEC, and it now accounts for the major share of EEC imports and exports. The enlargement of the EEC reduced transatlantic interdependence, as Great Britain turned to EEC partners for food and other imports. The structure of West European exports in the postwar period turned increasingly toward manufactures. The largest markets for these manufactures are the less developed countries, the United States, and, increasingly, the Eastern trading area. While the EEC has a substantial trade surplus in manufactures, it also has a large trade deficit in primary products; its greatest deficit is with the developing countries, which are almost the exclusive suppliers of its raw materials.

The most notable feature of this scene is the growing trend toward intra-EEC trade, and it must be remembered that more nations are knocking on the EEC door. Still more striking is the rapid increase in trade with countries to which the EEC has granted preferential treatment, as in the Lomé Agreement. Exports to Eastern Europe and to the Soviet Union more than doubled between 1970 and 1973, and continued growth is foreseen.

## CURRENT TRADE PROBLEMS IN AGRICULTURE

Bountiful harvests in the United States and in other major agricultural nations, with accompanying price weakness, the enactment of the Food and Agriculture Act of 1977, and the leveling of U.S. agricultural exports are the dominating facts of the American agricultural scene.(8) The Food and Agriculture Act basically extends the 1973 Farm Act and embodies subsidy, set-aside and grain-reserve provisions, as well as continuation of price support loan programs. The 1977 Act continues the Food for Peace Program and provides for a farmer-held grain reserve for wheat and feed grains. On-farm storage is fostered by providing loans up to $50,000, with a ten-year repayment period, for farmers who will construct storage facilities for designated products.

In signing the 1977 Act, President Carter conceded that it will be much more expensive than he wanted. One cost-restraining factor is that, although 1979 target prices will be based on changes in cost of production for the covered crops, land prices are not included in the cost of production despite notable pressure from farmers in favor of such inclusion. It is likely that the higher support prices engendered by the Act will intensify the general rate of inflation in the United States and will hamper efforts to widen foreign markets for American farm commodities. This tendency is especially unfortunate in its timing in view of the unprecedented U.S. trade deficit and the pledge by the United States to Japan to expand American exports.

There may be worse news to come in this sector. Certain events in January 1978 suggest the possibility that the new Act may later be liberalized even further to mollify militant farmers.(9) Thousands of farm strikers marched in Washington, while hundreds of them besieged the Department of Agriculture, demanding large price increases. Furthermore, the Carter

Administration, which had sought a 10 percent reduction in feed grain acreage, is disturbed by the latest reports of feed grain planting intentions, which are down by only one percent overall. The 10 percent reduction in feed grain acreage is technically voluntary, but farmers who fail to comply will become ineligible for federal loans and price support payments.

Thus far, the Administration's official position is that it will not approve any major new price support legislation. President Carter hopes to temper the farmers' wrath with some $7.3 billion to be paid as price supports in the current year and with other measures, including the removal of almost seven million tons of grain from the current huge, price-threatening, domestic stocks to create a special reserve for world food emergencies. Should these pacifiers prove inadequate to calm the farmers, there remains the possibility that Congressmen from the farm belt, facing November elections in 1978, may press for new and much more inflationary farm price legislation.

Programs to increase domestic agricultural prices above international prices are likely to require special interference with imports and exports. In the case of commodities that are normally exported, the rise in domestic prices leads to a loss of exports or resorting to export subsidies. Over the years, the U.S. government has in fact employed export subsidies for a wide variety of farm products. This step having been taken, there is then the problem of preventing reentry of the subsidized exports, and this leads to the establishment of import quotas, as was in fact done for cotton, wheat, peanuts and manufactured dairy products.

It is not really a long journey from domestic farm programs to export subsidies and import quotas. However, no export subsidies have been paid on corn since 1962, or on cotton since the mid-1960s, though subsidies were continued on most wheat exports until the program was suspended in September 1972.

Agriculture provides a peculiarly poignant scene of conflict between the EEC and the United States. In the agriculture group of the multilateral trade negotiations during 1976, the U.S. concern for expanding trade and the EEC's concern for stabilizing trade were in collision. Under the Trade Act of 1974, the United States is obliged to negotiate for agriculture in conjunction with industry. The EEC insists on separate treament for the two areas, arguing that the Common Agricultural Policy (CAP) is a domestic matter not subject to negotiation. To avoid helpless confrontation, the United States and the EEC, in 1975, compromised with a provision for notifications and consultations in regard to agricultural products not covered by specific subgroups.

The endless train of prickly agricultural issues between these mighty trading areas may be symbolized by the importunings of redundant chickens in the United States and of irrepressible cows in the EEC. On behalf of the former, the United States, following special negotiations related to the entry of the United Kingdom, Denmark and Ireland into the Common Market, unilaterally made a sharp cut in the tariff on imported brandy for two years to encourage a greater spirit of accommodation in the EEC with respect to a number of outstanding trade disputes, and, in particular, to win for U.S. poultry improved access to the EEC. At the end of the two-year period, EEC barriers to imports of U.S. poultry were higher than at the outset. Both sides made renewed efforts to reach a solution. In November 1976, the President partially restored the U.S. tariff on brandy.

In the EEC, a surplus of dairy products is a perennial fact of life, and the side effects of its disposition precipitate clashes with other countries. In March 1976, the EEC, seeking to dispose of a great hoard of nonfat dry milk from reserve stocks, tried to encourage feed manufacturers to use more dry milk in livestock rations, through a system of subsidies on the purchase of dry milk and refundable deposits on the purchase of vegetable meal. The United States filed strong protests on the grounds that an equivalent amount of U.S. vegetable protein would thereby be displaced in the EEC. The compulsory requirement of the EEC program ended in October 1976, but a GATT-established panel was to hold hearings to investigate the legality of the EEC move.

Conflicts of interest within the EEC post serious obstacles to reformation of the CAP, and examples are not far to seek. In 1977, the EEC announced discontinuance of subsidized butter exports to Eastern Europe for the foreseeable future. This about-face emerged from disclosure, mainly in the British press, of plans of a French exporter to ship surplus butter to the USSR at a cost to the EEC exceeding $150 million.

When viewing the EEC in an agricultural issues context, special note must be taken of the growing restiveness, particularly in West Germany, concerning the guaranteed farm product prices which redistribute income to the weaker members, especially Britain and Italy. British imports of food from the EEC are estimated to receive a 40 percent subsidy. These same guaranteed prices have brought unprecedented prosperity to Irish agriculture, where beef and dairy product prices have trebled during four years of membership in the EEC.

Agricultural policies in the Atlantic Community fall short of what is needed because they are based predominantly on domestic interests. The lack of supranational coordination plays a partial role in an erratic series of global shortages and surpluses of certain goods, as well as in price fluctuations that accompany the shifting physical quantities.

The less developed countries (LDCs) seek wider access to the EEC and U.S. markets, and the Lomé Agreement moved a short distance in that direction. Subsequent developments will be examined below in a general review of North/South issues.

## NONTARIFF BARRIERS

Over the years, as tariffs receded and lost much of their significance as barriers, nontariff barriers arose to achieve importance. These latter barriers are notable for variety and elusiveness: safety and labeling standards, export subsidies, government procurement policies, quotas, export and import controls, and taxes. Amid their differences, one arresting common trait stands out: they all can distort trade patterns. Elimination of them is much more difficult than in the case of tariffs because individual policies are rarely comparable. They also render the operation of the principle of reciprocity more difficult, if not impossible. Among the relevant measures, two present issues are of special importance to the Atlantic Community: government procurement and export subsidies.

## GOVERNMENT PROCUREMENT(10)

The United States is severely criticized for its Buy American Act, but national procurement policies are no strangers to the EEC either. Admittedly, American procurement policy has much greater impact because of the scale of the U.S. defense market. In the postwar period, the United States has become the dominant exporter of aircraft, computers, integrated circuits, and other sophisticated military equipment. At the same time, American multinationals gained dominant shares in European commercial markets for office equipment, electronics and aircraft.

Nonetheless, it is far from clear that the foregoing developments owe a great debt to Buy American policies. The success of American multinationals in European markets was surely the outcome of many factors, such as the scale of American firms and the favorable dollar exchange rate during the 1960s, which induced direct American investment in Europe. Moreover, the EEC failed to create a common market for high-technology products, and transnational mergers have been rare, despite the encouragement given to them in Brussels. In fact, American procurement policy may have been a minor factor in the ascendancy of American high-technology industries in the European milieu.

The Buy American Act supplies rationalizations for European restrictions on government procurement and militates against an efficient transatlantic division of labor. European governments subsidize high-technology industries to enable them to compete with their American counterparts. Political tensions and wasteful duplication of research and development efforts are the regrettable side-effects. In the interests of economic efficiency and improved Atlantic relations, government procurement policies ought to be discussed to identify the areas where comparative advantages in high-technology industries reside.

### Export Subsidies

Competition among the countries of the Atlantic Community operates vigorously in the arena of export subsidies. In the wake of the fourfold increase in petroleum prices and its massive impact on the balance of payments situations of the OECD nations, and the allure of rapidly growing OPEC markets, export subsidies have come to be regarded as appealing solutions to unemployment and payments problems. But the device is not new.

The United States has granted export credits since 1953 through the Export-Import Bank. The Japanese established a bank with similar purposes, and in 1975 the EEC submitted a proposal to the Council for an EEC export-credit bank. The primary concern has been to promote exports to developing countries. But soon the fallacy of composition rears its durable head: When most developed countries have export-promoting banks, their differential advantage becomes minimal and at last only the importers benefit from increased competition among the suppliers.

Loans to importing countries are similar in effect to export credits given to domestic exporters. In the past, loans to importers were granted to developing countries solely in the form of tied aid. The United States and, to a lesser extent, France and Great Britain administered aid so as to have almost negligible effects on the balance of payments. In the OECD countries, with the rise of unemployment and decline of exports in 1974 and 1975, some countries concluded trade agreements with the Soviet Union. France and Britain both extended large trade-credits to the USSR. Part of the price of gaining sales and jobs in this way is the enhanced leverage gained by the Soviet Union over these economies.

June 1976 saw a notable event in regard to export financing, with the adoption by the United States and six other major trading countries of a policy of issuing Unilateral Declarations on official export credits. Designed to soften international competition, the Declarations provide for a 15 percent minimum of cash payments by foreign buyers, minimum interest rates for credits over five years (7.5 percent to LDCs, 8 percent to highly developed countries), and for most exports, maximum repayment terms (ten years to LDCs, eight-and-a-half years to others). The practice of issuing Declarations will be in effect for one year, at the end of which time participating nations will decide anew on a future agreement with respect to official export credits.

In November 1976, the DISC (Domestic International Sales Corporation), a feature of the United States tax code permitting U.S. exporters under certain conditions to defer imposition of federal income taxes on half of their export profits, was found by a panel of tax experts to constitute an export subsidy in violation of Article XVI (4) of the GATT. A similar finding was made with respect to certain export tax practices of France, Belgium and the Netherlands. For its part, the United States has responded with a proposal for multilateral and bilateral consultations to reach an internationally acceptable solution to possible trade distortions deriving from direct tax practices.

## Quantitative Controls

Quantitative controls are a special variant of nontariff barriers in that they are highly visible and predictable in effect. Generally, GATT prohibits quantitative controls, but there are important exceptions to the rule: quantitative controls may be imposed in the agricultural sector as well as in cases where imports prove to be disruptive. Moreover, countries may invoke balance-of-payments difficulties and national security considerations to justify quantitative controls. The use of export controls and import restrictions under Article 19 has increasingly become an object of concern in recent years.

## Safeguards

The inadequacy of GATT rules is best seen in the ways the safeguard mechanisms of Article 19 are applied or circumvented in emergency situations. Discriminatory measures against countries responsible for market disruption were expected to be temporary. In practice, however, inefficient producer countries of certain goods have proved reluctant to face up to the social costs of introducing structural changes in the relevant industries, and so the temporary import restrictions have become permanent.

Present policy – for example, in the GATT cotton textile agreement – plainly shelters inefficient industrial sectors in the Atlantic Community. Still, it is difficult to set a time limit on safeguard measures, since it is difficult to predict the time needed by an efficient industrial sector to adjust to global competition. Because wage levels still differ greatly, without offsetting productivity differentials between developed and undeveloped countries, developed countries need some protection against market disruption if certain threatened sectors are to survive.

The lack of a clear and widely accepted definition of market disruption makes Article 19 inadequate. The United States apparently defines it as a sudden and sharp increase of imports threatening the domestic producers. The EEC specifies three elements in its definition: sharp increase in imports, excessive quantity, and excessively low prices. The Japanese, against whom the EEC import restrictions are primarily directed, acknowledge only the first condition as valid grounds for invoking Article 19.

Article 19 is also lacking in that the importing countries are not permitted to confine the penalties exclusively to the country causing the market disruption. The nondiscrimination principle, a cornerstone of GATT, must be observed when import restrictions are applied under Article 19. This weakness of Article 19 led to a proliferation of bilateral orderly marketing agreements, also known as voluntary export controls, which are perhaps the newest expression of protectionist chic. In recent years, voluntary export controls have increasingly been used by the United States and the EEC in lieu of straightforward Article 19 measures, in order to avoid penalizing all supplier countries.

Voluntary export controls have the added advantage of not constituting an open violation of GATT rules. The Japanese were particularly pressed to institute a variety of these controls in order to avoid import quotas or other restrictive measures by the EEC and the United States. Some observers have argued that voluntary export controls are an alternative to quantitative controls and are preferable to them. Yet this overlooks the ease with which such controls are instituted. In the United States, a confidential complaint by a threatened industry may precipitate voluntary export controls, whereas the invocation of import quotas would require public hearings. Thus, there may not be very many bilateral orderly marketing agreements which, if terminated, would be replaced by import quotas. GATT seems to have sanctioned the device of bilateral orderly marketing agreements by providing a forum for the negotiation of the Long Term Arrangement on Cotton Textiles, in which the industrialized countries compelled low-cost producers of cotton to restrain their exports.

Proliferating voluntary export controls seriously erode international commercial rules and procedures by violating the most-favored-nation principle. Moreover, those who are the enforcers of these controls are frequently powerful traders such as the United States and the EEC: Those who are coerced to reduce their exports are not usually in a position to retaliate. Article 19 should be revised to facilitate structural adjustment of threatened industries in advanced countries, and to require a case-by-case international examination of the evidence of market disruption.

### Export Controls

Since 1973, export controls initiated by the exporting country have become an issue among the Atlantic countries, as well as between developing and developed countries. GATT categorically prohibits the use of export controls as a strategic weapon; but even before the petroleum cartel, Article 11 had become an ineffective deterrent through the depredations of many historical precedents.

Export controls for economic reasons are vividly remembered from recent experience. In 1973, the United States banned the export of soybeans. Both Europe and the United States limit exports of scrap steel and certain farm products. The aim is to transmit inflationary pressures abroad by restraining exports of scarce materials.

The U.S. Export Administration Act of 1969, which expired in September 1976, provided a legislative basis for the exercise of export controls for reasons of national security, foreign policy and short supply, and required domestic firms to report to the Department of Commerce the receipt of requests to participate in restrictive trade practices or boycotts against countries friendly to the United States. Pending the introduction of legislation to amend and renew the Export Administration Act, the President, by executive order, kept in full force the administration of export controls and the requirement for reporting requests for boycott participation.

Export controls, especially where foodstuffs are involved, are destructive of the character of Atlantic relations, even where the inflationary impact on importing countries may be negligible in the short run. The importing country risks interruption of supply, the exporting country chances loss of valuable markets, and thus all countries should have some interest in avoiding shortsighted export controls. Persistence in such practices encourages self-defeating national hoarding and shortages with adverse implications for worldwide inflation.

## TARIFFS

Although tariffs on industrial goods were significantly reduced in the Dillon and Kennedy Rounds, there still remains scope for further reduction. Relative to LDCs, Atlantic countries have low tariffs in general, but some tariffs are still high in absolute terms. Nominal tariffs are a misleading measure. Effective tariffs, which take account of the value-added content of goods, turn out to be more protective than a survey of nominal rates might indicate.

Labor-intensive goods tend to have high tariffs, and further reductions would benefit primarily the less developed economies. A precondition of tariff cutting may be a more effective safeguard mechanism, such as the textile agreement, enabling industrial countries to shelter their labor-intensive industries against low-cost imports. Total abolition of tariffs does not seem to be a realistic goal, if for no other reason than the political importance to the EEC countries of their common external tariff.

During 1976, the Multilateral Trade Negotiations (MTN) Tariffs Group sought to frame a comprehensive tariff negotiation plan to guide its work in 1977. The chief elements of the plan were three: an agreed tariff-cutting formula, and the forms of special and differential treatment to be administered to developing nations in tariff negotiations. The U.S. proposal, the first to be tabled, sought final tariff cuts no less ambitious than those of the Kennedy Round – 35 to 40 percent after exceptions. It envisioned broad and deep cuts in all tariffs subject to limitations in the Trade Act, with special emphasis on cutting between 5 and 15 percent those duties where most trade occurs among developed countries. The proposal applied to agricultural as well as industrial tariffs, with a minimum of exceptions.

The EEC's proposal stressed harmonization, namely, the reduction of high tariffs by a greater percentage than lower ones. Tariffs below 5 percent would be reduced very little, and the proposal applies to industrial but not to agricultural products. On balance, the EEC proposal would yield a much smaller cut than the U.S. formula. The Japanese formula is similar to the EEC proposal in terms of tariff reductions yielded. The Canadian proposal pursues the elimination of tariff rates less than 5 percent, indicating Canadian preoccupation with expanding exports of processed primary products, which are usually dutiable at low rates.

In view of high unemployment in many industrial countries, there is an impression at Geneva that protectionist restraints have held at bearably low levels, all things considered. Quotas and other barriers are often intended as placebos for unions and managements, with little practical effect on imports. The dependence of weaker economies on IMF credit restricts their freedom to indulge in broad-gauge or severe limits on imports. Moreover, there may even be a way to cope with European anxiety over the incursion of Japanese products without much sacrifice by Japan. It is argued that Japan could reduce its own mass of import barriers without risking a great rise of imports because of the high quality of many products made in Japan.

## NORTH-SOUTH PROBLEMS

The Tokyo Declaration, outlining the agenda for the current GATT Round, placed special emphasis on the interests of the developing countries and on the importance of trade agreements between LDCs and industrial countries. For both sides of the Atlantic, the developing countries rank as highly important export markets and import sources. A substantial regime of interdependence links the developing and the Atlantic countries. The LDCs need capital investment, technology and markets for their raw materials. Both parties have major stakes in trade negotiations.

LDCs are interested in concessions in three areas: stabilization of export earnings from raw materials, market access for their industrial goods, and transfer of labor-intensive industries to the developing countries. To the Atlantic countries, major concerns are assured supplies of raw materials, trade liberalization in the LDCs, and adequate safeguard clauses so that they can protect vulnerable industries from the competition of low-cost imports.

The developing countries have pressed for enhanced access to the markets of developed countries not only in GATT but elsewhere as well. At

UNCTAD IV (United Nations Conference on Trade and Development) and CIEC (Conseil International des Employeurs du Commerce), LDCs pursued permanent preferential treatment and a wide range of special allowances. The United States and other developed countries have stood firmly on the proposition that proposals for such special treatment must be negotiated in the MTN. While favoring measures to improve the competitive position of LDCs in world markets, the United States has expressed concern that these measures be of such nature as to minimize distortion to the system of trade.

As part of the MTN's Tariff Group negotiations to cut tariffs generally, special treatment of the LDCs might take the form of cuts exceeding the general formula on products of special concern to LDCs. The United States is also exploring ways to provide differential treatment for LDCs in respect to nontariff barriers such as subsidies and countervailing duties, tropical products safeguards, standards and government procurement. A form of special treatment that has already been implemented for the LDCs is the GSP (Generalized System of Preferences), under which the developed nations concede preferential access to their markets on a temporary basis for a wide range of products from LDCs. The U.S. system took effect on January 1, 1976, and eighteen developed countries have such a system in effect. The U.S. system provides 140 countries and territories duty-free access to U.S. markets for over 2,700 products worth more than $2.5 billion. The U.S. system is to expire in 1985. In response to LDC representations that GSP should be expanded and made permanent, the United States holds that GSP is temporary and unilateral, and that a permanent two-tiered system of world trading would harm developed and developing nations alike.

It is in the case of tropical products that MTN has come the longest way. Early in 1976, the United States tabled an offer to grant permanent tariff reductions on products of export interest to participating developing countries encompassing about $7 billion of U.S. imports, on condition that beneficiary countries make some reciprocal concessions. The GSP improvement offers of most other developed countries were not tied to requests for reciprocity.

At the Seventh Special Session of the UN in 1975, the United States proposed substantial assistance to developing countries to stabilize their export earnings. In the same year, the IMF expanded and improved its Compensatory Financing Facility, which offers financing to IMF members experiencing temporary and largely unavoidable lapses in export earnings and related need for balance of payments financing. In the first seven months of 1976, drawings from the Facility exceeded the total drawn during the prior thirteen years of existence.

The Paris-based North-South dialogue was to have been completed in December 1976, but the final session was postponed to allow the Carter Administration to formulate its own policies. Previously, the major oil producers had suggested that their price policies would depend partly on the generosity shown by the industrialized nations to the poor developing countries. Later the oil cartel announced its price increases, and the North-South dialogue was put off until March 1977, in the expectation that the final round of sessions would begin with a meeting on April 6 of the group of industrial countries. Thereafter, a strict timetable of sessions was planned to climax in a ministerial-level meeting on May 30-June 1, 1977.

As planned, the ministerial-level representatives met their deadline on June 1, 1977, and the 18-month Conference on International Economic Cooperation came to a close. To a considerable extent, the agreements arrived at covered over rather than resolved some of the basic differences of outlook between rich and poor nations, but the industrial nations did concede more than they had intended to on the vital issue of commodities price support.(11)

A common fund for commodities price support has been one of the most intransigent of the Third World's demands. In the past, there has been strong resistance to this conception on the part of the developed nations. The United States has opposed indexation by formula on the grounds that such an innovation would intensify inflation, introduce arbitrary rigidities into the price structure, and, on balance, severely injure developing countries which are net importers of commodities. Japan and West Germany, too, have opposed the common fund approach as inferior to a case-by-case procedure for individual raw materials. The Soviet bloc nations, also cool to the common fund route, argue that the real gains would go to the multinational companies.

The Conference marks the first time that the industrial nations explicitly agreed that a common fund should be a key instrument in achieving such Third World objectives as stable prices and higher incomes. In the past, the rich nations had been amenable to considering a fund approach only in the sense of a clearinghouse for integrating the operations of funds that might be established for individual commodities.

It was also agreed that the details of any common fund would be left for negotiation at the United Nations Conference on Trade and Development in Geneva. It may be noted that none of the foregoing contains any explicit recantation of the persistent objective of the rich nations to any fund powerful enough to interfere unacceptably with the workings of free markets.

In the matter of government aid to the Third World from the wealthy nations, it was agreed that 0.7 percent of the annual gross national product of the donor nation should be the target to be approached in stages by substantially increasing aid. This target is not, however, a definite commitment on the part of all industrial nations. Japan promised to double its current 0.2 percent over a five-year period. Secretary of State Vance promised to request Congress to make a substantial increase in aid during the next five years. It was generally agreed that, insofar as possible, the amount of aid should not vary with budgetary or balance of payment problems in donor nations.

In the matter of demands for a moratorium on debt repayments by developing nations, the industrial nations refused firmly to accept the concept of a general forgiveness of these debts. The creditor nations contended that they already consider debtors on a case-by-case basis and will continue to do so. In the end, all that was agreed to was the proposal that appropriate bodies, such as the World Bank, should continue to study the question of debt repayments. The industrial nations did pledge special aid of one billion dollars to the poorest nations. This sum would approximately equal the debt repayments of such nations for one year.

Although common interests between developing and developed countries are readily perceived in the area of raw material trade, the issues of market access and tariff point up persistent conflicts. United States and EEC tariffs are relatively low, but there were few tariff reductions for items of special concern to the LDCs (i.e., semimanufactured goods) in the Kennedy Round. Therefore, products from LDCs generally face higher tariff barriers than products of industrial countries. The EEC generalized preference scheme, which grants special tariff treatment to selected LDC exports, is limited to a few items. The U.S. tariff preference scheme proposed in the 1974 Trade Act does not apply to semimanufactured goods and processed primary materials. These are not genuine concessions since the Atlantic countries have such clear competitive advantages in manufactures. Since the U.S. offer of permanent GSP improvements is conditional upon reciprocal concessions from LDCs in the tropical products case, it will be a major task of current multilateral negotiations to identify those sectors in LDCs which warrant a lowering of extensive trade barriers.

Transfer of labor-intensive industries to LDCs is a thorny issue for the Atlantic countries, as this demand conflicts with domestic pressures for maximum employment. One way or another, this transfer will occur at some future time, given the abundant labor resources of developing nations. Political realism requires that it be a gradual process. The Atlantic countries have little incentive to hasten this evolution unless they can invoke safeguard clauses or, temporarily, restrict imports. The abiding question is whether the labor force of an uncompetitive sector can be absorbed by other sectors, at what cost, and in what time span. Present unemployment rates in the Atlantic countries make this a difficult adjustment.

## EAST-WEST TRADE ISSUES

Among the notable events of the 1970s in the area of trade, surely a high place must be accorded to the remarkable growth of the exchanges between the centrally planned economies of Eastern Europe and Asia and the industrialized nations of the West.(12) From $15.7 billion in 1970, the two-way level of East-West trade grew to somewhat over $50 billion in 1976. In view of lagging demand and fierce competition for markets among the developed countries of the West, and the clamoring needs of the communist nations for Western technology and agricultural products, it would appear that both sides have much to gain from continued high growth in trade volume. Nonetheless, the dominant clues on the contemporary scene mostly seem to say that the pace of growth must slow considerably during the next few years.

Financial constraints and difficulty in expanding exports have brought the East to a crucial turning point in trade policy. During the period 1973-1976, the USSR and Eastern Europe incurred large and consistent trade deficits with the West. These deficits have been financed by heavy borrowing on the part of the USSR and most East European countries, since most communist countries have largely excluded direct foreign investment and do not have convertible currencies. In the foregoing circumstances, rapidly rising debt is a self-terminating game and the debtors are soon driven to press either for increased exports, curtailed imports, or both. The mode of adjustment in the case at hand is visibly beginning to take shape.

No one knows the exact magnitude of the indebtedness of the CMEA countries to the West, but all informed observers agree that it is very large, with estimates ranging up to $40 billion.(13) For their part, the East Europeans, and especially the Soviet Union, have made some strides toward adjustment. Trade data for the first three quarters of 1976 show the Soviets cutting or leveling imports, while launching a strong drive to expand exports. All this has made only a slight reduction in the Soviet trade deficit with fourteen major trading partners; the deficit still exceeds $2.2 billion for the first three quarters. In evaluating this, it must be borne in mind that perhaps $1.5 billion of that deficit stems from Soviet grain imports, purchased during the meager harvest of 1975, but delivered during the first nine months of 1976. Preliminary 1976 data show a major drop in Soviet grain imports. Although the Soviets are committed to grain imports from the United States ranging between six and eight million tons for several years, all this would still be much less than the 1976 purchases. If this pattern of curtailed grain imports can be maintained, the Soviet trade deficit will be commensurately reduced. Moreover, aside from the case of the United States and Canada, Soviet nonfood imports from the other twelve hard currency nations were reduced from 1975 levels. Collaterally, the Soviets achieved a 25 percent increase in exports, chiefly petroleum and natural gas, during the first nine months.

Efforts to expand Eastern exports to the West run into severe problems. Relevant Soviet exports consist of a few raw and semiprocessed materials, with petroleum and petroleum products supplying almost one-third of hard currency earnings. In contrast to the Soviet case, East European exports mostly feature a variety of manufactured and agricultural products, although Poland accounts for substantial coal and copper exports. Unprecedented efforts must be summoned to develop the supply capabilities to meet the quality and quantity requirements of Western markets in respect to the foregoing range of goods. The great pressure of domestic requirements in the communist countries competes strongly with export priorities, and the limited marketability of many Eastern products in Western markets for reasons of quality remains a hard fact of life.

In the struggle for hard currency earnings, the growing significance of compensation or buy-back arrangements must be noted. These are devices whereby Soviets and East Europeans pay for plant and equipment imports from the West with the subsequent output of these capital goods. In the case of the Soviet Union, and to some extent Poland, natural resource development is the relevant sphere. With Poland, Romania, and Hungary, manufactured goods predominate. It is possible that these payment arrangements may engender many billions of dollars of added hard currency earnings in the coming decade. The prospects are less clear for a similar rise in exports of East European manufactured goods.

The case of China is singular in several respects. Despite the rapid growth of China's total foreign trade during 1971-1975, less than 5 percent of China's GNP is thus accounted for, in contrast to the Soviet case (8 percent) and the East European countries (ranging from 20 to 50 percent of GNP). The best estimates of China's debt suggest that it is very small, probably on the order of $2 or $3 billion of medium-term and short-term credits. The mode of financing is unusual to the extent that no direct bank financing is involved. The Western supplier typically arranges for credit with commercial banks and government-supported credit institutions, and settles for repayment on a deferred basis from China.

China has considerable potential for expanding imports substantially through credit, and Chinese leaders have expressed interest in expanded foreign trade in the next few years, but the magnitudes are highly uncertain.

The precise mix of import, export and debt changes that will characterize East-West trade in coming years cannot be divined with respectable certitude. If some prediction must be forthcoming, however, the most probable one foreshadows a notable slackening in the growth of trade in the next few years. Should this forecast prove true, there may be heightened tension in the West concerning the long-standing irritant of trade credits and exportsubsidy competition among the Atlantic countries, from which the communist countries have derived great benefit. It has been the recurrent practice of some Western governments to subsidize trade credits. The United States had hoped to persuade the EEC to raise the interest rate charged to Eastern countries by allowing the Ex-Im Bank to raise its rates to 7 and 8.5 percent. Both Britain and France persistently undercut U.S. and German interest rate charges to contrive a differential advantage for their exporters; these countries also furnish major credits to the Soviet Union below the market rate. Aside from distorting trade patterns, such trade credits have the added demerit of entailing substantial risks for the granting countries. British and French policies have given the Soviet Union considerable leverage over their economies by cultivating a posture of dependency.

A few years ago, the EEC sought to regulate East-West trade to protect the EEC countries from the potential risks involved. It was proposed that the CMEA countries should negotiate only with the Community as a whole. East-West trade regulation was to be an important part of the Common Commercial Policy (CCP), and was aimed at denying the Soviet Union the chance of playing Western countries off one against another. Nonetheless, shortly after this CCP decision, the Soviet Union and Poland each separately negotiated ten-year agreements with some EEC countries with respect to industrial and technological cooperation. The protests of the EEC Commission that these agreements violated the spirit of the CCP were unavailing, and no agreement on East-West trade has been reached within the EEC.

The export of technology by Western firms carries special risks because of the inherent advantages of a state trading monopoly in negotiations with a free market system. Faced with skillful Soviet negotiating tactics, Western firms resort frequently to cutting prices to win major contracts. As research and development cost often have been allocated to previous sales, the bids of Western firms tend to decline to bargain levels. In such fashion does the Soviet Union acquire Western technology without having to pay the costs of research.

In the absence of intergovernmental agreements on export credits and the terms of technology transfer, the Eastern bloc can play Western countries and companies off one against another. Cheap credits and low prices are, in effect, the poor scores that the Western players have to show for their rounds in this fateful game with the winning Eastern teams. It is past time for Western governments and firms to take a hard look at practices which slant the benefits of trade so precipitously in the direction of the importing nations. Looking, of course, will not suffice, but it is a necessary preface to the changes in the institutional arrangements for trading that can cope with the vulnerabilities of the West.

## THE INADEQUACY OF GATT

Many would agree that GATT played a substantial role in the process of liberalizing trade in the postwar period. Many would also now add that GATT has lagged in adapting its rules to new trade issues; meanwhile loophole discovery has become a fine art with many practitioners.

Several developments in international trade give new urgency to the growing pressures for reform of GATT as an institution. First, there is a disturbing tendency toward the formation of trading-blocs, which violate the nondiscrimination principle. In addition, the enlargement of GATT to include a considerable number of less developed countries has also fostered an erosion of GATT rules, since most of these countries were unable to meet their trading obligations. Furthermore, the reciprocity principle invoked in GATT negotiations is less than adequate for the kinds of trade obstacles, especially nontariff barriers, which characterize the 1970s. GATT rules have become an insufficient foundation for further liberalization of trade. But constructive reform is elusive because of the large number of members and the lack of a small influential body – such as the Group of Ten within the IMF – which could add direction and momentum to the process of fashioning needed amendments.

Recent years have seen the most-favored-nation rule of GATT interpreted in a very lax manner. This is a symptom of a tendency of the international trading system toward regional trading blocs. The EEC preference system is deeply in conflict with the GATT nondiscrimination rule. The EEC common external tariff is far from common in its application: Greece and Turkey, formerly NATO partners, benefit from special agreements, as do Israel, Malta, Morocco, Tunisia and Spain. These bilateral agreements stem from historical ties between Mediterranean countries and the EEC, and the desire of France to counterbalance the influence of Germany and Britain in the Community. Former colonies of the European countries have special trading relationships with the EEC. In 1975, the EEC granted freer market access to forty-six African, Pacific and Caribbean countries in the Lomé Agreement. Although the EEC does not require reverse preferences, the Agreement allows these countries to treat imports from the EEC differently from third-country imports. Although presented to GATT under the rubric of an association agreement, the foregoing arrangement is clearly discriminatory and contradicts Article I of GATT.

The Lomé Agreement is the most flagrant breach of GATT rules, but political considerations have influenced trade agreements in other cases. United States quotas are not usually applied uniformly to all countries. The oil quotas in the 1950s treated Canada differently from the Middle East countries, and the voluntary textile quotas were applied in different ways to European and Asian suppliers. But the Lomé Agreement is sui generis in view of its sweeping scale; it might encourage association arrangements among the United States and Latin America and Canada, as well as between Japan and Southeast Asia, and so endanger the bedrock rationale of nondiscrimination on which the whole GATT trading system is supposed to be based.

The decolonization of Africa and Asia was another major development of the postwar period. Membership in GATT was all but automatic for the newly-developed countries. There is a certain awkwardness in their full membership in GATT, since they are not in a position to fulfill the trading obligations imposed by GATT to the extent that developed countries can. Increasingly it is arguable whether the developed countries should continue to refrain from requiring reciprocity in trade concessions. There is a tendency to perpetuate the use of quantitative import controls in developing countries. Infant industries, sheltered by tariff and quota barriers, have an all too familiar tendency to prolong childhood interminably. In the end, the framework of GATT and UNCTAD may have to suffice as the device for seeking solutions to problems between developed and developing countries, if the latter hold that they cannot, in the foreseeable future, liberalize their trade policies. The hard institutional fact remains that the size of GATT membership makes efficient decision-making and the attainment of consensus difficult.

The success of the Kennedy Round was due largely to the reciprocity rule governing these negotiations. Political leaders could defend trade concessions granted to other countries by pointing out concessions obtained in return. Tariff concessions can easily be juxtaposed, as tariffs are linearly reduced. For nontariff barriers (NTBs), no corresponding advantage may be readily demonstrable for concessions made. Both the effect and the intention of NTBs may be difficult to identify. Each country has its own range of NTBs, which do not match the assortment that other countries have. New procedures are required to deal with such intractable bargaining material. The lumping together of similar NTBs may offer a solution, or tradeoffs may be effected by a package approach. In view of the demonstrated inventiveness of nations in the area of trade-barriers, consideration should also be given to establishing GATT rules and procedures which will preempt new barriers.

## NOTES

(1) New York Times, January 22, 1978, section 6, p. 28.

(2) The Economist, December 31, 1977, p. 75.

(3) New York Times, January 1, 1978, p. F13.

(4) Wall Street Journal, January 2, 1978, p. 12.

(5) Ibid., May 25, 1977, p. 16.

(6) Ibid., January 10, 1978, p. 48.

(7) Ibid., January 16, 1978, p. 3.

(8) New York Times, January 8, 1978, section 12, p. 28.

(9) Wall Street Journal, January 23, 1978, p. 18.

(10) The issues of U.S.-European competition and collaboration in high-technology procurement are analyzed in Chapter 15.

(11) Wall Street Journal, June 2, 1977, p. 16.

(12) International Economic Report of the President Transmitted to the Congress, January 1977 (Washington, D.C.: GPO, 1977), p. 63ff.

(13) Wall Street Journal, March 16, 1977, p. 24.

# 15 Trade and the Atlantic Community— Some Avenues of Resolution

Lawrence Bell

Lord Keynes was wont to remind his contemporaries that we can promise to be good but we cannot promise to be clever. The matter in hand, with its hard choices and poignant tradeoffs, makes one wonder if we can promise either outcome. The study of trade policy long has been one of the great schools for cynics; preachment and practice so commonly diverge. Often, goals are oriented to destructive kinds of redistribution, e.g., exporting inflation or unemployment to other countries so there will be less in the exporting country. The pursuit of openness for the national economy has to be balanced against the risks of international interdependence. Even Adam Smith, the great apostle of laissez-faire, long ago noted that opulence may have to defer to defense. Trade policy is also the natural habitat of outlooks obsessed with short-run benefits and unmindful of steep deferred payments lying ahead.

Traditionally, economics has asserted a major advisory jurisdiction in trade matters, but, as always, one must decide who is to be followed. This is not the place for a comprehensive review of the range of teachings relevant to trade policy, but at least enough should be said to give some sense of the complexity and tentativeness of available professional advice. In the end, it is difficult to be good or clever, even with the best of advice.

A typical contemporary updating of the traditional position, which was oriented to fostering worldwide specialization through unrestricted trade, exhibits troublesome complications.(1) The familiar theses emerge: unilateral protection is an illusion, since other nations can and will retaliate; restraints of trade only redistribute employment within the economy, without a net gain in jobs as a whole to the nation; moreover, there are other and preferable ways of achieving employment goals without resorting to protectionism. The problem is said to be one of establishing a mechanism for redistributing enough of the gains of international trade within the nation to make openness acceptable.

The first-choice recommendation calls for appropriate use of monetary and fiscal policies, combined with transitional assistance to labor and capital displaced by imports. A second-best solution is to subsidize production in industries injured by imports; this alternative is preferred to tariffs or quotas because it would not raise prices to consumers of the affected products, as the latter devices would. But in the case of large countries which have the possibility of affecting terms of trade, it is less certain in which direction a tariff imposed by the large country will affect living standards within its borders, save for the extreme case where the tariff is high enough to eliminate all imports. By extension, there are quotas and voluntary export agreements which could be the equivalent of the tariff, and a similar uncertainty may be noted with respect to effects on living standards.

Still other complications lurk nearby. The foregoing view centers on a faith in monetary and fiscal policy as the chief reliance for coping with unemployment or inflation. Many contemporary economists now believe that the high degree of interdependence among the national units of today's world economy has greatly undermined the individual nation's capacity to manage its macroeconomy with a separately determined monetary and fiscal policy, and international coordination of these devices would surely not be more feasible than negotiating mutual advances to more open trade. Indeed, within the United States, no one has yet found a way to coordinate federal fiscal policy with the motley assortment of state and local government fiscal policies.

Writing in the 1960s, in his now classic study,(2) Richard Cooper focused on the central task of reconciling the pursuit of the benefits of extensive international trade with the concern for reserving enough domestic freedom to seek political and economic objectives considered either necessary or attractive. In an era of high and rising interdependence, he portrayed the erosion of autonomy in policymaking. Cooper saw the Atlantic Community confronted with three broad alternatives:

1. It could accept integration and the consequent loss of national freedom, and to determine economic objectives and policies jointly. This could imply making some decisions at the level of the Atlantic Community rather than at the national level, and would require either a high degree of labor mobility among the members of the Community, or else foreign aid programs within the Community.

2. It could accept integration but attempt to preserve national autonomy through provision of financial accommodation for prolonged payments deficits. This way of protecting domestic economic objectives against threats from balance-of-payments difficulties is an incomplete solution, since it does not protect members entirely against policy competition in the areas of regulation and taxation.

3. It could reject integration by deliberate imposition of barriers to the integrating forces, freedom of foreign trade and international capital movements. This last solution implies the orderly use of restrictions on international payments, combined with limited means of financing deficits. It also calls for a flexible but well-defined code of good behavior fashioned for application by members of the Atlantic Community, but under close international scrutiny, with the aim of using restrictions only to protect the balance of payments, not special interests within individual countries.

Cooper saw the third solution as winning by default. Others may share the belief that some variant of the third solution may come closest to what is attainable at this juncture in history.

The current Multilateral Trade Negotiations (MTN) differ markedly from previous trade negotiations: the number of actors has increased, the scenario is more complex, and the setting has profoundly changed. The Kennedy Round was dominated by the Atlantic countries; other OECD countries and less developed countries were sidelined. In contrast, the Tokyo declaration of September 1973 specifies one MTN goal as the securing of additional benefits for the international trade of the developing countries. OPEC's subsequent success with its petroleum cartel and its demand for raw material negotiations, unlike those of the Kennedy Round, which were confined to tariff cutting, also embrace nontariff barriers, agriculture, safeguards, export controls and other sensitive issues. All this augurs harder bargaining, as the impact of these issues on employment, prices and social policy far outranks that of mere tariff changes.

The current economic environment does not facilitate concessions. Appreciation of some European currencies relative to the dollar has made the related exports less competitive. The previous chapter noted the harsh impacts of oil prices and world recession on the balance of payments of most European countries. Floating exchange rates have brought a certain measure of instability. The MTN are a stern test of the Atlantic countries' will to cooperate.

## AGRICULTURAL POLICY

Basically, four choices face the Atlantic countries in dealing with agricultural problems such as surplus-dumping, supply interruption, and excessive price instability. All involve some tradeoff between economic efficiency and national political and social concerns.

The optimal solution in terms of economic efficiency calls for greater international division of labor. The Common Agricultural Policy (CAP) protects wheat, coarse grain, sugar, beef, poultry and dairy products through a system of variable levies. Heavy indeed are the costs of this policy in terms of inflation, surplus storage, price supports and misallocated resources. The United States has import quotas for sugar, meat and dairy products. Previous studies of U.S. farm commodity programs have shown that they have little effect upon output, and that a large fraction of benefits have been capitalized into land values and, furthermore, a substantial part of the benefits have gone to people or corporations who do not operate farms.

Since the Atlantic partners on both sides of the ocean are inefficient producers of meat, sugar and dairy products, increased specialization in them would not be economic. The economically optimal long-term solution is a gradual phase-out of the variable levy and import quotas, granting market access to such efficient producers as New Zealand, Australia and Argentina. This approach would leave for separate treatment the problem of poor farm families. The evidence is clear, in any case, that commodity programs do not make any significant difference in the economic status of low-income farm families, since it is not low farm product prices but limited resources which are the key to their problem. Rural poverty appears to be related strongly to advanced age, mental and physical handicaps, and low levels of education, and these factors commonly are reinforced by limited land and capital. The problems of this group and, more broadly, of medium or small farms should be addressed by policies to foster mobility through retraining and reeducation, where removable barriers to mobility are prime obstacles to adjustment. For those whose situation cannot be remedied in such fashion, the negative income tax offers a suitable approach. The foregoing approach would accelerate the consolidation of small, uneconomic farms and, for the remaining farmers, would open the way to economies of scale, with favorable effect upon the prices of dairy and meat product prices.

In grain, where both Atlantic partners are relatively efficient, the return of abundance has greatly complicated and worsened the prospects of moving to an international solution dominated by considerations of economic efficiency. The previous situation was already sufficiently difficult, even when world grain prices were much higher, because some degree of self-sufficiency in wheat has been regarded widely as a matter of national security. West Germany stores wheat as an element of strategic stockpiling.

Other things being equal, concentration on grain production on both sides of the Atlantic would create the possibility of an agreement on stockpiling, and such agreement is essential to ward off sudden and disruptive returns to national self-sufficiency in a bad crop year. In 1973, the U.S. ban on soybean exports induced the EEC to encourage the use of wheat and skim milk powder as animal feeds. Holding reserves would serve the long-term interests of the exporting countries and assure greater price stability. In one model, the Atlantic countries could establish target prices for wheat, soybeans and corn. When prices fell below the targets, these countries would buy agreed quantities of the affected commodities. If prices exceeded target levels, stocks would then be released. There is, of course, no use in pretending that either the domestic or international politics of these maneuvers would be easily manageable.

From what has been said about the first option, giving high priority to considerations of economic efficiency and preparing to pay the price for the orientation, it is readily seen that the required structural changes in the various economies may prove too hard to bear in the contemporary setting of high unemployment rates and sluggish recovery.

A second choice would stress coordination of agricultural policies among the Atlantic countries. These policies are dominated currently by domestic considerations or, in the EEC case, Community considerations. This going along separate ways produces a curious <u>melange</u> of shortages in some products and surpluses in others. Logically, this calls for coordination of the respective supply management programs of the United States and the EEC, with concessions on both sides, e.g., some lowering of price support on one side in exchange for relaxation of an import quota on the other side. Hopefully, the parties could then avoid a major portion of the heavy surplus storage costs, and there would be less occasion for trans-Atlantic charges of surplus dumping.

Candor does require caution against easy optimism about timetables or even the basic attainability of the foregoing proposals. At a minimum, one must see clearly the grave technical obstacles and negotiating preconceptions that stand in the way. The technical obstacles are a large subject in themselves, but two may be noted here. Careful studies of U.S. farm supply management programs suggest that the net effect on the total value of farm output has been small. Moreover, there is much uncertainty about the magnitude of typical price elasticity of demand for U.S. farm output. One reputable estimate puts its long-run value close to unity. If this is true, the management of U.S. farm output would have little effect on either gross or net farm income.

As for negotiating preconceptions, both in government and in farm organizations in the United States, one has long heard the argument that other industrial nations have little interest in the sort of farm products that we protect, and there is something to this view in the cases of peanuts, rice, sugar and wool. But this surely ignores the strong European interest in manufactured dairy products. Often Americans are surprised to discover that in Europe, American agriculture is thought to be almost as protected as that of the EEC.

A third choice would have the Atlantic countries stockpile on a national basis, if multilateral stockpiling with agreed international intervention prices proves unattainable. Here the objective of trade negotiations in agriculture is that of minimizing the risk of shortages, price fluctuations and the cost of surpluses. A useful device would be long-term supply contracts between the United States on the one hand and EEC, Japan and the Soviet Union on the other. These contracts would cover soybeans, wheat and other animal feed. Better planning should then be possible since external demand would be known approximately.

The most damaging option that the EEC could select, from the standpoint of fruitful Atlantic relationships, would be the pursuit of an import substitution strategy in grain. The Community faces a choice between encouraging grain production or increasing vegetable, fruit, and sugar output. Some LDCs would be injured by supply expansion in vegetables and fruit, while a stress on grain production would harm American export prospects. Some observers have felt that the Lomé Agreement signals a trend away from Atlantic interdependence and toward closer European-African trade relations.

If domestic production in the EEC came to replace the major part of its import requirements from the United States, the United States would then have to intensify export efforts directed toward communist or wealthy, less developed countries. The political consequences for the Atlantic relationship would not be constructive. The United States is under heavy compulsion, one way or another, to expand its exports of major farm products. The prospects, in the absence of improved market access for these goods, are for export availabilities (in the case of wheat and feed grains) to grow much more rapidly than demand during the remaining years of the 1970s.(3)

## NONTARIFF BARRIERS

A GATT survey of nontariff barriers has identified more than 800 ways of obstructing trade under this category. Detailed negotiaton of each issue is not a realistic prospect. If, however, kindred trade practices are grouped, three manageable categories emerge: government participation in trade, packaging and labeling standards, and charges on imports. Disclosure of such practices is the first necessary step, followed by the harmonization of the practices insofar as possible. Finally, there is need to formulate a code of conduct to which the Atlantic countries would have to commit themselves.

In the instance of government participation in trade, disclosure of present policies is uniquely important. Some countries, e.g., the United States, have explicitly tied aid and public procurement policies, whereas most European countries have not gone public with their practices. In this situation, criticism concentrates upon those who have confessed, while countries without published procurement procedures are spared. Given multinational disclosure of government procurement and the tied aid policies of the Atlantic countries, the costs of these policies should be examined. Atlantic procurement, instead of national, would almost certainly reap economies of scale. As for tied aid, a system similar to that of the World Bank is worth considering: upon receipt of a loan, an LDC would finance imports from any member of the Atlantic community. This would permit the LDC to buy from the most efficient producer, without endangering greatly the balance of payments position of any Atlantic country. This development of an Atlantic market for government procurement and aid to LDCs would foster Atlantic specialization and yield lower costs for Atlantic defense and other public procurement.

In the area of export subsidies, Atlantic cooperation, with Japanese participation, is still more important. While export subsidies may be profitable in the short run for the exporting country, they entail heavy costs in the long run for all developed countries. Ultimately, the communist countries, and probably OPEC too, are the real winners in this irrational sort of competition. This issue is so grave that it merits high priority in the MTN. The Atlantic countries, with Japan, must identify what constitutes artificial stimulation of exports, and an operational definition should be incorporated into the GATT articles.

The need to harmonize packaging and labeling standards, administrative entry procedures and similar matters should prove highly amenable to negotiation. All exporters suffer from heterogeneous national standards, and there should be wide interest in reaching agreement on uniform standards.

Concerning charges on imports, once again disclosure is basic. Ultimately there may come an equalization of countervailing and other duties, but the fundamental problem of different tax policies will remain. All in all, the prospect is for slow progress in negotiations over nontariff barriers.

## SAFEGUARD MECHANISM AND QUANTITATIVE CONTROLS

### Safeguard Mechanism

High unemployment rates intensify the sensitivity of the issue of disruption of domestic industry by imports. The GATT article specifying acceptable measures for coping with disruption is vague and has been interpreted very loosely. Most countries bypass entirely Article 19 by threatening the exporter with imposition of import controls. Although voluntary export controls are meager substitutes for an equitable trade policy, it can be said for the Atlantic countries that the limited adjustment assistance available makes it very difficult to adhere to an alternative course of action.

The safeguard mechanism problem could be approached in several different ways: a highly explicit GATT article detailing the conditions under which safeguards can be adopted; a time limit on safeguard measures; national adjustment assistance; international adjustment assistance.

To be effective, the GATT article must define market disruption in operational terms. This can be done by declaring a certain rate of increase in imports disruptive or by setting a limit on the market-share which foreign producers are allowed to reach. The market-share approach is especially adapted to key capital goods industries, such as steel, where national control of a major share of production is considered to be of strategic importance. In the case of consumption goods, some consensus must be sought as to an acceptable rate of import increase. Such an article might have preventive as well as remedial properties, since exporting countries would know _ex ante_ what the importing countries consider a tolerable level of imports. An operational definition should allow the Atlantic countries to impose multilateral or bilateral import controls, depending upon the number of countries which exceeded the allowed rate of import increase.

Limiting the time span within which safeguard measures can be adopted is another option. The time limit would vary with the size of the assistance. For a substantial scale of assistance, the time span might be on the order of six months to one year. Already negotiated agreements, such as the Long-Term Arrangement on Cotton Textiles, could remain unchanged while exporters and importers found a compromise acceptable to all parties.

Most countries have national adjustment programs, but they differ considerably in scale. Such adjustment assistance should seek to accomplish the transfer of workers into more productive sectors of the economy. The assistance should be sufficient to permit progressive migration of employees and depreciation of productive assets. Ideally, adjustment assistance would be so structured that it would, at first, permit the threatened industry to maintain its scale, and later, through a gradual tapering of assistance, engender an orderly transfer of labor to other sectors of the economy. Alternatively, adjustment assistance could be administered on an international basis. This would free the national government from domestic pressures to continue adjustment assistance indefinitely, and would spread the burden of adjustment assistance to all developed countries.

## Export Controls

Safeguard mechanisms and the possibility of import controls are realistic preconditions for further trade liberalization. However, export controls have recently become more noteworthy than import controls and have become a device for exporting inflation to importing countries. It is essential for the Atlantic countries to cope vigorously with the problem of arbitrary cutoff of scarce supplies. The International Energy Agency (IEA) emergency sharing agreement is one model for allocation of scarce resources, but may prove less than adequate for emergency sharing of products other than petroleum, since there is a fixed percentage distribution system in the latter case. Perhaps a more generally acceptable way of allocating scarce supplies would be to distribute them to importing countries according to past export shares of total exports. Such an arrangement would strengthen Atlantic trade links and would distribute the costs of shortages among exporting and importing countries.

## TARIFF NEGOTIATIONS

The crux of disagreement is not whether further tariff reduction is desirable, but which negotiating approach is preferable. A choice must be made among three negotiating strategies: across-the-board reduction, harmonization of tariffs, and sector-by-sector negotiation.

The U.S. 1976 proposal to the MTN Tariffs Group pursued tariff cuts comparable to those of the Kennedy Round – 35 to 40 percent after exceptions. Subject to limitations in the Trade Act, broad and deep cuts in all tariffs were sought, with particular emphasis on cutting between 5 and 15 percent those duties where most trade occurs among developed countries. Agricultural as well as industrial tariffs are encompassed with a minimum of exceptions.

While overall tariff levels in the United States and the EEC are comparable, the range in tariffs is greater in the United States. Europeans are reluctant to negotiate across-the-board reductions for fear that the United States would still emerge with relatively high tariffs on certain goods. The EEC's proposal stressed harmonization, that is to say, the reduction of high tariffs by a greater percentage than lower ones. Tariffs below 5 percent would be reduced very little, and the proposal applies to industrial but not to agricultural products. The EEC's aim is to reduce the disparities of the tariff range. The chief difficulty with this approach is that each quid pro quo must be laboriously negotiated, yielding long and cumbersome dealings when compared with the making of a uniform tariff cut. The harmonization approach may also conflict with the reciprocity principle of GATT, which assumes comparable tariff ranges and levels. The EEC insistence that the situation of agricultural products is a domestic matter not subject to negotiation also poses serious obstacles.

The conflict over negotiation methods may, in the end, lead to sector-by-sector negotiations. This approach was characteristic of pre-Kennedy rounds, and this awkward bargaining strategy may have had something to do with limited achievements in trade liberalization. The chief hope seems to lie in the linear approach, with a maximum tariff range.

Also at issue in the MTN are the preferential agreements which the EEC has concluded with associated countries. There have been U.S. hints that it favors total abolition of tariffs, which would by indirection eliminate the various preferential agreements of the EEC. For its part, the EEC has espoused trade liberalization only insofar as it does not conflict with EEC principles. The common external tariff is not considered expendable in the name of trade liberalization, and, realistically, it appears that at least nominal tariffs must be accepted. The United States must consider whether EEC trade agreements with countries such as Greece, Israel and Morocco have policitical benefits for the Atlantic Community which justify the economic costs for the United States.

## NORTH-SOUTH TRADE

Recent discussions of the commodity issue have centered on three policy goals: price stabilization, income stabilization, and stabilization of the purchasing power of less developed countries. Each of these alternatives is based on a set of different assumptions about the nature of the raw material problem.

Price stabilization proposals commonly regard commodity price fluctuations as intrinsically undesirable. The functional role of price changes in the adjustment processes of markets is slighted, and great stress is laid upon the role of speculators in the events of commodity markets. Advocates of price stabilization programs press for floor and ceiling prices on the grounds that producers and consumers alike would benefit from some degree of price stability. In practice, price stabilization programs can readily generate cycles in which high prices and production, leading to a new round of high prices, and so on. It is far from certain that higher prices will mean higher incomes for the LDCs, since falling volume, in response to higher prices, may more than offset the tendency of higher prices to raise income. The issue here turns upon the magnitude of price elasticity of demand. Typical estimates suggest that demand for most commodities is such that higher prices are likely to be associated with lower income.

Income stabilization programs are a second alternative and may be illustrated by the Lomé Agreement, which embodies a system of compensatory financing. Any shortfall in earnings is made good, whether it is due to a negative change in price or in the quantity exported by an LDC. The crucial variable in such a scheme is the average income which is to be expected from exporting a given commodity. If this figure is set at a reasonable level, the costs of compensatory financing are acceptable, especially when allowance is made for two great strengths of this alternative: it does not involve storage or other intervention costs, nor does it interfere with the vital allocative function of price.

Recently, LDCs have escalated their demands, insisting upon stable real incomes, not mere stabilization of money income. The fundamental problem is seen to be that of terms of trade, and it is argued that the purchasing power of the LDCs' export proceeds has declined steadily during the past decade. Indexation for raw materials is sought. For many reasons, this proposal must be rejected: its malignant mechanism for intensifying the cumulative, self-perpetuating tendencies already present in the process of worldwide inflation; the rigidities it would introduce into relations among subgroups of prices; and the derangements of the processes whereby the system of markets responds to the endless shifts of particular supplies and demands. Also it would injure those LDCs that are net importers of commodities.

The chief devices available for the stabilization of commodity markets are buffer stocks, purchase contracts and quotas. The effectiveness of the buffer stock approach depends on the degree of price flexibility and output control implied. In the absence of floor and ceiling prices, the quantity demanded would not be affected by the existence of buffer stocks. Administration of the buffer stock would in such case be confined to influencing supply: selling when demand is high, and buying when demand is low. In practice, this mode of administration would meet strong objections, as the exporting countries are reluctant to allow sales when demand and prices are high. Another difficulty, if supplies are not regulated, is that producers have no incentive to avoid excess production, and the buffer stock administration ends with having to buy great quantities of commodities. Buffer stocks can work only if they are reinforced by production or export quotas.

Long-term purchase contracts are another means for stabilizing raw material markets. The chief advantage is that the free market system for regulating supplies is not displaced. The main disadvantage lies in the two-price system created. This arrangement presents great temptations to exporting countries to evade their obligations when world prices are unusually high, as did some sugar producers in 1975.

Imposition of production or export quotas is a third type of stabilization device. The attractions of quotas lie in the fact that they prevent excess production and do not require financing of buffer stocks. Their disadvantages are not slight. Quotas readily yield misallocation of resources since market shares must be assigned to participants. Inefficient producers are helped to remain in production, while efficient producers supply less than optimal output. Quotas may also cause shortages and explosive price rises in bad crop years. This device consequently must be supplemented by some kind of buffer pool arrangement and so loses one of the major attractions noted above.

The method of financing commodity arrangements is an added and important issue for the Atlantic countries. The scale of requisite financing and the optimal allocation of the financial burden depend on the type of agreement acceptable to the developed countries. The required sum varies among commodities and so does the optimal strategy. Commodities which face effective competition from synthetic substitutes cannot, realistically, be priced at high levels. On the other hand, minerals facing price-inelastic demand may react to the conclusion of an agreement with a major rise in price. It is here assumed that the stabilization arrangement adopted by the Atlantic countries would be a type corresponding to a compensatory finance program.

In the absence of a broad commodity agreement, responsibility for compensatory finance could be taken by the importing countries on a national basis. The covered items, the volume and the norm could then be determined bilaterally by means either of a purchase contract or of export quotas by the exporting countries. Mineral trade would be a likely setting for such an arrangement, the situation being one where demand in the developed countries is not very price-elastic. The Atlantic countries could establish an institution to oversee fulfillment of commitments and to ensure that exporting countries keep their part of the bargain in periods of high demand.

Alternatively, the Atlantic countries could decide jointly upon national stockpiles in certain key commodities. With joint financing of such stockpiles borne by all the participating countries, prices could be managed through joint buying or releasing of stocks by the Atlantic countries. For the less developed countries, this would approximate the case of floor and ceiling prices, but they would not control sales. These practices may be compared to the open market operations of central banks, which ease or restrict supply according to market conditions.

If a broad agreement on commodity trade, covering most raw materials, is reached, the appropriate mode of funding would be multilateral. The cost of the agreed program could be shared by OPEC and the Atlantic countries. The International Monetary Fund (IMF) might be given responsibility for administration of the agreement. Now that OPEC has an increased share in the IMF, the burden could be distributed according to voting shares.

Alternatively, the financing of buffer stocks could be made the responsibility of the surplus countries. The advantage of this plan is that OPEC would contribute significantly to the stabilization effort, while Atlantic countries, such as the United Kingdom and Italy, in difficult balance-of-payments positions, would be spared added deterioration in their external positions. Still another alternative would be to set aside the proceeds of the IMF gold sale for commodity market intervention. In any event, these proceeds were destined for the Third World, and if most LDCs prefer commodity agreements to aid, a change of use for these proceeds would be called for.

The foregoing alternatives are broad types of commodity trade mechanisms. In the end, one must stress that a case-by-case approach is essential. Differing export dependencies, currency systems, demand elasticities and substitutes veto a single agreement or a single stabilization mechanism.

At long last, what is most important for the Atlantic Community is that the EEC and the United States coordinate their approaches to the commodity issue. Development of the Third World matters for both Atlantic partners. Long-term benefits warrant short-term concessions. A strategy of income stabilization, in tandem with buffer stocks and flexible prices or export quotas, would bear fruit for the Atlantic Community in political and economic advantages.

## EAST-WEST TRADE OPTIONS

East-West trade raises two fundamental issues: What balance should the Atlantic countries strike between their balance-of-payments and employment concerns and their security interests? How can private firms be prevented from supplying technology on terms that tilt the benefits of trade disproportionately in favor of the East?

One may discern two ways for the Atlantic countries to harmonize the terms of the trade credits they grant to the communist countries. The Rambouillet agreement on export loans, by analogy, provides one model. The Atlantic countries might establish a gentlemen's agreement with respect to floor levels of export credits to Eastern countries. The individual countries would then retain some discretion as to the exact rate to be charged. But will the supply of gentlemen be unfailing on all sides? The pressure of balance-of-payments problems may tempt some countries to violate the agreement.

An alternative approach would be a formal agreement on credit terms to be charged by the Atlantic countries. The OECD supplies a ready-made framework for this purpose, since it already has procedures for information on exchange credits. The Atlantic countries could determine floor rates or could impose one rate, subject to periodic review as interest rates and credit ratings of communist countries change. The floor rate option has a differential appeal in that it allows Western countries to charge lower rates to countries such as Yugoslavia. Such an arrangement, monitored by OECD or a similar agency, should end the current credit competition among Atlantic countries and ensure that the Eastern countries pay a market rate of interest.

## Military Application of Technology

There is a clear duty at this point to warn of the inadequacy of available knowledge in regard ot the broad question of the transfer of technology, and not only technology with military applications. Intensive, wide-ranging research is acutely needed; meanwhile, policymaking limps. Several kinds of problems involved in the transfer of technology may be identified.(4) The extent of transfer is not accurately measured by the transfer of a given number of publications, blueprints or documents. Much of technology is not written explicitly and frequently there is no substitute for person-to-person training for extended periods of time. Moreover, effective transfer often requires adaptation of technology to special circumstances in the receiving country, and this can be an exceedingly difficult task. Furthermore, the process of transferring technology itself can be very costly, and this important question is one that regretably has received inadequate attention.

It is clear that there has been a notable increase in the scale of U.S.-USSR technology transfer. Although the USSR commits substantial resources to research and development and has scored many noteworthy successes, Soviet technology falls short of that of the United States in many areas, including computers, integrated circuits and telecommunications. The benefits and costs to the United States of still greater transfer are not at all accurately known. For example, many experts have argued that relaxing controls on some large computer systems would have little effect on Soviet capabilities. Still other experts are much less sanguine about the wisdom of such relaxation. Viewing transfer in an economic context, there is no lack of economists to question whether the United States is getting anything of corresponding value in return. United States corporations have fretted about effects on patent rights and have argued for retroactive patent recognition. Also there has been concern about the bargaining advantage to the USSR in a structure where the State Committee on Science and Technology is arrayed against American firms. The most impressive rationale in favor of all of this invokes the alleged political or diplomatic benefits of increased transfer, but these are exceptionally difficult to predict or evaluate.

The most disturbing issue implicit in technology transfers resides in the potential military applications of technology. The 1974 amendment to the

Export Administration Act authorizes the secretary of defense to determine whether proposed exports increase significantly the military potential of communist countries. With only thirty days to make this decision, the secretary lacks the opportunity to analyze carefully the long-range impact of the technology to be transferred. Moreover, the heterogeneous standards of European countries for technology transfers provide the communist country the chance to get from one country the technology it was denied by another.

As an attempt to deal with this situation, the United States might seek to strengthen the International Export Control Coordinating Committee and thus bring to an OECD level the matters of technology transfer and reexport transfer standards and procedures. It must be conceded that this agency might well lack the requisite authority in view of the limited willingness of European and Japanese governments to cooperate more closely with the United States on this issue.

If technology transfers must be monitored on a national level, the American reviewing and evaluating process must lay more stress upon coordination. Several agencies and committees are involved in this process without central authority and unambiguous policy guidelines. The current emphasis of the Carter Administration upon the general reorganization of government, in the interests of greater effectiveness, may provide a highly favorable opportunity to designate some agency to assume the coordinating function for technology transfers. This agency could, conceivably, exchange information with European agencies, with the possibility of some interagency harmonization.

## Pricing of Exports to Communist Countries

Communist countries have been skillful about extracting favorable terms by pitting Western firms against one another. There are three ways of dealing with this issue.

One alternative is to exempt from antitrust prosecution firms which collude for the purpose of dealing with communist countries. Since most communist countries operate a bid system, information exchange among the bidding firms would permit charging average rather than marginal costs to communist buyers. Coordination of bids would ensure that profit levels on sales to communist countries would approximate those on domestic sales. One disadvantage of this approach is that the competitors may use this communication process to conspire about prices in the home market as well.

A second option would have an agency such as the Bureau of East-West Trade gather information on bids. The agency would circulate information to the bidding firms after the bidding deadlines. This would prevent diffusion of false information in regard to the actual levels of bids and reduce the possibilities of buyer-induced price cutting.

The system might also be operated on an Atlantic level. The gathering of bids by an agency such as OECD could arrange for the communist countries to pay for the research and development costs of the technology they acquire. Sellers would be encouraged to charge average costs. The buyers would be handicapped in price cutting strategies, since full information on the range of bids would be available to Western firms.

## OVERCOMING THE CULT OF DEFENSIVE ECONOMIC NATIONALISM

Against a background of the wide range of trade issues and policies considered in the foregoing pages, we come now to the choice of a model for Atlantic trade relations in the coming decade. The requirements of functional adequacy are deeply in conflict with those of political acceptability among the members of the Atlantic Community. No approach model is optimal with respect to both of these sets of considerations, and some compromises must be accepted.

The requirements of functional adequacy have grown more stringent in the postwar period. There was a time when optimal trade policy was viewed by the received tradition in economics primarily in terms of promoting worldwide specialization, competition and efficiency in the expectation of maximizing the rise of real income. Openness and interdependence among nations were to be pursued to heroic limits. But interdependence means vulnerability of the domestic economy to disturbances originating in foreign countries, and, clearly, some sort of shock-absorbing mechanisms were necessary.

It once was believed widely that flexible exchange rates would effectively insulate individual economies and make it possible for a domestic stabilization policy to be pursued separately by each nation. That faith has been shaken severely by the events of recent years. Now it is argued commonly that flexible exchange rates are poor insulators against foreign disturbances, and, furthermore, that the force of some disturbance is intensified in the presence of flexible rates.

All of this suggests that the Atlantic Community and Japan need to submit to extraordinary changes in the institutional arrangements and practices which frame and administer trade policy and domestic stabilization policy. To be more specific, it means that the monetary and fiscal policies of the member nations must be closely coordinated. In the absence of effective insulating devices, there appears to be no other way to reconcile a high degree of openness in trade and finance with the maintenance of tolerable unemployment and inflation rates. Nationally determined monetary and fiscal policies have become increasingly anachronistic in a world where the macroeconomic excesses of some nations quickly become the induced instabilities of other nations.

To say all this is to state the requirements of a functionally adequate trade relations model in extraordinarily demanding terms. Nothing less than a partnership model, hopefully fortified by Japanese cooperation, seems adequate for such a vast departure from nationally determined stabilization policies.

We come at last to the question of political acceptability. What is functionally adequate for the needs of the case far exceeds what is likely to be acceptable in the Atlantic Community, where the ideology of openness and interdependency is unmistakably on the defensive. On every side, a rival ideology, defensive economic natonalism, enjoys a strong ascendance. One has only to reflect on the current loss of momentum and the elusiveness of consensus on vital matters within the EEC to sense the utopian character of any proposal to coordinate monetary and fiscal policies throughout the

Atlantic Community in order to make the world safe for openness and interdependence. It is difficult to envision much more than the cooperative-competitive model with its wide scope for the play for national interests.

Unless sanity and a more enlightened selfishness prevail on both sides of the Atlantic, the cult of defensive economic nationalism foreshadows a decade in which the ingenuity of governments will be lavished on the mutual destruction of trade opportunities and the unconscious sabotage of the growth of world trade, all in the name of macroeconomic autonomy. In the end, it is doubtful that the nations involved will like any better the mixture of unemployment and inflation as well as real income per capita that they will get in this way.

## NOTES

(1) Monthly Economic Letter -- Citibank, March 1977, p. 9 et seq.

(2) Richard N. Cooper, The Economics of Interdependence (New York: McGraw Hill, 1968).

(3) D. Gale Johnson, Farm Commodity Programs (Washington, D.C.: American Enterprise Institute, 1973), p. 76.

(4) Edwin Mansfield, "East-West Technological Transfer Issues and Problems" The American Economic Review, May 1975.

# 16 Conclusion

Walter F. Hahn
Robert L. Pfaltzgraff, Jr.

The "Atlantic Community" emerged from World War II as a geographical-cultural description and as an ideal for the unity of democratic societies on both sides of the Atlantic. As a description, the term included those parts of the Western world that, in the aftermath of the "great fratricidal conflict," joined together in the face of a new danger arising over Europe's devastated landscape. In a geographical sense, the Atlantic Community embraced essentially the countries to the west of the Iron Curtain that was drawn through the center of Europe after World War II. The significance of the adjective "Atlantic" (rather than simply "Western") related to the momentous decision by the United States to link its own destiny permanently with kindred nations in Western Europe and thus to abandon the isolationism of the earlier twentieth century.

The Atlantic Community concept embodied the heritage of Hellenism, the Judeo-Christian religions, the spirit of scientific inquiry, the tenets of pluralism, and representative government, all of which represent values central to Western civilization. Yet, it seems fair to generalize in retrospect that this "cultural cement" was subsumed under the "cement of fear." In its initial manifestation, the Atlantic Community was essentially a defensive concept, which found tangible expression in the military realm – in the North Atlantic Treaty Organization.

The Atlantic Community as an ideal was based upon the need to exploit the impetus of fear and to reach beyond it toward lasting institutions of unity. As is succinctly pointed out in the initial chapters of this volume, the ideal has been blighted to a large extent by the variegated nature of its appeals and interpretations. It has inspired "Atlanticists" and "Europeanists" – the latter being distinguished from the former, not necessarily by their denial of the Atlantic Concept writ large, but by their inordinate emphasis on the evolution of Europe as the determining factor in the transatlantic relationship. Both "Atlanticists" and "Europeanists" have espoused various models grouped around federal and confederal precepts.

Perhaps the inescapable fact to emerge from the conceptual history of the

Atlantic Community is that the community concept as a structured ideal has faded from the official dialogue among the countries of Western Europe and North America as an inspiration of practical politics. The last real clarion summons to a more or less explicit structure of transatlantic relations came in President Kennedy's "Grand Design" of 1962, which featured the model of a partnership of equals between the United States and a unifying Western Europe.

It may be argued that the Nixon Administration's notion of partnership with allies represented a refurbishment of the ideal from the American vantage point. Central to the concept of partnership in the Nixon-Kissinger era was the emergence of new centers of power, notably Western Europe and Japan, which might share more equitably the burdens borne since World War II by the United States. Nevertheless, the Nixon-Kissinger partnership notion did not provide a specific structure for relationships among allies. In contrast to previous U.S. Administrations, President Nixon did not "view our allies as pieces in an American 'grand design,' "(1) but rather as parts of an emerging global system based upon a diffusion of power. In such a system the United States supposedly gained greater flexibility and maneuverability in dealing both with allies and adversaries.

This is not the place to engage in an extended critique of the Atlantic policies of U.S. Administrations, past or present. All American presidents since World War II have attached high priority to the transatlantic relationship. There is no question, nevertheless, that the trends since the early 1960s have featured a lowering of that priority relative to other emergent policy concerns, particularly the growth in U.S.-Soviet bilateralism, the U.S. preoccupation with the conflict in Southeast Asia, and the spate of economic problems besetting the industrialized world in the wake of the October War in the Middle East.

Especially after the traumatic American withdrawal from Southeast Asia, President Carter could assume office in 1977 with a restatement of U.S. emphasis on alliance relations within a trilateral framework of collaboration among the United States, Western Europe and Japan in coping with the great issues of the late twentieth century – allegedly more economic than military-political in nature. After more than one year of the Carter Administration, however, this emphasis has yet to be expressed concretely in U.S. policies. Indeed, American policy, in the present context, displays the elements of unpredictability for which previous administrations have been justly criticized – yet, continues to display them in an era in which the overall military balance is shifting to the disadvantage of the West. Hence, the United States and its Atlantic allies face the prospects of a weakened alliance relationships without having achieved a central goal of American (and European) policy: namely, a position vis-a-vis the Soviet Union adequate to the security needs of the states of the Atlantic Community. Such is the ominous trend noted in several of the chapters of this volume.

(1) Cited in Walter F. Hahn, "The Nixon Doctrine: Design and Dilemmas," ORBIS, Summer 1972, p. 369.

## THE FADING OF THE COMMUNITY IDEAL

What accounts for the waxing and waning of ideals such as the Atlantic Community? Historians, sociologists, political scientists, and psychologists who have attempted to probe the ideological variable in human behavior generally have been baffled by the phenomenon. They tend to agree that the ideal as an inspirational force is a function, not so much of the compelling logic or inherent magnetic quality of the ideal itself, but rather of the human needs and goals which it purportedly serves. In those terms, a rudimentary distinction can be drawn between the transcendental ideals of personal redemption that infuse the world's great religions and the temporal ideals of social and political movements and ideologies. Both set of ideals rise and fall with the intensity of perceived human needs. Yet, since transcendental ideals, by definition, relate to human spiritual needs that function more or less independently of the social and political, their half-life in the historical span tends to be longer. By contrast, temporal ideals are much more at the mercy of societal change.

To that extent, Maslow's "individual need hierarchy," noted in Chapter 2 of this volume to describe the evolution of the psychological environment of the Atlantic Community, provides a convenient framework of historical analysis. National behavior and national policies never mirror perfectly the attitudes and predilections of constituencies, but in democratic societies they reflect at least the dominant themes in those attitudes and predilections. There is no question, furthermore, that the Atlantic ideal, as an expression of postwar aspirations, particularly on the European side of the Atlantic, has been dimmed to a large extent by its own success – even though partial. It was in an Atlantic framework that the historic experiment of the Marshall Plan generated the economic recovery which met the "physical needs" of a war-ravaged continent. And it was in an Atlantic framework, namely NATO, that the "security needs" were met, thus permitting Western Europe greater potential for the pursuit of other goals in the generation after World War II.

These simple categories of evolution admittedly do not tell the whole story; they cannot account fully for the variable that might be called leadership caprice. Neither the Atlantic Ideal nor the European Ideal has recovered from the battering that each received from De Gaulle and Gaullism in the 1960s. Although Europeanism and Atlanticism had different emphasis and priorities, both aimed at a broad and logical confluence: unity of the Western peoples within an Atlantic framework. De Gaulle's historic disservice was twofold: he set forces of Atlanticism and Europeanism against one another, and he reintroduced the virus of nationalism into European and transatlantic relationships. Were both inevitable manifestations of the European drive for "self-actualization"? Could not the drive have been channeled into directions more compatible with the Atlantic Ideal?

A sense of history may sustain a reasonable continuum of attitudes and behavior in a society from one generation to the next, but that continuum is vulnerable to the advent of a leadership elite with a substantially different experience from its predecessors. The new elite that is ascending to positions of power on both sides of the Atlantic (if not yet the very highest levels of government) has no direct memories of the traumatic period that spawned the

Atlantic Ideal: World War II and its immediate aftermath.

With some exceptions to be sure, this new elite differs from its predecessors in the conception it holds of the emerging world of the late twentieth century. For example, there is a fashionable tendency in this rising generation to view the forces shaping this world as primarily economic and social ones. Military capabilities supposedly count for little in a global system in which security must be defined in far broader terms. The Soviet Union is held to be largely irrelevant to the great issues of the emergent future – those essentially of a North-South relationship. In such a world view, the Atlantic Community concept of the post-World War II era appears as an anachronistic Cold War leftover and as an impediment to the development of an agenda for action to deal effectively with the problems of the future.

This generational gap may be deeper in the United States than in Western Europe. Historically, American foreign policy vistas have ranged westward at least as much as eastward as a logical extention of the manifest destiny which drove America's expansion and national development ot the Pacific shores: it was reinforced psychologically by antipathy to the injustices, power politics and social stratification of Europe that had propelled the waves of immigrants to the New World. To generations of Americans, Europe represented a past with limited opportunities that had been rejected for the promise and ideals of a New World. Thus, the belated American entry into World War I was followed by a return to isolationism symbolizing the rejection by the United States of full participation in the interwar system that was still largely Eurocentric.

Therefore, the post-World War II American leadership generation – in the words of former Secretary of State Dean Acheson, those "present at the creation" of the postwar accords – was in many ways unique. It was a generation imbued with the memories of World War II, the failure of efforts, symbolized by the Munich agreements, to appease Hitler, and the devastation of World War II. This direct historical experience led the postwar leadership generation of the United States to link its future security directly to a permanent participation in European affairs – and to a massive involvement symbolized by the Truman Doctrine following Great Britain's retrenchment in 1947.

The postwar generation is passing from the scene. Its most prominent members have already departed from positions of influence on both sides of the Atlantic. The implications of this transition, to be sure, may be overdrawn. Even if the centrifugal tendencies in the Atlantic Community are more manifest, they are mitigated by the residual pull of European and Atlantic institutions and by the force of global events. The emerging elites in Western Europe may not instinctively "think Atlantic," but the entwined economies, lowered barriers to the flow of people and commerce, and, perhaps most important of all, the sweep of instant communications, together with unprecedented human mobility, predispose them in one measure or another to "think European."

In the United States as well there are countervailing trends against the neoisolationist mood that asserted itself markedly in later phases of the American engagement in Vietnam. The value structures and intuitive priorities of the rising leadership generation in the United States differ substantially from those of a generation or even a decade ago. This new generation not only has no real links with World War II and its direct aftermath, but has been influenced in one measure or another by the great rebellion of the 1960s against the assumptions of the Munich generation – a rebellion that was nurtured by the intellectual fashion of historical revisionism and reached a peak in the protest movements of the Vietnam era. Even in the United States, however, a person in his or her thirties, who is nearing positions of power and influence, may remember the fashions and experiences of formative adulthood. Nevertheless, he or she must face a certain logic of trends and their policy implications. The economist must be sensitive to the interdependence of the American economy and those of the other industrialized nations, especially those of Western Europe. The foreign policy specialist must pay due attention to Western Europe – especially to the extent that the disillusionment that blighted U.S. policy in Southeast Asia has refocused the attention of U.S. policy upon Western Europe.

Notwithstanding such mitigating factors, however, the implications of trends on both sides of the Atlantic are clear and must be confronted realistically by even the most dedicated Atlanticists. In terse formulation, these implications are the following:

1. It is true that especially since Vietnam, the United States has placed priority on the structuring of its military capabilities for contingencies related to Western Europe. Except for defense, however, the Atlantic Community is no longer the priority framework for policy in the United States and Western Europe, and, as noted in several chapters, trends in comparative NATO and Warsaw Pact force levels do not augur well for the Atlantic Alliance. Since a new elite generation on both sides of the Atlantic does not identify with the Community concept in any ideological sense, the commitment of the United States to the security of Western Europe, in a period of strategic-military parity or worse, rests upon weaker foundations than it did a generation ago.

2. It follows from the above that what has been characterized as the Atlantic Ideal – the concept of some permanent institutional structure embracing North America and Western Europe – no longer can exert as great appeal as it did in the post-World War II period. Only a "catalytic event" might be sufficient to restore this appeal. Such a "catalytic event" could come about in the unlikely contingency of a new war in Europe, or the emergence of the measure of imbalance in East-West military power that would in effect recreate the cement of fear as a dominant and unifying consensus on both sides of the Atlantic. The "catalytic event" could also be in the form of a devasting economic crisis sweeping the industrialized world in the wake of energy shortages and other dislocations.

3. Although the Atlantic Community, strictly defined, no longer provides a compelling framework for common action – especially in the crucial period immediately ahead – nevertheless, there is no escaping the continued priority of the transatlantic relationship in dealing with the problems of the next decade that have been the object of analysis in this volume. In defense, the nature of the problem can be summarized succinctly: to continue to harness the capabilities of the United States and its Atlantic allies to prevent the utilization by the Soviet Union of preponderant military power against

Western Europe for political gain – Finlandization. For this purpose, the Atlantic Alliance remains indispensable.

4. United States relations with Asian states are crucial to transatlantic relationships as well as a coherent framework of global policies. The Sino-Soviet split has provided American diplomacy with potential leverage against Moscow and Peking. Both the United States and Western Europe, as well as Japan, have benefited from the division between the two states whose recombined power would alter fundamentally, and perhaps irreversibly, the power balance in Eurasia. Hence, the future course of the Sino-Soviet schism holds implications for the security of Western Europe and the principal allies of the United States in East Asia, notably the Republic of Korea and Japan.

5. Security relationships between the United States and Western Europe affect the security relationships between the United States and Japan and vice versa. But this is not to suggest a broadening of the Atlantic Alliance beyond its present geographic bounds, or to propose that the security of Japan be linked institutionally with that of Western Europe. The linkage between Asian/Pacific security and European security must continue to lie in the commitment of the United States to the security of Western Europe and East Asia – to maintain adequate levels of American capabilities in both the North Atlantic and the Asian/Pacific areas. In light of the formidable Soviet military power arrayed against the rimlands of Europe and China, only the United States has the potential, assisted by its allies, to provide countervailing power. The projection of American power for the protection of allies and other states is as indispensable to the United States in the late twentieth century as it was in an earlier era.

6. While the framework for NATO defense must of necessity remain specifically Euro-American, the Atlantic Community states and Japan form the central grouping in the resolution of major economic issues of the twentieth century. These include the continued increase of trade, the stimulation of economic growth, the management of inflation, the resolution of monetary problems, the most effective utilization of existing energy supplies, and the development of new sources of energy.

7. For the above purposes the two indispensable prerequisities are, first of all, enlightened leadership on both sides of the Atlantic that transcends popular vagaries and apathy (a prerequisite that admittedly is more easily summoned than fulfilled) and, secondly, an emphasis on pragmatism. In this context, pragmatism connotes the avoidance of comprehensive "grand designs" and the careful tuning of basic models of relationships to the requirements of functional problem areas. Expressed differently, the model of "partnership," while it may have validity in economic relationships between the United States and the European Community, cannot accommodate the problems facing the Atlantic Alliance in the military-security realm. In turn, an Atlantic framework remains indispensable to the Alliance's military posture and deployments, but can be expected to have little relevance to U.S.-West European economic interaction and the general flow of policy cooperation (e.g., with respect to such volatile issue areas as the Middle East, Africa and the Third World more broadly).

## DEFENSE AND THE ATLANTIC IMPERATIVE

It is a principal thesis of this volume that the military sphere – embracing the U.S.-Soviet strategic-nuclear balance, the theater confrontation between NATO and the Warsaw Pact, as well as the emergence of threats to NATO lifelines outside the North Atlantic area – represents the decisive arena in terms of the survival of the Atlantic nations as independent and viable entities, and the most dangerous arena in the light of plausible projections over the next decade-and-a-half of Soviet-Warsaw Pact military power relative to that of the United States and its allies.

This thesis runs counter to assumptions that have become conventional in the West during the past decade – assumptions noted earlier in this chapter regarding the growing inutility of military force in the contemporary political environment and the alleged primacy of economic and social factors in determining both national power and the systemic competition between the West and East. These assumptions have played a substantial role in pushing and in rationalizing the relative decline of Western military power from its apex in the early 1960s to a point where the West contemplates Soviet and Warsaw Pact superiority across the full spectrum of military capabilities – from the strategic-nuclear to the conventional levels.

As pointed out in Chapter 3, notions about the relative inutility of military force have abounded, particularly in the United States. Together with a sense of overconfidence and faulty projections regarding both Soviet intentions and military programs – and exacerbated by the American preoccupaton with the Vietnam war – these notions contributed to the fateful decisions in the 1960s that led to the decline in U.S. strategic power and in general purpose forces relative to the Soviet Union. The strategic transformation has been abetted by a sincere but myopic American arms control approach to both strategy and weapons – an approach that has led to an underestimation both of the capabilities adequate to wage war and of an opponent who rejects the deterrence concepts so prevalent in the West in favor of strategic-military superiority across-the-board. Although concern is mounting in the United States over the growing vulnerability of U.S. fixed land-based ICBMs to a Soviet disarming first strike, there still seems to be a generally inadequate grasp – even at the decision-making levels of the United States government – of the implications of an accelerating strategic transformation for the tides of international politics and specifically for the linkage between U.S. strategic forces and the deterrence of conflict in Europe.

Notwithstanding internal problems and recurrent factional rivalry, Soviet strategy remains geared to (1) a coherent sense of purpose and objectives; (2) an orthodox view of the purpose and role of military force – a view that has not been basically shaken by the advent of nuclear weapons; and (3) a sensitivity to the interaction between the trends of power and the trends of politics (the correlation of forces). Moscow has made military power into the spearhead of political aspirations; there simply is no other plausible explanation for the unrelenting Soviet and Warsaw Pact military buildup in the face of flagging Western armament efforts of the past decade.

The trajectory of Soviet aspirations is a more controversial subject. Yet, both Soviet pronouncements and East-West military trend projections point to a possible denouement in the mid-1980s, when a substantial and a clear-cut margin of superiority in the strategic-nuclear equation and at the European theater level could induce the Soviet Union to press its objectives more ambitiously and daringly. The likelihood remains low that the Soviet Union will invoke military force in open combat and direct conquest (although the contingency of a lightning "smash grab" in NATO Europe for territorial and/or political objectives cannot be discounted, nor can Soviet military action in areas peripheral but critical to NATO, e.g., Yugoslavia). The stronger probability is that Moscow will continue to use the imposing shadow of Soviet military capability to (1) effect the decoupling of the American strategic deterrent from the defense of Western Europe; (2) press expanding inroads of political and economic influence into NATO Europe; and (3) hold superiority at the strategic-nuclear level as the ultimate counter-deterrent against an American reaction to the "inexorable processes of history."

There is also a defensive cast to the Soviet military buildup – defensive, but not in the traditional military sense. If one reads between the lines of some of the Soviet leadership's statements (particularly Brezhnev's confident remarks in Prague in 1973 about the ultimate rewards of Soviet strategy), one gains at least the inference that Moscow embraces in the goal of unchallenged military superiority and its hegemonial implications the promise also of settling the internal problems of the Soviet Union and the socialist camp more generally. From the vicarious vantage point of Moscow, the reasoning could be as follows: There are stumbling blocks on the road to the perfect socialist society, particularly in the economic realm. Detente is designed to help ease these problems in the short run, especially in the form of technological transfusion from the West. But detente also helps to stir "residual bourgeois dissidence" in the socialist system. In the longer term, military superiority, and the power it radiates, will solve these problems. Political-military hegemony will reap an economic harvest; it will also stifle dissidence (or render it irrelevant) by depriving it of any hope of external support.

In any event, NATO faces probably the climactic phase of its existence as an alliance during the next ten years. Given current trends in the Alliance, the prognosis posited in Chapter 3 must be accepted as realistic: namely, that despite a heightened recognition of danger, the governments of the Alliance are not likely to allocate funds of the magnitude that would be adequate to meet the challenge head-on – comparable, say, to the crash military buildup inaugurated in the early 1950s. The only alternative available to the Alliance is a holding strategy based upon tactical and doctrinal adaptation and exploitation of the existing, but narrowing, Western edge in technological proficiency.

Various measures to stem the erosion of NATO forces relative to the Warsaw Pact are detailed in the military section of this study and need not be repeated here. Essentially they fall into the following categories:

1. <u>Sustaining, or restoring, a linkage between U.S. strategic forces and the defense of Europe</u>. It has been emphasized that this critical imperative for the Alliance relates as much to image and perception as to objective capabilities. But the continued linkage between U.S. strategic forces and

European security is increasingly in doubt as the Soviet Union acquires by the mid-1980s the capacity to place at risk most, and perhaps all, of the fixed land-based U.S. strategic force. The modernization and expansion of NATO regional nuclear systems, with emphasis on weapons capable of reaching targets to the Soviet Union, will become an even more pressing priority for NATO in light of the development of Soviet strategic systems targeted against the United States as well as the new generation Soviet nuclear Eurostrategic systems, especially the SS-20 and the Backfire bomber, targeted against Western Europe. The accent here is on the underlying rationale of deterrence: to the extent that the credibility of the extended deterrent function of the U.S. strategic force is weakened, the visible tokens of the risk of escalation in Europe need to be magnified. Stated differently, the impressive growth of Soviet-Warsaw Pact forces, based on a structure and posture calling for surprise and preemption to strike before full NATO mobilization can be achieved, provides a potential for waging, and perhaps winning, a future war in Europe. Soviet doctrine draws no distinction between nuclear and conventional phases of warfare. This runs counter to some views in the U.S. strategic community that have drawn the opposite conclusion in favor of progressive denuclearization in Europe.

2. Blunting a potential Warsaw Pact surprise attack. The vast scope of modernization and expansion of Soviet-Warsaw Pact forces over the past decade has created a military capability far in excess of purely defensive needs in East-Central Europe. As the authors of Chapter 5 note, the emphasis of Soviet-Warsaw Pact military doctrine and force posture is on the primacy of offensive action. Soviet-War Pact forces are configured for high-speed maneuver with a sustained combat capability and utilize a combined arms concept. In continuous daytime and nighttime operations, the Warsaw Pact would attempt to overrun forward NATO positions, especially stores of tactical nuclear weapons and the supply lines linking U.S. forces in the south of Germany with other NATO units. The immense growth of Soviet airpower and naval capabilities increasingly places in doubt the ability of the United States and its NATO allies to control the air space over Western Europe and the transatlantic sea lanes – indispensable as they would be to the reinforcement of NATO front-line forces. The massed Soviet-Warsaw Pact mechanized and armor formations – in particular Soviet tanks, armored personnel carriers, and advanced armored fighting vehicles – are designed to overrun Western Europe in days and weeks, not months, as has been postulated in NATO planning.

Unlike NATO, Warsaw Pact doctrine does not draw clearcut distinctions between the conventional and nuclear phases of combat in Europe. Warsaw Pact forces are trained to use not only nuclear weapons, but chemical warfare. In light of the quantitative and qualitative growth of Pact forces, the question facing NATO is whether adequate warning time could be available in advance of an attack. Could the Warsaw Pact launch a surprise strike from a standing start or under the guise of maneuvers? As the authors of Chapter 5 conclude, NATO forces in their present configuration, based upon the assumption that adequate warning time will be available, make such a Warsaw Pact strategy highly suitable from the Soviet perspective, since it strikes Western forces when they are at their weakest and so maximizes the opportunities for swift and decisive victory.

Thus, NATO faces the prospect of a decisive shift in the theater military balance within Europe at a time when the credibility of a U.S. strategic nuclear guarantee for Europe is in doubt. It is in this context that the unfolding trends in the European theater balance become ominous for NATO, for the threat of escalation to the superpower level has provided a fundamental premise of the U.S.-West European defense relationship in the Atlantic Alliance: the ability of the United States to inflict unacceptable levels of damage upon the Soviet Union in the event of a Warsaw Pact attack against Western Europe.

Hence, NATO forces available at an early, indeed the earliest, stage in a NATO-Warsaw Pact conflict must be strengthened. These include tactical airpower to ensure control of airspace in Europe; the creation of greater mobility for existing divisions; the stockpiling of equipment for additional tank divisions; greater protection for stockpiled materials in Europe; and the upgrading of NATO firepower by means of new generation weapons, including precision-guided munitions, cruise missiles and theater nuclear weapons.

It is the central thesis of this study that these urgent tasks in the military arena can be accomplished only within an Atlantic framework. The concept of a true partnership within NATO – of a relationship of near-equals between the United States and some form of West European defense community – is an idea whose time either is past or has yet to come. In the present and emerging environment, the idea founders against several hard and immovable facts. The continuing, and heightened, need for a U.S. commitment to European security, which even in theory could be replaced only by formidable European nuclear deterrent capabilities; the impressive growth of Warsaw Pact capabilities which can be countered only by an augmented and integrated NATO effort and force posture-in-being at the front lines; and the faltering progress in Western Europe toward the level of political unity that is essential for the support of a common West European defense establishment and decision-making machinery.

The same caveat applies – albeit with more qualifications – to the technological base of the Alliance which must sustain the concerted effort in the decade ahead. The basic conclusion of the analysis contained in Chapters 6 to 8 is relatively simple: a heightened measure of intra-European and transatlantic cooperation in defense research, development and procurement is mandatory, not only as part of a more rational NATO technological strategy – especially if the Alliance is to meet the hard military requirements that have been outlined – but also of the economic strength of the nations involved. The initiatives undertaken in this respect under the auspices of the NATO Eurogroup are salutary. The United States must contribute to a two-way street in NATO defense R&D and procurement. Yet, there are limits to the traffic on this "two-way street." These parameters are set, on the one hand, by American proficiency in certain key sectors of high technology and, on the other, by the national and particularist restraining walls in Western Europe, as well as the intrinsic narrowness of the domestic markets of Western Europe.

In the final analysis, the limits of an institutionalized "two-way street" are determined by time and urgency. NATO needs a more rational and efficient division of labor in expanding and exploiting its technological base. Yet, the urgency of the technological task that has been outlined – and the leadtimes involved – militate against any preoccupying search for perfect models of cooperation. What is needed in the critical short run is (1) a consultative mechanism at the highest levels of the Alliance that determines the priority technological requirements and identifies the on-the-self technologies able to meet them, and (2) an increased technological effort by all NATO members. There is no reason why the search for longer-range models for economic and political unity and cooperation cannot proceed in tandem; it cannot, however, be allowed to detract from the urgency of the more immediate needs if NATO is to provide an adequate counterpoise to growing Soviet-Warsaw military capabilities.

## THE ARENA OF ECONOMICS AND RESOURCES

During the past decade, economic issues have gained a certain dominance in the transatlantic relationship. They have impinged directly upon defense, to the extent that Atlantic states have confronted constraints upon defense spending arising from other demands upon economic capabilities and resources. As noted elsewhere in this volume, the principal economic issues facing the Atlantic Community include the increase in inflation, the breakdown of an international monetary system based on fixed exchange rates in the early 1970s, the quest for new means of financing world trade, and the continued need to guard against a revival of protectionism and to expand world trade. Each has been the object of efforts at the European level and, on a broader basis, Western Europe, Canada, the United States, and, since the early 1960s, Japan. Postwar efforts embodied in the Marshall Plan to speed European recovery from World War II, the formation of the European Community to maximize the potential for trade within Western Europe, and the efforts of the United States and the European Community to reduce barriers to trade have represented policy issues of central importance to the transatlantic relationship. Without the dynamism displayed by the economies of Western Europe and the United States, the unprecedented growth of the international economic system in the generation after World War II would not have been possible.

In the decade of the 1970s all industrialized states have faced formidable economic problems. The economic achievements of the 1960s have not been sustained in the growth patterns of the 1970s. The energy crisis of 1973-1974, with its fourfold increase in oil prices, resulted in drastically lowered growth rates in all industrialized states and a recession of proportions unprecedented since the interwar period. The heavy dependence of Western Europe and Japan and, to a lesser extent, the United States upon oil imports pointed up their vulnerability to externally generated inflation in the form of higher oil prices. In the aftermath of the October War, industrial states opted for a variety of measures, some on a unilateral basis, others with the collaboration of most industrialized states. The greater the perceived need for immediate solutions to the energy crisis, as suggested in Chapter 13, the greater the emphasis on strictly unilateral action by energy import-dependent states.

In the period ahead, economic issues will continue to loom large in the transatlantic relationship, as the authors of several chapters of this volume have pointed out. In the absence of more efficient energy utilization, the United States will continue to import oil in substantially greater amounts than at the time of the Middle East war of October 1973.

The precipitous decline in the value of the dollar in international currency markets, the revival of inflationary pressures in the United States, and the huge balance of payments deficits experienced by the United States in 1977-1978 do not augur well for the transatlantic relationship in the period ahead. Already they have produced frictions – in particular, U.S. efforts to prod the Federal Republic of Germany and Japan to pursue expansionary policies to reflate their economies. In turn, the United States itself has been the object of criticism for allegedly having permitted the value of the U.S. dollar to decline substantially in order to increase the competitiveness of U.S. exports and to produce an effective decline in the price of oil which is denominated in U.S. dollars. At the same time, the United States has experienced a rapid rise in direct investment by foreigners – Europeans, Japanese, and nationals from oil-producing states. Essentially two reasons account for this phenomenon: the favorable exchange rate for foreign investors purchasing dollars and the relative safety of the United States as a haven for those concerned about future political stability in their own countries.

Whether the economic issues, existing and emergent, hold the potential for a major new recession, or depression, in the industrialized world is problematical. At the very least, they provide evidence of the need for continuing efforts, described elsewhere in this volume, to concert the economic policies of Atlantic Community states and Japan. The onset of economic crisis – a "crash" of the early 1980s – would complicate immensely, and perhaps hopelessly, the necessary efforts that have been prescribed earlier in this chapter with respect to the common military defense.

Energy-related issues will continue to pose formidable problems for the transatlantic relationship in the next decade. The continuing dependence of Western Europe and Japan upon imports of oil from the Persian Gulf, together with the increased U.S. demand for oil imports, may place greater burdens upon existing oil producers. It is conceivable that the Soviet Union and East European states will become dependent upon imports of oil from the same sources as the West in the 1980s. Such a projection, discussed in Chapter 13, poses the prospect of resource competition among Atlantic Community states, and between the Soviet Union and theWest. Hence, the growing Soviet potential for the projection of military power to the Persian Gulf, the Horn of Africa and Southern Africa, together with the emergence of greater Soviet naval power in vitally important sealanes, constitute an ominous development that could confront the United States, Western Europe and Japan with a serious threat to their energy supplies in the 1980s.

The effect of the rise in oil prices during the mid-1970s has been to increase the economic feasibility of alternative energy sources, notably North Sea oil and nuclear power. The former has already begun to provide, for Britain and Norway, oil reserves of importance for their economies. But the respite for the British economy, in particular, afforded by oil revenues from the North Sea is likely to be short-lived. In the absence of a restructuring of

Britain's economyto achieve sustained rates of growth and industrial modernization, the North Sea oil boom will leave a bitter legacy in the form of payments deficits stemming from import demand spawned during the 1980s. The inability of Britain to reverse her long-term economic decline, even with the aid of North Sea oil, would undoubtedly strengthen those forces which already seek protection for British industry in a low-grade economy.

Nuclear power holds the potential for reducing substantially the dependence of the United States, Western Europe and Japan upon oil for certain energy needs, especially the generation of electricity. But nuclear energy also has become a divisive issue within the Atlantic Alliance. The European Community and Japan will develop the fast breeder reactor as a means of reducing dependence upon imports of oil and uranium – the latter a resource that could be exhausted by the early twenty-first century. Because of potential shortages of uranium, the energy import-dependent allies of the United States are determined to press development of the fast breeder reactor and to reduce their dependence upon imports of uranium, or at least in the short term to diversify their sources of supply. The United States, however, seeks to retard the development of the fast breeder reactor because of the possibility that weapons-grade enriched plutonium will be produced, and to tighten safeguards for the use of enriched uranium exported to Western Europe. Because of the growing interest in, and dependence upon, this energy source in the late twentieth century, nuclear power is likely to give rise to future discord at the transatlantic level.

From the analysis contained in the economic chapters of this volume, several specific policy conclusions emerge as central to the resolution of the economic issues confronting the states of the Atlantic Community in the period just ahead:

1. As Brian Griffiths suggests in Chapter 12, the growth of the money supply has been closely related to the increase in inflationary pressures that have plagued most industrialized states in recent years. Although the causes of inflation are numerous, those countries which have experienced high rates of inflation have had great increases in money supply. Moreover, there is a relationship between the rate of growth of the money supply, the rate of growth of money income, the balance of payments and exchange rates, the level of interest rates and the rate of inflation. Thus, the need exists, both within Atlantic Community states, and in collaboration among them, to evolve monetary policies that control the money supply more effectively and provide at the same time for stable monetary growth. Such policies at the national level cannot be pursued in isolation from their effects on other states. In consultation with their counterparts in other Atlantic Community states central banks should set for themselves specific targets for monetary growth for periods of at least one year.

2. Continued efforts should be made on both sides of the Atlantic to reach agreement on tolerable (low) levels of inflation as an important prerequisite to monetary union, especially in the European Community, but also as a key element in the economic recovery of Atlantic Community states.

3. A return to fixed exchange rates is neither a likely, nor necessarily desirable, prospect in the period ahead, although, as pointed out in Chapter 12, periods of fluctuating exchange rates have usually been followed by a

return to fixed rates. The experience of recent years, as Lawrence Bell suggests, have shaken the earlier faith that flexible exchange rates could effectively insulate individual economies and make it possible for each nation separately to pursue its own domestic stabilization policy. If, as it is now more fashionable to argue, flexible exchange rates are poor insulators against externally generated disturbances in domestic economies, then the states of the Atlantic Community and Japan must, as noted above, coordinate their monetary policies.

The states of the Atlantic Community must also engage in more effective collaboration in the development of their respective fiscal policies. There is no other effective way to reconcile the growth of trade based upon lowered barriers – itself an important and continuing goal of the Atlantic Community and Japan – with the maintenance of tolerable levels of unemployment and inflation. In short, at a time when economic nationalism has attracted renewed attention in most industrialized states, such a solution would be less adequate, and more self-defeating, than ever in coping with the formidable economic problems of the late 1970s and beyond. Despite the problems confronting the EEC in consensus formation in recent years, the European Community provides the basis for a partnership model in addressing economic issues in cooperation with the United States, with Japan as a full participant.

4. To the extent possible, commodity markets should be stabilized. Atlantic countries should decide jointly upon national stockpiles in certain key commodities in which they are large-scale importers. In particular, stockpiles of oil should be increased to provide six-month supplies both as a hedge against a temporary embargo and as a reserve for wartime use. Many types of commodity trade mechanisms are possible. As noted in Chapter 14, differing levels of import dependence, demand elasticity, and substitute potential make infeasible a single agreement or stabilization mechanism. What is crucial, however, is coordination of the approaches of the European Community, Japan and the United States. A strategy of income stabilization for producer states, in conjunction with buffer stocks, if possible on a long-term basis, could redound to the advantage of producer and consumer states.

5. The indispensable element in economic recovery and continued growth in the North Atlantic area is the United States itself. The economic futures of Western Europe and Japan are linked inextricably to that of the United States. Thus, the first priority for American policy is the development of an economic strategy designed to control inflation and to reduce drastically the balance of payments deficit of the 1977-1978 period. Central to the economic future of the United States, moreover, are investment policies that provide adequately for R&D – in which the lead enjoyed by the United States has diminished significantly in recent years. No amount of prodding of allies by the United States to reflate their economies will provide an adequate substitute to a strengthened American domestic economy as a vital ingredient in the sustained economic vitality of the noncommunist industrialized world.

## A CONFLICT OF PHASING

The thrust of analysis contained in this volume has been toward a holding strategy for the community of Atlantic nations. The central underlying thesis is that, on the one hand, a series of crises is emerging which threatens to put the Atlantic Alliance – and the residual Atlantic Community concept – to the most excruciating test since the immediate postwar period. On the other hand, the evolution of political and psychological trends militates against the success of any new, mobilizing appeal to pull the Atlantic Community together. The task for statesmanship is to navigate the treacherous currents of the next decade-and-a-half, and to accomplish this within the constraints of resources, the competition of other priorities, and a weakened fabric of consensus both within Atlantic Community countries and among them.

The prognosis is somber, particularly in the near-term, but it should not be confused with Spenglerian notions of unarrestable decline. The Atlantic nations continue to command unfathomed resources of material strength and political vitality. If current projections concerning the more distant horizons of the industrialized world are valid, then the development of the Community concept in full institutional meaning may be the only viable long-range prescription available. In the meantime, however, urgent priorities loom immediately ahead.

The priorities relate primarily to a climactic phase in the systemic competition between the East and West. In this competition, the Atlantic nations have recourse not only to untapped reserves of physical strength but also to the powerful forces of political, social, spiritual, and human values. These values have been blurred by confusion and discord in the West, but ironically they have been mirrored more accurately (and their power demonstrated) in the camp of the adversary.

Let us return once again in this connection to the thesis adumbrated in Part IV of this volume. In somewhat restated form, this thesis is that the Soviet Union is striving for a synthesis of its external objectives of dynamic expansion and hegemony and its internal requirements of economic growth and social control. The external policy has been furthered by a strategy of detente (or, rather, "peaceful coexistence"), which has also benefited Soviet domestic objectives by providing badly needed infusions of trade and technology from the West. Yet detente has also produced, in the Soviet language of dialectics, the antithesis of increased discontent and human aspirations within the communist systems of the Soviet Union and Eastern Europe. No matter how diligently the Soviet leadership has tried to control the process of detente and to shield the domestic arena from ramifications of external policies, the inevitable "windows to the West" have taxed the Closed Society far more than had undoubtedly been anticipated. The Soviet dilemma has been particularly conspicuous in the context of the Conference on Security and Cooperation in Europe (CSCE), the Helsinki Declaration of 1975, and Moscow's attitudes toward compliance with CSCE.

The Soviet leadership is sensitive to the dilemma. It is endeavoring to contain it in the short run by stiffening controls to the point where the internal problems remain manageable, but not to the extent where the controls damage the image and requirements of external detente. It is hoping to resolve the dilemma in the longer term by means of expanding and unchallenged power.

In the meantime, the Soviet leadership continued to face the problem of balancing carefully its internal and external requirements and objectives.

There is little question that the unexpected offensive on human rights by the Carter Administration has exacerbated the problem. Yet the offensive has been flawed by its own contradictions of practical applications and their consequences, particularly by the penalties to United States relations with key non-European countries.

As was pointed out in Chapter 11, there is no need for these contradictions. A double standard in the application of human rights criteria bespeaks not cynicism but logic. It is clear that the standards of human rights – no matter how defined – cannot be applied indiscriminately to countries at differing milestones on the road of nation-building and/or under various measures of internal or external attack. The standards can and should be applied, however, to societies such as the Soviet Union whose established nationhood and level of economic development offer little justification for continued reliance upon instruments of terror and repression to achieve the legitimate goals of the state.

Thus, the challenge confronting the United States and its allies in the Atlantic Community is twofold: to devise a strategy for the short term to surmount the formidable problems of the period just ahead, and to create the minimal preconditions for dealing effectively in the longer term with the principal problems confronting the world of the future. Indispensable to this task is the shoring up of the ramparts of security and thus creating the essential prerequisites for the exploitation of the inherent advantages of the Atlantic Community – those that accrue from the human values and freedom central to the Atlantic Community concept. But if we are to preserve these values in societies where they now exist and to exploit the vulnerabilities of our adversaries where the values lie latent, we must sustain political, military and economic strength of its core area, the states of the Atlantic Community. Herein lies the indispensable, minimum condition for meeting the longer term challenges of building a world structure more adequate to the needs of the late twentieth century and beyond.

# Index

# About the Contributors

WALTER F. HAHN is Deputy Director of the Institute for Foreign Policy Analysis, and Editor-in-Chief of Strategic Review, the quarterly journal of the United States Strategic Institute. He has served as Deputy Director of the International and Social Studies Division of the Institute for Defense Analysis. He is the author and co-author of numerous books and monographs on international and military affairs, including American Strategy for the Nuclear Age (1960); Nuclear Politics: America, France and Britain (1973); Between Westpolitik and Ostpolitik: Changing West German Security Views (1975); and Soviet Shadow Over Africa (1976).

ROBERT L. PFALTZGRAFF, JR., is Professor of International Politics at The Fletcher School of Law and Diplomacy, Tufts University; Director of the Institute for Foreign Policy Analysis; and President of the United States Strategic Institute. He is author, co-author or editor of ten books, including Contending Theories of International Relations (1971); SALT: Implications for Arms Control in the 1970s (1973); The Superpowers in a Multinuclear World (1974); The Other Arms Race: New Technologies and Non-Nuclear Conflict (1975); and The Study of International Relations (1977). He has also published articles in many periodicals and scholarly journals. Dr. Pfaltzgraff has been a consultant to the Department of Defense, the U.S. Information Agency, and the Department of State.

LAWRENCE J. BELL is Professor of Economics at Saint Joseph's College in Philadelphia, and co-author of a paper, "The Politics and Economics of the Hunger Question," in a book he co-edited, Hunger and the American Conscience (1976).

FRANK T.J. BRAY is a Research Associate of the Institute for Foreign Policy Analysis, and a Ph.D. candidate at the Fletcher School of Law and Diplomacy, Tufts University. He is the author of Defense Technology and the Atlantic Alliance: Competition or Collaboration? (1977), and has published articles in several journals.

JACQUELYN K. DAVIS is Assistant to the Director and to the Deputy Director of the Institute for Foreign Policy Analysis, and Foreign Affairs Editor of Strategic Review, the quarterly journal of the United States Strategic Institute. She is co-author of SALT II: Promise or Precipice? (1976); The Cruise Missile: Bargaining Chip or Defense Bargain? (1977); and Soviet Theater Strategy: Implications for NATO (1978).

JAMES E. DOUGHERTY is Professor of Political Science at Saint Joseph's College in Philadelphia, and Senior Staff Member of the Institute for Foreign Policy Analysis. Co-author of Building the Atlantic World (1963), The Politics of the Atlantic Alliance (1967), and Contending Theories of International Relations (1971), he has lectured frequently in Europe and America on NATO affairs and problems of arms control.

BRIAN GRIFFITHS is Professor of Banking and International Finance and Director of the Centre for Banking and International Finance at The City University, London. He is the author of many articles and books, including Money (1972), Invisible Barriers to Invisible Trade (1975), and Inflation -The Price of Prosperity (1976).

MICHAEL MOODIE is Associate Director of the Institute for Conflict and Policy Studies and a consultant on international security affairs in Washington, D.C. He is co-author of Defense Technology and the Atlantic Alliance: Competition or Collaboration? (1977), and has published several articles on security problems in Africa and the Indian Ocean and on international political terrorism.

DIANE K. PFALTZGRAFF is Associate Professor of Political Science at the Philadelphia College of Textiles and Science, and a consultant to the Institute for Foreign Policy Analysis. She received her Ph.D. from the University of Pennsylvania where she was the recipient of a Pennfield Fellowship. She has also been an Earhart Fellow and has been engaged in the study of European-American relations and Italian politics and foreign policy.